The Jewish Time Line
Encyclopedia

The Jewish Time Line Encyclopedia

New Updated Edition

Mattis Kantor

JASON ARONSON INC.
Northvale, New Jersey
London

This book was written by Yitzchak Mattityahu (Kantor) ben Moshe Pinchas ben Yitzchak Mattityahu, who was a (maternal) grandson of Yitzchak Mattityahu (see 1884) and a son-in-law of Mordechai Aizik ben Yisrael Zev Horowitz (see 1861). Writing began on the 24th Elul 1983 and ended exactly three years later, including a break of one year.

The material was gathered and edited on a microcomputer, using standard database processing programs (the quality of which improved immensely over the three-year period).

Library of Congress Cataloging-in-Publication Data

Kantor, Mattis.
    The Jewish time line enclopedia / by Mattis Kantor.—New updated ed.
        p.   cm.
    Includes bibliographical references and index.
    ISBN 0-87668-229-8
    1. Jews—History—Chronology. I. Title.
DS114.K36 1992
909ʹ.04924ʹ 00202—dc20   92-33635

Manufactured in the United States of America. Jason Aronson Inc. offers books and cassettes. For imformation and catalog write to Jason Aronson Inc., 230 Livingston Street, Northvale, NJ 07647.

Contents

UNIVERSAL DISPERSION

How to Use This Book

This is an encyclopedia. Although it is presented in chronological order, it was not really designed for reading from cover to cover.

Most readers will immediately turn to an era or a year which interests them and read that section, but here are a number of other suggestions on how to benefit from the information in this book.

1. Browse

2. Specific Search

Use the index to find the item of interest, and read each entry. It is important to use the index to cover the whole matter, because although there is cross-referencing within the text, those references will not necessarily give a comprehensive listing on the item of interest to you.

3. Historical Perspective

This book was designed to give the researcher or reader a sense of historical perspective. It begins with a one-page chart of the various eras of Jewish history, moves on to a time line of its highlights, and then continues with a more detailed time line of major events before proceeding with the detailed text, which is also in chronological order.

To gain a proper perspective, it is possible to zero in on an event (or person), and then withdraw to the broader perspectives for a telescoping effect. The book does not concentrate on biographical detail, but it is more concerned with placing events in their proper chronological setting.

Square brackets [ ] have been used to enclose reference material of importance to scholars.

Many items and "snippets" of information have been enclosed in parentheses to indicate either (a) the secondary importance of the information or (b) that the documentation of that information is not as sound as the rest of the statement.

For "Living in the Year" charts where the dates are uncertain, the earliest estimate has been given for the date of birth and the latest estimate for the date of death.

Outline

Jewish history is divided here into four sections. Each section is subdivided into the various eras (tekufot), each being presented as a chapter.

Some eras are subdivided into chapters because of natural historical demarcations, or to reduce excessive length. In such instances the breaks have been placed at some point of significance.

Time lines are presented to enhance the reader's perspective of Jewish history.

Time Line 1: The Total Spectrum of Jewish History. This is a listing of the four major sections into which history is divided here and the fifteen eras and their subdivisions. It gives a wide-angle view of Jewish history on one page.

Time Line 2: Highlights of Jewish History. This five-page listing adds only the very major and/or familiar events to the previous time line. Because of the addition of detail, the reader's focus needs to narrow down, although the wide-angle view is still there.

Time Line 3: Major Events in Jewish History. This eight-page listing adds more detail yet, and may therefore be somewhat daunting to a reader not very familiar with Jewish history. After having read through a portion of the main text, the reader will find this time line useful for stepping back and seeing it all within a larger framework. (Segments of this time line appear at the start of every chapter, some of them with even more detail.)

Significant events are highlighted within these time lines, to add further dimension to their usefulness. This highlighting allows for two levels of increased significance: (1) bold, all upper case (2) bold, upper and lower case.

Preface

This book is a digest of the history of biblical and talmudic times, post-talmudic scholars (major events in their lives), and events that affected Jewish life in general until this day. The major objective of this book is to cover over 5,700 years of Jewish history, listing events that occurred, and to allow the reader to develop a sense of perspective and milieu.

It is otherwise concerned with the endeavors of individual Jews or organizations, where these affected the general flow of Jewish history or served as an indication of trends in Jewish life, but does not devote any detailed attention to the personalities and developments of nontraditional or secular Jewish trends. Similarly, it does not concern itself with the particulars of non-Jewish persons or governments, even when those details had some bearing on the events of Jewish history (and particularly when those details only confuse the flow of events). For example:

> (1) Outstanding Jewish personalities such as Albert Einstein are not mentioned in this book (he had no direct impact on Jewish history). (2) Details with regard to many Jewish personalities who were very prominent in the development of current secular or nontraditional movements are not listed. (3) Details concerning the Roman procurators who ruled in Eretz Yisrael prior to the destruction of the second Beit Hamikdash have been omitted because they were well documented from Roman sources, and such detail would only serve to overpower the impact of the not-so-well-documented Jewish personalities and events of that period.

The scope of this book, then, is very specific. It is an indexed chronological listing or digest of events and people in biblical, talmudic, and post-talmudic Jewish history (quoting the sources of information until the end of the Talmud era), which places emphasis on the proper sequence of events. Events are listed in their year of occurrence unless otherwise indicated.

It is an attempt to list in a clear, but very brief, manner all the important information available, presenting it in a readable manner to the lay reader. For the sake of clarity, it has been necessary to omit certain details that would only inject confusion, not clarity.

This book does not attempt to chronologically synchronize events that occurred prior to the secular year 1, based on biblical and talmudic sources with events from other sources. That is the scope of an entirely different book.

It is important to note that the Talmud and Talmudists share two fundamental differences with the prevailing attitudes to history.

(1) The Talmud maintains that the overall quality of the intellectual and *spiritual* caliber of people has declined as the generations have proceeded [Tal.Shab.112b,Eruv.53a /Igg.R.Sher.G.]; Talmud scholars of a particular era (tekufa) have always maintained a deep and somewhat mystical respect for the scholars in preceding eras [Tal.B.B.12a, Ramban /See Appendix D].

(2) The Talmud considers unwritten communication to be superior to written material. In fact, written material was viewed as a concession to the lower standards of later generations [Tal.Tem.14b, Ket.103b /Rashi B.M.33a /Mmn.Hakd.L'Yad /Hakd.S'MaG].

These two "axioms" deliver a different set of instruments with which to measure history and the importance of people and events.

* * *

In the presentation of the personalities and events of modern Jewish history, an attempt has been made to use the same perspectives as used for previous centuries. Many of today's notable events and personalities, therefore, have not been highlighted in a manner commensurate with their current prominence, and other events and personalities may have been projected into greater importance in this book than their current recognition warrants, either because their significance has not yet been felt, or because they will eventually be recognized as having a more lasting nature. It is entirely possible, therefore, that with the passage of time this book may become inaccurate in its perspective of current Jewish history.

* * *

Basically this book sets out to present:

(1) information on traditional Jewish history in a clear, concise form.

(2) Jewish history in a systematic manner, so that even the novice can develop a clear sense of perspective.

To achieve these aims, events have been listed with a finely balanced sense of importance. An event, for example, may be downgraded and not headlined because of the lack of clarity in the exact date. On the other hand, there are personalities in the Talmud for whom a relative abundance of biographical detail is available, yet they have not necessarily been given prominence in direct relation to that information, but have been considered in the perspective of their total impact on Jewish history.

This book emphasizes the chronological placement of events and people, but only deals very briefly with biographical details of personalities. Often more details are given about less-famous people than famous ones, because it is assumed that the reader has some prior knowledge of the famous or has access to reliable biographical material elsewhere. It is also considered unlikely that brevity would distort the historical impact of the famous.

In instances of massacres of Jews, a total number of casualties is often given and then instances of specific incidents are chronologically listed. The specifics are not comprehensive and include only major incidents or those incidents that serve to illustrate the nature of the occurrences.

Time Line 1: The Total Spectrum of Jewish History

THE BEGINNINGS

THE NATION

RIVERS OF BABYLON, CONVULSIONS IN YEHUDA (JUDEA)

UNIVERSAL DISPERSION

Time Line 2: Highlights of Jewish History

THE BEGINNINGS

Chapter 1 THE NEW WORLD

Jewish Year		Secular Year
1	THE CREATION OF THE WORLD AND ADAM AND CHAVA (EVE)	− 3760
1656	THE GREAT FLOOD COVERED THE EARTH	− 2105

Chapter 2 THE FOREFATHERS

1996	Dispersion from Bavel (Babel) after the tower was built	− 1765
2018	THE COVENANT (BRIT BEIN HABETARIM) WITH AVRAHAM	− 1743
2084	THE AKEDA: YITZCHAK WAS PREPARED TO BE A SACRIFICE	− 1677
2229	Yosef became viceroy of Egypt	− 1532
2238	YAAKOV AND HIS FAMILY WENT TO EGYPT	− 1523

Chapter 3 LIVING IN EGYPT

2332	THE ENSLAVEMENT IN EGYPT BEGAN	− 1429
2447	Moshe saw the burning bush	− 1314
2448	THE CHILDREN OF ISRAEL LEFT EGYPT	− 1313

THE NATION

Chapter 4 MOSHE THE LEADER

2448	THE REVELATION ON MOUNT SINAI	− 1313
2488	Moshe died	− 1273

Chapter 5 JUDGES AND EARLY PROPHETS

2488	Bnei Yisrael crossed the Jordan into Canaan	− 1273
2503	The apportionment of Eretz Yisrael was completed	− 1258
2516	Yehoshua died	− 1245
2533	The rule of the Shoftim (Judges) commenced	− 1228
2654	Devorah became leader	− 1107
2694	Gideon became leader	− 1067
2810	Shimshon (Samson) became leader	− 951
2871	Shmuel became leader	− 890

Chapter 6 KINGS AND THE FIRST BEIT HAMIKDASH

2882	Shaul was appointed king	− 879
2892	DAVID BECAME KING OF ISRAEL IN YERUSHALAYIM	− 869
2924	Shlomo became king	− 837

RIVERS OF BABYLON, CONVULSIONS IN YEHUDA (JUDEA)

Chapter 7 EXILE IN BABYLON

Chapter 8 THE SECOND BEIT HAMIKDASH

Greek Cultural Domination

Kingdom of Yehuda (Judea) – Dynasty of the Chashmona'im

Roman Client Kings and Rulers – The Herodian Dynasty

Chapter 9 THE TALMUDIC ERA: THE MISHNA

Chapter 10 THE TALMUDIC ERA: THE GEMARA

Chapter 11 THE TALMUDIC ACADEMIES OF BAVEL

The Rabbanan Savurai

The Ge'onim and Arabic Dominion

UNIVERSAL DISPERSION

Chapter 12 THE RISHONIM – EARLY SCHOLARS

Early Rishonim, Tosaphot, and the Crusade Massacres

Later Rishonim, Persecutions, and Expulsions

The Independent State of Israel and the Current Era

Jewish Year		Secular Year
5708	**THE STATE OF ISRAEL WAS ESTABLISHED IN ERETZ YISRAEL**	**1948**
5709	**The War of Independence (in Eretz Yisrael) ended**	**1949**
5717	Jewish forces invaded Egypt and conquered the Sinai	1956
5727	**YERUSHALAYIM REUNITED UNDER JEWISH RULE IN SIX DAY WAR**	**1967**
5734	2,500 Jewish soldiers were killed in Yom Kippur war	1973
5742	Massive enemy arsenals were discovered in Lebanon	1982

Time Line 3: Major Events in Jewish History

THE BEGINNINGS

Chapter 1 THE NEW WORLD

Jewish Year		Secular Year
1	**THE CREATION OF THE WORLD AND ADAM AND CHAVA (EVE)**	−3760
687	**Metushelach (Methuselah) was born**	−3074
930	**Adam died**	−2831
1056	**Noah was born**	−2705
1558	**Shem was born**	−2203
1656	**THE GREAT FLOOD COVERED THE EARTH**	−2105
1723	**Ever was born**	−2038

Chapter 2 THE FOREFATHERS

1948	Avraham (Abraham) was born	−1813
1996	Dispersion from Bavel (Babel) after the tower was built	−1765
2006	Noah died	−1755
2018	**THE COVENANT (BRIT BEIN HABETARIM) WITH AVRAHAM**	−1743
2023	Avraham came to settle in Canaan	−1738
2048	**Avraham circumcised himself and Yishmael**	−1713
2048	Sdom and Amorrah were destroyed	−1713
2048	Yitzchak (Isaac) was born	−1713
2084	**THE AKEDA: YITZCHAK WAS PREPARED TO BE A SACRIFICE**	−1677
2084	Sarah died	−1677
2108	**Yaakov (Jacob) and Eisav (Esau) were born**	−1653
2123	Avraham died	−1638
2158	Shem died	−1603
2171	**Yitzchak blessed Yaakov instead of Eisav**	−1590
2192	Yaakov married Leah and Rachel	−1569
2199	Yosef (Joseph) was born	−1562
2205	Yaakov left Charan	−1556
2216	**Yosef was sold**	−1545
2228	Yitzchak died	−1533
2229	**Yosef became Viceroy of Egypt**	−1532
2238	**YAAKOV AND HIS FAMILY WENT TO EGYPT**	−1523

Chapter 3 LIVING IN EGYPT

2255	**Yaakov died**	−1506
2309	Yosef died	−1452
2332	**THE ENSLAVEMENT IN EGYPT BEGAN**	−1429
2368	Moshe (Moses) was born	−1393
2406	Yehoshua (Joshua) was born	−1355
2447	Moshe saw the burning bush	−1314
2448	**THE CHILDREN OF ISRAEL LEFT EGYPT**	−1313

THE NATION

Chapter 4   MOSHE THE LEADER

Jewish Year		Secular Year
2448	**THE REVELATION ON MOUNT SINAI**	−1313
2449	Moshe came down Sinai with the second tablets	−1312
2449	The Mishkan (Tabernacle) was erected	−1312
2449	The spies returned from Canaan with bad news	−1312
2487	Aharon and Miriam died	−1274
2488	**Moshe died**	−1273

Chapter 5   JUDGES AND EARLY PROPHETS

2488	**Bnei Yisrael crossed the Jordan into Canaan**	−1273
2503	The apportionment of Eretz Yisrael was completed	−1258
2516	**Yehoshua died**	−1245
2533	**The rule of the Shoftim (Judges) commenced**	−1228
2654	**Devorah became leader**	−1107
2694	**Gideon became leader**	−1067
2810	**Shimshon (Samson) became leader**	−951
2830	**Eli (HaKohen) became leader**	−931
2854	David ben Yishai was born	−907
2871	**Shmuel became leader**	−890

Chapter 6   KINGS AND THE FIRST BEIT HAMIKDASH

2882	**Shaul was appointed king**	−879
2884	**David became king in Hevron (Hebron)**	−877
2892	**DAVID BECAME KING OF ISRAEL IN YERUSHALAYIM**	−869
2924	**Shlomo became king**	−837
2928	Building of the first Beit Hamikdash commenced	−833
2935	**THE FIRST BEIT HAMIKDASH WAS COMPLETED**	−826
2964	**SHLOMO DIED AND HIS KINGDOM WAS DIVIDED**	−797
3084	**Yeho'ash I (Joash) renovated the Beit Hamikdash**	−677
3142	**Yeshayahu (Isaiah) began his prophecies**	−619
3187	**First two of the ten tribes were exiled**	−574
3195	Two more of the ten tribes were exiled	−566
3199	Chizkiyahu (Hezekiah) became king of Yehuda	−562
3205	**THE LAST OF THE TEN TRIBES WERE EXILED**	−556
3213	Sancheriv invaded Eretz Yehuda	−548
3228	Menasheh (son of Chizkiyahu) became king of Yehuda	−533
3298	**Yirmiyahu (Jeremiah) began his prophecies**	−463
3303	Yoshiyahu (Josiah) renovated the Beit Hamikdash	−458
3319	**Yerushalayim was conquered, and Yehoyakim was exiled**	−442
3321	Yehoyakim burned Megillat Eycha	−440
3327	**Yerushalayim was conquered again and Yehoyachin was exiled**	−434
3331	Yirmiyahu persisted in prophesying calamity	−430
3332	Yechezk'el (Ezekiel) prophesied in exile	−429
3336	**The final siege of Yerushalayim**	−425
3338	**THE FIRST BEIT HAMIKDASH WAS DESTROYED**	−423

RIVERS OF BABYLON, CONVULSIONS IN YEHUDA (JUDEA)

Chapter 7 EXILE IN BABYLON

Jewish Year		Secular Year
3339	**Gedalyah ben Achikam was killed**	−423
3340	Daniel interpreted Nebuchadnetzar's dream	−421
3352	Yechezk'el prophesied about the future Beit Hamikdash	−410
3389	**Daniel read the writing on the wall**	−372
3389	Daniel was thrown into the lion's den	−372
3390	**Zerubavel led the return to Eretz Yisrael**	−371
3391	Building of second Beit Hamikdash began and was stopped	−370
3395	Achashverosh II made his great banquet	−366
3399	Esther was taken to the palace	−362
3404	Esther took action against Haman's decree	−357
3406	**MORDECHAI PROCLAIMED PURIM**	−355
3408	**Building of the second Beit Hamikdash was resumed**	−353
3412	**THE SECOND BEIT HAMIKDASH WAS COMPLETED**	−349

Chapter 8 THE SECOND BEIT HAMIKDASH

3413	**Ezra led the second return to Eretz Yisrael**	−348
3426	Nechemyah returned to rebuild the walls of Yerushalayim	−335
3448	**EZRA DIED**	−313
3448	Shimon HaTzadik met Alexander the Great	−313
3449	The Minyan Shtarot began	−313

Greek Cultural Domination

3488	Shimon HaTzadik died	−273
3515	**Seventy-two elders translated the Torah into Greek (Septuagint)**	−246
3621	**The revolt of Mattityahu the Chashmona'i**	−140

Kingdom of Yehuda (Judea) – Dynasty of the Chashmona'im

3622	Yehuda (HaMaccabi) ruled	−139
3622	The Second Beit Hamikdash was rededicated	−139
3623	**CHANUKA WAS DECLARED A FESTIVAL**	−138
3628	**Yehuda (HaMaccabi) was killed in battle**	−133
3700	**The Romans gained control of Yehuda (Judea)**	−61

Roman Client Kings and Rulers – The Herodian Dynasty

3725	**Herod I ruled and killed all the Chashmona'im**	−36
3728	**Hillel became leader of the Torah scholars**	−33
3742	**Herod I commenced rebuilding the second Beit Hamikdash**	−19
3750	Renovations of the second Beit Hamikdash were completed	−11
3768	Hillel died	8
3788	**The Sanhedrin moved from the second Beit Hamikdash**	28

Jewish Year		Secular Year
3810	Raban Gamliel I (son of Shimon, son of Hillel) died	50
3826	**Vespasian arrived in Yehuda to reassert Roman authority**	**66**
3829	**THE SECOND BEIT HAMIKDASH WAS DESTROYED**	**69**

Chapter 9   THE TALMUDIC ERA: THE MISHNA

3834	R.Yochanan ben Zakkai died	74
3846	The Sanhedrin began moving from place to place	86
3893	**Betar fell and Bar Kochba's revolt ended in tragedy**	**133**
3894	Judaism was banned, and R.Akiva was imprisoned	134
3949	**R.YEHUDA HANASSI COMPLETED THE MISHNA AROUND THIS TIME**	**189**

Chapter 10   THE TALMUDIC ERA: THE GEMARA

3979	**Rav left Eretz Yisrael and settled in Bavel (Babylonia)**	**219**
4007	Shmuel was the Talmudic authority in Bavel	247
4014	R.Yochanan was the leading Talmudic authority	254
4050	R.Huna was the leading Talmudic authority	290
4058	R.Yehuda was the leading Talmudic authority	298
4060	R.Chisda was the leading Talmudic authority	300
4069	Rabbah was the leading Talmudic authority	309
4081	R.Yosef was the leading Talmudic authority	321
4085	Abbayé was the leading Talmudic authority	325
4098	Rava was the leading Talmudic authority	338
4119	**Hillel II (who made the Jewish calendar) became Nassi**	**359**
4152	R.Ashi was the leading Talmudic authority	392
4187	**R.Ashi died after the compilation of the Gemara**	**427**
4235	**THE TALMUD WAS COMPLETE WHEN RAVINA II DIED**	**475**

Chapter 11   THE TALMUDIC ACADEMIES OF BAVEL

The Rabbanan Savurai

4311	Mar Zutra proclaimed Jewish self-rule in Babylonia	551

The Ge'onim and Arabic Dominion

4349	The Metivta of Pumpedita was reconstituted by R.Chanan	589
4369	The Metivta of Sura was reconstituted	609
4374	The Persians conquered Eretz Yisrael	614
4374	**JEWS WERE ALLOWED TO RETURN TO YERUSHALAYIM**	**614**
4389	The Byzantine (E.Roman) Empire reconquered Eretz Yisrael	629
4396	R.Yitzchak was the last Gaon of Neharde'a (Firuz-Shabur)	636
4397	**The Arabs conquered Eretz Yisrael**	**637**
4405	One of the *Takkanot HaGe'onim* was enacted	645
4515	R.Acha(i) Gaon left Bavel for Eretz Yisrael	755
4519	R.Yehudai became Gaon of Sura	759
4519	The *Halachot Gedolot* (BaHaG) was written at this time	759
4548	Another of the *Takkanot HaGe'onim* was enacted	788
4618	R.Amram (who wrote the Siddur) became Gaon of Sura	858

Jewish Year		Secular Year
4688	Rbnu.Saadya was appointed Gaon of Sura	928
4715	Four Captives were ransomed around this time	955
4728	R.Sherira became Gaon of Pumpedita	968
4757	R.Hai became (the last) Gaon of Pumpedita	997
4798	**R.HAI GAON DIED AND THE ACADEMIES OF BAVEL DECLINED**	**1038**

UNIVERSAL DISPERSION

Chapter 12 THE RISHONIM – EARLY SCHOLARS

Early Rishonim, Tosaphot, and the Crusade Massacres

4800	Rbnu.Gershom Me'or HaGola died	1040
4856	**THE FIRST CRUSADES DESTROYED JEWISH COMMUNITIES**	**1096**
4859	**Yerushalayim was captured by the Crusaders**	**1099**
4863	**The Rif died**	**1103**
4865	**RASHI DIED AND THE ERA OF THE TOSAPHOT BEGAN**	**1105**
4895	**THE RAMBAM (MAIMONIDES) WAS BORN**	**1135**
4904	**THE FIRST (RECORDED) BLOOD LIBEL TOOK PLACE**	**1144**
4907	**The Second Crusade attacked Jewish communities**	**1147**
4907	Rabbenu Tam was captured by the Crusaders	1147
4908	The Rambam's and the Radak's families left Cordova	1148
4925	The Rambam visited Eretz Yisrael	1165
4931	Rabbenu Tam died	1171
4935	The Rashbam died	1175
4944	The young son of the Ri was killed	1184
4948	**Jews were allowed to return to Yerushalayim**	**1187**
4949	R.Yaakov D'Orleans was killed in London	1189
4950	Jews were massacred in England in the Third Crusade	1190
4951	The Radak wrote his commentary	1191
4954	The Ramban (Nachmanides) was born	1194
4959	The Ra'avad died	1198
4965	The Rambam died	1204
4996	Rampaging mobs massacred Jews in France	1236
5002	**A massive burning of the Talmud took place in Paris**	**1242**
5004	Yerushalayim was sacked by Egyptians and Turks	1244
5012	The Inquisition began to use torture	1252
5030	The Ramban (Nachmanides) died in Eretz Yisrael	1270
5046	**The Maharam MeRothenburg was imprisoned**	**1286**
5050	**THE ERA OF THE TOSAPHOT CONCLUDED AROUND THIS TIME**	**1290**

Later Rishonim, Persecutions, and Expulsions

5050	**The Jews were expelled from England**	**1290**
5053	The Maharam MeRothenburg died in prison	1293
5058	**The Rindfleisch massacres began**	**1298**
5058	The Mordechai and Hagahot Maimoniyot were killed	1298
5065	The Rashba placed a limited ban on philosophy	1305
5065	The Rosh (and his son, the Tur) arrived in Spain	1305

Jewish Year		Secular Year
5066	The Jews were expelled from France	1306
5088	The Rosh died	1327
5096	Jews of Germany were massacred by the Armledder bands	1336
5098	The Ralbag wrote his commentary on the Bible	1338
5109	**THE BLACK DEATH MASSACRES SWEPT ACROSS EUROPE**	**1349**
5127	The Ran, Rivash, and other scholars were imprisoned	1367
5151	Jews of Spain were massacred — many became Marranos	1391
5151	The Rivash and Rashbatz left Spain	1391
5155	**The final expulsion of Jews from France**	**1394**
5173	R.Yosef Albo was in a forced debate with Christians	1413
5181	Jews of Austria massacred in the Wiener Gezera	1421
5235	**THE INVENTION OF PRINTING WAS USED FOR JEWISH BOOKS**	**1475**
5241	**The Inquisition was established in Spain**	**1481**
5248	R.Ovadya Bertinura settled in Yerushalayim	1488
5251	Columbus consulted R.Avraham Zacuto before his travels	1491
5252	**THE JEWS WERE EXPELLED FROM SPAIN AND SICILY**	**1492**

Chapter 13 THE KOV'IM, TORAH CONSOLIDATION, AND THE SHULCHAN ARUCH

5253	R.Yitzchak Abarbanel arrived in Naples from Spain	1493
5257	**The Jews were expelled from Portugal**	**1496**
5276	The *Eyn Yaakov* was printed	1516
5276	The Turks (Ottoman Empire) conquered Eretz Yisrael	1516
5285	R.Yosef Yoselman saved Jews during the Peasants War	1525
5314	A mass burning of Jewish books took place in Rome	1553
5323	**The Shulchan Aruch was completed by R.Yosef Karo**	**1563**
5330	**SHULCHAN ARUCH PUBLISHED WITH SUPPLEMENTS OF RAMO**	**1570**
5332	**The Ari'zal died in Tzfat (Safed)**	**1572**
5334	The Maharshal died	1573
5335	R.Yosef Karo died in Tzfat	1575
5359	The Maharal returned to Prague again	1599
5374	The Maharsha became Rabbi in Lublin	1614
5377	The Tosaphot Yom Tov commentary was concluded	1616
5382	The Shaloh arrived in Eretz Yisrael	1621
5389	R.Yom Tov Lipman Heller was imprisoned in Prague	1629
5400	R.Yoel Sirkes, the Bach, died	1640
5406	**The Shach and Taz (on Shulchan Aruch) were printed**	**1646**
5408	THE JEWS WERE MASSACRED BY CHMIELNITZKI'S FORCES	1648

Chapter 14 THE ACHARONIM—LATER SCHOLARS

5414	The first Jews settled in New Amsterdam (New York)	1654
5415	Jews killed in Russian and Swedish invasions of Poland	1655
5416	Jews were permitted to live in England	1656
5416	Baruch Spinoza was excommunicated	1656

Jewish Year		Secular Year
5433	The Magen Avraham (on Shulchan Aruch) was completed	1673
5437	**SHABBETAI TZVI DIED AS A MUSLIM**	**1676**
5449	The Beit Shmuel (on the Shulchan Aruch) was printed	1689
5458	**THE BA'AL SHEM TOV WAS BORN**	**1698**
5463	The Pnei Yehoshua's family was killed in an explosion	1702
5472	The Siftei Chachamim was arrested	1712
5484	R.Yaakov Culi (Me'am Lo'ez) arrived in Constantinople	1724
5487	The Mishneh LeMelech died	1727
5494	**Jews were massacred by the Haidamack bands**	**1734**

Acharonim and Early Chasidim

5501	The Or HaChayim arrived in Eretz Yisrael	1741
5507	R.Moshe Chaim Luzzatto (Ramchal) died in Acco (Acre)	1747
5510	R.Yonatan Eybeshutz became Rabbi in Hamburg	1750
5515	The Noda BiYehuda became Rabbi in Prague	1754
5518	**The Frankists instigated mass burnings of the Talmud**	**1757**
5519	Frankists supported blood libel charges against Jews	1759
5520	**The Ba'al Shem Tov died**	**1760**
5524	The Va'ad Arba Aratzot was discontinued	1764
5528	**The Haidamacks massacred thousands of Jews**	**1768**
5532	The Maggid of Mezeritsch died	1772
5546	R.Elimelech of Lizensk died	1786
5551	**The Pale of Settlement was established in Russia**	**1791**
5553	Jews suffered in the Reign of Terror of the French Revolution	1793
5558	The Vilna Gaon died	1797
5559	The Ba'al HaTanya was released from first imprisonment	1798
5559	Napoleon led an army expedition through Eretz Yisrael	1799
5566	The Chida (R.Chaim Yosef David Azulai) died	1806
5566	The Chassam Sofer became Rabbi in Pressburg	1806
5570	R.Levi Yitzchak of Berditchev died	1809
5571	R.Nachman of Bratslav died	1810
5574	R.Akiva Eger became Rabbi in Posen	1814
5575	Kozhnitzer Maggid and Yehudi of Pershisskha died	1814
5575	Chozeh of Lublin and R.Mendel of Rymanov died	1815
5579	Anti-Jewish (Hep! Hep!) riots spread throughout Germany	1819
5587	**Russia began conscripting Jewish children to the army**	**1827**
5600	Adm.R.Yisrael of Ruzhin was released from imprisonment	1840

Later Acharonim and Changing Society

5603	The Tzemach Tzedek was arrested in Russia	1843
5606	Sir Moshe Montefiore visited Russia to help the Jews	1846
5609	R.Yisrael Salanter left Vilna	1848
5611	R.Shimshon Rapha'el Hirsch became Rabbi in Frankfurt am Main	1851
5619	R.Menachem Mendel of Kotzk died	1859
5624	The Malbim was imprisoned and expelled from Rumania	1864

Jewish Year		Secular Year
5626	The Chidushei HaRim died	1866
5633	The *Chafetz Chaim* was published	1873
5634	The Minchat Chinuch died	1874
5638	Petach Tikva agricultural settlement was established	1878
5641	**MANY JEWS BEGAN LEAVING RUSSIA AFTER A WAVE OF POGROMS**	**1881**
5646	R.Shlomo Ganzfried (Kitzur Shulchan Aruch) died	1886
5652	R.Chaim (Brisker) became Rabbi in Brisk	1892
5665	The Sfass Emess died	1905
5665	**Many Jews were killed in (official) Russian pogroms**	**1905**
5671	*Chazon Ish* was published	1911
5674	**Over 500,000 Jewish soldiers fought in World War I**	**1914**
5678	**Over 60,000 Jews were killed during Russian Revolution**	**1918**
5684	*Daf HaYomi* study cycle commenced	1923
5687	The Lubavitcher Rebbe was released from Soviet prison	1927
5699	Jews were attacked in Kristallnacht pogrom in Germany	1938

Chapter 15   THE HOLOCAUST, THE INDEPENDENT STATE OF ISRAEL, AND THE CURRENT ERA

The Holocaust

5699	Germany started World War II and mass killing of Jews	1939
5701	**200,000 Jews were killed at Babi Yar and Ponary**	**1941**
5702	**400,000 Jews of Warsaw were sent to death camps**	**1942**
5703	**THE REMAINING JEWS IN WARSAW STAGED A MASSIVE UPRISING**	**1943**
5703	Jewish uprisings at Treblinka, Sobibor, and Bialystok	1943
5704	300,000 Hungarian Jews were killed in three months	1944
5705	Uprising in Auschwitz death camp just before freedom	1944
5705	Nazi Germany was conquered and World War II ended	1945
5705	**6,000,000 JEWS WERE KILLED BY THE NAZIS DURING THE WAR**	**1945**

The Independent State of Israel and the Current Era

5707	Publication of the Talmud Encyclopedia was commenced	1947
5708	The United Nations divided Eretz Yisrael	1947
5708	Arabs attacked in Eretz Yisrael to gain territory	1947
5708	**THE STATE OF ISRAEL WAS ESTABLISHED IN ERETZ YISRAEL**	**1948**
5708	**Eretz Yisrael was invaded by many Arab countries**	**1948**
5709	**The War of Independence (in Eretz Yisrael) ended**	**1949**
5710	The Jews left the ancient Jewish community of Iraq	1950
5710	The Jews of Yemen emigrated to Eretz Yisrael	1950
5717	Jewish forces invaded Egypt and conquered the Sinai	1956
5727	**YERUSHALAYAIM REUNITED UNDER JEWISH RULE IN SIX DAY WAR**	**1967**
5734	2,500 Jewish soldiers were killed in Yom Kippur war	1973
5742	Massive enemy arsenals were discovered in Lebanon	1982

The Beginnings

CHAPTER 1

The New World

The first chapter in Jewish history begins with the creation of the world as *mentioned* but not *described* in the Bible. It ends with the birth of Avraham, where an important new chapter begins.

This book assumes that the reader is conversant with the basic text of the Bible (Chumash), and therefore makes reference to many events without describing them.

For centuries Jews have counted their beginnings from Biblical creation. In our century, so far science has effectively proven that the earth appears to be very much older than the 5749 years we count in Jewish history.

Science, however, has not yet proven that it was not created as a "complete" world as mentioned in the Talmud [Chul.60a.], a world which on its first day was already well into its evolutionary process, with mature trees, a mature man, and mature rock formations.

In fact philosopher Bertrand Russell has argued that there is no proof, scientific or otherwise, that can disprove the statement that "the world was created two days ago." Our memories, this book, everything around us would all be part of that creation. The trees would have many rings to show their apparent age, and old people would have wrinkles to indicate the many years they appear to have lived. The fact that our experience is so real to us does not serve as a *logical* proof that the world is any older than two days, frustrating as this argument may be.

Russell was, of course, only presenting an argument in which neither he nor anyone truly believes, but it is an argument useful in illustrating the limitations of scientific proof for what is essentially a philosophical notion – that the earth is (or is not) as old as it appears to be.

Or in the words of Albert Einstein (in a letter to a friend), "The truth is by no means given to us; given to us are the data of our consciousness."

THE NEW WORLD

1	**THE CREATION OF THE WORLD AND ADAM AND CHAVA (EVE)**	**− 3760**
130	Sheit (Seth, son of Adam) was born	− 3631
235	Enosh (son of Sheit) was born	− 3526
325	Keynan (son of Enosh) was born	− 3436
395	Mehalalel (son of Keynan) was born	− 3366
460	Yered (son of Mehalalel) was born	− 3301
622	Chanoch (son of Yered) was born	− 3139
687	**Metushelach (son of Chanoch) was born**	**− 3074**
874	Lemech II (son of Metushelach) was born	− 2887
930	**Adam died**	**− 2831**
1056	**Noah (son of Lemech II) was born**	**− 2705**
1536	Noah began construction of the ark	− 2225
1556	Yaphet (son of Noah) was born	− 2205
1557	Cham (son of Noah) was born	− 2204
1558	**Shem (son of Noah) was born**	**− 2203**
1656	Metushelach died	− 2105
1656	**THE GREAT FLOOD COVERED THE EARTH**	**− 2105**
1658	Arpachshad (son of Shem) was born	− 2103
1693	Shelach (son of Arpachshad) was born	− 2068
1723	**Ever (son of Shelach) was born**	**− 2038**
1757	Peleg (son of Ever) was born	− 2004
1787	Re'u (son of Peleg) was born	− 1974
1819	Serug (son of Re'u) was born	− 1942
1849	Nachor I (son of Serug) was born	− 1912
1878	Terach (son of Nachor I) was born	− 1883

1 / −3760

Creation of Adam and Chava (Eve).

The world was created in six days and upon completion had the appearance of being fully developed and aged. Adam was created as a fully mature man [Tal.Chul.60a,Tos./Mid.Rab.Br.14.7/Ramban Br.5.4.] The first day of creation was the 25th Elul in the Jewish year -1, or as some call it 0 or 1. Adam and Chava (Eve) were created on the 1st Tishrei. [Mid.Rab.Vay.29/Pir.Dr.El.8/RaN.R.H.3a/Mmn.Hil.Kid.Hach.6.8, Shmitt.10.2]

41 / −3720

Kayin and Hevel (Cain and Abel) were born with twin sisters whom they later married. Kayin had many children [Tal.San.58b/Mid.Rab.Br.Br.22.2. Koh.6.3/Rashi Yer.Yev.11.1(61a)]. Kayin's twin was Kalmana; Hevel's twin was Balbira [Abarbanel Br.4.1]. All children were born with twins in the first generations [Sed.Had.]. Kayin killed Hevel in the year 41 [Mid.Tan.Br.Br.9].

130 / −3631

Sheit (Seth, son of Adam) was born in 130. [Bible Br.5.3]. Kayin had a son Chanoch (and built a city in his name). Chanoch in turn had Irad, who had Mechuyael, who had Metushael, who had Lemech I – names similar to the children of Sheit [Bible Br.4.17, 18].

235 / −3526

Enosh (son of Sheit) was born in 235 [Bible Br.5.6]. He was the first to introduce idolatry [Bible Br.4.26/Mmn.Hil.A.Z.1.1], some say in 266 [Pane'ach Raza.q. Sed.Had.], and others say after Adam died in 930 [Ramban/Sed.Had.]. A third of the world was engulfed by the ocean in his lifetime [Mid.Tan.Sh.Yit.16, Rab.Br.23.7].

325 / −3436

Keynan (son of Enosh) was born in 325 [Bible Br.5.9]. Some say that Keynan ruled wisely over all the people. He predicted a flood if they continued in their immoral behavior and engraved this prediction in stone [Yuch.1.1235/Sed.Had.].

395 / −3366

Mehalalel (son of Keynan) was born in 395 [Bible 5.12]. Lemech I, the descendant of Kayin, had three sons: Yaval, the first nomadic shepherd; Yuval, who invented musical instruments; and Tuval Kayin, the first to work with metals [Bible 4.20–22]. He also had a daughter Na'ama; see 1554/-2207.

460 / −3301

Yered (son of Mehalalel) was born [Bible Br.5.15].

622 / −3139

Chanoch (son of Yered) was born in 622 [Bible Br.5.18]. Chanoch was a man of high moral standing and was asked to rule over the people (according to some), which he did for 243 years. He waged a war (they say) against the descendants of Kayin and suggested different diets and lifestyles for various geographic locations [Sed.Had.].

687 / −3074

Metushelach (Methuselah) was born.

Metushelach (son of Chanoch) was born in 687 [Bible Br.5.21]. Metushelach, who lived 969 years, was the longest living person (see 1656/-2105) on record [Bible Br.5.27]. Only those recorded in the Bible lived such long lives; others had normal lifespans [Mmn.Gd.Ppl.q.Sed.Had.].

874 / −2887

Lemech II (son of Metushelach) was born [Bible Br.5.25].

930 / −2831

Adam died.

Adam died in 930 [Bible Br.5.5] and was buried in Ma'arat Hamachpelah at Hevron (Hebron) [Mid. Rab.Sh.58.4].

974 / −2787

Na'ama (daughter of Chanoch) was born in 974 [Sed.Had.], and later became the wife of Noah (see 1554/-2207).

987 / −2774

Chanoch died in 987 [Bible Br.5.23], and (some say) Metushelach succeeded him as ruler (see 622/-3139) [Sed.Had.].

1042 / −2719

Sheit died in 1042 [Bible Br.5.8], and (some say) he was buried in Arbe'el [Sed.Had.].

1056 / −2705

Noah was born.

Noah (son of Lemech II) was born [Bible Br.5.28,29]. Some say Lemech II married Ashmua, daughter of Elishua, who was the son of Chanoch. Noah was named by Metushelach (his paternal grandfather and maternal great-uncle), but they say his father called him Menachem [Sed.Had.].

1140 / −2621

Enosh died [Bible Br.5.11].

1235 / −2526

Keynan died in 1235 [Bible Br.5.14] and (some say) he was buried in the Indian islands [Yuch.1.1235].

1290 / −2471

Mehalalel died in 1290 [Bible Br.5.17].

1422 / −2339

Yered died in 1422 [Bible Br.5.20].

1536 / −2225

Noah began construction of the ark in 1536 [Bible Br.6.3/Sed.Had.], and is also credited with inventing agricultural equipment [Zoh.Br.Br.58b/Rashi Br.5.29].

1554 / −2207

Noah married Na'ama (some say) in 1554 [Sed.Had.]. There were two women named Na'ama. One was the daughter of Chanoch (see 974/-2787); the other (see 395/-3366) was the sister of Tuval Kayin (and a descendant of Kayin). There are differing opinions as to which one was Noah's wife [Mid.Rab.Br.23.3/Rashi Br.4.22, Sif.Chach/Sed.Had.].

1556 / −2205

Yaphet (son of Noah) was born in 1556 [Bible Br.5.32, Rashi]. One of the sons of Yaphet (see 1651/-2110) was Yavan [Bible Br.10.2], for whom the Greeks were named. The others were Gomer (see 1787/-1974), Magog, Maday (Medians), Meshech, and Tiras [Bible Br.10.2]. Tiras was the ancestor of the Persians [Tal.Yom.10a/Mid.Rab.Br.37.1].

1557 / −2204

Cham (son of Noah) was born in 1557 [Sed.Had.]. One of the sons of Cham (see 1651/-2110) was Kush after whom the black people of Africa were named; another was Mitzrayim, the antecedent of the Egyptians; another was Put, and the fourth was Canaan. [Bible Br.10.6].

1558 / −2203

Shem was born.

Shem (son of Noah) was born in 1558 [Bible Br.11.10]. The descendants of Shem are still called Semites. Shem was also called MalkiTzedek king of Shalem, a town later called YeruShalem (see 2084/-1677) [Bible Br.14.18/Tal.Ned.32b./Mid.Yal. Br.22.102]. One of Shem's sons (see 1651/-2110) was Ashur (see 1996/-1765), after whom the Assyrians were named; another was Aram. The others were Lud, Eylam, and Arpachshad (see 1658/-2103) [Bible Br.10.22].

1651 / −2110

Lemech II (father of Noah) died in 1651 [Bible Br.5.31]. Some say that construction of the ark was speeded up in this year [Sed.Had.]. Some say that the three sons of Noah married three daughters of Elyakum, the son of Metushelach [Sed.Had.].

1656 / −2105

The great flood covered the earth.

Metushelach died on the 11th Cheshvan (the 7th day before the flood began) [Bible Br.7.4/Tal.San.108b]. Some maintain that Kayin also died this year [Mid.Rab.Sh.31.17]. If so, he outlived Metushelach by many years. Kayin was killed by his descendant Lemech I (see 130/-3631), who was blind. He had gone hunting with his son, Tuval Kayin, who directed his aim, but mistook Kayin's movement in the distance for an animal. Lemech I was so upset he killed his son in his frenzy [Rashi Br.4.23].

The great flood began on the 17th Cheshvan 1656 when the ark had just been completed (see 1536/ 2225, 1651/-2110) [Bible Br.7.5-7]. All the people perished in the flood except Noah and his family. However, Sichon and Og, the giants (see 2487/ 1274), were not affected by the flood. [Mid.,Rab. Dev.11.10/Tal.Nid.61a].

It rained for forty days and the rain ended on the 28th Kislev. The waters began receding on the 1st Sivan, 150 days later, and the ark came to rest on the mountaintop on the 17th Sivan. On the 1st Av the mountains appeared out of the water. On the 10th Elul Noah sent the raven, and on the 17th he sent the first dove. On the 24th Elul he sent the second dove which returned with a small olive branch, and on the 1st Tishrei he sent the third dove, which did not return [Bible Br.7.17,24; 8.4-14, Rashi/Mid.Rab.Br.33.7].

1657 / −2104

Noah and all who were with him stayed in the ark until the earth's surface was hard, coming out on the 27th Cheshvan [Bible Br.8.14]. They had been in the ark for one full lunar year and eleven days, the equivalent of one solar year [Mid.Rab.Br.33.7]. The ark settled on the mountains of Ararat in Armenia [Bible Br.8.4, Targ.Yer./Yuch.5.2/ Sed.Had.]. Noah and his sons named the constellations [Mmn.Hil.Yes.Hat.3.7]. After the flood, Noah was permitted (in a revelation) to eat meat (Adam had been forbidden). He was also given a code of seven laws for all humanity to live by [Bible Br.9.1-7/Tal.San.59b, 56a].

1658 / −2103

Arpachshad (son of Shem) was born in 1658 [Bible Br.11.10]. Canaan once saw his grandfather Noah naked and drunk and reported this to his father Cham. Cham had been concerned that Noah might have more children, so he decided to castrate him. When Noah realized what had happened, he cursed them both [Bible Br.9.21-27, Ralshi/Tal. San.70a/Mid.Rab.Bam.10.2/Rashi Br.9.25].

1693 / −2068

Shelach (son of Arpachshad) was born in 1693 [Bible Br.11.12]. Some say that Aner and Eshkol were also sons of Arpachshad [Sed.Had.]. They were allies of Avraham [Bible Br.14.13, 24].

1723 / −2038

Ever was born.

Ever (son of Shelach) was born in 1723 [Bible Br.11.14]. Some say the name "Hebrews" comes from Ever, and others say it is because Avraham came to Canaan from the other side of the river (Ever HaNahar). [Mid.Rab.42.8].

1757 / −2004

Peleg (son of Ever) was born in 1757 [Bible Br.11.16]. Ever had another son, Yaktan, who in turn had thirteen sons. One was called Yovav and another, Avimael (see 2218/-1543). [Bible Br.10.25-29].

1787 / −1974

Re'u (son of Peleg) was born in 1787 [Bible Br.11.18]. Ashkenaz was born one year before Re'u (1786)

[Tzem.Dav.]. He was the son of Gomer who was the son of Yaphet, and the Germanic peoples were named after him [Tal.Yom.10a/Mid.Rab.Br.37.1]. Nimrod, son of Kush (see 1557/-2204), became king in 1788 (according to some) [Sed.Had.].

1819 / −1942

Serug (son of Re'u) was born [Bible Br.11.20].

1849 / −1912

Nachor I (son of Serug) was born [Bible Br.11.22].

1878 / −1883

Terach (son of Nachor I) was born [Bible Br.11.24].

CHAPTER 2

The Forefathers

The second chapter in Jewish history begins with the birth of Avraham and ends with Yaakov's going into Egypt with all his family, covering the period dominated by the forefathers.

THE FOREFATHERS

Jewish Year		Secular Year
1948	Avraham (son of Terach) was born	— 1813
1958	Sarah (daughter of Haran) was born	— 1803
1973	Avraham married Sarah	— 1788
1996	Dispersion from Bavel (Babel) after the tower was built	— 1765
2000	Terach left Ur Kasdim with his family	— 1761
2006	Noah died	— 1755
2018	**THE COVENANT (BRIT BEIN HABETARIM) WITH AVRAHAM**	**— 1743**
2023	Avraham came to settle in Canaan	— 1738
2034	Yishmael (son of Avraham) was born	— 1727
2048	**Avraham circumcised himself and Yishmael**	**— 1713**
2048	Sdom and Amorrah were destroyed	— 1713
2048	Yitzchak (Isaac) was born	— 1713
2084	**THE AKEDA: YITZCHAK WAS PREPARED TO BE A SACRIFICE**	**— 1677**
2084	Sarah died	— 1677
2108	**Yaakov (Jacob) and Eisav (Esau) were born**	**— 1653**
2123	Avraham died	— 1638
2158	Shem (son of Noah) died	— 1603
2171	**Yitzchak blessed Yaakov instead of Eisav**	**— 1590**
2185	Yaakov went to Charan	— 1576
2187	Ever (great-grandson of Shem) died	— 1574
2192	Yaakov married Leah and Rachel	— 1569
2195	Levi (son of Yaakov) was born	— 1566
2199	Yosef (Joseph) was born	— 1562
2205	Yaakov left Charan	— 1556
2208	Binyamin was born	— 1553
2216	**Yosef was sold**	**— 1545**
2228	Yitzchak died	— 1533
2229	**Yosef became viceroy of Egypt**	**— 1532**
2235	Kehot (son of Levi) was born	— 1526
2238	**YAAKOV AND HIS FAMILY WENT TO EGYPT**	**— 1523**

1948 / −1813

Avraham was born.

Avraham (son of Terach) was born in Nissan or in Tishrei in the city of Kutha (in Aram) which was west of Ur Kasdim. If he was born in Tishrei, it was probably before the 10th (see 2048/-1714). Terach had two other sons besides Avraham, Nachor II and Haran. He later moved eastward to Ur Kasdim where Haran was born. Nachor II remained in the land of Aram [Bible Br.11.31; 24.10Tal.R.H.10b,11a/Bachya Br.11.28/Sed.Had.]. Avraham's mother was Amathla'a, the daughter of Karnevu [Tal.B.B.91a]. Haran, the son of another wife, died before his father did. [Bible Br.11.27, 28; 20.12, Rashi].

1958 / −1803

Sarah was born.

Sarah (daughter of Haran) was also known as Yiska; she was Lot's sister and Avraham's niece [Bible Br.11.27-29/Tal.Meg.14a].

Avraham was hidden by his father Terach for the first ten years of his life, because the astrologers had warned Nimrod (see 1787/-1974) that this child would become powerful [Tal.B.B.91a/Sed.Had.]. Avraham came out of hiding (with his mother) this year at the age of 10. Some say that she took him to Noah and Shem, where he spent many years learning from them [Sed.Had.]. He had already refused to believe in idols at the age of three (see 1996/-1765) [Tal.Ned.32a/Kes.Mish.Hil.A.Z.1.3].

1973 / −1788

Avraham married Sarah [Mid.Yal.Br.15.78/Sed.Had.].

1996 / −1765

Peoples were dispersed from Bavel (Babel) after building the tower.

Construction of the Tower of Bavel ended in 1996 [Mid.Yal.D.H.I 1073] Until this time all the people had spoken one common language besides their own [Tal.Yer.Meg.1.9/Mid.Tan.Dev.2/Tor.Tem.Br.11.1] Ashur left the country because he did not approve of the tower construction (which was led by Nimrod), and he established the towns of Nineveh, Rechovot, and Kalach [Bible Br.10.11/Mid.Rab.Br.37.4].

Some say that Avraham recognised the concept of one G-d in this year [Mid.Rab.Br.64.4/Sed.Had.], and others say eight years earlier when he was 40 (see 1958/-1803) [Mmn.Yad Hil.A.Z.1.3, Hag.Mm., Kes.Mish].

Peleg died [Mid.Yal.1073] and Hevron (Hebron) was built during this year [R.Saadya.q.Sed.Had.].

1997 / −1764

Nachor I died [Bible Br.11.25].

2000 / −1761

Avraham destroyed the idols of Terach and aroused the anger of Nimrod (see 1958/−1803) who subsequently sought to destroy Avraham in a furnace. Avraham was miraculously saved, and Terach decided to leave the country [Mid.Rab.Br.38.13/Sed.Had.]. Some say that Terach left Ur Kasdim with his family (see 1948/−1813) in this year [Sed.Had.]. Terach planned to settle in Canaan but stopped on the way and settled in Charan (see 1948/−1813) [Bible Br.11.31]. Some say that Terach had another wife (see 1948/−1813), Pelilah, and had a son called Tzova, who had a son Aram, who had a daughter Machalat (see 2218/−1543). [Sed.Had.2075].

2006 / −1755

Noah died in 2006 [Bible Br.9.29].

In 2008, the people of Sdom and Amorrah rebelled against Kedarla'omer, and thirteen years later in 2021 he retaliated in the war of the five kings against four (see 2018/−1743) [Bible Br.14.4/ Tos.Ber.7b].

2018 / −1743

The covenant (Brit Bein HaBetarim) was made with Avraham.

Avraham had lived in Charan for three years (see 2000/−1761) when he went on to Canaan, the original destination, in 2003, and settled there. It was during this stay in Canaan that the Brit Bein HaBetarim was made on the 15th Nissan 2018 (see 2023/−1738). Avraham went back to Charan after the Brit and stayed there for no longer than five years. If it was a full five years, then the war between the four and five kings must have been in 2023 after he returned (see 2006/−1755) [Mech.Sh. 12.40, Rashi/Sed.Ol./Tos.Ber.7b, Shab.10b./Mrsha.Meg.9a/Sed.Had.].

2023 / −1738

Avraham came to settle in Canaan.

When Avraham came to Canaan (see 2018/−1743), the Canaanite people spoke Hebrew, while he spoke Aramaic [Ramban Br.45.12 Manscpt.Ed.]. There was a famine in Canaan this year [Bible Br.12.4, 10], and Avraham went to Egypt, where on the 15th Nissan he had trouble over the abduction of Sarah, his wife [Bible Br.12.10, Rashi/Mid.Yal.Br.12.68]. Some say that the Brit Bein HaBetarim (the Covenant) was this year (or slightly later) [Bible Br.15.1-9/Mid.Rab.Br., 46.2/Rashi Br.15.1; 21.1]. However, this raises many questions [Mech.Sh.12.40], (see 2018/−1743). Avraham wandered through the land for a few months before he settled [Bible Br.12.8,9].

2026 / −1735

Re'u (son of Peleg) died [Bible Br.11.21].

2034 / −1727

Avraham married his second wife Hagar, who was the daughter of Pharaoh [Mid.Yal.Br.12.68, Rashi Br.16.1,3], and Yishmael was born in 2034 [Bible Br.16.16]. Some say that Avraham was the first person to have white hair; others say he was the first to grow a beard [Tal.B.M.87a, Mrsha/Mid.Rab.Br.65.9, Yef.To.q.O.Hat.4.1556].

2048 / −1714

Avraham circumcised himself and Yishmael.

Avraham circumcised himself and his son Yishmael on the 10th Tishrei [Bible Br.17.24/Mid.Y.16.80]. Yishmael was 13 years old and Avraham was 99, and his 100th birthday was the following Nissan or Tishrei (see 1948/−1813) [Sed.Had.]. Some say the circumcision took place on the 13th Nissan [Mid.Rab.Br.50.12]. In an earlier revelation, Avraham and Sarah had their names changed (from Avram and Sarai). On the third day after the circumcision, three angels predicted that Yitzchak would be born within a year [Bible Br.17.5,15; 18.10/Tal.B.M.86b].

Sdom and Amorrah were destroyed.

Lot's wife, Irith, looked back at the destruction of Sdom because her two married daughters were left behind [Bible Br.18.16; 19.1, 13, 24/Mid.Yal.Br.19.84/B.Turim Br.19.26]. Isolated in a cave, Lot's two rescued daughters believed that the whole world had been destroyed, and therefore conceived two children from him, Mo'av and Ben Ami (Amon) [Bible Br.19.31, 37, 38]. Avraham moved to the land of Plishtim in this year and had trouble with Avimelech over the abduction of his wife [Bible Br.20.1, 2]. He lived there for 26 years [Rashi Br.21.34].

2048 / −1713

Yitzchak (Isaac) was born.

Yitzchak was born on the 15th Nissan of a Jewish leap year [Tal.R.H.11a]. Accordingly Yitzchak would have been born in the seventh month of pregnancy (from Tishrei, see 10th Tishrei 2048/

16

−1714). Avraham made a banquet to honor the occasion of Yitzchak's development (some say when he was eight days old–his circumcision day, others say at the age of 2, and others at 13). To this banquet (some say) he invited all the great people (Shem, Ever, Avimelech, king of the Plishtim) and also his father Terach, and brother Nachor II, both of whom came from Charan to celebrate the occasion [Bible Br.21.8/Mid.Rab.53.10, Mat.Keh./Sed.Had.].

2049 / −1712

Serug (grandfather of Terach) died in 2049 (after his son Nachor I, see 1997/−1764 [Bible Br.11.23]. Nachor II (son of Terach) married Milka his niece (daughter of Haran, see 1958/−1803) and had many sons. One was called Utz and another Betuel. Among the children of Betuel was a son Lavan and a daughter Rivka (Rebecca) [Bible Br.22.20–23]. Iyov (Job) was the son of Utz [Mid.Rab. Br.57.4/Yal.Reuv.q.Sed. Had.] Others say Iyov lived many years later (see 2449/−1312 9th Av) [Tal.B.B.15b/Sed.Had.].

2061 / −1700

Avraham sent Yishmael and his mother away in 2061 [Mid.Rab.Br.53.13, Mat.Keh.]. Yishmael had two wives, who (some say) were called Meriva and Fatima (or Malchut), and he eventually settled in the land of Plishtim near his father [Sed.Had.]. Eliezer, the servant of Avraham, was a descendant of Canaan [Mid.Rab.Br.59.9]. Some say he was the son of Nimrod (the nephew of Canaan, see 1557/ −2204, 1787/−1974) [Pir.Dr.El./Me'am Lo'ez Br.24.2].

2083 / −1678

Terach died [Bible Br.11.32].

2084 / −1677

The Akeda. Yitzchak was prepared to be a sacrifice.

Yitzchak was 36 or 37, depending on the day in Nissan that the Akeda took place (see Nissan

2048/−1713) [Mid.Rab.Br.55.4, Sh.15.11/Sed.Had.]. Avraham named the place of the Akeda "Yir'eh," and this was added to its previous name "Shalem" (see 1558/−2203), hence the name "Yerushalayim" [Bible Br.22.14/Mid.Yal.Br.22.102]. Sarah heard that Avraham had taken Yitzchak to offer him as a sacrifice, and she traveled to search for them. When she reached Hevron (Hebron), she was informed that he had not been sacrificed. The good news was too overwhelming for her, and she died [Bible Br.23.1, 2, Rashi/Mid.Rab.Br.58.5, Vay.20.2/Sed.Had.]. Avraham negotiated the purchase of the Ma'arat Hamachpela in Kiryat Arba (see 930/−2831), near Hevron, and he buried her there [Bible Br.23.19,20]. Yitzchak married Rivka (see 2049/ −1712) shortly thereafter. Some say that Rivka was 10 years old at that time [Sed.Had.]. Some also say that Nachor II (brother of Avraham) died at around this time and that Avimelech, king of the Plishtim, also died, and his son Benmelech was made king and renamed Avimelech as was the custom [Sed.Had.].

2096 / −1665

Arpachshad (son of Shem) died in 2096 [Bible 11.13]. Avraham married a woman named Keturah (some say in the year 2088), and they had six sons. One of them was Midyan, and the others were Zimran, Yakshan, Medan, Yishbak, and Shuach [Bible Br.25.1,2/Sed.Had.]. Some say that Keturah was actually Hagar, who had changed her name [Mid.Rab.Br.61.4].

2108 / −1653

Yaakov (Jacob) and Eisav (Esau) were born [Bible Br.25.26].

2123 / −1638

Avraham died.

On the day Avraham died (some say in Tevet), Eisav came home tired (because he had killed someone), and it was on that day that he sold his rights as the firstborn to Yaakov [Bible Br.25.7/ Tal.B.B.16b]. Some say it was Nimrod (who was out hunting) that he killed [Mid.Rab.Br.65.16/Sed.Had.]. At this time Yitzchak moved to the land of Plishtim and had difficulties with Avimelech the king (see 2084/−1677) over his wife Rivka [Bible Br.26.6-10].

2126 / −1635

Shelach (grandson of Shem) died [Bible Br.11.15].

2158 / −1603

Shem died, but he had outlived eight of the next nine generations of his descendants: his son Arpachshad (see 2096/−1665), Shelach (see 2126/−1635), NOT Ever (see 2187/−1574), Peleg (see 1996/−1765), Re'u (see 2026/−1735), Serug (see 2049/−1712), Nachor I (see 1997/ −1764), Terach (see 2083/−1678), and Avraham (see 2123/−1638) [Bible Br.11.11]. Eisav married Yehudit (daughter of Be'eri), and Basmat (daughter of Eylon), both Chitites (descendants of Canaan), in 2148 [Bible Br.26.34].

2171 / −1590

Yitzchak blessed Yaakov instead of Eisav.

Yitzchak blessed Yaakov on the 15th Nissan, and Yaakov had to leave Be'er Sheva because of Eisav's anger [Bible Br.27.42-44/Pir.Dr.El./Rashi Br.27.9]. He spent fourteen years studying with Ever, before he went to Charan. Yishmael died this same year, before Eisav married his daughter Machalat [Bible Br.28.9, Rashi/Tal.Meg.17a].

2185 / −1576

Yaakov went to Charan, and it was at this time that he had the dream of the ladder [Bible Br.28.12, Rashi 28.9].

2187 / −1574

Ever (great-grandson of Shem) died [Bible Br.11.17].

2192 / −1569

Yaakov had to work for seven years in Charan before he married Lavan's daughter Leah in 2192. He married Rachel one week later. He also married Zilpah and Bilhah [Bible Br.29.23-30/Rashi Br.28.9]. Some say that it was in 2191 [Sed.Had.] that Eisav married Ahalivamah who was officially the daughter of Anah, who was the son of Tzivon, a descendant of Canaan. Actually Ahalivamah was the illegitimate daughter of Tzivon (her grandfather), and even her official father was Tzivon's illegitimate son. (Tzivon had previously had an illegitimate son called Anah with his own mother. He then had Ahalivamah from this son [Anah's] wife) [Bible Br.36.2, Rashi].

2195 / −1566

Levi was born on the 16th Nissan 2195 [Bible Sh.6.16, Mid.Yal.1]. Reuven, the oldest son of Yaakov, was born on the 14th Kislev. Shimon was born on the (21st or) 28th Tevet, Yehuda on the 15th Sivan, Yissachar on the 10th Av, Zevulun on the 7th Tishrei, Dan on the 9th Elul, Naftali on the 5th Tishrei, Gad on the 10th Cheshvan, Asher on the 20th Shvat [Mid.Yal.Sh.1/Bachya Sh.1.6], Yosef (Joseph) (see 2199/−1562), and Binyamin (see 2208/ −1553). Dinah was a twin of Zevulun [Ibn Ezra Br.30.21].

2199 / −1562

Yosef (Joseph) was born on the 1st Tammuz [Mid.Yal.Sh.1].

2205 / −1556

Yaakov left Charan.

Lavan pursued Yaakov when he left Charan in 2205 [Bible Br.31.23, 38], and (some say) he also sent messengers to Eisav to stir up his anger at Yaakov (see 2171/−1590) [Sed.Had.]. Yaakov's subsequent confrontation with Eisav on his return to Canaan was on the 9th Av [Rashal Br.Vayish.q.Sed.Had.]. Yaakov was given the additional name of Yisrael (Israel) in a revelation [Bible Br.33.29; 35.10]. Dinah, who was captured in Canaan by Sh'chem, became pregnant and had a daughter called Osnat. Yaakov sent Osnat away because her uncles did not treat her kindly. She was adopted by Potiphera in Eygpt (see 2229/−1533) [Mid.Yal.Br.34.134].

2208 / −1553

Binyamin was born on the 11th Cheshvan [Mid.Yal.Sh.1, Rab.Bam.14], and his mother Rachel who died at his birth was buried in Beit Lechem [Bible Br.35.18,19]. Rivka had died around 2207 [Rashi Br.33.17; 35.8]. Some say that Dinah married Iyov (Job) (see 2049/−1712) [Mid.Rab.Br.57.4]. Yaakov and his sons fought some battles with the local Canaanites who attacked them because of what they had done to the city of Sh'chem [Rashi Br.48.22/Ramban Br.34.13/Bachya Br.35.6/Sed.Had.].

2216 / −1545

Yosef was sold.

Yosef spent his first year in Egypt as a servant of Potiphar before he was imprisoned for twelve years because of Potiphar's wife who (some say) was called Zuleicha [Mid.Rab.Sh.7.1, Bam.15.12/Sed.Had.]. Leah died this year [Mid.Yal.Br.34.135/Sed.Had.], and (some say) that Reuven married Elyoram the daughter of Chivi (the Canaanite) [Sed.Had.]. Eisav had many children, and Eliphaz his son had an illegitimate daughter Timna (from the wife of Seyir). Eliphaz then had a son from his daughter Timna who was called Amalek [Bible Br.36.12, Rashi].

2218 / −1543

The twelve sons of Yaakov married (according to some): Reuven (see 2216/−1545); Yehuda mar-

ried Eilat, the daughter of Shua; Levi married Adina the daughter of Yovav (see 1757/−2004) and Yissachar married her sister Arida; Dan married Aphlala, daughter of Chamudan; Gad married Utzit, daughter of Amoram who was the son of Utz (see 2049/−1712); and Naftali married her sister Merimat; Asher married Adon, the great-granddaughter of Yishmael, and after she died he married Hadura, the daughter of Avimael (see 1757/−2004), who had a girl, Serach, from her first husband (Malkiel, son of Eylam, see 1558/−2203); Zevulun married Merusha, the granddaughter of Midyan (see 2096/−1665); Binyamin married Machalat, the daughter of Aram in 2218 (see 2000/−1761) [Sed.Had./Targ. Yon.Bam.26.46].

2228 / −1533

Yitzchak died [Bible Br.35.28].

2229 / −1533

Yosef became Viceroy of Egypt.

Yosef was released from prison on the 1st of Tishrei, and became viceroy of Egypt [Bible Br.41.46/Tal.R.H.11a] . Yosef married Osnat, his niece, the adopted daughter of Potiphera (see 2205/−1556) [Mid.Yal.Br.34.134]. Pharaoh gave him the Egyptian name of Tzaphnat Pane'ach [Bible Br.41.45]. Some say that graduates of a special university in Khartoum were the Khartumim who acted as Pharaoh's advisers [Pirush Inyaney Chalom Par'oh Br.41.8].

2235 / −1526

The seven years of plenty came to an end and the famine began [Tal.Toseph.Sot.10.3]. Kehot (ben Levi) was born [Ralbag q.Sed.Had.]. Menasheh and Ephrayim (Yosef's sons) were born before the famine years [Bible Br.41.,50].

2238 / −1523

Yaakov and his family went to Egypt.

Yocheved, the daughter of Levi, was born as
Yaakov and his family were entering Egypt [Bible
Br.47.9/Tal.B.B.123b]. Yaakov was never told that his
sons had sold Yosef [Ramban Br.45.27].

CHAPTER 3

Living in Egypt

The third chapter of Jewish history begins when the children of Yaakov (Yisrael) came to a foreign land. It ends with the Children of Israel leaving as a nation for a great new dream under the leadership of Moshe.

LIVING IN EGYPT

Jewish Year		Secular Year
2255	**Yaakov died**	**−1506**
2309	Yosef died	−1452
2332	**Levi died and the enslavement began**	**−1429**
2368	Moshe (Moses) was born	−1393
2406	Yehoshua (Joshua) was born	−1355
2447	Moshe saw the burning bush	−1314
2448	**THE CHILDREN OF ISRAEL LEFT EGYPT**	**−1313**

2255 / −1506

Yaakov died.

After living in Egypt for 18 years, Yaakov died and was taken to Canaan to be buried, but Eisav attempted by force to stop his sons from burying him in Ma'arat Hamachpela. In the ensuing fight, Chushim the son of Dan killed Eisav, and Yaakov was buried on the 15th Tishrei [Bible Br.47.28/Tal.Sot.13a/Sed.Had.]. Amram (ben Kehot) was born before the death of Yaakov [Tal.B.B.121b] and married Yocheved (see 2238/−1523) who was 22 when Yaakov died. Yaakov could have told her what he had heard from Avraham, who had heard from Noah, who had heard from Lemech II, who had heard from Adam.

2309 / −1452

Yosef died.

Yosef died on a Shabbat afternoon [Bible Br.50.26/Zoh.Sh.156a], the first of his brothers to die (see 2332/−1429) [Tal.Ber.55a]. All the sons of Yaakov (according to some) died on the same day of the same month they were born (see 2195/−1566) [Siddur Yavetz].

2332 / −1429

The enslavement in Egypt began.

The enslavement process of the Children of Israel (Bnei Yisrael) began after the death of Levi on the 16th of Nissan; he was the last of the brothers to die (see 2309/−1452) [Bible Sh.6.16/Mid.Yal.Sh.1/Sed.Ol.3/Rashi Sh.6.16]. Yaakov had appointed Levi as the guardian of all the knowledge and tradition he had received from his father Yitzchak, who had in turn received it from Avraham. The children of Levi continued this tradition [Mmn.Hil.Av.Z.1.3].

2361 / −1400

Miriam (the daughter of Amram) was born [Sed.Ol.3/Sed.Had.].

2365 / −1396

Aharon ben Amram was born [Bible Sh.7.7, Bam.33.39].

2368 / −1393

Moshe (Moses) was born.

Moshe was born on the 7th Adar [Bible Sh.7.7.Tal.Kid.38a]. His father (Amram) called him Chaver, but Kehot his grandfather (who died this year) called him Avigdor [Mid.Yal.Sh.2.166/Ralbag/Sed.Had.]. Moshe was placed on the river on the 6th Sivan [Tal.Sot.12b]. His mother, Yocheved, could tell him things that she had heard of (dating back to creation) at no greater distance than the sixth (reliable) word of mouth (see 2255/−1506).

2406 / −1355

Yehoshua (Joshua) was born in 2406 [Yuch.1/Tzem.Dav.]. Amram (Moshe's father) died before 2392, and Achiyah Hashiloni (see 2964/−797) was born before Amram died [Tal.B.B.121b].

2410 / −1351

Kalev (ben Yefuneh) was born in 2410 [Bible Ysh.14.10]. Yefuneh was Chetzron, the son of Peretz ben Yehuda [Bible D.H.I 2.9/Tal.Sot.11b]. Moshe had killed the cruel Egyptian about two years earlier in 2408 [Mid.Rab.Br.100.10].

2418 / −1343

The Children of Yisrael (Israel) knew of (the prediction of) a 400-year duration to their exile in Egypt [Bible Br.15.13]. The descendants of Ephrayim had calculated that the exile had begun in 2018, the year of the Brit Bein HaBetarim (when the exile was first mentioned); they decided the time had already come. They left Egypt, but many perished in their unsuccessful attempt to reach Canaan (under the leadership of Gon) [Bible D.H.I 7.21/Tal. San. 92b/Mid.Yal.Sh.227, D.H.I 7.1077/Pir.Dr.El.48/ Sed.Had.].

2447 / −1314

Moshe saw the burning bush.

Moshe had a revelation in the burning bush on the 15th Nissan, and exactly one year passed until the Exodus from Egypt. The plagues commenced on the 1st Av and continued on the first of each month until the last plague on the eve of the 15th Nissan [Mid.Yal.Sh.4.176/Bachya Sh.10.5]. Bnei Yisrael were free from slave labor from the 1st Tishrei 2448 [Tal.R.H.11b, Tos.]. Bnei Yisrael were told that in commemoration of their redemption, Nissan would henceforth be reckoned as the first month, the month of redemption (instead of Tishrei) [Bible Sh.12.2, Ramban].

2448 / −1313

The Children of Israel (Yisrael) left Egypt.

The Children of Israel (Yisrael) who left Egypt on the 15th Nissan included 600,000 men between 20–60 years of age. In normal demographic extensions, this would add up to a population of approximately 2,000,000 people. This exodus from Egypt was exactly 430 years after the Brit Bein HaBetarim in 2018 and exactly 400 years after Yitzchak was born (see 2418/−1343) [Bible Br.15.13, Sh.12.40, 41, Mech.].

[2448/−1313 is continued in Chapter 4.]

26

The Nation

CHAPTER 4

Moshe the Leader

The fourth chapter of Jewish history is distinct from all others in that it (a) covers only forty years, and (b) is named after a person.

The events of this 40-year-period were significant enough to stand as a chapter on their own, and the leadership of Moshe (Rabbenu) was so great that the events that occurred during his rule comprise a separate chapter in the history of the people.

The chapter begins with Bnei Yisrael leaving Egypt and ends with the death of Moshe only days before they entered Canaan.

MOSHE THE LEADER

Jewish Year		Secular Year
2448	The Children of Israel crossed the reed sea	− 1313
2448	**THE REVELATION ON MOUNT SINAI**	**− 1313**
2448	Moshe broke the Tablets	− 1313
2449	Moshe came down from Sinai with the second Tablets	− 1312
2449	The Mishkan (Tabernacle) was erected	− 1312
2449	The spies returned from Canaan with bad news	− 1312
2487	Aharon and Miriam died	− 1274
2488	**Moshe died**	**− 1273**

[2448 / −1313 is continued from Chapter 3]

The Children of Israel (Bnei Yisrael) crossed the reed sea.

Pharaoh sent observers to supervise the immediate return of Bnei Yisrael after the three days of freedom they had requested. These supervisors returned to Pharaoh on the fourth day to report that Bnei Yisrael had no intention of returning. The Egyptians pursued them on the fifth and sixth days and on that night (entering the seventh day, the 21st Nissan) Bnei Yisrael crossed the sea [Tal.Sot.12b/Mech./Sed.Ol./Rashi Sh.14.5].

Bnei Yisrael arrived on the 23rd Nissan at Marah where, through a miracle, the water became sweet and drinkable [Bible Shm.15.22]. Bnei Yisrael received ten laws there, including the law of Shabbat [Tal.San.56b]. It was only seven days later (on the 1st day of Iyar), when someone transgressed the law of Shabbat by removing trees and collecting wood [Bible Bam.15.32, Rashi/Sifri/Mid.Yal.Bam.15.749/Tal.Shab.96b, Yer.San.5.1].

Bnei Yisrael arrived at the desert of Sinn on the 15th Iyar, and the morning after their arrival the Mann (Manna) came down for the first time [Bible Sh.16.1, 7, 13/Tal.Kid.38a]. It was then that Moshe instituted the first blessing for Birkat HaMazon (grace after meals) [Tal.Ber.48b].

The Revelation on Mount Sinai.

Bnei Yisrael arrived in the desert of Sinai on the 1st Sivan [Bible Sh.19.1/Tal.Shab.86b]. On the 5th Sivan Moshe built an altar [Bible Sh.24.4, Rashi]; the Torah was given in a revelation on Sinai on the 6th; and on the 7th Moshe went up on the mountain for forty days [Bible Dev.9.9/Tal.Shab.86b, Tan.28b/Sed.Ol./Tos.B.K.82a.Sed.Had.]. Bnei Yisrael had calculated he would come down on the 16th Tammuz and when he did not appear they thought he had died, and they made the golden calf. Moshe then came down from the mountain (and broke the Tablets) on the 17th [Bible Sh.32.1/Tal.Shab.89a/Mid.Rab.Bam.15.21]. He went up Mount Sinai again on the next day

(18th Tammuz), and he remained there for another forty days. He came down on the 29th Av and went up once again on the 30th for forty days [Sed.Ol./Rashi Dev.9.18/Tos.B.K.82a/Sed.Had.].

2449 / −1313

Moshe came down from Mount Sinai with the second tablets.

Moshe placed the second tablets in a special ark when he brought them down on the 10th Tishrei (Yom Kippur). They were later transferred to the Holy Ark built by Betzalel (the great-grandson of Kalev) [Bible Sh.40.20, Rashi, Dev.10.1-5, Rashi 10.1, D.H.I 2.19/Sed.Ol./Rashi Sh.18.13]. On the very next day (the 11th Tishrei) Bnei Yisrael began bringing gifts for the building of the Mishkan (Tabernacle) [Mid.R. Sh.51.4, Tan.Sh.Pek.11/Sed.Ol.]. Moshe sat (in court) to hear cases and pass judgment, and he was advised by his father-in-law Yitro to institute a judicial system [Bible Sh.18.13,19, Rashi].

2449 / −1312

The Mishkan (Tabernacle) was erected.

Some say the Mishkan was completed on the 25th Kislev; others say on the 1st Adar [Mid.Tan.Sh.Pek.11, Pesikta Rab.6.5]. It was initially erected on the 23rd Adar, and dismantled daily for seven days, until it was permanently erected on the 1st Nissan, the same day that Nadav and Avihu (two of Aharon's sons) died. The daily sacrifices and contributions brought by the leaders of the twelve tribes commenced (with Nachshon ben Aminadav of the tribe of Yehuda) on that day [Bible Sh.40.17/Tal.Shab.87b/ Mid.Rab.Vay.20.12, Bam.12.15/Sed.Ol./Rashi Vay.9.1].

On the 2nd Nissan, Moshe prepared the sacrifice of the first Para Aduma (Red Heifer) [Bible Bam.19.2/Sed.Ol.]. The Pesach sacrifice (the first after the Exodus from Egypt) was brought on the 14th Nissan [Bible Bam. 9.1,2]. Moshe was instructed to count Bnei Yisrael on the 1st Iyar [Bible Bam.1.1]. Those who could not bring their Pesach sacrifices on time because of their ritual impurity brought them on the 14th Iyar [Bible Bam.9.11]. Eldad and Medad (see 2516/−1245) became prophets at the end of Iyar [Calculated from: Tal.Tan.29a, Bible Bam.11.26; 33.16; 33.19, Rashi]. Moshe sent the spies on the 29th Sivan, and they returned with bad news on the 8th Av. That night (9th Av), Bnei Yisrael bemoaned their plight [Bible Ba.14./Tal.Tan.29a/Sed.Ol.]. Iyov (see 2049/−1712) died just before the journey of the spies [Rashi Bam.14.9]. The rebellion of Korach took place soon thereafter [Bible Bam.16/Sed.Ol.8]. Nachshon also died this year [Mid.Yal.Shof.42.3].

2487 / −1274

Aharon and Miriam died.

The Bible does not describe any events that took place from the return of the spies in 2449 until the death of Miriam on the 10th Nissan 2487, but it does list the twenty places where Bnei Yisrael stayed during those thirty-eight years. The first nineteen of these years were spent in Kadesh Barne'a, where they were encamped when the spies were sent [Bible Dev.1.46, Rashi, Rashi Dev.2.17/ Tzem.Dav./Sed.Had.]. Aharon died on the 1st Av, and

he was succeeded as Kohen Gadol (High Priest) by his son Elazar [Bible Bam.33.38]. It was at this point that Bnei Yisrael had their various wars mentioned in the Bible, including the incident with Balak, king of Mo'av, and Bil'am the sorcerer. They conquered (and settled) the eastern bank of the Jordan River including the territories of the giants, Sichon and Og (see 1656/−2105), who were killed in the battle [Bible Bam.20.28; 22.2-21; 24.10-14; 21.21-35].

2488 / −1273

Moshe died.

Moshe began reviewing the Torah with Bnei Yisrael on the 1st Shvat, and finished on the 6th Adar [Bible Dev.1.3/Mid.Yal.Ysh.1/Sed.Ol.]. On Shabbat, the 7th Adar, he gathered all of Bnei Yisrael once again and entered them into a covenant. He prepared them for his imminent death by reciting the Shira (poem) of Ha'azinu, and by blessing them. He then went up to the peak of Mount N'vo, and saw the promised land [Bible Dev.32.1; 33.1; 34.1/Tal.Kid.38a/Mid.Yal.Ysh.1/Zoh.Sh.156a]. Before he died, he had completed the writing of the Chumash (Bible) [Tal.B.B.15a].

[2488/−1273 is continued in Chapter 5.]

CHAPTER 5

Judges and Early Prophets

The fifth chapter in Jewish history begins when Bnei Yisrael entered the promised land of Canaan and ends with the appointment of the first king, which indicates that there was a significant strengthening of political self-perception.

JUDGES AND EARLY PROPHETS

Jewish Year		Secular Year
2488	**Bnei Yisrael crossed the Jordan into Canaan**	**−1273**
2503	The apportionment of Eretz Yisrael was completed	−1258
2516	**Yehoshua died**	**−1245**
2533	**The rule of the Shoftim (Judges) commenced**	**−1228**
2533	Othniel ben Knaz became leader of Bnei Yisrael	−1228
2573	Ehud ben Gerah became leader	−1188
2654	Shamgar ben Anath died	−1107
2654	**Devorah became leader**	**−1107**
2694	**Gideon became leader**	**−1067**
2734	Avimelech (son of Gideon) became leader	−1027
2737	Tolah ben Pu'ah became leader	−1024
2758	Ya'ir HaGil'adi became leader	−1003
2779	Yiphtach (HaGil'adi) became leader	−982
2792	Eylon became leader	−969
2802	Avdon ben Hillel became leader	−959
2810	**Shimshon (Samson) became leader**	**−951**
2830	**Eli (HaKohen) became leader**	**−931**
2854	David ben Yishai was born	−907
2871	**Shmuel became leader**	**−890**

[2488/−1273 is continued from Chapter 4.]

Bnei Yisrael crossed the Jordan into Canaan.

Bnei Yisrael mourned the death of Moshe for 30 days (until the 7th Nissan) during which time Yehoshua sent the two spies, Pinchas (ben Elazar) and Kalev (see 2516/−1245). Rachav, the woman who assisted them (in Yericho), converted and later married Yehoshua [Rashi Ysh.2.1/Mid.Tan.Bam. Shl.1,Yal.Ysh.2.9/Tal.Meg.14b, Zev.116b].

For three days Bnei Yisrael prepared themselves for the westward journey into the promised land, and they crossed the Jordan River on the 10th Nissan [Bible Ysh.4.19]. Under Yehoshua's guidance, all Bnei Yisrael who had not been circumcised in the desert were circumcised on the 11th Nissan [Tal.Yev.71b]. On the 14th Nissan they made the Pesach sacrifice. The Mann (Manna) had stopped coming down from the day of Moshe's death but supplies lasted until the 16th Nissan, when they started using local grains [Bible Ysh.5.9–12/Tal.Kid.38a]. Yehoshua then instituted the second blessing in Birkat HaMazon (grace after meals) (see 15th Iyar 2448/−1313) [Tal.Ber.48b].

Bnei Yisrael erected the Mishkan at Gilgal (as well as erecting the twelve stones they took from the Jordan, before the seven-day "siege" of the city of Yericho, which began on the 22nd Nissan [Bible Ysh.4.5/Sed.Ol.11/Sed.Had./D.YbY].

2495 / −1266

Bnei Yisrael ended their conquests.

Bnei Yisrael ended their conquests in 2495 [Tal.Zev.118b]. Yehoshua conquered the thirty-one kings who did not accept his terms [Bible Ysh. 12.24/Tal.Yer.Shvi.6.1.16b/Mmn.Hil.Mel.6.5, Kes.Mish, Radvaz]. Many kings from other countries had maintained palaces in this land [Sifri/Rashi Dev.33.17]. At this time, some of the Canaanites migrated to Allemani, which much later became a German dukedom [Ibn Ezra Ovad.1.20/Rashi Dev.3.9/Radvaz Hil.Mel.6.5]. Shovach,

king of Armenia, contacted Yehoshua [Yuch.5.10]. Elazar and Yehoshua began the task of apportioning the land (including that which was not yet conquered) [Bible Ysh.14.1].

2503 / −1258

The apportionment of Eretz Yisrael was completed.

When the apportionment was completed in 2503, the Mishkan was moved from Gilgal and erected at Shilo with stone walls instead of the original wooden beams [Bible Ysh.18.1/Tal.Zev.112b, 118b]. The counting for the seven-year Shmitta cycles and the fifty-year Yovel commenced in 2503 [Sed.Ol.11/ Mmn.Hil.Shmitt.10.2]. The tribes of Reuven, Gad, and half of Menasheh's tribe returned to their families (east of the Jordan) and expressed concern about (the possibility of) being disenfranchised from the rest of Bnei Yisrael [Bible Ysh.22].

2516 / −1245

Yehoshua died.

Yehoshua completed the writing of Sefer Yehoshua before he died on 26th Nissan [Tal.B.B.14b/ TBY.O.C.580.1/Yuch.1]. The last passage cites the death of Elazar, which occurred around this time [Mid.Yal.Ysh.24.35]. After Yehoshua, leadership was assumed by the Zekeinim (Elders) [Bible Ysh.24.31, Shof.2.7] and included Kalev as the main figure [Tal.Naz.56b]. Other notables were Pinchas (Kohen Gadol, succeeding his father Elazar), Eldad, and Medad (see Iyar 2449/−1312) [Mid.Rab.Bam.3.7/ Yuch.1]. The leadership of the Zekeinim lasted for seventeen years, until 2533 [Sed.Ol./Yuch.1/TBY. O.C.580.1].

2533 / −1228

The rule of the Shoftim (Judges) began.

The last of the Zekeinim (Elders) died on the 5th Shvat, and Othniel ben Knaz became leader of

Bnei Yisrael for forty years [Bible Shof.3.11/Sed.0l./ Yuch.1/T BY.O.C.580]. He was the first of fifteen consecutive leaders called Shoftim, whose leadership continued for almost 350 years, until the first king was appointed (see 2882/−879). Othniel was Kalev's half-brother [Bible Shof.1.13/Tal.Sot.11b,Tem.16a], and he was also called Yavetz [Tal.Tem.16a]. For eight years Kushan Rishatayim, king of Aram Naharayim, dominated Bnei Yisrael, until Othniel overpowered him [Bible Shof.3.8,9].

2573 / −1188

It was during the rule of Othniel that Michah (see 2964/−797) made his idol called Pessel Michah (see 2870/−891), and the controversy with the tribe of Binyamin about the Pilegesh BeGiv'a took place [Bible Shof.17-21/Mid.Yal. Shof.68/Sed.0l.12/Rashi Shof. 17.1,Radak]. One hundred people from the tribe of Binyamin consequently settled in Europe (according to some) in what is now Italy and Germany [Rashi Shof.20.45]. Othniel died in 2573, and Ehud ben Gerah (who was from the tribe of Binyamin) became (Shofet, Judge) for eighty years [Bible Shof.3.15; 3.30/Sed.0l./Yuch.1]. For eighteen years Bnei Yisrael were dominated by Eglon, king of Mo'av, until (after eleven years of rule) Ehud gained entry to his palace and killed him [Bible Shof.3.14-25/ Mid.Yal.Shof.42.3/Sed.0l.12].

2654 / −1107

Devorah became leader.

Shamgar ben Anath (a Kohen) was a Shofet (Judge) who ruled during the last years of Ehud's rule [Bible Shof.3.31/Mid.Yal.Shof.42.3/Tzem.Dav./Sed.Had.], and they both died in 2654 [Tol.Am.0l.1.41]. Some say Shamgar ruled after Ehud, as it appears in the Bible [Radak Shof.4.1].

After Ehud and Shamgar, Devorah (the prophetess) ruled for forty years [Bible Shof.5.31/Sed.0l./Yuch.1], together with her husband Barak (ben Avinoam),

who was also known as Lapidut [T.D.B.E.9/Mid.Yal. 424]. For twenty years of her rule, Bnei Yisrael were dominated by Yavin, king of Canaan, and Sisra, his general, until Devorah and Barak waged war against them [Bible Shof.4/Mid.Yal.Shof.42.3/Sed.0l.12].

Although Devorah was considered one of the Shoftim (Judges), she never actually acted as a judge on legal matters, but instructed the judges during her rule. [Tos.Nid.50a].

2694 / −1067

Devorah died and Gideon became leader.

After Devorah died in 2694, Gideon (ben Yo'ash, from the tribe of Menasheh) became Shofet for forty years [Bible Shof.8.28/Sed.0l./Yuch.1]. He is also referred to as Yerubaal, because (on the 15th Nissan) he destroyed an altar used for the worship of the Baal idol [Bible Shof.6.32, Mid.Yal.62]. For seven years of his rule, Bnei Yisrael were dominated and harassed by the people of Midyan until Gideon overpowered them in a surprise night attack [Bible Shof.6.2-6; 7.19/Ralbag Shof.8.28/Sed.Had.].

2734 / −1027

Avimelech succeeded his father Gideon as Shofet in 2734 and ruled for three years [Bible Shof.9.22/ Sed.0l./Yuch.1].

2737 / −1024

Tolah (ben Pu'ah, of the tribe of Yissachar) succeeded Avimelech and ruled for twenty-three years [Bible Shof.10.1,2/Sed.0l.]

2758 / −1003

Ya'ir HaGil'adi (of the tribe of Menasheh) became a Shofet in 2758, and he ruled for twenty-two years [Bible Shof.10.3/Sed.0l./Yuch.1]. The beginning and the end of his leadership actually overlapped with that of Tolah and Yiphtach [Yuch.1]. The eighteen-year domination and harassment of Bnei Yisrael at the hands of the people of Amon began during his rule, in 2764 (see 2779/−982) [Sed.Ol.].

2779 / −982

Eli (the Kohen) was born in 2772 [Tzem.Dav./ Sed.Had.], and Yiphtach HaGil'adi became Shofet for six years in 2779 [Bible Shof.12.7/Sed.Ol./Yuch.1]. The domination and harassment by the people of Amon ended in 2782 (see 2758/−1003), when Yiphtach overpowered them in battle. Although Yiphtach ranked lowest among the Shoftim, he was nevertheless a prophet [Tal.R.H.25b/Mid.Rab.Vay.37.3, Yal.Shof.67, 68].

2785 / −976

Ivtzan, also called Bo'az, succeeded Yiphtach in 2785, and he ruled for seven years [Bible Shof.12.9/ Tal.B.B.91a/Yuch.1]. He married Ruth in his later years. Bo'az was the son of Sal'mon who was the son of Nachshon ben Aminadav. Aminadav was the son of Ram, who was the son of Chetzron, and Chetzron was the son of Peretz the son of Yehuda [Bible Rut.4.18-20].

2792 / −969

Eylon HaZevuloni (from the tribe of Zevulun) succeeded Ivtzan as Shofet in 2792, and he ruled for ten years [Bible Shof.12.11/Yuch.1].

2802 / −959

Avdon ben Hillel HaPir'atoni, who was from the tribe of Ephrayim, succeeded Eylon and ruled for eight years [Bible Shof.12.13-15/Yuch.1].

2810 / −951

Shimshon (Samson) became leader.

Shimshon ben Mano'ach of the tribe of Dan succeeded Avdon, and he ruled for twenty years (see 2830/−931) [Bible Shof.16.31/Yuch.1]. Before his birth, his mother Tzal'lephunit was told that he should be a Nazir [Bible Shof.13.3-5/Tal.B.B.91a/Bam.Rab.10.5]. He was famous for his great physical strength despite the fact that he was lame in both legs [Tal. Sot.10a/Med Yal.Shof.13.69]. He was the wisest of the wise in his generation, and for twenty years after his death the Plishtim remained subdued, until they were certain that he had no sons who had inherited his strength [Tal.Sot.10a,R.H.25b,Yer./Sed.Had./Mid.Yal.Shof. 16.71/Mrsha.Sot.10a (2) (5)].

2830 / −931

Eli HaKohen became leader, and Shmuel was born.

Eli ruled as a Shofet for forty years and he also succeeded Pinchas as Kohen Gadol (see 2516/ −1245) [Bible Shm.I 4.18/Yuch.1/Mmn.Hakd.L'Yad]. He was one of the descendants of Ithamar, the son of Aharon [Rashi Shm.I 2.30]. On the very day that Eli became leader, Chanah (Hannah) came to Shilo and prayed for a son (Shmuel) who was born in the same year [Sed.Ol.13/Rashi Naz.5a, Shm.I 1.9, 22]. Both she and her husband Elkana were prophets [Tal.Meg.14a, Rashi/Sed.Ol.20/Mid.Rab.Bam.10.5]. Shimshon (see 2810/−951) died in the year 2831 [Tzem. Dav./Sed.Had.].

2854 / −907

David (ben Yishai) was born.

David, who was born in 2854 [Tzem.Dav./Sed.Had.] was the son of Yishai who was the son of Oved, the son of Bo'az (see 2785/−976) and Ruth [Bible Rut.4.20]. Ruth was the daughter or granddaughter of Eglon, king of Mo'av (see 2573/−1188), who

41

was a descendant of Balak (see 2487/−1274) [Tal.San.105b, Sot.47a, Hor.10b, Naz.23b].

2870 / −891

Eli died on the 10th Iyar 2870 or 2871 [TBY.O.C. 590.1/Tzem.Dav./Sed.Had]. He died on learning (from Shaul) that the Holy Ark had been captured by the Plishtim and his two sons were killed in the battle [Bible Shm. I 4.18/Mid.Yal.Shof.4.102/Rashi Shm.I 4.12/ Sed.Had.]. On the day that Eli died, the Mishkan was destroyed [Tal.Zev.118b]. Pessel Michah (see 2573/ −1188) was worshiped by some until this time [Bible Shof.18.31, Rashi 17.1].

2871 / −890

Shmuel became leader.

Shmuel, who had already gained acceptance as a leader during the life of Eli, succeeded him as

Shofet in 2781 [Bible Shm.I 4.1/Radak Shof.18.1/Tzem. Dav./Sed.Had.]. The Mishkan was reconstructed at Nov (see 2870/−891) [Tal.Zev.118b/Sed.Ol.13]. The Holy Ark remained in the hands of the Plishtim for seven months until they returned it to Beit Shemesh [Bible Shm.I 6.1,15]. It was then brought by Bnei Yisrael to the house of Avinadav at Kiryat Ye'arim, where it remained for twenty years, even though the Mishkan was at Nov [Bible Shm.I 7.1−2].

2881 / −880

Shmuel had appointed his two sons, Yoel and Aviyah, as leaders but they were not following his ways. In 2881 Bnei Yisrael asked Shmuel to appoint a king, an idea he did not immediately approve [Bible Shm.I 8.1−7/Tal.Naz.5a,Tem.14b.]. Shmuel himself was considered a leader without peer among the prophets [Mid.Shochar Tov 90.4.].

SHOFTIM – JUDGES AND EARLY PROPHETS

Jewish Year		Secular Year
2488	Yehoshua (Joshua)	−1273
2516	Zekeinim (Elders)	−1245
2533	Shoftim (Judges)	−1228
2533	Othniel ben Knaz	−1228
2573	Ehud ben Gerah	−1188
2654	Shamgar died[1]	−1107
2654	Devorah	−1107
2694	Gideon	−1067
2734	Avimelech	−1027
2737	Tolah ben Pu'ah	−1024
2758	Ya'ir HaGil'adi	−1003
2779	Yiphtach	−982
2792	Eylon	−969
2802	Avdon ben Hillel	−959
2810	Shimshon (Samson)	−951
2830	Eli (HaKohen)	−931
2871	Shmuel	−890

[1]All others listed at beginning of reign.

CHAPTER 6

Kings and the First
Beit Hamikdash

The sixth chapter in Jewish history begins when the first king was appointed and ends when the last king was dethroned, and the first Beit Hamikdash was destroyed.

This book assumes that the reader is familiar with the major occurrences described in the T'nach (Bible), and therefore makes reference to many events and people without describing them.

The events occurring at the end of this chapter are scattered throughout the T'nach (notably in Melachim/Kings, Divrei Hayamim/Chronicles, and Yirmiyahu/Jeremiah) and therefore require more detailed attention in this book.

KINGS AND THE FIRST BEIT HAMIKDASH

Jewish Year		Secular Year
2882	Shaul was appointed king	−879
2884	David became king in Hevron (Hebron)	−877
2892	DAVID BECAME KING OF ISRAEL IN YERUSHALAYIM	−869
2924	Shlomo became king	−837
2928	Building of the First Beit Hamikdash commenced	−833
2935	THE FIRST BEIT HAMIKDASH (see also 2928) WAS COMPLETED	−826
2964	SHLOMO DIED AND HIS KINGDOM WAS DIVIDED	−797
2964	Rechav'am (son of Shlomo) became king of Yehuda	−797
2964	Yerav'am ben Nevat became king over Yisrael	−797
3084	Yeho'ash I (Joash) renovated the Beit Hamikdash	−677
3142	Yeshayahu (Isaiah) began his prophecies	−619
3187	First two of the ten tribes were exiled	−574
3195	Two more of the ten tribes were exiled	−566
3199	Chizkiyahu (Hezekiah) became king of Yehuda	−562
3205	THE LAST OF THE TEN TRIBES WERE EXILED	−556
3213	Sancheriv invaded Eretz Yehuda	−548
3228	Menasheh (son of Chizkiyahu) became king of Yehuda	−562
3298	Yirmiyahu (Jeremiah) began his prophecies	−463
3303	Yoshiyahu (Josiah) renovated the Beit Hamikdash	−458
3319	Yerushalayim was conquered, and Yehoyakim was exiled	−442
3321	Yehoyakim burned Megillat Eycha	−440
3327	Yerushalayim was conquered again and Yehoyachin was exiled	−434
3331	Yirmiyahu persisted in prophesying calamity	−430
3332	Yechezk'el (Ezekiel) prophesied in exile	−429
3336	The final siege of Yerushalayim	−425
3338	The walls of Yerushalayim were penetrated	−423
3338	The sacrifices ceased in the Beit Hamikdash	−423
3338	THE FIRST BEIT HAMIKDASH WAS DESTROYED	−423

2882 / −879

Shaul (Saul) was appointed king.

Shaul ben Kish who was from the tribe of Binyamin was the first of forty-three kings who reigned (some concurrently) for a total of 456 years until the destruction of the first Beit Hamikdash (see 3338/−423). He had been anointed by Shmuel in 2881 [Bible Shm.I 10.1/Tal.Tem.14b], and appointed in 2882 [Tzem.Dav./Sed.Had.]. Although he was chosen because he was a very outstanding person, nevertheless he had to prove himself (in the successful battle against Nachash the Amoni) before he was universally accepted [Bible Shm.I 9.2; 10.24; 11.12–14].

2883 / −878

When Shaul did not completely fulfill his duties, Shmuel sought another lineage for future kings [Bible Shm.I 13.13,14; 15.17,23,26,28]. This was done discreetly in order not to arouse Shaul's anger [Bible Shm.I 16.2]. Shmuel anointed David (ben Yishai, see 2854/−907) in 2883 [Sed.Had.]. He was the seventh of eight brothers [Bible Shm.I 16.10; 17.12 D.H.I 2.15, Rashi, Radak]. When David killed Golyath (Goliath) he received all the praise, and Shaul had to give him his daughter Michal as he had promised. Shaul then became jealous of David [Bible Shm.I 17.25; 18.27].

2884 / −877

Shmuel aged early and died on the 28th Iyar 2884, four months before Shaul [Rashi Shm.I 12.2, 1.22, Tem.15a/TBY.O.C. 580.1/Sed.Had.]. He had transformed his leadership role into that of prophet only in his later years and relinquished political leadership to others (his sons, then Shaul, and then he appointed David). Shmuel wrote the books of Shoftim, Ruth, and Shmuel [Tal.B.B.15a]. After the death of Shmuel, David married Avigayil, the widow of Naval [Bible Shm.I 25.1, 2, 40–42].

In the last part of his life, Shaul became obsessed with jealousy of David (his son-in-law), who was also his son Yehonatan's best friend, and he hunted him all over the country. The prophet Gad assisted David with advice when he was evading Shaul [Bible Shm.I 19–24; 26; 22.5]. Avner was Shaul's general, and Do'eg Ha'adomi was the Av Beit Din (Chief Justice) [Bible Shm.I 17.55; 21.8, Rashi]. When Shaul saw his three sons killed in a losing battle against the Plishtim, he attempted to take his own life [Bible Shm.I 31.2–6; II 1.6–9/Tzem.Dav./Sed.Had.].

David became king in Hevron (Hebron).

David was 30 years old when he became king in Hevron upon the death of Shaul, and he ruled over his tribe of Yehuda. His reign in this limited form lasted for seven and one-half years [Bible Shm.I 2.5/ Tzem.Dav./Sed.Had.]. The Mishkan at Nov was destroyed the year that Shmuel died and was rebuilt at Giv'on. The Holy Ark remained at Kiryat Ye'arim until 2892 (see 2871/−890) [Tal.Zev.118b/ Rashi Tzem.Dav./Sed.Had.].

2892 / −869

David became king of Israel in Yerushalayim.

From 2884 until 2889 no one had ruled over all of Bnei Yisrael (see 2884/−877). In 2889, Avner appointed Ish Boshet (son of Shaul) as king of Bnei Yisrael, and he ruled for two years. Six months after Ish Boshet was assassinated, all of Bnei Yisrael accepted David as their king [Bible Shm.II 2.8–10; 4.7; 8.1–3/Rashi San.20a/Tzem.Dav./Sed.Had.]. David captured the fortress of the people of Yevussi within Yerushalayim and called it Ir (city of) David. During the festive procession accompanying the Holy Ark to the new Ir David (in 2892), Uzah (ben Avinadav, see 2871/−890) disgraced the Ark and died. David then left it with Oved Edom Hagiti (the Levi) for three months, before continuing to Yerushalayim [Bible Shm.II 5.9; 6.10–11/D.H.I 26.4,5/Tal.Sot.35a/Tzem.Dav.]. David instituted a third blessing in Birkat HaMazon (grace after meals) (see 2488/−1273) [Tal.Ber.48b/Kes.Mish. Hil.Ber.2.1]. Natan the prophet told David that his son (not he), would build the Beit Hamikdash [Bible D.H.I 17.1–15].

2912 / −849

The incident with David and Bat Sheva (the daughter of Eliyam ben Achitofel) was on the 24th Elul after Uriya her husband had given her a conditional divorce on the 7th Sivan. David was forgiven on the 10th Tishrei (Yom Kippur) [Bible Shm.II 11/Tal.Shab.56a, Tos./Zoh.Ber.Hakd.8a/Sed.Had.]. Shlomo was born in 2912 and was her second son. The first son had died [Bible Shm.II 11.3; 12.18,24/Tal. San.69b/Tzem.Dav./Sed.Had.]. The incident with Amnon (David's son) and Tamar (his stepdaughter) occurred in 2913 [Bible Shm.II 13/Tzem.Dav.].

2921 / −840

Avshalom (David's son) fled to Geshur in 2915 after he took revenge on his half-brother Amnon (for the incident with Tamar, see 2912/−849). He then returned to Yerushalayim for two years before going to Hebron and declaring himself king in 2921 with the support of David's former adviser, Achitofel (see 2912/−849). Avshalom died at the hands of Yo'av (David's general and nephew) and his men, when he was caught by his hair in a tree [Bible Shm.II 13.28,38; 14.28; 15.9–12; 18.14, 15, D.H.I 2.16/Tal.Naz.5a, Tos./Tzem. Dav./Sed.Had.]. Sheva ben Bichri also attempted a rebellion against David [Bible Shm.II 20.1,22].

2924 / −837

David died and Shlomo became king.

In the last years of his rule, David ordered a census of Bnei Yisrael, which showed there were 1.3 million men under arms and which indicated more than 5 million people (see 2448/−1313) [Bible Shm.II 24.9, D.H.I 21.5,6].

In the last days of David's life Adoniyahu (his spoiled son) proclaimed himself king with the backing of Yo'av (see 2921/−840). Natan the prophet advised Bat Sheva to inform David of this and to remind him of his promise that Shlomo (her son) would become king. David subsequently

dispatched Tzadok (the Kohen Gadol) Natan and Benayahu (an important figure) to publicly anoint Shlomo (who was only 12 years old). When word of this spread, everyone deserted Adoniyahu [Bible Mel.I 1.5–49, Ralbag Mel.I 1.38/Sifri/Sed.Had.].

David died (in Ir David) on the Shabbat afternoon of Shavu'ot (which some say was on the 7th Sivan that year) [Bible Mel.I 2.10/Tal.Shab.30b, Yer.Chag.2.3/Zoh.Sh. Ter.156a/Tos.Chag.17a/Rashal Vay.q.Sed.Had./Lik.Sich.8.22.Note 8]. David wrote the *Tehillim* (Psalms) which include some verses by ten elders [Tal.B.B.14b–15a, Rashi].

2928 / −833

Building of the Beit Hamikdash commenced.

David had prepared many of the supplies needed for building the Beit Hamikdash, and he also gave Shlomo instructions [Bible D.H.I 22]. Building began in Iyar, and Hiram, king of Tzur (Tyre) who was friendly with David, helped supply wood from Lebanon [Bible Shm.II 5.11, Mel.I 5.24; 6.1, 37]. The components of the Mishkan made by Moshe in the desert were buried under the Beit Hamikdash [Tal.Sot.9a/Mid.Rab.Br.42.3]. Shlomo added to the third blessing in Birkat HaMazon (grace after meals) (see 2892/−869) [Tal.Ber.48b/Kes.Mish.Hil.Ber.2.1].

2935 / −827

The First Beit Hamikdash was completed.

On the 7th Tishrei, Shlomo gathered all of Bnei Yisrael to celebrate the arrival of the Holy Ark into the new Beit Hamikdash. The festivities lasted for seven days (and included eating, even on Yom Kippur), and they then celebrated Sukkot [Bible Mel.I 8.65/Tal.M.K.9a, Shab.30a]. The finishing touches to the new building were completed in Cheshvan [Bible Mel.I 6.38, Ralbag, D.H.II 7.10,11]. Shlomo who was a disciple of Shim'i (who had cursed David during Avshalom's uprising) cunningly found grounds to have him killed. Shlomo subsequently married the daughter of Pharaoh [Bible Mel.I 2.37–46/Mid.Rab.Bam.10.3/ Radak Mel.I 2.8/Sed.Had.].

2964 / −797

Shlomo died, and his kingdom was divided.

Hiram the king of Tzur (Tyre) (see 2928/−833) had exchanged gifts and territories with Shlomo in 2948 [Bible Mel.I 9/Tzem.Dav./Sed.Had.]. When Yerav'am ben Nevat criticized Shlomo for his wrongdoing, Achiyah HaShiloni (who was already Eliyahu's [Elijah's] mentor at that stage) prophesied that Yerav'am would be king of ten tribes [Bible Mel.I 11.26, 31/Yuch.1/Sed.Had.]. Shlomo had composed *Mishli* (Proverbs), *Kohelet* (Ecclesiastes), and at the end of his life, *Shir Hashirim* (Song of Songs) [Rashi B.B.14b, Tos., Mrsha.15a]. Shlomo died in 2964 and Rechav'am was to be his successor. He rejected the advice of the older advisers and accepted the advice of his friends, when he informed Bnei Yisrael that he would rule with a stronger hand than had his father Shlomo. Bnei Yisrael then turned to Yerav'am I to be their king in the north [Bible Mel.II 12.8,19/Tzem.Dav./Sed.Had.]. Rechav'am subsequently ruled over the tribes of Yehuda and Binyamin in the south for seventeen years [Bible Mel.I 14.21/ Tzem.Dav./Sed.Had.].

Yerav'am's father, Nevat, was also known as Michah (see 2573/−1188) and Sheva (ben Bichri) (see 2921/−840) [Tal.San. 101b, Mrsha]. For three years, Bnei Yisrael made visits to the Beit Hamikdash in Yerushalayim, thus strengthening the rule of Rechav'am [Bible D.H.II 11.16,17]. Yerav'am I made two golden calves for Bnei Yisrael to worship and set up border guards on the 23rd Sivan to prevent them from going to the Beit Hamikdash, in order to retain their loyalty to him [Bible Mel.I 11.23/TBY.O.C.580.1].

2981 / −780

In 2969, Shishak, king of Egypt, invaded Yerushalayim and took treasures from the Beit Hamikdash and the palace [Bible Mel.I 14.25, 26/ Tzem.Dav./Sed.Had.]. Rechav'am was succeeded (in 2981) by his son Aviyah (Aviyam), who battled constantly with Yerav'am I, king of Yisrael [Bible Mel.I 15.1,7, D.H.II 13.2/Tzem.Dav./Sed.Had.].

2983 / −778

Assa succeeded his father Aviyah as king of Yehuda in 2983, but unlike his father and grandfather he was a righteous person, similar to his ancestor David. Peace reigned between Yehuda and Yisrael for the first ten years of his rule (see 2986/−775) [Bible Mel.I 15.11, 16, 32, D.H.II 14.5/ Tzem.Dav./Sed.Had.]. The largest battle recorded in the Bible took place in 2998 when Zerach HaKushi invaded Eretz Yehuda with over one million troops and was defeated by Assa [Bible D.H.II 14.8/ Tzem.Dav./Sed.Had.].

2985 / −776

Ido who had been a prophet since the time of Shlomo criticized Yerav'am I. He was subsequently killed by a lion [Bible Mel.I 13.1-4; 14.24/Rashi 13.1/Sed.Had.]. Yerav'am I secretly sent his wife to consult Achiyah HaShiloni about the sickness of his rebellious son Aviyah (who often went to the Beit Hamikdash, see 2964/−797). Achiyah HaShiloni prophesied to her that Yerav'am I's dynasty would not last long (see 2986/−775) [Bible Mel.I 14.1-10/Tal.M.K.28b].

Yerav'am I was succeeded by his son Nadav as king of Yisrael in 2985 [Tzem.Dav/Sed.Had.].

2986 / −775

Ba'asha ben Aviyah, from the tribe of Yissachar, assassinated Nadav and the whole family of Yerav'am I in 2986 (see 2985/−776) and proclaimed himself king of Yisrael [Bible Mel.I 15.33/ Tzem,Dav./Sed.Had.]. He continued to maintain Yerav'am's golden calves for worship [Bible Mel.I 16]. In 2993 he waged a battle against Assa, king of Yehuda (see 2983/−778) [Tzem.Dav./Sed.Had.].

3009 / −752

Elah succeeded his father Ba'asha as king of Yisrael in 3009 [Bible Mel.I 16.6/Tzem.Dav./Sed.Had.]. Yehu ben Chanani prophesied to Elah (and to Ba'asha) that their dynasty would not last long because they were following in the ways of Yerav'am I [Bible Mel.I 16.1,7].

3010 / −751

Zimri was a (cruel) servant in the palace of Elah. He killed Elah the king of Yisrael and all his family in 3010 (see 3009/−752), and pronounced himself king [Bible Mel.I 16.9,15/Radak 16.9/Tzem.Dav./Sed.Had.].

When the people heard that Zimri had killed Elah and made himself king, they countered by proclaiming Omri, a general, as king. Omri led an attack on the palace and the trapped Zimri (who had been king for seven days) set the palace afire and perished in the flames. Nevertheless, part of Yisrael did not accept Omri but instead followed Tivni (ben Ginat) for more than four years (until he was killed in 3014) and then all Yisrael accepted Omri as king [Bible Mel.I 16.16–24, Rashi 16.22, 23/Mid.Yal.Mel.I 15/Sed.Ol./Tzem.Dav./Sed.Had.].

Omri built up Shomron as the capital of Yisrael in 3020 [Bible Mel.I 16.24].

3021 / −740

Ach'av succeeded his father Omri as king of Yisrael in 3021. He and his wife Izevel (Jezebel) turned further from the way of the Torah than had all the preceding kings, and they were almost successful in their attempt to kill all the prophets.

Eliyahu publicly refuted the priests of Ba'al (on Mount Carmel) and killed them. Izevel then sought to kill Eliyahu despite the fact that he had just predicted the end of a three-year drought.

Ovadya, a wealthy convert from Edom, became a prophet when he rescued 100 prophets from Ach'av by hiding them in caves and spending all his money to support them [Bible Mel.I 16.30; 21.25; 18.4,19,44; 19.2/Tal.San.39b/Mid.Rab.Sh. 31.4/Tzem.Dav./Sed. Had.].

3024 / −737

Assa (king of Yehuda), whose legs were stricken with illness in 3022, died in 3024 and was succeeded by his son Yehoshaphat [Bible Mel.I 15.23, D.H.II 16.12/Tzem.Dav./Sed.Had.]. Yehoshaphat, who had great respect for Torah scholars, followed in his father's ways (see 2983/−778) [Bible Mel.I 22.42].

In 3027, Yehoshaphat sent messengers throughout Yehuda (Ovadya and Michiyahu were among them) to teach his people [Bible D.H.II 17.7/Tal.Mak.24a/ Tzem/Dav./Sed.Had.].

3041 / −720

When Eliyahu prophesied earlier to Ach'av (see 3021/−740) that his dynasty would be wiped out (because Izevel had Navot killed for his vineyard) Ach'av showed remorse [Bible Mel.I 21.21,29].

Michiyahu ben Yimla, the prophet (see 3024/ −737), assisted Ach'av in the war against Ben Haddad I, king of Aram, until Ach'av (in victory) treated Ben Haddad I like a brother. In the final battle in 3041 (after a 3-year break), Ach'av was killed as Michiyahu had predicted, and his son Achazyahu I succeeded him as king of Yisrael [Bible Mel.I 20.13,22,25,32; 22.17,27/Tzem.Dav./Sed.Had.].

3043 / −718

Achazyahu I had been seriously injured when he fell from an attic balcony in 3043, two years after he succeeded his father as king of Yisrael. Eliyahu's prophecy that he would not recover was conveyed to him shortly before Eliyahu went up in a chariot of fire (leaving Elisha behind) [Bible Mel.II 1; 2.11/ Sed.Ol.17/Tzem.Dav./Sed.Had.].

Achazyahu I was succeeded by his brother Yehoram I because he had no sons [Bible Mel II 1.17].

3047 / −714

Yehoram II became king of Yehuda in 3047 two years before his father Yehoshaphat died [Sed.Ol.17/ Rashi Mel.II 8.16/Tzem.Dav./Sed.Had.]. He was married to Athalya (the daughter of Ach'av, king of Yisrael) [Bible Mel.II 8.18]. Yehoram II originally conducted his affairs in the proper manner, but he later strayed severely and followed the ways of his father-in-law, Ach'av [Bible Mel.II 8.27, D.H.II 21.6/Tal.Hor.11b].

3055 / −706

Achazyahu II became king of Yehuda in 3055 when his father Yehoram II became very sick (as was prophesied in Eliyahu's letter). Yehoram II died a year later, at the age of 40 [Bible D.H.II 21.12-20/Rashi Mel.II 9.29/Tzem.Dav./Sed.Had.].

Elisha had prophesied to Yehu (son of Yehoshaphat, son of Nimshi) that he would become king. Yehu ben Nimshi (as he was called) rebelled against Yehoram I, king of Yisrael (in 3055) and killed him, Izevel, and all the remaining family of Ach'av (see 3056/−705). The prophecy of Eliyahu (see 3041/−720) had been delayed for a generation, because Ach'av had shown remorse. Yehu pronounced himself king and stamped out the Ba'al worship that Ach'av had introduced [Bible Mel.I 21.29; II 9; 10/Tzem.Dav./Sed.Had.].

3056 / −705

In the rebellion against Yehoram I, king of Yisrael (see 3055/−706), Yehu also killed Achazyahu II, king of Yehuda. Athalya (Achazyahu's mother, see 3047/−714) then killed almost all the rest of the royal family of the House of David and named herself queen in 3056. However, Yehosheva managed to save a baby nephew (the son of her brother Achazyahu II) from its grandmother Athalya. Yehosheva, who was the wife of Yehoyada, the Kohen Gadol (see 3098/−663), hid this year-old boy (Yeho'ash I) in the Beit Hamikdash where he remained for six years [Bible Mel.II 9.27; 11.1-3/Sed.Had.].

3061 / −700

After hiding Yeho'ash I in the Beit Hamikdash for six years (see 3056/−705), Yehoyada made him king of Yehuda in 3061, and in the process, Athalya was killed [Bible Mel.II 11.4-16, D.H.II 23/Tzem. Dav./Sed.Had.].

3083 / −678

Yeho'achaz I succeeded his father Yehu as king of Yisrael. Yona, who had been Elisha's messenger to anoint Yehu (see 3055/−706), prophesied that his dynasty would last for four generations [Bible Mel.II 9.1, Rashi, 10.30, Rashi].

Eretz Yisrael was invaded by Chaza'el, the king of Aram, and his son Ben Haddad II, and was occupied for most of the reign of Yeho'achaz I. The invaders were to be ousted later by Yeho'ash II, his son (see 3098/−663) [Bible Mel.II 13.3-5, Radak, Mel.II 13.17-25/Tzem.Dav./Sed.Had.].

3084 / −677

Yeho'ash I renovated the Beit Hamikdash.

Approximately 155 years after Shlomo had begun building the Beit Hamikdash, Yeho'ash considered it necessary to strengthen and redecorate the structure [Bible Mel.II 12.7/Sed.Ol.18/Tzem.Dav./Sed.Had.].

3098 / −663

Yeho'ash II succeeded his father Yeho'achaz I as king of Yisrael in 3098 [Bible Mel.II 13.9,10/Tzem.Dav./ Sed.Had.]. Elisha and his disciple, Yehoyada Kohen Gadol (see 3061/−700), both died in 3098 [Bible Mel.II 13.14/Mid.Yal.Naso.q.Sed.Had./Yuch.1/Sed.Had.].

Yeho'ash I had respected Yehoyada and followed his advice. However, after Yehoyada's death, Yeho'ash I allowed himself to be idolized (because he had lived in the Beit Hamikdash for six years [see 3056/−705]), and he subsequently strayed from his previous ways [Bible D.H.II 24.17, Radak/ Mid.Rab.Sh.8.2].

3100 / −661

Zecharyah ben Yehoyada had succeeded his father as Kohen Gadol (see 3098/−663) but was killed on the orders of Yeho'ash I (king of Yehuda) on Yom Kippur (which was also Shabbat). Because of that incident Yeho'ash I was killed in his bed by his servants [Bible D.H.II 24.21,22,25/Mid.Rab.Eych.2.4].

Amatzya succeeded his father Yeho'ash I, although he had already ruled for one year during his father's life. He overpowered Edom in 3112 and then instigated a battle with Yeho'ash II (king of Yisrael) and lost [Bible Mel.II 14.1,7–13/Sed.Ol.18/Tzem.Dav./Sed.Had.].

3115 / −646

Yerav'am II became king of Yisrael in 3115, three years before his father Yeho'ash II died [Rashi Mel.II 15.8/Tzem.Dav./Sed. Had.], and he extended the borders of Eretz Yisrael as had been prophesied by Yona (see 3083/−678) [Bible Mel.II 14.25]. He later attempted to banish Amos the prophet (see 3142/−619) because of his prophecy that his dynasty would not last [Bible Amos 7.10–17, Rashi].

Uziyahu (son of Amatzya) became king of Yehuda after a rebellion against his father in 3115 (see 3130/−631). Uziyahu, who was also called Azaryah, continued to rule for the fifteen years of his father's life [Bible Mel.II 14.19;15.1,D.H.II 26.1/Rashi Mel.II 15.8/Tzem.Dav./Sed.Had.].

3130 / −631

After the rebellion (see 3115/−646) Amatzya fled into exile, where he was killed fifteen years later (in 3130) during his son Uziyahu's rule [Bible Mel.II 14.19/Rashi Mel.II 15.8]. Uziyahu captured and rebuilt the city of Eilat after the death of his father [Bible Mel.II 14.22].

3142 / −619

Yeshayahu (Isaiah) began his prophecies.

Amos had begun his prophecies in 3140 (see 3115/−646), and Hoshea had prophesied before him [Rashi Hosh.1.2, Amos 1.1/Tal.B.B.14b].

When in 3142 Uzihayu attempted to burn incense in the Beit Hamikdash for a sacrifice (normally a function of the Kohanim), he was struck with leprosy and seriously incapacitated [Bible Mel.II 15.5, D.H.II 26.16–21/Sed.Ol.19].

At that time (the same day) Yeshayahu (Isaiah) made his first prophecy [Targ.Yon.Yesh.6.1, Rashi 1.1,6.4]. Amotz, the father of Yeshayahu, was a brother of Amatzya (see 3100/−661). [Tal.Meg.10b].

3153 / −608

Zecharyahu succeeded his father Yerav'am II as king of Yisrael but only ruled for six months [Bible Mel.II 15.8].

3154 / −607

Shalom ben Yavesh rebelled against Zecharyahu (and killed him publicly) in 3154, thus fulfilling Yona's prophecy (see 3083/−678). Shalom declared himself king of Yisrael [Bible Mel.II 15.10–13/Tzem.Dav./Sed.Had.].

Menachem ben Gadi rebelled against Shalom after he had ruled for only one month, and forcefully established his own rule [Bible Mel.II 15.14, 16]. Phul, king of Ashur, invaded Eretz Yisrael, and Menachem was forced to pay a very high tribute in order that Phul withdraw his forces [Bible Mel.II 15.19,20].

3164 / −597

Pekachya succeeded his father Menachem as king of Yisrael [Tzem.Dav./Sed.Had.].

3166 / −595

Pekach ben Remalyahu, the general, rebelled against Pekachya and became king of Yisrael in 3166 [Bible Mel.II 15.25/Tzem.Dav./Sed.Had.].

3167 / −594

Yotam succeeded his father Uziyahu as king of Yehuda in 3167 [Bible Mel.II 15.32/Tzem.Dav./Sed.Had.].

Michah began his prophecies during the reign of Yotam; at that time there were four major prophets–Hoshea, Yeshayahu, Amos, and Michah (see 3142/−619) [Bible Yesh.1.1, Hosh.1.1, Mich.1.1/Tal.Pes.87a].

3183 / −578

At the end of Yotam's rule (see 3167/−594), the kingdom of Yehuda had protracted battles with Retzin, king of Aram, and Pekach, king of Yisrael (see 3187/−574) [Bible Mel.II 15.37,38, Rashi, Radak, Ralbag].

Achaz succeeded his father Yotam in 3183, but did not follow in the ways of King David. He tampered with the sanctity of the Beit Hamikdash and destroyed Sifrei Torah (scrolls) [Bible Mel.II 16.2–4, 14–18/Tal.San.103b/Tzem. Dav./Sed.Had.].

3187 / −574

First two of the ten tribes were exiled.

Achaz (king of Yehuda) had provided through a bribe that Tiglath Pil'esser (king of Ashur) should help him in his protracted war against Aram and Pekach (king of Yisrael) [Bible Mel.II 16.7,8].

At the end of the reign of Pekach (in 3187), Tiglath Pil'esser invaded Eretz Yisrael, conquered territory, and expelled the tribes of Gad, Reuven, and half of the tribe Menasheh (see 2503/−1258) [Bible Mel.II 15.29/Mid.Rab.Eycha Petichta 5/Rashi Mel.II 17.1/Tzem. Dav./Sed.Had.].

When (Reuven) the tribe of Hoshea ben Elah was expelled, he rebelled against Pekach and became king of Yisrael [Bible Mel.II 15.30/Sed.Had.]. He was nominally the last king of Yisrael but in reality merely the local representative of the king of Ashur until he rebelled against him (see 3195/−566) [Bible Mel.II 17.3,4, Ralbag 17.1]. On the 15th Av he removed the border guards (see 2964/−797) and thus became the only king of Yisrael to allow his people to go to the Beit Hamikdash [Tal.Git.88a, Tan.30b–31a].

3195 / −566

Two more of the ten tribes were exiled.

Hoshea ben Elah, king of Yisrael, rebelled in 3195 against Shalmanessar, king of Ashur, who retaliated by expelling the tribes of Zevulun and Naftali from Eretz Yisrael [Bible Mel.II 17.4–6/Mid.Rab.Eycha Petichta 5/Rashi Mel.II 17.1/Tzem.Dav./Sed.Had.].

3199 / −562

Chizkiyahu (Hezekiah) became king of Yehuda.

Chizkiyahu succeeded his father Achaz in 3199 and became one of the most righteous of all the kings of Yehuda, (some say more than King David). He made sure that all the people were well educated in the laws of the Torah, and he refused to be dominated by the king of Ashur as his father was (see 3187/−574). He also repelled the Plishtim from Eretz Yehuda [Bible Mel.II 18.1,5,7,8/Tal.San.94b/Mel.II 18.5, Radak, Ralbag/Tzem.Dav./Sed.Had.].

Chizkiyahu and his peers recorded the books of *Yeshayahu, Mishli* (Proverbs), *Shir Hashirim* (Song of Songs), and *Kohelet* (Ecclesiastes) (see 2964/−797) [Tal.B.B.15a, Maharsha].

3205 / −556

The last of the ten tribes were exiled.

Shalmanessar invaded Eretz Yisrael in 3202 (see 3187/−574, 3195/−566) and by 3205 had completely conquered it and destroyed the capital, Shomron (see 3010/−751). He then expelled the remainder of the ten tribes [Bible Mel.II 18.9–11; 17.6, Radak 17.24, Rashi, 17.1/Tzem.Dav./Sed.Had.].

The king of Ashur settled other conquered peoples around Shomron, the people of Kutha (see 1948/−1813) and Bavel (Babylonia) among them. When the Kuthim were later attacked by lions, they saw it as an omen and requested to be taught the religion of the land, which they did not then fully accept (although some say they subsequently did and then rejected it again at a later stage) (see 4046/−286) [Bible Mel.II 17.25,33/Tal.San.85b, Rashi, Kid.75b, Min.42a, Rashi, Tos/Tos.Suk.8b].

3213 / −548

Sancheriv invaded Eretz Yehuda and retreated.

Sancheriv, king of Ashur, was expanding his empire and resettling all the peoples of his conquests (see 3205/−556). He invaded Eretz Yehuda and approached Yerushalayim. Chizkiyahu was terminally ill at the time, but was informed by Yeshayahu that he would live for another fifteen years [Bible Mel.II 19.35-37; 20.1-6, Yesh.37.38/Sed.Ol.23/Tal. San.96a, Ber.28a/Tzem.Dav./Sed.Had.].

He insisted that Chizkiyahu marry and have children and so Chizkiyahu married Yeshayahu's daughter [Tal.Ber.10a, Hag.Bach].

On the third day of his illness Chizkiyahu recuperated as Yeshayahu had prophesied. On that night (15th Nissan), when Bnei Yehuda were celebrating with their Pesach sacrifices, Sancheriv miraculously (and hastily) withdrew. On his return home, he was killed by his sons while worshipping at his idol (a board from Noah's ark) [Bible Mel.II 19.35-37; 20.1-6, Yesh.37.38/Sed.Ol.23/Tal.San.96a/Mid. Rab.Sh.18.5/Tzem.Dav./Sed.Had.]. Sancheriv left some Egyptian prisoners in Eretz Yehuda in his hasty withdrawal, who then converted and returned to Egypt [Tal.Min.109b/Rashi Yesh.19.18].

3228 / −533

When Chizkiyahu befriended a delegation from Bavel (Babylonia), Yeshayahu prophesied about the future exile of his descendants and the royal household to that country [Bible Mel.II 20.14,18].

Menasheh succeeded his father Chizkiyahu as king of Yehuda in 3228, and initially he was the worst of all the previous kings of Yehuda. He placed a statue in the Beit Hamikdash on the 17th Tammuz [Bible Mel.II 21.2-7/Tal.San.103b, Tan. 26b, Rashi, Yer.Tan.4.5(23b)/ TBY.O.C.549/Tzem.Dav./Sed.Had.]. He killed his grandfather Yeshayahu (see 3213/−548) [Tal.Yev.49b], and was warned by the prophets Nachum and Chabakuk that his deeds would

cause the destruction of Yehuda [Bible Mel.II 21.10-14, Rashi/Mid.Yal.Chab.1].

3283 / −478

Menasheh's reign was the longest of both Yehuda and Yisrael. He was captured by the armies of Ashur in 3250 and taken to Bavel (Babylonia) for a while and there he changed his ways [Bible D.H.II 33.11, 12/Sed.Ol.24/Tai.San.103a/T.D.B.E.19].

Amon succeeded his father Menasheh in 3283. He conducted his affairs in a very bad way and was killed by his servants, who in turn were subsequently killed by the people. The people then proclaimed Yoshiyahu (Josiah) king (see 3285/−476) [Bible Mel.II 21.23,24].

3285 / −476

Yoshiyahu, the son of Amon was only 8 years old when he was proclaimed king of Yehuda in 3285 (see 3283/−478) [Bible Mel.II 21.24/Tzem.Dav./Sed.Had.]. He began to follow the ways of King David in earnest in 3293, and in 3297 he began cleansing Yehuda of idol worship, a program that he intensified after the prophecy of Chuldah (see 3303/−458) [Bible D.H.II 34.3/Radak Mel.II 23.4, Ralbag 23.25/ Tzem.Dav./Sed.Had.].

3298 / −463

Yirmiyahu (Jeremiah) began his prophecies.

Yirmiyahu ben Chilkiyahu HaKohen (who some say was Chilkiyahu the Kohen Gadol, see 3303/−458) began his prophecies in 3298 [Bible Yir.1.1, Radak/Tos.B.K.16b/Sed.Had.]. In 3302 Yirmiyahu returned some of the people of the ten tribes from their exile to live under the rule of Yoshiyahu [Tal.Erch.12b, 33a, Tos./Rashi Mel.II 23.22, San.110a/Sed.Had.].

Tzephanya, a descendant of Chizkiyahu, was also a prophet during the reign of Yoshiyahu [Bible Tze.1.1].

3303 / −458

Yoshiyahu renovated the Beit Hamikdash.

In 3303 Yoshiyahu began renovations on the Beit Hamikdash (218 years after Yeho'ash I, see 3084/ −677). Chilkiyahu, the Kohen Gadol, found a Sefer Torah which had been hidden during the period when Achaz would have destroyed it (see 3183/−578). Yoshiyahu consulted Chuldah, the prophetess (wife of Shalum ben Tikva), and she confirmed (see 3285/−476) that there was significance in the fact that the scroll had been opened to the dire predictions of exile [Bible Mel II 22.4,5,13-15, D.H.II 34.8/Rashi Mel.II 22.8/Tzem.Dav./Sed.Had.].

3316 / −445

Yoshiyahu had been concerned about the numerous prophecies of the destruction of the Beit Hamikdash, and he consequently buried the Holy Ark and other holy items in an underground chamber built by Shlomo [Tal.Cri.5b, Yom52b, Hor.12a/ [Mmn,Hil.B.Hab.4.1].

N'cho, Pharaoh of Egypt, invaded Eretz Yehuda and killed Yoshiyahu in 3316. The people of Yehuda anointed Yeho'achaz II (his younger son) as king and after he had served for three months, Pharaoh N'cho took him into captivity (where he eventually died) [Bible Mel.II 23.29-34/Tzem.Dav./Sed.Had.].

N'cho appointed Elyakim (an older son of Yoshiyahu) as king and renamed him Yehoyakim [Bible Mel.II 23.34].

In 3317, because of the prevailing uncertainties, Yehoyakim appointed his son Yehoyachin (who was also called Yechanya) to rule after him [Bible D.H.II 36.9, Mel.II 24.8, Radak].

3319 / −442

Yerushalayim was conquered and Yehoyakim was exiled.

In 3318, Nebuchadnetzar, the king of Bavel (Babylonia) (who some say was an exceptionally short man) rebelled against the king of Ashur who dominated Bavel (see 3205/−556). In 3319 he successfully conquered Eretz Yehuda and Yerushalayim, plundered the Beit Hamikdash, and expelled Yehoyakim to Bavel together with Daniel (who was 15), Chananyah Misha'el, and Azaryah, among others. He returned Yehoyakim to rule over Yehuda (under his dominion) which Yehoyakim did for three years [Bible Dan.1.1-6/Ibn Ezra 1.4/Tal.Erch.12a/Mid.Yal.Dan.4/T.D.B.E.Rab.31/Radak Mel. II 24.1/Tzem.Dav./Sed.Had.].

3321 / −440

Yehoyakim burned Megillat Eycha.

Yirmiyahu constantly prophesied about an imminent calamity unless the people changed their ways. In 3320 he wrote his prophecy of *Megillat Eycha* (Lamentations) and distributed it through Baruch ben Neriyah (his disciple), because he had been imprisoned by Yehoyakim. The people proclaimed a fast because of the serious message it conveyed, but Yehoyakim read it, tore it up, and then threw it into the fire on the 28th Kislev [Bible Yir.36.5,9,10,22,23; 45.1, Rashi 36.5; 37.4/TBY.O.C.580.1/Tzem. Dav./Sed.Had.].

3327 / −434

Yerushalayim was conquered again, and Yehoyachin was exiled.

Uriyah the prophet fled to Egypt after prophesying imminent disaster. Yehoyakim had him returned and killed [Bible Yir.26.20-23].

Yehoyakim rebelled against Nebuchadnetzar in 3323 and four years later was defeated in battle. He died while being led in prisoners' chains [Bible Mel.II 24.1,2, Radak/Mid.Yal.Mel.II 24/Ibn Ez.Dan.1.4/ Tzem.Dav./Sed.Had.].

Yehoyachin then succeeded his father Yehoyakim (see 3316/−445) as king of Yehuda, but he ruled for only three months (and ten days) before

Nebuchadnetzar laid siege to Yerushalayim for the second time, and Yehoyachin surrendered peacefully. Nebuchadnetzar plundered the Beit Hamikdash again, and the palace, and he took the leaders of the people, including Yehoyachin, Yechezk'el (the prophet), and Mordechai, to Bavel (Babylonia) [Bible Mel.II 24.8-16, D.H.II 36.9,10,Yech.1.1,2, Est.2.6].

Nebuchadnetzar returned Tzidkiyahu from exile and appointed him king of Yehuda and ruler of his surrounding conquests [Bible Mel.II 24.17, Yir.27.3, Rashi/Sed.Had.].

Tzidkiyahu (whose name was also Matanya and Shalum until Nebuchadnetzar changed it) was the third son of Yoshiyahu to be king and was an uncle to Yehoyachin, whom he succeeded. He was the last king of the House of David [Bible Mel.II 24.17, D.H.I 3.15, D.H.II 36.10, Rashi/Tal.Git.5b/Tzem.Dav./ Sed.Had.].

At this time, Nebuchadnetzar was training the intelligent young exiles in Bavel (see 3319/−442) for civic leadership. Daniel and his friends who were among them agreed to eat only certain vegetables [Bible Dan.1.1-6,12].

3331 / −430

Yirmiyahu persisted in prophesying calamity.

Yirmiyahu, who was released from prison by Tzidkiyahu, continuously prophesied an imminent destruction [Bible Yir.37.4, Rashi, 28]. In Av 3331 he debated with Chananyah ben Azur who had prophesied that Nebuchadnetzar and his armies would soon leave Eretz Yehuda. Yirmiyahu exclaimed that he too wished it be so, but that unless the people changed, there would be disaster. He also prophesied that Chananyah would die that year, and he did [Bible Yir.28/Mid.Yal.Yir.28].

3332 / −429

Yechezk'el (Ezekiel) prophesied in exile.

Yechezk'el's first recorded prophecy on the 5th Tammuz 3332 did not pertain to Yerushalayim.

However, on the 5th Elul 3333, he prophesied about the imminent calamity of the Beit Hamikdash [Bible Yech.1.1,2, Rashi, 8.1].

On the 10th Av 3334, he was consulted by the elders who were struggling to find meaning in their religious life in exile [Bible Yech.20.1, Rashi]. Yirmiyahu also addressed that uncertainty by sending a letter telling the people not to return, but to settle down to a normal life for seventy years [Bible Yir.29.1-11/Mmn.Pir.Mish.Hakd.-Begin.].

3336 / −425

The final siege of Yerushalayim.

Tzidkiyahu rebelled against Nebuchadnetzar, who then returned to Yerushalayim to recapture it on 10th Tevet 3336 [Bible Mel.II 24.20; 25.1/Yech. 24.1,2/Tzem.Dav./Sed.Had.]. Many people had taken refuge in Yerushalayim before the siege, and food became extremely scarce [Bible Yir.8.14, Eycha 1.11/T.D.B.E.30]. The army of Yehuda inside the walls of Yerushalayim inflicted heavy casualties on the Babylonian army outside [Mid.Yal.Eycha 1009].

3337 / −424

Yirmiyahu was accused of treason (because his prophecies were demoralizing), and Yir'iyah (the grandson of Chananyah, see 3331/−430) falsely testified that he had seen him conspiring with the enemy. Some ministers had Yirmiyahu lowered into a dungeon, but Tzidkiyahu saved him and placed him in a courtyard prison. He continued to prophesy about exile (and future return) and about how the Egyptians, who were on their way to assist, would soon retreat [Bible Yir. 32.1-2; 37.7,13; 38.1-6, 10,13/Mid.Yal.Yir.28].

Yirmiyahu cursed the day he was born (which was the 9th Av), because he despised being a prophet of doom for the land and the people that he loved [Bible Yir.11.14; 15.10; 20.14/Mid.Yal.Yir.36/Sed. Had.3298].

3338 / −423

The First Beit Hamikdash was destroyed.

The attack on Yerushalayim was led by Nebuzradan, one of Nebuchadnetzar's ministers [Bible Mel.II 25.8,9], and on the 9th Tammuz the walls of Yerushalayim were penetrated [Bible Yir.52.6/Tzem. Dav./Sed.Had.]. On the 17th Tammuz sacrifices ceased in the Beit Hamikdash [Tal.Erch.11b].

Tzidkiyahu attempted to escape via an eighteen-mile-long tunnel, but was captured by some enemy troops who, while chasing a deer, saw him coming out at Yericho. He was taken to Nebuchadnetzar, encamped in Rivlah (Antioch) [Bible Mel.II 25.3-7, Rashi 25.4/Tal.Eruv.61b/Mid.Rab.Bam.2.9, Yal.Mel.251.25].

On Friday the 7th Av, the enemy entered the Beit Hamikdash, where they feasted and vandalized until late into the 9th, when they set the structure afire. The fires burned for twenty-four hours [Bible Mel.II 25.8, Yir.52.13/Tal.Tan.29a].

The invading armies confiscated the archives of Yehuda including the writings of Shlomo and took them for the scholars of Babylonia [Kuz.1.63; 2.66, Otz.Nechm./Mmn.Gd.Ppl.1.71/Tor.Ha01.3.7].

Only a small number of Yehudim (Jews) remained in Eretz Yehuda. Many had died of hunger and disease during the siege; vast numbers were killed by enemy troops, and many were taken to exile in Bavel (Babylonia). Others fled to what was later to become France, Germany, and Spain [Bible Mel.II 25.11,12, Yir.52.15,16,30, Yech.5.2,12, Ovad.1.20/Tal.Git.57b, 58a, San.96b/Sed.Had.5380-3].

[3338/−423 is continued in Chapter 7.]

KINGS 2882–2924	
	Jewish Year
Shaul	2882
David (limited rule)	2884
Ish Boshet	2889
David	2892
Shlomo	2924

KINGS OF YEHUDA

	Jewish Year
Rechav'am	2964
Aviyah	2981
Assa	2983
Yehoshaphat	3024
Yehoram II	3047
Achazyahu II	3055
Athalya Ruled	3056
Yeho'ash I	3061
Amatzya	3100
Uziyahu	3115
Yotam	3167
Achaz	3183
Chizkiyahu	3199
Menasheh	3228
Amon	3283
Yoshiyahu	3285
Yeho'achaz II	3316
Yehoyakim	3316
Yehoyachin	3327
Tzidkiyahu	3327

KINGS OF YISRAEL

	Jewish Year
Yerav'am I	2964
Nadav	2985
Ba'asha	2986
Elah	3009
Zimri	3010
Omri	3010
Ach'av	3021
Achazyahu I	3041
Yehoram I	3043
Yehu	3055
Yeho'achaz I	3083
Yeho'ash II	3098
Yerav'am II	3115
Zecharyahu	3153
Shalom	3154
Menachem	3154
Pekachya	3164
Pekach	3166
Hoshea	3187

KINGS 2964–3327

King	Jewish Year	Kingdom
Rechav'am	2964	Yehuda
Yerav'am I	2964	Yisrael
Aviyah	2981	Yehuda
Assa	2983	Yehuda
Nadav	2985	Yisrael
Ba'asha	2986	Yisrael
Elah	3009	Yisrael
Zimri	3010	Yisrael
Omri	3010	Yisrael
Ach'av	3021	Yisrael
Yehoshaphat	3024	Yehuda
Achazyahu I	3041	Yisrael
Yehoram I	3043	Yisrael
Yehoram II	3047	Yehuda
Achazyahu II	3055	Yehuda
Yehu	3055	Yisrael
Athalya Ruled	3056	Yehuda
Yeho'ash I	3061	Yehuda
Yeho'achaz I	3083	Yisrael
Yeho'ash II	3098	Yisrael
Amatzya	3100	Yehuda
Uziyahu	3115	Yehuda
Yerav'am II	3115	Yisrael
Zecharyahu	3153	Yisrael
Shalom	3154	Yisrael
Menachem	3154	Yisrael
Pekachya	3164	Yisrael
Pekach	3166	Yisrael
Yotam	3167	Yehuda
Achaz	3183	Yehuda
Hoshea	3187	Yisrael
Chizkiyahu	3199	Yehuda
Menasheh	3228	Yehuda
Amon	3283	Yehuda
Yoshiyahu	3285	Yehuda
Yeho'achaz II	3316	Yehuda
Yehoyakim	3316	Yehuda
Yehoyachin	3327	Yehuda
Tzidkiyahu	3327	Yehuda

Rivers of Babylon, Convulsions in Yehuda (Judea)

CHAPTER 7

Exile in Babylon

The seventh chapter in Jewish history begins with the destruction of the first Beit Hamikdash and the forced exile of the people (now called Jews rather than Children of Israel) to Bavel (Babylonia). The chapter ends with the completion of the second Beit Hamikdash and the return of some Jews to Eretz Yisrael.

EXILE IN BABYLON

Jewish Year		Secular Year
3339	**Gedalyah ben Achikam was killed**	**− 423**
3340	Daniel interpreted Nebuchadnetzar's dream	− 421
3352	Yechezk'el prophesied about the future Beit Hamikdash	− 410
3389	**Daniel read the writing on the wall**	− 372
3389	Daniel was thrown into the lion's den	− 372
3390	**Zerubavel led the return to Eretz Yisrael**	− 371
3391	Building of the Second Beit Hamikdash began and halted	− 370
3395	Achashverosh II made his great banquet	− 366
3399	Esther was taken to the palace	− 362
3404	Esther took action against Haman's decree	− 357
3406	**MORDECHAI PROCLAIMED PURIM**	**− 355**
3408	**Building of the Second Beit Hamikdash was resumed**	**− 353**
3412	**THE BEIT HAMIKDASH WAS COMPLETED**	**− 349**

[3338/−423 is continued from Chapter 6.]

Nebuchadnetzar commanded his people to take care of Yirmiyahu. He was released from the courtyard jailhouse, but insisted on chaining himself to the people being led into exile. However, he decided later to remain in Eretz Yisrael rather than live a privileged life in Bavel as he had been promised [Bible Yir.39.11–14; 40.4/Mid.Yal.Teh.137/Rashi Meg.13a]. Gedalyah ben Achikam, who was appointed ruler, instructed the people who were left in Eretz Yisrael to live peacefully under the new circumstances [Bible Mel.II 25.22,24].

3339 / −423

Gedalyah ben Achikam was killed.

Yishmael ben Netanya (whose mother was a member of the royal family) accepted the advice of Ba'aliss, the king of Amon, that he should be ruling, not Gedalyah [Bible Yir.40.14/Tal.Meg.15a, Yer.Hor.3.8]. Yochanan ben Kari'ach then warned Gedalyah of a plot. Gedalyah, because of his honesty, did not believe he was being deceived by Yishmael but while they sat together at dinner on the 2nd Tishrei, Yishmael killed him [Bible Yir.40.14; 41.1–2, Radak/TBY.O.C.549].

After that, Yishmael killed Gedalyah's local supporters as well as the Babylonian troops who were in the vicinity. He then began leading the remaining people to Amon. When Yochanan, a leader of some irregular troops, heard what Yishmael had done, he pursued Yishmael who escaped with only a handful of people. Yochanan, afraid that the Babylonians would retaliate, led the people (including Yirmiyahu) to Egypt. This was against the advice of Yirmiyahu (whom he had initially consulted) [Bible Yir.41; 42; 43]. Plato had discussions with Yirmiyahu in Egypt (according to some) [Tor.HaO1.1.11/Sed.Had.3300].

All the children of Tzidkiyahu were killed in his presence at Rivlah (see 3338/−423). Then he was blinded on the 7th Cheshvan and led into exile [Bible Mel.II 25.7, TBY. O.C.580.1].

Serayah (the Kohen Gadol), a descendant of Pinchas (ben Elazar), was also killed at Rivlah [Bible Mel.II 25.18–21, Radak, Ralbag].

3339 / −422

On the 5th Tevet, a messenger came to inform Yechezk'el and the other Jews (Yehudim) who were already in Bavel (see 3319/−442, 3327/ −434) that the Beit Hamikdash had been destroyed [Bible Yeh.33.21].

Led to exile after the destruction of the Beit Hamikdash, the Jews did not go directly to Bavel but were diverted in different directions. Despite their continuous march they only arrived in Bavel much later [Mid.Rab.Br.82.10, Eycha 2.4, Yal.Teh.137/Rashi Tze.2.8]. Many died when they drank the water of the Euphrates [Mid.Yal.Teh.137].

On the 1st Adar, Yechezk'el prophesied about the fall of Egypt [Bible Yech.32.1, Radak].

3340 / −421

Daniel interpreted Nebuchadnetzar's dream.

Nebuchadnetzar asked Daniel to remind him of the dream he had had as well as to interpret it; he subsequently wanted to idolize him for having been successful in both. However, he rewarded him with a powerful position ' instead [Bible Dan.2.46,48, Rashi Dan.2.1/Sed.01.25/Mid.Yal.Dan.1060.2]. On the 10th Tishrei (Yom Kippur), Chananyah, Misha'el, and Azaryah, who were given positions of power at Daniel's request [Bible Dan.2.49], refused to bow down to Nebuchadnetzar's new idol but were miraculously saved from the fire into which they were thrown.

On that day Yechezk'el prophesied about the dry bones [Bible Dan.3, Yech.37/Mid.Yal.Sh.Hsh.7.9/Tal.San.92b].

3342 / −419

Tzur (Tyre) was conquered by Nebuchadnetzar and those Jews who had taken refuge in Tzur (and also in Amon and Mo'av) were now also taken to Bavel [Bible Yir.52.30, Rashi]. Normal life continued in exile, and eventually some Jews became very wealthy and influential. They settled in many cities including Hutzal and Neharde'a (where they built notable synagogues), and also in Tel Aviv. They also excelled in the study of Torah (in Aramaic) [Bible Yech. 3.15/Tal.B.K.80a, Meg.29a, Git.6a/Ralshi B.K.80a/Tos.B.K.80a, Git.6a, Yev.115a/T.D.B.E.Rab.5, 23/Igg.R. Sher.Gaon/Mmn.Hil.Nizk.Mam.5.8]. The use of Hebrew as a language declined at this stage [Mmn.Hila.Tfi.1.4].

3346 / −415

Egypt was conquered by Nebuchadnetzar, and Yirmiyahu and Baruch ben Neriyah were taken to Bavel with the few survivors of those who had gone to Egypt in 3339 [Bible Yir.44.28, Radask/Sed.01.26]. The whole region conquered by Nebuchadnetzar was totally desolate. Nebuchadnetzar sacked and looted but never seriously concerned himself with dominion over those conquests) [Bible Chab.1, Metz.Dav.]. None of the groups surrounding Eretz Yisrael and Yehuda were successful in settling the country [Ramban Vay.26.32].

3352 / −410

Yechezk'el prophesied on Yom Kippur about the future Beit Hamikdash (see 3340/−421) [Bible Yech.40.1; 43.10−11, Rashi 43.11, Radak 43.10/MmnHil.Mel.4.8, Radvaz, Hil.Mas.Hak.2.14, Lech.Mish.].

Yirmiyahu wrote the books of *Melachim I* and *II* and *Yirmiyahu* (also Eycha, see 3321/−440) before he died [Tal.B.B.15a]. Nebuchadnetzar had had another dream, which Daniel interpreted to mean that Nebuchadnetzar would become insane for seven years and live in the wilderness. Fearing this, he had followed Daniel's advice and distributed provisions for needy Jews in Bavel for a period of 12 months [Bible Dan.4/Tal./Sot.20b−21a, Rashi]. The seven years would have been at around this time.

3364 / −397

Ehvil M'rudach, Nebuchadnetzar's son, was not eager to succeed his father's rule when Nebuchadnetzar died on the 25th Adar, following his earlier experience when Nebuchadnetzar had disappeared for seven years into the wilderness (see 3352/−410). He had then suddenly reappeared and punished his son for his relatively benevolent rule [Bible Yir.52.31, Dan.4.30, Metz.Dav./Mid.Rab.Vay.18.2, Yal.Chab.1.562, Yal.Dan.2.1059].

Ehvil M'rudach released Yechanya (Yehoyachin) and his uncle, the blind Tzidkiyahu, from prison on the 27th Adar, but Tzidkiyahu (the last ruler of the House of David) died that same day [Bible Mel.II 25.27/Tal.M.K.28b/Mid.Yal./Yir.34, Dan.2.1059]. Yechanya was treated with respect for the rest of his life [Bible Mel.II 25.30].

3386 / −375

Daniel's first prophetic dream predicted the fall of Bavel and the rise of other powerful nations [Bible Dan.7, Ibn Ezra 7.1].

Ehvil M'rudach died this year, and Belshatzar his son became king [Sed.01.29]. His style of rule was similar to that of his grandfather Nebuchadnetzar (see 3364/−397) [Tal.Meg.11a./Mid.Yal.Dan.4].

3389 / −372

Daniel read the writing on the wall.

Daniel had again dreamed (see 3386/−375) of the future powerful kingdoms of the world (and a mystical number of 2,300 was revealed to him). He did not disclose his dreams clearly, as a prophet would disclose prophecies, and although he was shaken for a number of days he nevertheless continued his palace duties without interruption [Bible Dan.8.14,20−24, 22, 27, Rashi].

Bavel had been invaded by Darius I (Daryavesh I, son of Achashverosh I, king of Media) in alliance with his son-in-law Cyrus (Coresh, king of Persia), but their initial attack was repelled. [Rashi Dan.5.1; 9.1].

Belshatzar gave a banquet after repelling the invasion and in his euphoria he brought out the captured vessels of the Beit Hamikdash. A hand appeared and wrote a cryptic message on the wall which no one could read. It was in Aramaic, in a calligraphic style (Ashurit) used only for very holy writings, and had not been seen or used since Yoshiyahu had buried the ark and Moshe's Torah scroll (see 3316/−445). The message as decoded by Daniel predicted the imminent fall of Bavel [Bible Dan.5./Rashi San.22a]. On that night, the Medians under Darius I and the Persians under Cyrus returned for battle, and in the ensuing confusion Belshatzar was killed by his own troops [Bible Dan.5.30/Mid.Rab.Sh.Hsh.a3.4]. Darius I then became king of the empire, and Babylonia ceased to be the center of power [Bible Dan.6.1].

Daniel was thrown into the lion's den.

Darius I appointed three viceroys to oversee the kingdom. One of them was Daniel who excelled in statesmanship and became the most prominent of them. This led to jealousy and intrigue, in which Darius I was maneuvered into proclaiming that no one was permitted to address any formal requests for anything at all, except to the king. Predictably, Daniel continued his daily prayers, which was a breach of the decree, and was consequently thrown into the lions' den (on the 15th Nissan), from which he miraculously emerged untouched, to the relief of Darius I [Bible Dan.6].

3390 / −371

Zerubavei led the return to Eretz Yisrael.

Darius I was killed in battle after ruling for only one year [Rashi Dan.6.29]; Cyrus became king and the power of the empire (see 3389/−372) moved to Persia. Cyrus immediately encouraged the Jews of Bavel to return to Eretz Yisrael and to rebuild the Beit Hamikdash [Bible D.H.II 36.22,23, Ez.1.1–4].

Over 40,000 people returned with Zerubavel (who was of the royal family), including Yehoshua (the Kohen, a nephew of Ezra), Nechemyah, and Mordechai but the majority remained behind (see 3413/−348) [Bible Ez.2.64, 65, D.H.I. 5.40, 41, Rashi/Mid.Tan.Sh.Tetz.13/Ibn Ez.Cha.1.1/ Tal.Kid.69b, Rashi/ Ran.Meg.1b].

3391 / −370

The building of the second Beit Hamikdash commenced and was halted.

Zerubavel the leader and Yehoshua the Kohen began building the altar when they arrived in desolate Yerushalayim [Bible Ez.3.1–3/Ibn Ez.Cha.1.1/ Rashi Kid.69b]. Although the foundation stones of the second Beit Hamikdash were not yet laid, they began the daily sacrifice services on Rosh Hashana, 3391 [Bible Ez.3.1–6/Tal.Zev.62a]. More than one fourth of those who returned to Eretz Yisrael with Zerubavel were from tribes other than Yehuda and Binyamin [Sed.01./Rashi Ez.2.64]. Zerubavel and Yehoshua (now the Kohen Gadol) organized the construction of the Beit Hamikdash, which began in Iyar. They also organized a choir of Levi'im (Levites) to sing (as was the practice during services in the Beit Hamikdash) while the building progressed [Bible Ez.3.5,10]. The Kuthim (Samaritans) (see 3205/−556) asked to help in the reconstruction but were discouraged. They subsequently disrupted the rebuilding and persuaded Cyrus to withdraw his authorization to build. Construction ground to a halt, and the Kuthim actively sought to have the ban continued (see 3395/−366) [Bible Ez.3.6,8; Rashi 4.1,7/Rashi Meg.16a].

3392 / −369

The prophets Chagay, Zecharyah, and Malachi (Ezra) were with Daniel, who was still a viceroy of the empire on the bank of the River Chidekel when he was overcome on the 24th Nissan by another mystical vision (which they did not see) [Bible Dan.6.29; 10; 11; 12/Tal.Meg.15a]. In this vision he was given two mystical numbers (1,290 and 1,335) [Bible Dan.12.11,12]. Chagay and Zecharyah went to Eretz Yisrael (see 3408/−353, 3412/−349) and Malachi went later (see 3413/−348).

3395 / −366

Achashverosh II made his great banquet.

Achashverosh II (who was not of royal descent) became emperor in 3392 after the death of Cyrus. He maintained and confirmed the moratorium on building the Beit Hamikdash, after being so persuaded by the Kuthim (see 3391/−370) [Bible Ez.4.6/Tal.Meg.11a, Rashi 16a, 11a/Sed.Ol./Rashi Est.9.10]. In the third year of his reign he made an elaborate banquet at which he had his wife (Vashti the daughter of Belshatzar) killed for not obeying his orders [Bible Est.1/Tal.Meg.11b/Mid.Yal.Est.1.1049/Sed.Ol.24,28/ Sed.Had.].

3399 / −362

Esther was taken to the palace.

Esther (Hadassa), who was 40 (some say even older) when taken to the palace in Tevet, realized, once she was selected to be Achashverosh's wife, that there must be some special purpose to her life [Bible Est.2.7,16/Mid.Rab.Est.6.6, Br.39.13/Sed.Had.].

Mordechai (a prophet) had come to Bavel three times: the first time with Yehoyachin (see 3327/−434), the second after the destruction of the first Beit Hamikdash, and the third time probably with Nechemyah (see 3426/−335) after work on the second Beit Hamikdash was halted in 3391 [Bible Est.2.5,6, Ez.2.2/Tal.Meg.13a,15a, Rashi 13a/Mid. Yal.Est.1053].

3404 / −357

Esther took action against Haman's decree.

The decree to exterminate the Jews was issued by the king on the 13th Nissan at the instigation of Haman (the prime minister), and Mordechai com-

municated the contents to Esther through Daniel (Hatach) who, although retired, still had access to the palace [Bible Est.3.8; 4.5-10/Tal.Meg.15a]. At Esther's request, the Jews of Shushan fasted on the 13th, 14th, and 15th Nissan (even though the 15th was Pesach) [Bible Est.4.15-17/Tal.Meg.15a/Mid.Rab.Est.8.7,Yal.4, Pir.Dr.El.53]. On the last day of the fast, Esther invited Achashverosh II and Haman to dinner that evening and again on the next. At the second dinner, she finally revealed that she was Jewish and had been clandestinely keeping to her religion. She pleaded the case for her people with Achashverosh II. Haman was disgraced and consequently hanged and Esther then attempted to have the decree withdrawn (see 3405/−356) [Bible Est.2.20;5.1-8; 7.1-10/Tal.Meg.13a/Mid.Yal.1053].

3405 / −356

Achashverosh II was unwilling to send out proclamations withdrawing Haman's decree but he permitted Mordechai and Esther to send out supplementary proclamations, which they did on the 23rd Sivan 3404. The new proclamations authorized the Jews to fight anyone who attempted to implement the previous decree. Consequently, on the 13th (and 14th) of Adar 3405 the Jews had to fight some people, although many non-Jews were impressed with their stand and converted to Judaism. On the 14th (and 15th) the Jews rejoiced in their relief (see 3406/−355) [Bible Est.8.8,9,11,17; 9.1-5,17,18].

3406 / −355

Mordechai proclaimed Purim.

After the 15th Adar 3405, Mordechai wrote and distributed the Book of Esther declaring the celebration of Purim. In 3406 (the same year that Achashverosh II died), Esther and Mordechai sent out reminders about the forthcoming celebration of Purim [Bible Est.9.20-23,29, Rashi]. The Anshei Knesset Hagdola (see 3426/−335, 3448/−313) accepted Mordechai's proclamations [Tal.B.B.15a]; he became a statesman, which subsequently diminished his influence in Jewish circles [Tal.Meg.16b/ Rashi Est.10.3].

3408 / −353

Building of the second Beit Hamikdash was resumed.

Chagay conveyed a prophecy to Zerubavel and Yehoshua (on the 1st Elul) that they should not be concerned with previous obstructions to rebuilding the Beit Hamikdash. In 3408, Darius II (Daryavesh II, the son of Esther and Achashverosh II, who succeeded his father in 3406) allowed the building of the second Beit Hamikdash to continue. This was seventy years after the destruction of the first [Bible Ez.5; 6/Mid.Rab.Est.8.3/Sed.Had.].

On the 24th Elul preparations began, and on the 24th Kislev building resumed [Bible Cha.1.1,2,15; 2.18, Rashi].

3412 / −349

The second Beit Hamikdash was completed.

On the 4th Kislev 3410, Zecharyah had prophesied (in Eretz Yisrael) that there was no longer any need to mourn the destruction of the first Beit Hamikdash [Bible Zech.7.1-7; 8.19, Rashi 7.2].

The second Beit Hamikdash was completed on the 3rd Adar 3412 [Bible Ez.6.15].

The King of Persia insisted that an engraving of the city of Shushan be placed in the Beit Hamikdash as a clear indication of who had authorized the rebuilding, and it was placed on the eastern gate, which was consequently called Sha'ar Shushan [Tal.Min.98a, Rashi, Mido.1.3, Mmn.Pir. Mish].

CHAPTER 8

The Second Beit Hamikdash

Greek Cultural Domination

Kingdom of Yehuda (Judea) – Dynasty of the Chashmona'im

Roman Client Kings and Rulers – The Herodian Dynasty

The eighth chapter in Jewish history covers the convulsive life of Jews in Eretz Yisrael, reduced in size to Eretz Yehuda (Judea) and under almost continuous pressure from within and without. This chapter ends with the destruction of the second Beit Hamikdash, when the Jewish people suffered a severe blow to their national standing.

THE SECOND BEIT HAMIKDASH

3412	**THE SECOND BEIT HAMIKDASH WAS COMPLETED**	**−349**
3413	**Ezra led the second return to Eretz Yisrael**	**−348**
3426	Nechemyah returned to rebuild the walls of Yerushalayim	−335
3448	**EZRA DIED**	**−313**
3448	Shimon HaTzadik met Alexander the Great	−313
3449	The Minyan Shtarot began	−313

Greek Cultural Domination

3488	Shimon HaTzadik died	−273
3515	**Seventy-two elders translated the Torah into Greek (Septuagint)**	**−246**
3621	**The revolt of Mattityahu the Chashmona'i**	**−140**

Kingdom of Yehuda (Judea) – Dynasty of the Chashmona'im

3622	Yehuda (HaMaccabi) ruled	−139
3622	The Second Beit Hamikdash was rededicated	−139
3623	**CHANUKA WAS DECLARED A FESTIVAL**	**−138**
3628	**Yehuda (HaMaccabi) was killed in battle**	**−133**
3628	Yonatan (son of Mattityahu) ruled	−133
3634	Shimon (son of Mattityahu) ruled	−127
3642	Yochanan Hyrkanos (son of Shimon) ruled	−119
3668	Yehuda Aristoblus (son of Yochanan Hyrkanos) ruled	−93
3670	Alexander Yannai (son of Yochanan Hyrkanos) ruled	−91
3688	Shalomit (Queen Salome, wife of Alexander Yannai) ruled	−73
3696	Aristoblus II (son of Alexander Yannai) ruled	−65
3700	**The Romans gained control of Yehuda (Judea)**	**−61**
3700	Hyrkanos II (son of Alexander Yannai) ruled	−61
3721	Antigonus (son of Aristoblus II) ruled	−40

Roman Client Kings and Rulers – The Herodian Dynasty

3725	**Herod I ruled and killed all the Chashmona'im**	**−36**
3728	**Hillel became leader of the Torah scholars**	**−33**
3742	**Herod I commenced rebuilding the second Beit Hamikdash**	**−19**
3750	Renovations of the second Beit Hamikdash were completed	−11
3761	Archelaus (son of Herod I) ruled	1
3768	Hillel died	8

Jewish Year		Secular Year
3770	Archelaus was deposed by the Roman Emperor	10
3781	Agrippa I (grandson of Herod I) ruled	21
3788	**The Sanhedrin moved from the second Beit Hamikdash**	28
3804	Agrippa II (son of Agrippa I) ruled	44
3810	Raban Gamliel I (son of Shimon, son of Hillel) died	50
3826	**Vespasian arrived in Yehuda to reassert Roman authority**	66
3829	**THE SECOND BEIT HAMIKDASH WAS DESTROYED**	69

3413 / −348

Ezra led the second return to Eretz Yisrael.

Baruch ben Neriyah was too old and weak to make the journey to Eretz Yisrael, and his disciple Ezra (the son of Serayah, see 3339/−423) did not leave Bavel (Babylonia) until after his death [Bible Ez.7.1.-7/Tal.Meg.16b, R.H.3b/Mmn.Hakd.L'Yad].

Ezra was the head of the Sanhedrin known as Anshei Knesset Hagdola, and this court went to Eretz Yisrael with him [Rashi b.B.8a, 15a/Mmn.Hakd. .'Yad].

Ezra emphasized clarification of family lineage (in Bavel and in Eretz Yisrael), and he arrived in Yerushalayim on the 1st Av. He arrived with only a small group of Jews, compared with the numbers that came in the first return with Zerubavel. The majority of Jews (including great Torah scholars) chose to remain in Bavel (see 3390/−371) because of the harsh conditions prevailing in Eretz Yisrael [Bible Ez.7.8,9; 8/Tal.Yom.9b, Suk.20a, Rashi/RaN.Meg. b/SMaG Hakd.].

Ezra officially gave the months Babylonian names (Nissan, Iyar, etc., instead of 1st month, 2nd, etc.), as a form of commemoration of the exile that had been (see 2447/−1314) [Tal.Kid.69a-b, Rashi 69b, Yev.86b, Yer.R.H.1.2/Tos.R.H.7a/Ramban Sh.12.2].

3414 / −347

Ezra addressed a three-day assembly of all the Jews on the 20th Kislev, and they accepted his admonitions that they adhere firmly to their religious practices. They set up courts, which sat on the 1st Tevet to investigate and assess the intermarriage problem. On the 1st Nissan they reported that only 17 Kohanim and 96 others had taken non-Jewish wives [Bible Ez.10]. Ezra made the second Para Aduma (Red Heifer) (see 2449/−1312) [Tal.Par.3.5].

The Jews of Eretz Yisrael still referred to themselves as "Bnei HaGola" (exiles) [Bible Ez.10.7].

3426 / −335

Nechemyah returned to rebuild the walls of Yerushalayim.

Nechemyah had returned to Babylonia and become an important minister to Darius II. He received disturbing reports on conditions in Eretz Yisrael, particularly dealing with problems of safety in Yerushalayim (whose wall had not been repaired since the destruction in 3338). In Nissan he gained the support of the king to go to Yerushalayim and rebuild the walls. During this reconstruction, they had to keep a continuous guard against their enemies, the Kuthim (Samaritans) [Bible Nech.1.1-3; 2.1,5-8,10,19; 4.1,2,10-17]. After the walls were completed (on the 25th Elul) and the gates were fitted (on the 7th Iyar), they celebrated with two concurrent parades led by Ezra and Nechemyah [Bible Nech. 6.15; 12.27-42/Tal. Shev.15b]. The gates of Yerushalayim were opened at certain times only, because many houses were still uninhabited, and the Kuthim continued their antagonism (see 3391/−370, 3395/−366) [Bible Nech.7.1-4]. Ezra and the Anshei Knesset Hagdola excommunicated the Kuthim from Shomron (see 3205/−566, 4046/−286) [Mid.Yal. Mel. II 17, Pir.Dr. El.38]. The 120 elders of the Anshei Knesset Hagdola (80 of them were prophets) included Ezra (Malachi, see 3392/−369) as head, Zecharyah, Chagay, Daniel, Chananyah, Misha'el, Azaryah, Nechemyah, Mordechai, Zerubavel, and Shimon Hatzadik [Tal. Meg.17b, Av.1.1, Yer.Ber.2.4 17a, Yer.Meg.1.5 6b/Rashi B.B. 15a, Chul.139b/Mmn.Hakd.L'Yad].

They instituted, among other things (see 3406/−355, 3413/−348, 3448/−313), daily prayer, the Shmona Esrei (eighteen) blessings of prayer, Kiddush, Havdala, and the regular individual blessings [Tal.Ber.33a-b, 26b, Rashi, Meg.17b/Mmn.Hil.Tfi.1.3,4].

3438 / −323

Jews began returning to Yerushalayim, although the numbers still remained very small and Nechemyah was recalled to Bavel by Darius II. When he returned to Eretz Yisrael (the third time, see 3426/−335) after a short absence, he set out to correct the worsening religious and safety problems. He also induced the wealthy to support the poor [Bible Nech.5, 13].

The Jewish birthrate was very high at this time (and for a number of generations later), exponentially increasing the population of Eretz Yisrael [Mid.Rab.Sh.Hash.1.16.3, Eycha 1.2].

3448 / −313

Ezra died.

Ezra died on the 9th Tevet; Chagay and Zecharyah had already died, and Nechemyah returned again to Bavel (see 3438/−323) where he also died. This marked the end of prophecy [Tal.San. 11a, Yom.9a/Yuch.1.14/Kuz.3.39,65,67/Yuch.1/Mag.Av.O.C.580.6].

Ezra the scribe (and the head of the Anshei Knesset Hagdola) had officially publicized (published) all 24 books of the Torah (some had been previously unavailable) in accurate original holy writing (see 3389/−372). He had clarified every detailed letter and incorporated the last prophets as well [Tal.B. B.15a Rashi, San.22a, Rashi, Av.Dr.Nat.1.4, Rashi Shab.6b/Mid. Tan.Sh.Besh.16].

Alexander (the Macedonian) who conquered Persia (see 3390/−371 sought to extend the empire. All the archives of Yehuda (Judea) originally confiscated by the Babylonians (see 3338/−423) were transferred to Alexander, and to Aristotle his mentor [Tal.A.Z.9a/Kuz.1.63, Otz.Nech.; 2.66/Tor.Ha01.3.7/ Tzem.Dav./Sed.Had.].

Shimon HaTzadik met Alexander.

The Kuthim (Samaritans) (see 3426/−335) received Alexander's permission to destroy the Beit Hamikdash when they described it as a symbol of rebellion against the empire [Tal.Yom.69a]. Shimon HaTzadik, the last of the Anshei Knesset Hagdola, was chosen to meet Alexander and attempt to change his mind [Tal.Av.1.1, Mach.Vit./Mmn.Hak.L'Yad Dor.Har.1.197]. When he went out to meet him on the 25th Tevet, adorned in the garments of the Kohen Gadol, Alexander jumped off his horse and bowed to him, explaining to his surprised (and angry) generals that he often had visions of a similar man leading him into battle. After visiting the Beit Hamikdash and seeing the services conducted there, Alexander withdrew his support of the destructive plans of the Kuthim [Tal.Yom. 69a A.Z.9a/Yuch.1.13]. The Kuthim later built their own temple on Mount Gerizim [Yuch.1.14/Sed.Had.].

Canaanite and Yishmaelite tribes made representations to Alexander claiming the territory of Eretz Yisrael. Geviha (the hunchback) successfully argued the Jewish case on the 24th Nissan [Ta. San.91a/Mid.Rab.Br.60.7].

Alexander, a Macedonian, was raised in the culture of the neighboring Greek city-states. He spread this culture wherever he went, and after his conquest of the Middle East the Greek letters (Alpha, Beta, etc.) were used for identification purposes in the Beit Hamikdash [Tal.Shek. 3.2 Riv'van].

3449 / −313

The Minyan Shtarot began.

Alexander requested that his statue be placed in the Beit Hamikdash. Shimon HaTzadik explained how disagreeable this would be to Jewish religious feelings and suggested that the Jews could bestow an even greater honor on him by naming all the male Kohanim born in that year "Alexander." They would also accept that year (of his conquest of the empire) as the first year of counting in all legal documents. This system, Minyan Shtarot, commenced on the 1st Tishrei 3449, was still in use 1500 years later although it was not formally discontinued until an even later date (see 5277/−1517) [Tal.Yom.69a, A.Z.9a, Rashi/Sed.01. 30/ Mmn.Hil.Kid.Hach.11.16, Hil.Gir.1.27/Yuch.1.13/Dor.Har.1.109].

3454 / −307

Alexander died and his kingdom was divided among four of his generals who ruled over separate (warring) states. Eretz Yisrael was geographically caught between two of them, the Egyptians, ruled by a dynasty of kings (most of whom were called Ptolemy) and the Syrians (whose kings were mostly called Seleucius, Antiochus, and Demetrius). There were many wars between these two states, and Eretz Yisrael was usually dominated by one or the other [Rashi Dan.11.4.17].

The Ptolemy who reigned after Alexander's death attempted (unsuccessfully) to have the Torah translated by five scholars (see 3515/−246) [Tal.Sof.1.7, 8/Tzem.Dav.2.3454, 3484]. He also exiled over 100,000 Jews to Egypt [Yuch.5.154/Tzem.Dav./Sed.Had.], and Alexandria began to flourish as a Jewish center [Tal.Suk.51b, Hag.R.B.Rans., Yer.Suk.5.2/Yuch.1.13].

3488 / −273

Shimon HaTzadik died.

Shimon HaTzadik was Kohen Gadol for 40 years (and Av [head] of the Sanhedrin). If, as some say, he directly succeeded Ezra [Mmn.Hakd.L'Yad], then he died in 3488. If, as others say, he succeeded his father Chonyo I, who in turn succeeded his father Ido [Yuch.5.154], then he may have died after 3488 [Tal.Yom.9a/Dor.Har.1.197,199]. Antigonus (Ish Socho) succeeded him as Av of the Sanhedrin [Tal.Av.1.3/Dor.Har.1.199].

Shimon HaTzadik's son Chonyo II left for Egypt (see 3454/−307) after a jealous dispute with his brother Shim'i because the latter had become Kohen Gadol, and he built an altar (for sacrifices) in Egypt [Tal. Min.109b, Mmn.Pir.Mi./Tol.Am.01. 2.394].

Yehoshua ben Sira (who was still young) praised Shimon HaTzadik at the end of his book, Ben Sira although he referred to him only as Shimon the Kohen Gadol, see 3580/−181). This book was not accepted as a Torah writing, although the Talmud quotes phrases from it in a number

of places [Ta1. San.100b, Rashi/Toseph.Yad.2.5/Sed.Had.3298/Dor.Har.1.193].

3515 / −246

Seventy-two Elders translated the Torah into Greek (Septuagint).

In this second attempt to have the Torah translated (see 3454/−307), seventy-two great Torah scholars were gathered by the ruling Ptolemy, sequestered separately, and forced to translate the Torah into Greek. They produced seventy-two corresponding translations (including identical changes in thirteen places) on the 8th Tevet [Tal.Sof.1.7,8, Meg.9a/TBY.O.C.580.1/Tzem.Dav./Tol.Am.01. 2. 397]. Later published versions are not believed to be true to the originals [Sed.Had.]. Greek became a significant second language among Jews as a result of the translation [Mmn.Pir.Mi.Meg.17a/Tos.Y.T.Shek.5.3].

3530 / −231

Antigonus Ish Socho had died by this time, and Yosef (Yosee) ben Yochanan (his disciple) was appointed Av of the Sanhedrin [Tal.Av.1.4/Dor.Har. 1.173, 199]. The misinterpretation of Antigonus' teachings by two of his students (Tzadok and Baytuss) were further amplified by their students and eventually developed into a movement called Tzedukim (Sadducees), of which the Baytussim were a faction. Josephus (a sympathizer of theirs) described them [Ant.18.1.4] as a secularist movement believing only in the here and now [Tal.R.H.22b, Av.Dr.Nat.5.2/Dor.Har.2.361-3,372, 400,413,419-21,479].

3550 / −211

Chonyo II who had returned from Egypt (see 3488/−273) to become Kohen Gadol was petty and tight-fisted. He refused to hand over the taxes due to Egypt. Yosef ben Tuviyah then volunteered (to the ruling Ptolemy) to collect taxes for a commission, and his proposal was accepted. This averted a crisis but established him as the powerful, ruthless, and wealthy leader of an organized class of collaborating tax collectors who filled the power vacuum created by a weak Kohen Gadol [Yuch.5.6.155/Dor.Har.1.171,184].

In order to redeem some of the leadership lost by default from the office of the Kohen Gadol (who had also been responsible for such civil matters as tax collection), the Sanhedrin created the higher position of Nassi (president) of the Sanhedrin, and appointed another of Antigonus' disciples, Yosef (Yosee) ben Yo'ezer, to fill it. This was the first such combined leadership, Yosef ben Yochanan as Av (head) of the Sanhedrin and (above him) Yosef ben Yo'ezer as Nassi [Tal.Av.1.4/Mmn.Sef.Mitz.316, Hil. San.1.3/Dor.Har.1.199, 200].

3570 / −191

Yosef ben Yochanan died, and conditions in Eretz Yisrael were changed under the influence of the tax collectors (see 3550/−211), the Tzedukim (Sadducees) (see 3530/−231), the Hellenists (who promoted acceptance of "progressive" Greek culture), and the Kuthim (Samaritans). These groups shared a common antagonism to the majority of the Jews who maintained close adherence to the laws and traditions of the Torah under the guidance of the Sanhedrin and who were later called Perushim (Pharisees) [Yuch.5.6.156/Dor.Har.2.362-5,Note (3)].

3580 / −181

The cult of the Essenes emerged (some say around this time). They lived (mostly) in secluded agricultural communes. Many in this elitist group did not marry and have families, because they considered that to be too materialistic. According to Josephus [Ant.18.1.3, 5] (a sympathizer [Vita 2.]) their sacrifices were not accepted in the Beit Hamikdash because they had different laws of purity. There were similarities in intensity between the customs of the Essenes and those of the Kuthim(Samaritans) [Tal.Ber.47b/Yuch.5.6.157/Sed.Had.3460].

Chonyo II had died around this time, and his son Shimon II became Kohen Gadol. People began referring to the first Shimon as Shimon HaTzadik to distinguish between him and his grandson as

they were both named Shimon ben Chonyo Kohen Gadol [Dor.Har.1.181, 195].

3600 / −161

Eretz Yisrael was dominated by the Syrians at this time (see 3454/−307). Shimon II had died, and his son Chonyo III became Kohen Gadol. He reduced the political power of the Hellenists and the tax collectors (the descendants of Yosef ben Tuviyah, see 3550/−211). Both these groups differed essentially in the emphasis of their collaboration and identification with the ruling powers (Syrian Greeks) [Dor.Har.1.176, 184, 186; 2.393].

3610 / −151

In collaboration with the ruling Antiochus of that time, (Yeshua) Jason, a Hellenist, replaced his brother Chonyo III as Kohen Gadol. Chonyo III subsequently went to Egypt and built a temple for the altar of Chonyo II his grandfather (see 3488/−273), which stood for over 300 years [Tal.Meg.10a/Tos.Zev.119a(Zu)/Yuch.5.156/Tol.Am.01.2.404].

The Hellenists in collaboration with the Syrians (Greeks) conducted a harsh program to eliminate Jewish religious observance in Eretz Yisrael [Dor.Har.2.375]. Menelaus (who excelled in cultural collaboration) replaced Jason as Kohen Gadol and actively involved the Syrians in increasing the religious persecution and desecration [Dor. Har.2.374-6]. At first they forbade certain sacrifices to be brought to the Beit Hamikdash, but when they gained a more strategic foothold in Yerushalayim itself they completely stopped the holy services. Apustomus, one of the Syrian leaders, burned a Sefer Torah on the 17th Tammuz [Tal.Tan.26b,Rashi 28a, Mrsha].

The Syrians enforced severe penalties for Jews who kept the religious laws of the Torah, especially Shabbat, circumcision (mila), and marriage [Tal.Ket.3b, San.32b]. There were many incidents of death and destruction. Miriam (some say Chanah) and her seven sons were brutally killed [Tal.Git.57b

Mid.Rab.Eych.1.50, Haradal/Yuch.1.14/Tzem.Dav.]. Yosef ben Yo'ezer was killed. Yehoshua ben Perachya and Nitai Ha'arbeli (respectively) became Nassi (president) and Av (head) of the Sanhedrin [Tal.Av.1.6/ Mid.Rab.Br. 65.22/Dor.Har.1.160].

At this time the Jews in Bavel (see 3342/−419, 3413/−348) were living peacefully, free from the troubles that tormented the Jews of Eretz Yisrael and with scholarly leadership and direction.

The Jews in Egypt (see 3454/−307) were thriving, but not in Torah scholarship, even though they had established their own Sanhedrin [Tal. Ket.25a, Min.110a, Mrsha, Suk.51b, Rashi, Tos./Mid.Tan.Br.Noach /Yuch.5.156/Sed.Had./Dor.Har.1.101-2].

3621 / −140

The revolt of Mattityahu the Chashmona'i.

After years of physical and spiritual destruction in Eretz Yisrael, Mattityahu (the aging son of Yochanan), and his five sons (Yochanan, Shimon, Yehuda, Elazar, and Yonatan) staged a rebellion in Modi'in, when the Syrian (Greek) authority came to initiate his daughter before her marriage. The revolt quickly spread under his leadership [Meg. Tan.6/Yuch.1.14/Tzem.Dav./Sed.Had.].

Some say that the revolt of the Chashmona'im was in 3590, but this is inconsistent with the Talmud [See Appendix A] [A.Z.9a/Tzem.Dav.3590, 3621/Sed. Had.].

NESSI'IM – PRESIDENTS OF THE SANHEDRIN	
	Jewish Year
Yosef (Yosee) ben Yo'ezer	3550
Yehoshua ben Perachya	3610
Shimon ben Shatach	3688
Hillel	3729
Shimon (ben Hillel)	3769
Rbn. Gamliel I (ben Shimon)	3769
R.Shimon ben Gamliel I	3810
R.Gamliel II (ben R. Shimon)	3828
R. Elazar ben Azaryah[1]	3844
R.Shimon ben Gamliel II	3878
R.Yehuda HaNassi	3925
R.Gamliel III (ben R.Yehuda)	3949
R.Yehuda Nessia I (ben Gamliel)	3949
R.Gamliel IV (ben Yehuda)	3990
R.Yehuda Nessia II (ben Gamliel)	3990
R.Gamliel V (ben Yehuda)	4060
R.Yehuda Nessia III (ben Gamliel)	4069
Hillel II (ben Yehuda)	4119
R.Gamliel VI (ben Yehuda)	4189

[1]Approximately twenty years of his leadership were shared (see 3864), and he was the only Nassi from the time of Hillel, who was not his direct descendant.

3622 / −139

Yehuda (HaMaccabi) ruled.

After a year of leadership and many successful battles against the Syrians (Greeks), Mattityahu died and his son Yehuda become leader [Tal.A.Z.9a/Mid.Rab.Sh.15.6/Sed.Ol./Yuch.1.14/Tzem.Dav./Sed.Had./Ramban Br.49.10]. The small band of fighters had grown into a national movement and they gained control of the Beit Hamikdash, which they entered on the 24th or 25th Kislev [Tal.Shab.21b/Targ. Sh.Hash. 6.9/Mmn. Hil.Chan.3.2/Meiri Shab.21b (Jer.p25)].

The second Beit Hamikdash was re-dedicated.

The Beit Hamikdash had been misused (and desecrated) for years, and many things needed repair or replacement. Most of the holy utensils were ritually impure, and there were also no ritually pure supplies stored away for the services. The most difficult to obtain was oil but a small container was found, and although normally sufficient for one day, it miraculously burned for eight festive days in a makeshift Menora [Tal.Shab.21b, Min.89a A.Z.43a, Rashi, 52b/Meg.Tan.2, 9, Rashi Sh.27.21]. Yochanan ben Mattityahu became Kohen Gadol [See Appendix B] [Tal.R.H.18b/Mmn.Hakd.Pir.Mi.Zer.Chap.4,6,7/Roke'ach 225/Levush Hil.Chan.670]. Yehudit, his daughter, infiltrated the enemy camp and killed their leader [Tal.Shab.23a, Rashi/Mid.q. RaN Shab.10a (23a)/Shilt.Gib.Mord. 456.2/KolBo Chan.44 p.3c/Ramo O.C.670.2].

KINGS AND RULERS OF THE CHASHMONA'IM DYNASTY

	Jewish Year
Yehuda HaMaccabi	3622
Yonatan	3628
Shimon	3634
Yochanan Hyrkanos	3642
Yehuda Aristoblus	3668
Alexander Yannai	3670
Shalomit	3688
Aristoblus II	3696
Hyrkanos II	3700
Antigonus	3721

3623 / −138

Chanuka was declared a festival.

Yochanan Kohen Gadol composed the "Al Ha Nissim" prayer [Roke'ach 225/KolBo 44p4b, 122p926] and was responsible for the festival of Chanuka [Roke'ach 225/Levush Hil.Chan.670], together with his peers, the leaders of the Sanhedrin (Yehoshua ben Perachya and Nitai Ha'arbeli [Tal.Shab.21b/Mmn.Hil. Chan.3.3/Hak.Pir.Mi.chap.4,7].

The Chashmona'im won many successive victories, and those days were set aside and celebrated as commemorative days for some time without any specific laws or customs [Tal.R.H.19b/Meg.Tan.2,6, 9,12].

3628 / −133

Yehuda (HaMaccabi) was killed in battle.

The Chashmona'im had to fight many battles even after their initial victories in 3621-3622; in one of those battles Elazar was crushed by an elephant, and (later) Yehuda was killed. Yehuda had made friendly contacts with the Romans, who were already building an empire, and thought it useful to have allies in the strategic Middle East [Targ.Sh.Hash. 6.8,9/Ramban.Br.32.4; 49.10/Yuch. 1.14/Tzem.Dav./Sed.Had.]. Four months after Yehuda was killed in battle, his brother Yonatan became ruler of Yehuda (Judea). His was a relatively peaceful reign over what was now called the Kingdom of Yehuda (Judea) [Tzem.Dav./Sed.Had.]. Yochanan Kohen Gadol, his brother [see Appendix B], had sent delegations all over the country to inquire about religious practices and make many adjustments [Tal.Sot.47a, 48a, Par.3.5]. Jews from Egypt (see 3610/ −151) came to the Beit Hamikdash for festivals, and the visiting artisans helped to extend the skills of the local artisans [Tal.Yom.38a, 61a,b].

The Chashmona'im became well established, the Sanhedrin exercised its powers, and the Tzedukim could no longer be overt atheists (for fear of the penalties). They therefore claimed to adhere (only) to the Written Law of the Bible (available to these second and third generation secularists/Hellenists/Tzedukim in Greek (see 3515/−246), the only language they knew). Their interpretations of the Written Law was free and varied, and some say that this was the beginning of the sect of Kra'im (Karaites) (see 4523/763) [Mmn.Pir.Mi.Av.1.3, Hil.Mam.3.3/Yuch.1.14/Tzem.Dav.4515/Dor.Har.2.361-364, 387, 413].

3634 / −127

Yonatan was killed in battle and was succeeded as ruler of the kingdom of Yehuda by his brother Shimon in 3634 [Ramban Br.49.10/Yuch.1.14/Tzem.Dav./Sed.Had.].

The Perushim (see 3570/−191) who had remained in Eretz Yisrael during the many years of strife (before the revolt of the Chashmona'im) were impoverished by the continuous persecution, whereas the collaborating secularists/Hellenists/Tzedukim, many of whom were descendants of Yosef ben Tuviyah and his tax-collecting agents, retained their wealth and upper-class status [Tal.Av.Dr.Nat.5.2/Dor.Har.2.391].

3642 / −119

Shimon had lived in a wealthy manner and "outclassed" the wealthy secularists (see 3634/−127). He was killed by his son-in-law, or a Ptolemy from Egypt. Some say this was the same person. His two older sons were also killed, but his son Yochanan Hyrkanos (also called Yannai I) escaped and became ruler of Yehuda (Judea) [Tos.Yom.18a/ Yuch.5.6.156/Tzem.Dav./Sed.Had./Dor.Har.2.392/Tol. Am.01.2. 409]. Yochanan Hyrkanos also became Kohen Gadol, probably directly after his uncle, Yochanan Kohen Gadol, which some say was in 3628 [Tzem.Dav.3668].

He attempted to avenge his father's death but was restrained by a threat to kill his mother, who was killed anyway. He conquered territories and forced some Judaism on the conquered peoples; he fought battles against the south (Egypt) and the north (Syria). He opened the grave of King David and took some gold that was buried there to en-

courage the Antiochus of that time to leave Eretz Yehuda [Yuch.5.156/Tzem.Dav./Sed.Had./Dor.Har.2.392-3].

3648 / −113

The Romans took a dominant stand in their ties with Yehuda (Judea), in 3648 (see 3628/−133) [Taz.A.Z.8b]. Nevertheless, because of the successful battles of Yochanan Hyrkanos (see 3642/−119), there was peace and prosperity in the expanded kingdom of Yehuda.

Yochanan Hyrkanos (Yannai I) invaded Shomron, the capital of the Kuthim (Samaritans), and destroyed their temple on Mount Gerizim (see 3448/−313) [Yuch.1.14/Tzem.Davd./Sed.Had.]. On his return from a successful battle, he gave a banquet and also invited Tzedukim with whom he maintained cordial relations. One of them aroused his suspicions about how genuine the allegiance of the Perushim was (to his dual role as Kohen Gadol and ruler), and when one of the older Perushim inelegantly criticized him, Yochanan Hyrkanos became infuriated. The Tzedukim incited him to have the scholarly leaders of the Perushim killed, a challenge he eventually accepted [Tal.Kid.66a, Mrsha/ Dor.Har.2.391].

3668 / −93

Yochanan Hyrkanos later in life became a Tzeduki, after the incident at the banquet (see 3648/−113). He killed most of the Torah scholars. Yehoshua ben Perachya had fled to Egypt, and Shimon ben Shatach was hidden by his sister Shalomit (Salome I), the daughter-in-law of Yochanan Hyrkanos (see 3670/−91) [Tal.Kid.66a, Ber.29a, 48a, Ches.San.107b/Mag.Av.2.4/Sed.Had./Dor.Har.2460, 476]. After he died, in 3668 [Tzem.Dav.] or 3666 [Yuch.5.156], his son Yehuda Aristoblus succeeded him as ruler of Yehuda instead of his wife (as he had wished) [Dor.Har.2.454]. Yehuda Aristoblus, also a Tzeduki, demeaned the role of Kohen Gadol by appointing the highest bidder to that honorable position. Thus (with their money, see 3634/ −127) the Tzedukim gained control of the key political and religious positions of power, and appointed members of their own families to other important positions [Tal.Yom.8b, Mmn.Pir.Mi.18a, Pes.57a/ Mid.Rab.Vay.21.9]. The power-oriented Yehuda Aristoblus jailed his brother Alexander Yannai and his mother (who died in prison), favoring his younger brother Antigonus, whom he later had killed (because of a suspected revolt) [Tzem.Dav./Dor.Har.2.454-7].

3670 / −91

After he killed his younger brother Antigonus, (see 3668/−93), the sick Yehuda Aristoblus did not live long. He had no children and so his brother Alexander Yannai (also a Tzeduki) was released from imprisonment (see 3668/−93) and succeeded him [Tzem.Dav./Sed.Had.]. Some say that Shalomit was originally the wife of Yehuda Aristoblus, and that because they had no children she released Alexander Yannai, married him (*yibum*), and made him king of Yehuda (Judea) [Bible Dev.25.5-10/Dor.Har.2.460].

Shalomit (Salome I) arranged for her brother Shimon ben Shatach to be appointed to the Sanhedrin, which by that time was completely dominated by Tzedukim. He excelled over the others in scholarship and by careful strategy was able to replace them (one by one) with his disciples (see 3680/−81) [Meg.Tan.10].

3671 / −90

Yeshua ben Sitda, a student of Yehoshua ben Perachya, was rejected from the circle of scholars because of his undesirable behavior. He was later accused of idol worship and witchcraft and punished accordingly by the Sanhedrin [Tal.Ches.San. 43a, 67a, 107b/Yuch.1.16].

Some (manuscript) versions of the Talmud refer to him as Yeshu HaNotzri (the Nazarene), and relate events (mostly of his death) which bear similarities to those surrounding Jesus (see 3790/−30) [Tal. Ches.San.43a, 67a,103a, A.Z.17a, Ber.17b/Toseph.Shab. 11.15, Chul.2.6-end]. Many say or imply that this was, in

fact, Jesus, despite the lack of chronological synchronization (see 3790/−30) [Mmn.Igg.Teman(end)/ Sef.Hak.q.Sed.Had./Ramban Mil. Vik.22/Yuch.1.16/Sed.Had.3560, 3671, 3707, 3724, 3761]. Other claims that they are not the same person [Me'iri Sot.47a, (p.115 Jer. 1947), Hak.L'Avot (p.28, Jer. 1964)], could be supported by some of the references in the Talmud which appear to be contradictory in the chronological placement of Yeshu [Tal.Ches.A.Z.17a/Toseph.Chul2.6-end/Mid.Rab. Koh. 1.8#3]. Accordingly, events surrounding an earlier Yeshu may later have been used (or confused) to describe a later one. The history of Jesus (see 3790/−30) is shrouded in mystery; his historical prominence is not reflected in the writings of his time, and references to the early history of the church were often influenced by pressures brought to bear (see 5023/1263).

3680 / −81

Yehoshua ben Gamlah was appointed Kohen Gadol (after his wealthy wife Martha [Miriam] bat Baytuss paid an appropriate amount [see 3668/−93] to Alexander Yannai). Later (together with Shimon ben Shatach) he helped establish a national Torah educational system [Tal.B.B.21a, Yev. 6a, Tos., Yom.18a, Tos./Tal.Yer.Yom.5.1, Ket.8.11/Meg.Tan.12/ Mid.Rab.Eych.1.47/Yuch.1.15].

Shimon ben Shatach covertly sent a message to (his mentor) Yehoshua ben Perachya signaling that he could return from Egypt (see 3668/−93) [Tal. Ches.San.107b/Dor.Har.2.469]. He cleverly convinced Alexander Yannai to contribute to the expenses of the sacrifices of the poor [Tal.Yer.Naz.5.3/Mid. Rab.Br.91.3] and also managed to have him appear before the Sanhedrin over a charge of murder brought against a servant of his. The resultant confrontation of power (in the court) established a precedent that became law that a king should not participate in court proceedings [Tal.San.19a].

Alexander Yannai had a confrontation with the Perushim after someone threw an etrog at him, some say accidentally, during the Sukkot services (others say he ridiculed the services) in the Beit Hamikdash. He killed many of the Torah scholars, although some managed to escape and others fled the country [Tal.Suk.48b/Meg.Tan.12/Yuch.1.14/Tzem.Dav./Dor.Har.2.480-2].

Choni Ham'agel was a great Torah scholar who managed to remain prominent, yet survive [Tal.Tan.23a, Yer.Tan.3.9/Mmn.Hakd.Mi.Zer.Chap.4, 7].

3686 / −75

The people rebelled against Alexander Yannai (see 3680/−81) and fought open battles against him for six years during which at least 50,000 people were killed. He gruesomely killed 800 men and their families. When he was sick and dying, he expressed his regrets; nevertheless, his wife Shalomit considered retiring (with their two young sons) into private life and discontinuing the dynasty of the Chashmona'im [Dor.Har.2.484-92, 504-5].

3688 / −73

Shalomit (Salome I), also called Shalminin [Meg.Tan.10] and Shel Tzion [Shab.16b/Sed.Had.3670], succeeded her husband (see 3686/−75) as ruler of Yehuda (Judea). She was advised by him (before he died on the 7th Kislev) to rule until their sons (Hyrkanos II and Aristoblus II) were older, and also to associate with the Perushim because they could be trusted and would allow the dynasty (of the Chashmona'im) to continue [Tal.Sot.22b, Rashi/Meg.Tan.9 per Dor.Har. 2.678-9, 503-5/Tzem.Dav./Sed.Had.]. She appointed Hyrkanos to deal with matters of the Beit Hamikdash, and Aristoblus (a Tzeduki) as a regional governor outside of Yerushalayim [Tzem.Dav.].

Yehoshua ben Perachya and Nitai Ha'arbeli had died. Shimon ben Shatach convinced Yehuda ben Tabbai to return from Egypt, and subsequently they became leaders of the Sanhedrin as Nassi (president) and Av (head) [Tal.Yer.San.6.6/Dor.Har.2.470, 475-6]. During the peaceful years of Shalomit's rule, they made special judgments to reassert the authority of religious law [Tal.San.45b, 46a, Mak.5b, Chag.16b/Tzem.Dav.]. Shimon ben Shatach guided

Todos (Theodus), a leader of the Roman Jewish community [Tal.Ber. 19a, Pes.53a, Rashi].

3696 / −65

Even before his mother Shalomit died, Aristoblus II had begun wielding power with the army under his control. When she died, he took over the rule of Yehuda after a civil war with his brother Hyrkanos II which lasted for three months (until the elders made peace) [Tal.Sot.49b, Rashi/Yuch.5.156/Tzem.Dav./Sed.Had./Dor.Har.2.518-20]. Under his rule the Tzedukim regained political power (see 3688/−73) [Dor.Har.2.538].

Shimon ben Shatach and Yehuda ben Tabbai had already died, and Shem'aya and Avtalyon (descendants of converts and of Sancheriv) became the leaders of the Sanhedrin [Tal.Av 1.9,Git.57b, San.97b/Yuch.1.17/Dor.Har.1.71]. Hillel (a Babylonian Jew), who almost froze to death while listening at the window of their joint school of study (Beit Midrash) in his eagerness to learn, was a disciple of theirs [Tal.Yom.35b/Dor.Har.1.50].

3700 / −61

The Romans took control of Yehuda (Judea).

Hyrkanos II (stirred by Antipater, his adviser and a Roman sympathizer) regretted handing over the rule to his brother Aristoblus II (see 3696/−65). He waged a bitter civil war to gain control, and both brothers attempted to involve Pompey, whose Roman legions had been in the region for some time already. Pompey grasped the opportunity to exercise power and installed Hyrkanos II (who was weaker) as king, with Antipater as his minister [Tal.Min.64b, Sot.49b, Rashi/Rashi Sh.Hash.6.12, Rashi San.97b/Yuch.5.156/Tzem.Dav./Sed.Had./Dor.Har.1.1; 2.146].

Aristoblus II was led in captivity to Rome (which had already conquered and controlled a vast empire). Antipater (a schemer of Idumean descent, who married a non-Jewish Idumean) was in effective control of Judea through his friend Hyrkanos

II. They were sympathetic to the Perushim (due to political considerations), which meant that Torah scholarship could flourish as it had under the rule of Shalomit (Salome I), the mother of Hyrkanos II (see 3688/−73) [Tzem.Dav./Sed.Had./Dor.Har.2.544-6].

3714 / −47

R. Yochanan ben Zakkai was born in 3714 (see 3834/−74) during the reign of Julius Caesar, who respected Hyrkanos II [Tal.R.H.31b/Tzem.Dav./Sed.Had.].

3715 / −46

Shem'aya and Avtalyon had died, and Alexander II (a son of Aristoblus II) had rebelled against the Roman installation of his uncle Hyrkanos II as king, instead of his father (see 3700/−61). He was defeated with the assistance of Rome which, at the request of Antipater, also broadened the powers of Hyrkanos II to include all civil matters previously administered through the Sanhedrin in the Beit Hamikdash. This was, in effect, a dissolution of the highest court [Tal.Sot.48a, Yer.Sot. 9.11/Dor.Har.1.36, 55, 59, 61-63, 70]. No one was appointed to replace Shem'aya or Avtalyon as head of the Sanhedrin, but the respected family of Beteira was temporarily given leadership responsibilities [Tal.Pes.66a, B.M.85a/Yuch.1.18/Dor.Har.1.76].

Shamai, who had been a respected member of the high court, established his own school of study (Beit Midrash) [Dor. Har.1.76]. Admon and Chanan were (independently) famous judges for their rulings in two of the numerous lower courts [Tal. Ket.104b-105a/Mmn.Hakd.Mi.Zer.4].

Hyrkanos II reluctantly succumbed to public pressure to have Herod (son of his friend Antipater) brought to trial for participating in the slaying of a group of Jewish nationalists who had rebelled against the Roman occupation forces.

Herod arrogantly (and threateningly) appeared with some of his (armed) soldiers and only through the brave admonition of Shamai did the court proceedings continue. Hyrkanos II arranged, however, that the trial be postponed, and Herod escaped [Tzem.Dav./Sed.Had.3724/Dor.Har.1.46; 2.626-7, 630, 735].

3721 / −40

Antigonus, another son of Aristoblus II (see 3715/−46), engaged the help of the king of Partha (Persia), a successful warrior against the Romans, to conquer Yerushalayim and remove his uncle Hyrkanos II from Roman-sponsored power.

The attack succeeded and Hyrkanos II was taken to Partha as a captive but later released to lead the Jews in that area which included Bavel (Babylonia). However, the Romans later returned to remove Antigonus (the last ruler of the Chashmona'im dynasty) and reassert their control over Yehuda (Judea) (see 3725/−36) [Tzem.Dav./ Sed.Had.].

ROMAN CLIENT KINGS AND RULERS – HERODIAN DYNASTY	Jewish Year
Herod	3725
Archelaus	3761
Roman Procurators only[1]	3770-3781
Agrippa I	3781
Agrippa II	3804

3725 / −36

Herod I ruled and killed all the Chashmona'im.

The Emperor Augustus sent his Roman legions to forcefully install Herod I (see 3715/−46) as ruler of Yehuda in 3725 (see 3721/−40) [Sed.01./Tal.A.Z.9a/ Tzem.Dav./Sed.Had.].

Herod I realized that he would not be accepted because of his ancestry (see 3700/−61) and because of his ruthlessness (see 3715/−46), so he proceeded to kill all the Chashmona'im including, eventually, his own wife Miriam (daughter of Alexander II, see 3715/−46) and their children. He even encouraged Hyrkanos II to return from exile to Yerushalayim (see 3721/−40) so that he could kill him, thus eliminating all of the Chashmona'im [Tal.B.B.3b.Yuch.5.156/Tzem.Dav./Sed.Had.].

3727 / −34

For two years Herod I terrorized the Jews into accepting his reign (see 3725/−36). He restructured the country (building fortresses such as Massada) with the apparent intention of creating a secular kingdom in which the Jews would only be a part. Cities built with monies collected from Jews, he populated with non-Jews. On the completion of Caesarea he made a great celebration. He had apparently intended that this would be his

---

[1] There were no official Jewish leaders during this period – only Roman Procurators.

new capital, instead of Yerushalayim, but was thwarted by the Romans who suspected the strategic significance of his amibitions [Dor.Har.1.9-18].

3729 / −32

Hillel became leader of the Torah scholars.

Hillel (see 3696/−65), who was a descendant of King David [Tal.Ket.62b], had returned to Bavel but came to Eretz Yisrael in 3729 for Pesach. He was the only scholar to know a specific law relating to Pesach of that year. The family of Beteira (see 3715/−46) stepped aside, and Hillel was appointed leader of the scholars. He later became the Nassi of the Sanhedrin (with Shamai as Av), an office he elevated during the decline of the office of Kohen Gadol (see 3668/−93, 3550/−211, 3781/21) [Tal.Shab. 15a, Pes.66a, Suk.20a, Chag.16a, Rashi, Yom.Mish.1.6].

Hillel began his own Beit Midrash (separate from Shamai's see 3715/−46), a departure from the previous tradition (see 3696/−65). He did not wish to prematurely arouse the suspicions of Herod I that the central Sanhedrin was to re-emerge as a powerful and united voice under his leadership. In this manner Hillel quietly ushered in a new era, the era of the Tanna'im (first-generation Talmudists) [Tal.Suk.20a/Dor.Har.1.76, 77, 144; 2.548, 672]. Herod I (later) respected Hillel [Dor.Har.1.44].

3742 / −19

Herod I began to rebuild the second Beit Hamikdash.

When Herod presented the idea of rebuilding the second Beit Hamikdash, which was in bad repair after 334 years, the Jews were wary of his uncharacteristic suggestion (see 3727/−34), even though it had been raised by one of the Tanna'im, Bava ben Buta (who, although blinded, had survived Herod's massacre of the Tanna'im). The Jews feared that Herod was really scheming to demolish it. Some say it was a maneuver to mislead the Romans about his strategic ambitions in the region (see 3727/−34) [Tal.B.B.3b-4a/Tzem.Dav./Sed.Had./ Dor.Har.1.18-20].

3750 / −11

Renovation of the second Beit Hamikdash was completed.

The magnificent structure of (Herod's) Beit Hamikdash, completed in 3750, included gold taken from King David's grave (see 3642/−119) [Tal.B.B.4a, Suk.51b/Yuch.5.156/Tzem.Dav./Sed.Had.]. Herod I placed a religiously offensive (Roman) golden eagle above the entry (see 3760/−1).

Some say that due to Herod's cruel, disdainful treatment of the Jews (see 3725/−36, 3742/−19, 3760/−1, 3761/1), they became second-rate citizens in the eyes of the Romans; the international perception of the Jew irreversibly declined [Dor.Har. 1.27, 30, 35, 36; 2.673-8; 3.41].

3760 / −1

When Herod I lay dying, rumor spread that he had already died. A group of religious scholars (and students) tore down the religiously offensive golden eagle from above the gates of the Beit Hamikdash (see 3750/−11). These people were brought to Herod who had them burned alive.

Herod had a member of each Jewish family arrested and he ordered his sister Salome II (see 3761/1) to have them killed on the day he died, so that the Jews would mourn on that day [Meg.Tan.11 per Dor.Har.2.673-9].

3761 / 1

Herod I appointed his son Archelaus to rule over Yehuda (subject to the consent of the Roman emperor), after having killed some of his other sons [Tzem.Dav./Sed.Had.].

When Herod I died on the 2nd Shvat, his sister Salome II did not notify anyone, but sent word to the prison guard that the king had ordered the release of all the recent prisoners (members of each family) (see 3760/−1). When that had been done,

she announced that Herod was dead [Meg.Tan.11 per Dor.Har.2.678-9/Tzem.Dav./Sed.Had.].

When Archelaus succeeded his father many Jews were still languishing in prison, and Herod's non-Jewish officials were still in control.

Archelaus forcefully stopped the Pesach sacrifice on the 14th Nissan in a bloodbath where thousands were killed. The Jews sent a delegation (joined by many Roman Jews (see 3688/−73) to the emperor requesting that no king be approved. Archelaus went to Rome and he prevailed, although he was not approved as a full king by the emperor [Tzem.Dav./Sed.Had./Dor.Har.2.680-82, 688, 698-700].

While Archelaus was in Rome, the Roman High Commissioner of Syria sent in his legions to quell a 'possible' uprising in Yehuda. This was an unfounded charge but it gained Archelaus power. The general of these troops had his household guards ruthlessly extort money from Jews, creating a universal outcry for his withdrawal. The High Commissioner had him withdrawn, but this episode set an atmosphere of anarchy in Judea (see 3770/10, 3781/21) [Dor.Har.2.692-7].

3769 / 9

Hillel died.

Hillel, who had brought the Sanhedrin back to its original power (see 3715/−46), died and was succeeded by his son Shimon to the now elevated position of Nassi of the Sanhedrin (see 3729/−32). Shimon did not live long, and was succeeded by his son Raban Gamliel I, the first to be called "Raban." Thus the leadership of the Jews was in the hands of descendants of King David. [Tal.Shab.15a/Sifri Dev. 357/Tzem.Dav./Sed.Had.Vol.2/Dor.Har.2. 670-2,707-8].

Hillel's greatest disciple was Yonatan ben Uziel who made an Aramaic translation (Targum) of the Nevi'im (Prophets) (see Figure A, page 312). [Tal.Meg.3a, B.B.134a, Av.Dr.Nat.14.1].

3770 / 10

The Jews sent a delegation to the emperor to protest the extreme brutality of Archelaus. The emperor then removed him and sent him to exile [Tzem.Dav./Sed.Had./Dor.Har.2.705].

The anarchy which began with Archelaus' rule (see 3761/1), continued to spread. Arab gangs (taking revenge for Herod's brutality), small groups of soldiers expelled from Herod's army years earlier, and some corrupt Roman commanders, all plundered and killed throughout the country [Tzem.Dav./Sed.Had./Dor.Har.2.696-7, 700, 713].

With the removal of Archelaus,the Romans annexed Yehuda and installed their own governor (procurator). Antipas, the brother of Archelaus (son of Herod I), ruled in a limited way in the northern part of Yehuda) [Sed.Had.]. The Tzedukim became politically active at around this time, and they established their own 'sanhedrin' [Tal.San.52b/Dor.Har.2.632-3].

3775 / 15

Around this time there was an unusual disturbance (with anti-Semitic overtones, see 3750/-11) against the Jews of Bavel (Babylonia) as a result of the activities of two Jewish (private) militia leaders. Much of the (rural) Jewish population had to relocate and concentrate around the larger cities [Dor.Har.1.121-125,126].

3781 / 21

Agrippa I (grandson of Herod I), who spent much of his time in Rome, had been imprisoned for a lack of loyalty to the emperor. He was released with the ascent of a new emperor to the throne, and was sent to Yehuda to rule in a limited way. He became popular with the people, accepted by the Tanna'im, and broadened his original (territorial) mandate to rule. He became so popular that some people almost idolized him [Tal.Sot.41a, Ket.17a,

Pes.107b,Rashbam/Mid.Rab.Vay.3.5/Tos.Y.T.Bik. 3.4/Yuch.5.158/ Tzem.Dav./Sed.Had.].

The position of Kohen Gadol had long been a source of revenues (see 3668/-93, 3680/-81), and some of the Roman authorities increased their personal profit by appointing kohanim to this post sometimes several times a year (instead of their serving a full lifetime). Many of the corrupt ex-kohanim gedolim formed their own strong-arm groups (even militia), and this contributed further to the anarchy, lawlessness, and violence that plagued Yehuda (see 3761/1, 3770/10) [Tal.Yom.9a, Tos./Dor.Har.2.713, 715; 3.6].

3789 / 29

The Sanhedrin moved from the Beit Hamikdash.

With all the lawlessness, violence, and bloodshed (much of it stemming from the ex-kohanim gedolim, see 3781/21), the Sanhedrin despairingly decided to withdraw from a center of activities it could not control. They left their respected place in the Beit Hamikdash and moved to the Holy Mount. This automatically downgraded the spiritual and legal status of all the courts. (It was no longer possible to pass the death sentence.) [Tal.A.Z.8b, Shab.15a, R.H.31a-b, Rashi/Tzem.Dav./Sed.Had./Dor. Har.2.719; 3.112].

R.Tzadok, one of the Tanna'im, perceived the emerging national danger and began a daily fast, until 3829 [Tal.Git.56a-b/Zoh.1.149].

3790 / 30

Jesus, according to Christian tradition (see 3671/-90), had criticized the strong-arm groups of kohanim gedolim controlling the Beit Hamikdash (see 3781/21). They captured him and delivered him to the Romans, who later killed him on charges of treason.

3800 / 40

Emperor Caligula insisted on being worshipped, and ordered that a statue of him be placed everywhere, including the Beit Hamikdash and synagogues in Egypt (see 3610/−151). The Jews of Yehuda (Judea) expressed their religious objection, and Petronius the (Roman) Syrian high commissioner, convinced that this was not an expression of rebellion, sought to have the order withdrawn. Caligula was furious, but died before his cruel reply reached Yehuda.

Philo(n), a Jewish philosopher from Alexandria, made representation to Rome on this issue [Yuch.5. 158-9/Sed.Had./Dor.Har.3.25, 149].

3804 / 44

Agrippa II, son of Agrippa I, became a very limited ruler in 3804, when the Romans controlled Eretz Yehuda through their governors (procurators). He also gained some of the power of his uncle Herod II (a regional ruler). He collaborated with the Romans (see 3825/65), and aligned himself with some of the strong-arm groups of ex-kohanim gedolim as they had ways and means of collecting money (see 3781/21), which they shared with him and the Roman procurators (in return for political considerations) [Tal.A.Z.55a/Tzem.Dav./Sed. Had./Dor.Har. 2.633; 3.8, 14-15].

3810 / 50

Rbn.Gamliel I (ben Shimon, ben Hillel) died.

R.Shimon ben Gamliel I succeeded his father as the Nassi (president) of the Sanhedrin, and R.Yochanan ben Zakkai was the Av (head) Bet Din [Tal.Shab.15a, Sot.47a/Rashi R.H.31b/Tzem/Dav./Sed.Had.2/ Dor.Har.3.52].

Queen Helena and King Munbaz, from the vicinity of Bavel (Babylonia, Persia), converted to Judaism and came to see Yerushalayim. They later made contributions to alleviate food shortages there [Tal.B.B.11a/Mid.Rab.Br.46.10/Yuch.5.159-60/Sed.Had./ Dor.Har.1.99-101].

The sanhedrin of the Tzedukim was active at this time (see 3770/10) [Dor.Har.2.632-3]. The Kuthim (Samaritans) attacked Jews on their way to the Beit Hamikdash for the festivals [Dor.Har.3.58].

3815 / 55

Anarchy was increasing in Eretz Yehuda (Judea), and various political groups emerged. Some were hoping to restore peace and order even if it meant living under Roman rule, provided that rule was honest and allowed for basic human and religious freedom. Others (such as Agrippa II, the ex-kohanim gedolim, and the Tzedukim) were seeking wealth and power. Others, radical nationalists, sought to fight the Romans and expel them from Eretz Yehuda. There were many factions and splinter groups within these general categories [Dor.Har.2.715; 3.3, 10, 17, 34-5].

3825 / 65

A rebellion by most Jewish factions (see 3815/55) against the ruling Roman procurator (who was exceptionally greedy, brutal, and dishonest) was sparked by his disdainful handling of an incident concerning the harassment by local non-Jews of a synagogue in Caesarea.

Agrippa II (a collaborator, see 3804/44) disagreed with the findings of an independent Roman investigator who had concluded that this uprising was directed only against this procurator and not against the Roman empire. Agrippa II insisted that the procurator retain his position (because it suited his own power maneuvers) [Dor. Har.3.14-15, 19, 149].

Most of the Jews were so outraged that they took to the streets of Yerushalayim and forced Agrippa II to flee with the procurator. Agrippa II (and some power groups) then attempted to have the Syrian high commissioner intervene on the grounds that this was certainly a rebellion against Rome. They eventually succeeded after some radical kohanim

94

rejected a sacrifice sent by a Roman official. Roman legions together with the troops of Agrippa II marched on Yerushalayim. They had to withdraw after a bloody battle, and the radical nationalists then proclaimed Yerushalayim a "free" city [Tal.Git.56a/Sed.Had./Dor.Har.3.20-1, 25-8].

Factional infighting increased in Yerushalayim. Those who were hoping for a return to peaceful law and order (under the Romans) despaired when the Romans aligned themselves with Agrippa II and his corrupt power groups, while the defeat of Roman legions at the gates of Yerushalayim encouraged the radicals to believe that they could ultimately succeed in militarily driving out the Romans [Tal. Av.Dr.Nat.4.5/Dor.Har.3.35].

Emperor Nero sent a massive army under Vespasian and his son Titus, to restore Roman authority [Tzem.Dav./Sed.Had.]. Total anarchy reigned in Yehuda, and Jews were being killed by the local non-Jewish population [Tal.Toseph.Git.3.14/Dor.Har.3.28, 141-2].

3826 / 66

Vespasian arrived in Yehuda to reassert Roman authority

Yosef ben Mattityahu (Josephus) was a friend of Agrippa II, who in turn was an old acquaintance of Nero and Vespasian. He maneuvered himself into an important military position in the northern part of Yehuda from which R.Shimon ben Gamliel I (unsuccessfully) sought to have him removed because of this allegiance to Agrippa II and the Romans. He surrendered to the Romans not long after Vespasian began his military campaign in the north and subsequently travelled with them, recording the battles and the destruction of Yehuda, Yerushalayim, and the Beit Hamikdash, from inside the Roman camp [Tzem.Dav./Sed.Had./Dor. Har.1.43; 3.1, 10, 12, 15(7), 39, 179].

3827 / 67

With the fall · of the surrounding country to Vespasian's army, the infighting and power struggles in Yerushalayim turned into open and bloody civil war (see 3815/55), even though the many warring factions may have shared similar goals. Groups of militia set fire to the vast food storage facilities (which had enough to last for years); some groups also formed an internal siege, not letting anyone out. A number of groups (some say) even minted their own coins, each proclaiming a "free" state, under their own leader [Tal.Git.56a/ Mid.Rab.Eych. 1.31/Tzem.Dav./Sed.Had./Dor.Har.3.33-5].

Many Jews from all over Yehuda who had come to the Beit Hamikdash for Pesach were caught in the siege and could not return home [Dor.Har.3.80]. R.Shimon ben Gamliel I died during the siege, possibly in the civil war (see 3826/66) [see Appendix C] [Mrsha.Sot.49a/Dor.Har.3.179].

3828 / 68

R.Yochanan ben Zakkai (the last disciple of Hillel) escaped from the internal siege of Yerushalayim (see 3827/67) and from the later forced confrontation with the Romans. He personally negotiated an agreement with Vespasian to allow the continuance of the studies of the Sanhedrin under R. Gamliel II, son of R.Shimon ben Gamliel I, as Nassi in Yavneh.

Vespasian returned to Rome (after the death of Nero), and Titus laid siege to Yerushalayim, causing serious hunger and disease in the overpopulated city (see 3827/67) [Tal.Git.56a-b, Av.Dr.Nat.4.5; 6.3;14.1/Mid.Rab.Eych.1.31/Dor.Har.3.33-5, 61-3].

3829 / 69

The second Beit Hamikdash was destroyed.

All factions in Yerushalayim (see 3827/67) had no option but to unite and fight the Romans, which they did valiantly despite their weak and starved condition [Tal.Av.Dr.Nat.6.3/Dor.Har.3.38]. (A Roman historian, Dio Cassius, recorded that Titus was wounded during the fighting and that some Ro man soldiers deserted to the Jewish side because they did not believe they could conquer Yerushalayim.)

On the 17th Tammuz the walls of Yerushalayim were penetrated, and the Romans advanced with difficulty until they reached the Beit Hamikdash and set fire to it on the 9th Av 3829. The western wall was all that remained of the structure, and the Romans took many of the holy utensils to Rome (see 4215/455) [Tos.A.Z.9b/Mmn.Hak.L'Yad].

Vast numbers of Jews (over one million recorded) died in the battle, from hunger, and from disease [Tal.Tan.28b/Tzem.Dav./Sed.Had./Dor.Har.3.80].

Some say that the second Beit Hamikdash was destroyed in 3828 [Rashi A.Z.9b, Erch.12b].

[The secular date usually given for the destruction of the second Beit Hamikdash is 70 (3830/70). This one-year difference could be an adjustment based on the naming of the year 1. See 1/-3760].

[3829/69 is continued in Chapter 9.]

CHAPTER 9

The Talmudic Era: The Mishna

The ninth chapter in Jewish history focuses on the struggle for Jewish survival in Eretz Yisrael under Roman conquest and the development of the Mishna as a written body of Jewish law. The chapter ends with the completion of the Mishna. Later scholars adhered completely to the Mishna and would not consider overruling any of its statements.

THE TALMUDIC ERA: THE MISHNA

Jewish Year		Secular Year
3834	R.Yochanan ben Zakkai died	74
3846	The Sanhedrin began moving from place to place	86
3893	**Betar fell and Bar Kochba's revolt ended in tragedy**	**133**
3894	Judaism was banned, and R. Akiva was imprisoned	134
3949	**R.YEHUDA HANASSI COMPLETED THE MISHNA AROUND THIS TIME**	**189**

[3829/69 is continued from Chapter 8.]

Almost 100,000 Jews were taken to Rome as captives, and many of them were forced to fight wild animals in the Roman coliseums. The Romans were selective in their punishment of the various (factional) leaders of the revolution. Some were brutally killed while others were imprisoned, indicating that the Romans were aware that some of the leaders had been drawn into the conflict against their better judgment (see 3815/55, 3827/67, Av 3829/69) [Mid.Rab.Eych.1.45/Tzem. Dav./Sed.Had./Dor.Har.3.37-8, 48, 75, 80, 138].

Some Jewish fortresses resisted the Romans for one or two years after the destruction of the Beit Hamikdash (see 3831/71), while roaming bands of legionnaires killed many people in those parts of Yehuda already conquered. This random killing slowed after many prisoners (including some of the factional leaders) were taken to Rome specifically for Titus's triumphal march (approximately nine months after the destruction of the Beit Hamikdash) [Tal.Git.55b/Dor.Har.3. 37-8, 128, 138-9].

The Sanhedrin continued its studies (as an academy) in Yavneh (see 3828/68), under the leadership of R.Gamliel II (ben Shimon ben Gamliel I) as Nassi. R.Yochanan ben Zakkai, the Av Bet Din (see 3810/50), came only periodically to Yavneh (for sessions) because he had moved elsewhere, some say in order not to cast his shadow over the leadership of the inheritor of his mentor Hillel's dynasty (see 3810/50, 3828/68) [Tal.San.32b, Git.56b, Av.Dr.Nat.14.6/Toseph. Mas.2.2/Mid.Rab.Koh.7.7.2/Sed.Had.2/ Dor.Har.3.24, 61-71].

3830 / 70

R.Yehoshua (ben Chananyah) traveled to Rome (see 3841/81, 3856/96) to negotiate for the release of Jewish captives there and had many dialogues with the emperor and his daughter (see 3856/96) [Tal.Git.58a, Hor.10a, Shab.119a, Tan.7a, Chag.5b, Chul.59b-60a, Bech.8b/Tzem.Dav./Sed.Had.2/Dor.Har.3.48-50].

Josephus wrote his history in which he presented events from (and as a justification of) his political perspective (see 3826/66); he wrote this under the auspices of his friends in Rome and in consultation with Titus and Agrippa II, whom the Romans had appointed ruler in the Galil (which was considered separate from Yehuda). His (slanted) writings could not have served to decrease Roman anger and cruelty toward the Jews,whom he portrayed in a negative light [Tal.Kid.110a/Mmn.Hil.Kid.Hach.4.4, Ish.13.16, Shmitt.7.9/Dor.Har.1.15(9), 19-20(12), 70(35), 193-4; 2.693; 3.38-40, 85, 129].

The groups of ex-kohanim gedolim (see 3804/44, 3815/55) ceased to exist, and the remnants of the Herodian Dynasty (including Agrippa II) eventually disappeared through intermarriage with the Romans [Dor.Har.3.38-40, 51, 354].

3831 / 71

The Romans had conquered all of Yehuda (see 3829/69) (except for the fortress of Massada which fell later), order was restored, and the Roman troops stopped their wanton killings (see 3829/69).

Vespasian issued a decree (through his governor) that all properties left by Jews killed in the war were to be transferred to the emperor. The rightful heirs had great difficulties in subsequently securing their family estates and rightful inheritances from Roman officers [Tal.Shab. 116a-b, Git.55b, Yer.Git.5.7/Dor. Har.3.127-136, 140].

3834 / 74

R.Yochanan ben Zakkai died.

R.Yochanan ben Zakkai made adjustments to adapt Jewish life without a Beit Hamikdash to the laws of the Torah [Tal.R.H.29b-31b, Suk.41a/Dor.Har.3.122-125], and when he died (approximately five years after the destruction of the Beit Hamikdash), R.Yehoshua ben Chananyah (one of his five most prominent disciples) succeeded him as the Av Bet Din [Tal.Av.2.9, B.K.74b, Nid.7b, Yer.San.,1.2(6a)/Sed.Had.1,2/ Dor.Har.3.203, 210-11, 277(24), 307-11, 337].

R.Eliezer ben Hyrkanos, another of the five most prominent disciples (who married Iyma Shalum, a sister of R.Gamliel II), was author of the Midrash *Pirkei D'Rebbi Eliezer*, and he became the Chacham (supreme scholar) of the Sanhedrin Academy, a special appointment made out of respect and in recognition of his brilliant scholarship [Tal.Av.2.8, Bert.-end, Shab.116a, Mak.27a, Git.83a, Nid.7b, Yer.San.1.2(6a)/ Mid.Rab.Sh.Hsh.1.3.1/Pir.Dr.El.1, 2/Tzem.Dav./Sed.Had./Dor.Har. 3.210-11, 291-6].

When the three leaders of the Sanhedrin Academy, R. Gamliel II (Nassi), R.Yehoshua (Av), and R. Eliezer, gathered in Yavneh (after the death of R.Yochanan ben Zakkai), they began regular sessions of the Sanhedrin in order to consolidate and clarify the laws of Torah by ruling on the differences of opinion that had arisen(from the time of Hillel and Shamai) [Tal.Shab.138b, Eruv.13b, Yer.Yev.1.6 (9a),Av.Dr.Nat.14.6/Toseph.Ed.1.1/ Mid. Rab. Koh.7.7.2/Tos.B.K. 94b/Dor.Har.3.203-5, 210-12, 284].

Eliezer ben Yaakov I, who was known for his precise articulation, taught the accurate measurements of the Beit Hamikdash as part of the Mishna, and R.Shimon Ish HaMitzpeh taught the order of the Yom Kippur services (in the Beit Hamikdash) [Tal.Yom.14b, Yev.49b, Yer.Yom.2.2(12a)/Dor. Har.3.82, 181-2].

3835 / 75

The Jews began to regain some stability, but antagonistic Christians (many of whom belonged to Jewish Christian sects (see 3893/133) and therefore mingled freely among Jews) continuously "informed" the Romans on Jewish progress. The Roman governor, Tirentius Rufus I, attempted to capture and kill R.Gamliel II (a descendant of King David, see 3769/9). He also plowed under the whole city of Yerushalayim and the site of the Beit Hamikdash on the 9th of Av [Tal.Tan.29a, Yer. Tan.4.5(25a)/Dor.Har.3.71-78].

3836 / 76

As part of the Torah clarification (see 3834/74) Shimon HaPakuli (a Tanna) was entrusted by

R.Gamliel II to standardize the various versions of the eighteen blessings of Shmona Esrei (see 3426/-335). R.Gamliel II also wanted a nineteenth blessing added as prayer against "informers" (see 3835/75, 3877/117, 3894/134), and Shmuel HaKatan (another Tanna) composed it [See Appendix C] [Tal.Ber.28b, Meg.18a/Mmn.Hil.Tfi.2.1., Kes.Mish/ Dor.Har.3.145-7, 172-3].

3841 / 81

Titus became emperor after the reign of his father Vespasian, and he ruled in a surprisingly mild manner. R.Eliezer, R.Yehoshua, and R.Gamliel II, traveled to Rome to appeal for better conditions in Eretz Yisrael. However, Titus died while they were there, and he was succeeded by his cruel brother Domitian who drafted a decree to exterminate the Jews. He killed many Romans, but a powerful political acquaintance the Jewish leaders had made in Rome, gave his life to have the decree against the Jews suspended [Tal.Yer.San.7.13(41a) Mid. Rab.Dev.2.24, Yal.Teh.754/Dor.Har.3.275-8].

When the three leaders returned from Rome, having witnessed the ruthlessness of the new emperor (particularly toward Romans suspected of being friendly to Jews), they maintained a low profile in Yavneh and did not call any more full sessions of the Sanhedrin Academy, but decided on all matters among the three of them (after discussions in which R.Eliezer was respected as the supreme scholar [Tal. Git. 83a/Mid. Rab. Sh. Hsh.1.3.1/Dor. Har. 3.280-1, 283].

Onkelus II (who had converted to Judaism after his uncle Titus died) was a disciple of R.Yehoshua (ben Chananyah) and R.Eliezer (ben Hyrkanos). He translated the *Chumash* (five Books of Torah) into Aramaic based on their teachings (see Figure A, page 313). This was not the Onkelus I who was a disciple of Hillel and Shamai [Tal.Meg.3a, Git.56b-57a, A.Z.11a, B.B.99a/Zoh.Vay.73a/Rashi Kid.49a/Tzem.Dav./Sed. Had.2].

3842 / 82

R.Eliezer had ruled on matters of law without the prior consent of the other two leaders (see 3841/

81), and when he refused to withdraw these judgments (claiming that the others were insincere in their opposition), he was removed from the circle of scholars by R.Gamliel II, with the support of the others. R.Gamliel II and R.Yehoshua were thus the sole remaining leaders of Sanhedrin Academy affairs, and without the respected presence of R.Eliezer, friction emerged between them (see 3844/84) [Tal.B.M.59b, Git.83a, Nid.7b, Yad.4.3, Yer.M.K.3.1 (10b), Korb.HaE./Dor.Har.3.293-6, 302].

3844 / 84

R.Gamliel II dealt harshly with the Av Bet Din R.Yehoshua, who was also an astronomer, in a confrontation about the setting of the month, a function usually reserved for the Av Bet Din. More than a year later (at a public lecture) he was again harsh in his treatment of R.Yehoshua. Those present were most upset and offended and insisted that R.Gamliel be replaced as Nassi [Tal.R.H.2.7,2.8,Bert.,2.9,Rashi31b,Ber.27b-28a, Yer.Ber.4.1(32b)/ Dor.Har. 3.302-6, 318, 324, 330].

Seventy-two scholars were present when R.Elazar ben Azaryah (a young wealthy Kohen and direct descendant of Ezra) was appointed Nassi to replace R.Gamliel II, and they took this rare opportunity of a full session of the Sanhedrin Academy (see 3841/81) to decide on many issues. That session was referred to as "that day."

R.Elazar ben Azaryah later shared the leadership with R.Gamliel II who was reinstated [Tal.Ber.27b-28a, Zev.11b, Yad.3.5, 4.3/Dor.Har.3.319-24, 327, 338; 5.177].

3846 / 86

The Sanhedrin began moving from place to place.

The Romans increased their troops in Eretz Yisrael and continued to persecute the Jews there, particularly the scholarly leadership which had to leave Yavneh and move to Usha in the Galil (see 3830/70). Even while there, R.Gamliel II and his court were under pressure, and they moved to Teverya (Tiberius) and wandered from place to place [Tal.Shab. 115a, Eruv.101b/Toseph.Ter.2.13, San.2.6/Sifri Dev.33.3/Dor.Har.3.344,346-8].

3856 / 96

The ruthless emperor Domitian (see 3841/81) died. R.Gamliel II, R.Yehoshua, R.Elazar ben Azaryah, and R.Akiva traveled to Rome during Tishrei to make representation to the new emperor (the aging Nerva), for some relief and freedom from persecution (see 3841/81, 3846/86). Some say he subsequently removed the heavy tax being paid by the Jews of Eretz Yisrael [Tal.Mak.24a, Suk.23a, 41b/Dor.Har.3.349-50].

When the delegation of four elders arrived in Rome, they were questioned closely about their religion by many Romans who were fascinated by Judaism (particularly after Domitian's virulent anti-Jewishness, see 3841/81), and they were now free to inquire about it. R.Yehoshua was particularly well known for his brilliant dialogue in these matters (see 3830/70). Upon their return to Eretz Yisrael, they moved the Sanhedrin Academy back from the Galil to Yavneh (see 3846/86) [Tal.A.Z.54b, R.H.31a-b, Chag.5b, Eruv.53b, D.E.5/Sifri 33.3/Dor. Har.3.349-52].

3858 / 98

The Emperor Nerva died and was succeeded by Trajan who harbored a deep hatred for the Jews (his father had headed a legion in the action that led to the destruction of the Beit Hamikdash). The Sanhedrin Academy at Yavneh was abandoned once again and the elders settled (privately) in Lod, where they called days of fast and prayer because of the persecutions they were suffering [Tal.R.H.18b, 31a-b, Yer.Tan.2.12(12b), Betz.3.5/Toseph.Pes.3.9, 10.8/Dor.Har.3. 352-62].

3864 / 104

The Roman persecutions (see 3858/98) had become so extreme, that R.Akiva had to travel to

Bavel (Babylonia) to fulfil one of the functions of the Sanhedrin (setting of the new month). R.Gamliel II died in Lod, and R.Elazar ben Azaryah continued in the role of Nassi (see 3844/84) in Lod [Tal.M.K.27a, B.M.59b, Yev.122a, San.32b, Yad.4.3, Yer.Ber.3.1(22a)/Dor.Har.3.358-66].

3867 / 107

R.Elazar ben Azaryah presided over a minor regeneration of the Sanhedrin Academy (in Lod), where there were as many as thirty-two scholars attending sessions. However, the Roman persecutions (see 3858/98) forced them to leave and go to the Galil once again (see 3856/96), and even there they were forced into hiding in Tzippori (Sepphoris) [Toseph.Kel.B.B.2, Mik.8.6, Meg.2.2/Dor.Har.3. 363, 367-71].

3874 / 114

The Greek population of Egypt (part of the Roman Empire) took advantage of Trajan's hatred for the Jews (see 3858/98) which was magnified by the fact that the Jews of Bavel (see 3610/−151) had just participated in the fight against his invading forces. The Greeks conducted a massive massacre in Alexandria (see 3610/−151), which almost wiped out the entire community of over one million Jews (see 3454/−307), while the Romans did nothing to protect them [Tal.Suk. 51b, Yer.Suk. 5.1(23a)/Dor.Har.3.393-404, 407-8].

The Jews of Cyprus and those of Cyrene (North Africa, west of Egypt) were well organized and managed to fight off similar attacks by large local Greek populations, also under Roman control. The Greeks then attempted to incite the Romans by claiming that these counter-attacks were proof that the Jews were staging an international uprising; but their claims were not heeded by Trajan who was in Babylonia occupied with expanding the Roman Empire to its fullest size (see 3877/117) [Tal.Yer.Suk.5.1(23a)/Dor.Har.3.409-11, 414].

3877 / 117

When Trajan died, Hadrian became emperor and chose a relatively peaceful path for the Roman Empire. He withdrew from the furthest conquests and even granted permission to the Jews to rebuild the Beit Hamikdash. At the request of the surviving Jews of Egypt (see 3874/114) he brought to trial those responsible for the massacre in 3874, had them killed, and ordered that the Jewish section of Alexandria be rebuilt [Mid.Rab.Br.64.10/Dor.Har. 3.397-99, 404, 406-7, 426-32; 4.574-5].

Hadrian had the governor of Eretz Yisrael (his political enemy) killed, and some Jewish prisoners were subsequently released [Tal.Tan.18b, Sma.8.(47b)/Dor. Har.3.421, 423, 431]. However, Hadrian had a change of heart after he was advised, some say, by "informers" (see 3836/76) of the dangers of allowing the Jews too much independence. Permission for rebuilding the Beit Hamikdash was withdrawn [Mid.Rab.Br.64.10/Dor.Har.3.428(3), 432].

3878 / 118

R.Elazar ben Azaryah had died, and the Sanhedrin Academy came out of hiding (see 3867/107) and was established in Usha once again (see 3846/86) under the leadership of the elderly R.Yehoshua as Av Bet Din (see 3834/74), and R.Shimon ben Gamliel II as the "son of the Nassi," without the full responsibilities of Nassi (see 3550/−211) [Tal.R.H.31a-b, Toseph.Eruv.5.6/Mid.Rab.Br.64.10/Dor.Har.3.425-6, 432; 4.433-9, 445-47].

3880 / 120

When R.Yehoshua died (see 3878/118), a skilled voice was lost in debating the early Christians (see 3830/70, 3835/75, 3856/96). The elderly R. Akiva (who had lost thousands of disciples in a plague) succeeded him as Av Bet Din in Usha (see 3878/118) [Tal.Chag.5b, Yev.62b, Ket.62b-63a, Ned.50a, Eruv.53b, Smach.8.(47b)/Dor.Har.4.439-42, 574, 746, 763].

3883 / 123

Hadrian's change of heart toward the Jews in Eretz Yisrael (see 3877/117) became complete. He issued a decree against some major religious observances (Shabbat, mila, mikva), and revealed plans to rebuild Yerushalayim as a secular city (under another name), complete with a temple for worshipping Jupiter on the place of the Beit Hamikdash (see 3835/75). He also began deporting to North Africa some the (millions of) Jews who were still living in Eretz Yisrael (see 3438/−323) [Tal. Yev.72a, Rashi, B.B.60B, Rashi, Me'i.17a, Toseph.Ber.2.13/ Mid.Rab.Eych.4.5/Dor.Har.4.577-84].

Many Jews went into hiding in order to maintain those forbidden religious observances, and when the Romans came to seek them out they resisted with armed combat. This resistance developed into a revolution with Jewish guerrilla forces making sporadic surprise attacks against the Roman legions. The regular meetings of the Sanhedrin Academy ceased during these difficult times [Dor. Har.4.577-90, 603, 717, 744].

3887 / 127

The Jewish revolt against the harsh decrees of the Romans grew from its initial stages (see 3883/123), and the Jews built underground trenches and tunnels from which they staged successful attacks on the Roman legions. Under the leadership of Shimon Bar Kuziba (Bar Kochba) the attacks became increasingly audacious and successful until they emerged into open battle. Bar Kochba led the well-prepared forces (which included Jewish volunteers from other countries) to conquer cities from the Romans. He eventually conquered Yerushalayim, declared it a free city, and coins were minted for the new Jewish free state. R.Akiva (see 3880/120) then suggested that Bar Kochba appeared to be the Mashiach (Messiah) [Tal.Yev.72a, Rashi, San.93b, B.K.97b, Rashi, Yer.Mas.Shen. 1.1(4a), Yer.Tan.4.5(24a)/Mid.Rab.Eych.2.4/Dor.Har.4.580, 589-93, 600-3, 613-4, 620-1, 626-8, 632(85)].

3893 / 133

Betar fell and Bar Kochba's revolt ended in tragedy.

Bar Kochba (Bar Kuziba) ruled in Yerushalayim for over two years, and the Romans had to send reinforcements to recapture Eretz Yisrael. They did not engage in open battle with the apparently more powerful army of Bar Kochba, but staged sporadic attacks on outlying posts and towns [Tal.San.93b, 97b/Rashi Yev.72a/Dor.Har.4.585, 590-4, 601, 613-4].

R.Yishmael and R.Shimon ben HaSgan, who were captured and killed in the outlying areas, were the first two of the Asara Harugei Malchut (Ten Martyrs) [See Appendix C], and on hearing of their death, R.Akiva realized that Bar Kochba was not the Mashiach (see 3887/127).

The Romans continued their partial conquests, capturing many fortresses and towns (Hadrian himself came to supervise the conquest) until they had retaken much of Eretz Yisrael. They then captured Yerushalayim, and Bar Kochba and his forces withdrew to Betar (a fortress near Yerushalayim).

The Romans laid siege to Betar, but the battle continued for over three years amid death and starvation. Bar Kochba was killed in battle, together with 580,000 Jews. Many more died of starvation and many more were killed, when Betar fell on the 9th Av (Tisha B'Av).

The Romans then attacked and destroyed many cities, killing indiscriminately. Jews were forbidden to bury their dead (see 3908/148) and many were captured and sold as slaves [Tal.Tan.26, Git.57a, Av.Dr.Nat.38.3 (and Smach.8(47a) per Dor.Har.3.177-181), Yer. Tan.4.5/Mid.Rab.Eych.2.4/Tos.Y.T.Chal.4.10/Mmn.Hil.Tan.5.3/ Dor.Har.4. 590-4, 596, 598, 602-3, 613-4, 616-8, 634-41, 710].

The Jews were expelled from Yerushalayim (see 4374/614), and the Romans also began to discriminate against Jewish Christian sects (see 3835/75), which contributed to their decline [Dor.Har.4.664-5].

3894 / 134

Judaism was banned, and R.Akiva was imprisoned.

The Romans forbade all Jewish religious practices in a decree of "Shmad," and the very elderly R.Akiva was imprisoned on the 5th Tishrei. He remained imprisoned for an extended time, and his close disciple, R.Yochanan HaSandlar (a descendant of King David), asked him questions through the cell window.

A short while later, torture and death were instituted as punishments for keeping the religion; many Jews were discovered to be keeping religious practices. (The Romans learned of these through Jewish informers.)

R.Akiva was killed, as was R.Yishmael (see 3893/133) who had composed the *Mechilta* (a form of commentary on the *Chumash* (Bible); other Tanna'im, some of whom later became known as the Asara Harugei Malchut (Ten Martyrs), were also killed [See Appendix C].

The massacres (see 3893/133) continued (under Tinius Rufus II) until the total destruction of Yehuda. The country lay waste and all hope was lost. Jewish life in Eretz Yisrael did not recover for nearly 2,000 years [Tal.Ber.61b, Pes.112a, Yev.108b, San.12a,14a,A.Z.18a,Smach.8(47b),Yer.Pea.7.1(31b). Yer.Chag.2.1 (9b), Yer.Sot.5.5(25a), Yev.12.5(68b)/Tur B.Y.O.C.580/Dor.Har.3. 76-78; 4.628, 635-46, 658, 660-2, 664, 670-2, 679, 710, 793; 5.283].

The great Tanna'im of Yavneh (see 3867/107) had all died or been killed, and many of the younger Tanna'im (disciples of R.Akiva) fled from Eretz Yisrael [see Appendix C, note 2] and settled in Bavel (Babylonia) where R.Yehuda ben Beteira was (in Netzivin) [Tal.Ber.63b, San.14a, Sot.25a, Yer.San.8.6 (42b-43a), Chag.3.1(15a-b), Yev.62b, 108b/Sif.Dev.80(Re.28)/Dor. Har.4.635, 672-83, 691 696(20), 710].

3903 / 143

Hadrian had died, and when some Jews of Eretz Yisrael emerged from their hiding to return to normal life, some Romans interpreted this as a new uprising and the Jews were massacred once again.

Some time later the Tanna'im began to return from Bavel (see 3894/134), and they met in small gatherings, without reestablishing the formal Sanhedrin Academy (see 3883/123) [Tal.Yer.Chag.3.1 (15a)/Mid.Rab.Sh.Hsh.2.Sam.3(15a)/Dor.Har.4.704-10, 712-13].

3908 / 148

The Romans, confident that the Jews were no longer a threat, began a program of public construction, and normalization of commercial life in Eretz Yisrael.

The Tanna'im had cautiously called sessions of the Sanhedrin Academy (in Usha) in the Galil (see 3903/143), in order to reconstruct the process of clarification of the Torah laws previously begun in Yavneh (see 3834/74); and a group of Babylonian Tanna'im (headed by R.Natan, the son of the Reish Galuta (Exilarch), and some say the basic author of *Avot D'Reb Natan*) settled in Eretz Yisrael [Tal.Shab.33b/Tos. B. K. 94b/Sed. Had. 2.R.Natan/.Dor. Har.4.717-8, 722, 724, 727, 735, 768, 823-4, 829].

R.Shimon ben Yochai was sent to Rome to plead with the emperor (Antoninus Pius) to have the bans on Jewish observances officially lifted. He succeeded in this mission, and permission was also granted on the 15th Av to bury all the dead (see 3893/133). The Tanna'im gathered (temporarily) in Yavneh and instituted another blessing in Birkat HaMazon (grace after meals) (see 2928/ −833), in commemoration [Tal.Ber.48b, Yer.Ber.7.1 (52a), Tan.31a, Me'i.17a-b/Mid.Rab.Br.76.8/Dor.Har.4.736, 738-40, 743-4].

The Sanhedrin Academy was subsequently established (with caution) in Shepharam (in the Galil, near Usha), with R.Natan as the Av Bet Din, R.Meir as the Chacham (supreme scholar, see 3834/74), and R.Shimon ben Gamliel II (who was appointed later) as the Nassi (see 3878/118). Some say he was not active, or in regular attendance, for security reasons (the Romans could have interpreted his inherited presidency as a measure of self-rule and rebellion). The Academy continued the process of clarification of the law and organized the body of law into sections (called

Masechtot) [Tal.R.H.31a-b, B.M.86a, Eruv.13b, Hor.13b, Kel.30.4/Igg.R.Sher.G./Dor.Har.4.744, 764-8, 770-3, 775, 718-22; 5.81, 89-90, 105].

3909 / 149

R.Yehuda (Bar Ila'i) had privately praised the Romans for their renewal of commercial life in Eretz Yisrael (see 3908/148), and R.Shimon (ben Yochai) had countered that they had only done so out of self-interest. Word of this private discussion reached the Roman authorities, who declared that R.Yehuda should be honored with leadership, R.Shimon killed, and R.Yossi (ben Chalafta) (author of *Seder Olam*), who had been present at the conversation, but made no comment, should be placed under "house arrest" in Tzippori (Sepphoris) [Tal.Shab.33b].

This presented the Jews with an opportunity for officially sanctioned public appointment (see 3908/148). R.Yehuda was therefore appointed to the position of Rosh HaMedabrim (chairman) of the Sanhedrin Academy. R.Meir (also called R.Nehorai) was the outstanding scholar (see 3908/148), but he had lost popularity with the people, some say because he retained a respectful relationship with Elisha Acher ben Avuya his former mentor, who had been an informer (see 3894/134). R.Shimon (ben Yochai) escaped and hid in a cave (with his son, R.Elazar) for thirteen years [Tal.Shab.33b, Rashi, Eruv.13a, Chul.142a, Yer.Shvi. 9.1 (25a-b), Yer.M.K.3.1(10-b), Yer.Chag.2.1(9b)/Mid.Rab.Br.79.6/Tashbatz.1.33/Dor.Har. 4.640-1, 769-73, 775-80, 791-5].

Berurya, the learned daughter of R.Chanina ben Tradyon [see Appendix C], was the wife of R.Meir [Tal.Pes.62b, Toseph.Kel.(B.K.)4.9, Kel.(B.M.)1.3].

3925 / 165

The leaders of the Sanhedrin Academy (see 3908/148, 3909/149) had all died; the Romans, who were fighting defensive battles against the Parthians (the rulers of Persia, which included Babylonia), brought their legions through Eretz

Yisrael, and began again to suppress Jewish life. The Jews appealed, the oppressions were lifted, and some say R.Yehuda ben R.Shimon (ben Gamliel II) met the new emperor (Marcus Aurelius Antoninus), who agreed to the full and formal restoration of the Sanhedrin Academy, with an official active Nassi (see 3908/148). R.Yehuda thus succeeded his father and became known as R.Yehuda HaNassi (the first officially active Nassi since the decrees of Hadrian, see 3883/123), and he maintained a friendship with the emperor [Tal. Sot.49b/Igg.R.Sher.Gaon/Rashi B.M.33b/Dor.Har.4.809-17, 818-9].

R.Yehuda HaNassi (who was also called Rebbi) continued (to conclusion) the clarification of Torah laws (see 3908/148), most of which had already been clarified and organized by his father and R.Natan [see Tal. Suk19b, Rashi]. He consolidated the various opinions into one body of law, the Mishna, which, when edited in its specific succinct style of syntax, became established as the final word of Jewish law and jurisprudence [Tal.B.M.86a, Kel.30.4, Tif.Yis.Bo./Igg.R.Sher.G./Tos.B.K.94b/ Dor.Har.4.817-824, 829, 858-9, 866, 870, 873, 877; 5.79,89-90, 105].

Although the Jews of Eretz Yisrael were suffering continuous persecutions from the Romans, many scholars came from Bavel and strengthened the Jewish community and the Sanhedrin Academy there (and even established their own synagogue[s] in Eretz Yisrael, see 4098/338) [Tal.Git.55b, 58b-59a, Suk.20a, Ket.103b, Chul.86a, Yer.Ber.5.1(37b)/Dor.Har. 5.282-5, 289-91, 403].

3949 / 189

R.Yehuda HaNassi completed the Mishna around this time.

R.Yehuda HaNassi died around 3949. Some say he died around 3979 but this is generally due to a calculation based on the assumption that Rav settled, rather than visited, in Bavel (Babylonia), during R.Yehuda HaNassi's lifetime (see 3979/ 219). An associated error crept into the *Iggeret* of R. Sherira Gaon, which says he settled in Bavel during the life of R.Yehuda HaNassi instead of the life of R.Yehuda Nessia (Dor.Har.5.215). He completed the final editing of the Mishna before he died. [Sef.Hak.q. Tzem.Dav.3975/Dor.Har.4.687; 5.1-3, 32-33, 307-8].

He was succeeded by his son, R.Gamliel III, as Nassi after his death, and he was in turn succeeded by his son, R.Yehuda Nessia I after a short while [Tal.Ket.103b/Dor.Har.5.20-1].

Many of the colleagues (and major disciples) of R.Yehuda HaNassi (some of whom were still considered Tanna'im) continued the process of clarifi-cation of the law in the Sanhedrin Academy by teaching (orally) the total body of Mishna law and explaining the exact meanings of sections of the Mishna. Many explanations and clarifications were recorded in the form of *Beraitot* (by R.Chiya, R.Oshiya, bar Kappara, etc.); *Sifra* and *Sifri* (by Rav); and additional material was recorded in the Tosephta [Tal.Eruv.92a, Rashi, Nid.62b, Tos., Git.76b, Rashi, A.Z.35b, Rashi, 36a Tos.(Asher), 37a, Mak.21b, Rashi Chul.141a-b, Rashi, Yer.Shab.1.2(6a)/Igg.R.Sher.G./Rashi Eruv.19a (ben Zakkai), Betz 29a (Tanna deBey Shmuel), B.M.48a (UBadka Levi)/Rashbam B.B.52b-end/Tos.B.K.94b/Dor.Har.5.19-20, 34-36, 40-46, 48-9, 53, 55-57, 60, 77-79, 114, 126-136, 145-6, 153, 181, 253, 256].

CHAPTER 10

The Talmudic Era:
The Gemara

The tenth chapter in Jewish history focuses on the growth of the Talmud, as the Gemara explains, interprets, and extends the words of the Mishna. The chapter ends with the completion of the Gemara.

THE TALMUDIC ERA: THE GEMARA

3979 / 219

Rav left Eretz Yisrael and settled in Bavel.

The attacks and persecutions on the Jews of Eretz Yisrael (see 3925/165) intensified at this time, and it was dangerous for Jews in certain areas [Tal.Git.16b-17a, Shab. 145b-end, Yer.Dma.6.1(25a), A.Z.2.8(16a)/ Dor.Har.5.284-8].

Rav (Abba Aricha, "the tall Abba") was an elderly disciple of R.Yehuda HaNassi who had on previous occasions returned to Bavel (Babylonia, Persia), his country of origin [Tal.Git.59a, Yer.Sot.9.2(41a)/ Dor.Har.5.213-5, 223, 403]. In 3979 he returned once again and settled in Neharde'a, the major center of the Jews in Bavel, where R.Shila was head of the Babylonian scholars (since the death of R.Yehuda HaNassi) [Rashi Chul.173b/Igg.R.Sher.G. per Dor.Har.5.212-5/ Tzem.Dav./Sed.Had./Dor.Har.4.701; 5.165, 167-8, 182-4, 403, 411].

3986 / 226

Bavel was part of the Persian Empire ruled by the (centuries-old) Parthian government, which was overthrown (and replaced by the Sassanids) at this time. They allowed the rulers of the local provinces (satrapies) to continue (see 4311/551) under the central rule of a king, but the introduction of their religion caused conflict with the local Jewish population in Bavel (see 4229/469, 4234/474) [Tal.Git.16b-17a/Dor.Har.5.64, 409, 450; 6.101].

3990 / 230

R.Yehuda Nessia I had died, and his son R.Gamliel IV could not maintain the greatness of the Sanhedrin Academy under the dynastic leadership of the descendants of Hillel. R.Gamliel IV did not live long and was succeeded by his young son, R.Yehuda Nessia II. For centuries, the Sanhedrin Academy had asserted a leadership role among the Jews of Eretz Yisrael, as well as the Jews of Bavel through the direct contact it maintained with the political leader of Babylonian Jewry, the Reish

Galuta (Exilarch). With the decline of the leadership of the Nassi, a number of scholars of the Mishna established their own Metivta (Yeshiva) (see 3995/335) and continued their teaching and studies in different locations, which further eroded the centrality of the role of the Nassi and the Sanhedrin Academy. Eventually the Nassi in Eretz Yisrael retained a similar status to that of the Reish Galuta in Bavel. The latter was essentially not a role of scholarship but of political leadership (and the various incumbents were referred to in the Talmud by name only if they were also scholars in their own right). Furthermore, the Reish Galuta, who was (invariably) a descendant of the House of King David, was a (political) leader formally recognized by the Babylonian government, and he even wore the golden sash (kamara) of official Persian office [Tal.San.5a, Rashi, 11b, Hor.13b-end, Rashi Yer.Meg.1.5(7b), Pn.Mosh., Chal.4.4(25b-end)/Mmn.Hil.San. 4.12/Dor.Har.5. 23-4, 28-9, 34-39, 48, 210-12, 222-3, 228, 251, 253-254, 258, 332-5, 346-7, 406].

When R.Shila had died (see 3979/219), Rav left Neharde'a, leaving the succession there in favor of (his colleague's son) Shmuel, and he settled in Sura where (in the absence of any major scholarship there) he established a Metivta, began teaching the Mishna there, and eventually rejuvenated Jewish life in the whole vicinity. Shmuel established a formal Metivta in Neharde'a [Igg.R.Sher.G./Dor.Har.5.35 210-12, 222-5, 403, 407].

The scholars teaching the Mishna were called Amora'im (see 4111/351) and many of those mentioned in the Talmud had the same names (even though they lived in various generations) (see 4112/352, 4191/431) [Sed.Had.2/Dor.Har.5. 210, 228, 283, 582, 588; 6.12, 89-91].

3995 / 235

R.Yochanan established a Metivta in Teverya (the old city of Tiberius, which was in a different location from the "new" Tiberius) [Tal.Yer.Meg.1.1 (2b)/Dor.Har.5.72]. A few years later, after R.Oshiya (who had established a Metivta in Kessarin [Caesarea]) died, the Metivta of his disciple

R.Yochanan became the central focal point of Talmud study in Eretz Yisrael (see 4007/247, 4014/254) and eventually even for Bavel (see 4050/290) [Tal.Eruv.53a, B.K.117a/Tzem.Dav./Sed.Had./Dor. Har.5. 212, 253-5, 257-8, 298, 309-10, 329].

The Metivta (Yeshiva) acquired a special form. The scholars as well as the disciples of the Metivta would gather twice a year in the months of Elul and Adar, whch were called Yarchei Kalla, each scholar identifying with his own Metivta. (Other Yeshivot existed, but they were not central focal points as were the "official" Metivtot.) There was a specific protocol of titles and seating (in rows) in the official Metivta according to the hierarchy of learning. This continued the original system of the Sanhedrin (which originated with the seventy elders accompanying Moshe), and which (after the destruction of the second Beit Hamikdash) had evolved into the Sanhedrin Academy (see 3829/69, 3990/230). In the Metivtot of Bavel the Reish Galuta (Exilarch) took part in some of the cermonial proceedings [Tal.Bk.117a, Rashi, Meg.28b, Chul.137b/Mmn.Hil.San.1.3,7, 4.1/Dor.Har.6.156(2), 159, 192-3, 216-9, 221-3, 267-8].

4007 / 247

Shmuel was the Talmudic authority in Bavel.

Rav had died by this time, and no one was appointed to succeed him as the Rosh Metivta of Sura (see 3990/230). Shmuel, the Rosh Metivta in Neharde'a (see 3990/230), became the leading Talmudic authority in Bavel (Babylonia, Persia), while R.Yochanan was the leading authority in Eretz Yisrael (see 3995/235), where there was a renewal of persecutions against the Jews [Tal.Chul. 95b/Igg.R.Sher.G/Dor.Har.5.222(24), 272,315-7, 403, 408-11, 416, 481].

4014 / 254

R.Yochanan was the leading Talmudic authority.

Shmuel had died by this time in Neharde'a (see 4007/247). No one was appointed to succeed him

(see 4018/258, 4019/259, 4058/298) for a few years, so at this point (the elderly) R.Yochanan in Eretz Yisrael was the senior Talmudic authority (see 3995/235, 4050/290) [Igg.R.Sher.G./Dor.Har.5.222 (24), 408, 410-11].

4018 / 258

R.Huna became Rosh Metivta of Sura (see 4007/247) and the central Talmudic authority passed from Neharde'a to Sura (see 4014/254, 4019/259, 4050/290) [Dor.Har.5.411-2, 416-7, 481].

4019 / 259

The Jewish community in Neharde'a was destroyed (see 3979/219, 4014/254) by the cavalry and archers of Pappa bar Nazer, a (corrupt) military commander from Tadmor (Palmyra, N.Syria), when he invaded cities in Persia in support of Rome during a war between the Persians and the Romans [Tal.Ket.51b, Rashi/Igg.R.Sher.G./Dor.Har.4. 702-3; 5.250, 411, 413-4].

R.Yehuda (bar Yechezk'el) established a Metivta (see 3995/235) in Pumpedita (Bavel) at around this time (see 4798/1038) [Dor.Har.5.417].

4020 / 260

Twelve thousand Jews were killed (in one of the possessions of the Persian Empire) when Shabur of Bavel suppressed a revolt in which they participated [Tal.M.K.26a, Rashi].

4046 / 286

The Roman emperor Diocletian divided the Roman Empire into two separate parts (east and west) and he took control of the eastern part which included Eretz Yisrael. He was in Eretz Yisrael when he declared that all wines were to be nade sacramental except for Jewish wine. The Kuthim (Samaritans) did not choose to classify hemselves as Jews, and consequently they were urther removed (see 3426/−335) from being accepted in Halacha as Jews [Tal.Yer.A.Z.5.4(33b-end)/Dor.Har.5.340(46), 341, 344].

4050 / 290

R.Huna was the leading Talmudic authority.

R.Yochanan died at the approximate age of 110 around this time, a few years after R.Shimon ben Lakish, his brother-in-law (who had shared some of the leadership of the Metivta). R.Yochanan's Metivta had been the central place of Talmud tudy in Eretz Yisrael (see 3995/235). All the xplanations of the Mishna that he taught were what he had heard directly from R.Yehuda HaNassi (when he was a young orphan boy) and hen from his disciples. All this became the basis of the Talmud Yerushalmi (sometimes called he Talmud of Eretz Yisrael, see 4111/351) [Tal.Yom.82b, Kid.31b, B.K.117a, Rashi, Chul.137b/Dor.Har.5. 99, 302-3, 306-11, 321-3].

R.Ami succeeded R.Yochanan, yet the focal point of Talmud study moved to Bavel (Babylonia, Persia), to R.Huna (see 4018/258), who was the recognized leader of all scholars, and later to R.Yehuda (bar Yechezk'el) (see 4058/298) [Tal. Git.59b, Kid.70a,Yer.Chag.1.8(7a)/Dor.Har.5.332, 348, 417, 421]. The Amora'im of Bavel and Eretz Yisrael were always in close contact and consultation [Dor.Har.5. 58, 467-70, 472].

4058 / 298

R.Yehuda was the leading Talmudic authority.

R.Huna died (and was buried in Eretz Yisrael). Although he was succeeded by R.Chisda as Rosh Metivta of Sura, and R.Nachman I had reestablished the Metivta of Neharde'a (see 4019/259) in Mechuza, the central Talmudic authority passed

over to R.Yehuda in Pumpedita (see 4018/258, 4019/259) [Tal.Kid.70a, Rashi, M.K.25a, Rashi/Igg.R.Sher.G./Dor.Har.5.222, 269, 416(90), 417-9, 421, 481].

4060 / 300

R.Chisda was the leading Talmudic authority.

R.Yehuda (bar Yechezk'el) had died and was (reluctantly) succeeded by Rabbah (bar Nachmani) as Rosh Metivta of Pumpedita (with his colleague R.Yosef stepping aside), but the central Talmudic authority in Bavel passed over to R.Chisda in Sura (see 4058/298) [Tal. Hor.14a, Ket.42b/Igg.R.Sher.G./Sed.Had./Dor.Har.5222, 347-8, 421, 432-4,481].

R.Yehuda Nessia II died (after R.Yehuda) and was succeeded by his son R.Gamliel V, as Nassi of the Jews in Eretz Yisrael (see 3990/230) [Tal.M.K.17a/Dor.Har.5.347-8].

The elderly R.Ami (who had been a disciple of R.Oshiya) was the last of the famous Roshei Metivta in Eretz Yisrael (see 4050/290). He had to relocate the Metivta from Teverya (Tiberius) to Kessarin (Caesarea) (see 3995/235) because of Roman persecutions. He was (later) consulted by scholars of Bavel on difficult questions. R.Avahu was the senior scholar in Kessarin after R.Ami died [Tal.Git.63b, Chul.86b/Sed.Had./Dor.Har.5. 315-7, 349-52, 355-6, 373(62)].

4069 / 309

Rabbah was the leading Talmudic authority.

R.Chisda died and no one succeeded him as the Rosh Metivta of Sura. The central Talmudic authority passed to Rabbah in Pumpedita [Dor.Har.5. 222, 434,481]. R.Gamliel V had died previously and was succeeded as Nassi by his R.Yehuda Nessia III [Tal.M.K.22b-end/Dor.Har.5.347-8, 393-4].

4073 / 313

The Roman Emperor Constantine I who established his capital in Byzantium (later Constantinople) gave formal recognition to the Christian religion. He later had churches built on Christian holy places in Eretz Yisrael.

4081 / 321

R.Yosef was the leading Talmudic authority.

Rabbah (bar Nachmani) died in hiding after he had been slandered to the government. He was succeeded by his (blind) colleague R.Yosef (see 4060/300) as Rosh Metivta of Pumpedita and as central Talmudic authority [Tal.B.M.86a, Hor.14a Eruv.54a, Rashi/Igg.R.Sher.G./Dor.Har.5.306, 432-4, 437-8, 440-1, 447, 454-5].

4085 / 325

Abbayé was the leading Talmudic authority.

The persecutions increased in Eretz Yisrael (see 4073/313) and many of the Amora'im fled to Bavel from where many of them had originally come (see 3925/165) [Dor.Har.5.356, 390-1, 435, 455, 467-9, 473-4].

R.Yosef died in 4083 and some two years later, from among four candidates (two of whom were from Eretz Yisrael), Abbayé was selected to succeed him [Tal.Hor.14a/Igg.R.Sher.G./Dor. Har.5.432-3, 437-8, 440-1, 447, 461, 473-74].

The Christian Council of Nicaea (northwest Turkey) called by Constantine I (see 4073/313), passed measures to distance Christianity from Judaism and to limit the rights of Jews in the Roman Empire. They discussed the disengagement of the dates of Easter and Pesach (Passover) (which was dependent on the monthly decision of the Jewish Beit Din, as to when the new moon would inaugurate the month, see 4121/361). The council also discussed changing the Sabbath from Saturday to Sunday. Some twenty years earlier, a Council in Elvira (Spain) had forbidden Christians from keeping the Jewish Shabbat, eating with Jews, or marrying them.

4098 / 338

Rava was the leading Talmudic authority.

Abbayé had died by this time and Rava succeeded him as Rosh Metivta of Pumpedita. He moved the Metivta (and the central Talmudic authority) to Mechuza (see 4058/298) (where he had always lived) [Igg.R.Sher.G./Dor.Har.5.367, 437-8, 441, 494-6]. A number of Roman Jews (see 4715/955) settled in Mechuza and established their own synagogue (see 3925/165) [Tal.Meg.26b, Rashi/Dor.Har.5.496].

4111 / 351

Gallus, the (corrupt) Roman ruler in the east (see 4046/286), and his general (Ursicinus) waged a military campaign that was almost a religious crusade (see 4073/313, 4085/325) against the Jewish community in Eretz Yisrael, claiming that they were suppressing a rebellion (which was in fact raging elsewhere in the western Roman Empire). The Romans attacked and devastated cities and also prohibited the Jewish system of fixing the monthly calendar by the new moon (see 4121/361) [Tal.San.12a, Rashi/Yer.Meg.3.1(24a), Yev.16.3(82b)/Sed. Had./Dor.Har.5.286, 356, 366, 373-6, 378; 6.124-6].

Most of the Amora'im of Eretz Yisrael fled to Bavel (Persia). The basics of the Talmud of Eretz Yisrael, which came to be called the Talmud Yerushalmi, remained in its rudimentary form as it was being taught and memorized from the time of the end of the Mishna (see 4050/290, 4152/392). The Talmud Yerushalmi is in Hebrew and Western Aramaic (Galilean-Syrian) [Rashi Sot.49b/Dor.Har.5.373, 376, 390-1, 467, 472, 526-9, 535-6; 6.103, 106-137]. The Talmud Bavli (in the Eastern Aramaic language) had also taken form by this time (see 4152/392), based on the explanations of the Mishna that the early Amora'im had conveyed and the further comments of later Amora'im, particularly through the clarification of laws undertaken by Rava (Haviyot D'Abbayé VeRava) in Pumpedita, now the center of Talmudic authority (see 4069/309) [Tal.B.B.134a, Rashi Suk.28a/Rashi 29b-30a Rashi/Rashi Kid.13a (Linkutinhu),/Igg.R.Sher.G./Dor.Har.5.473, 480-4, 489-90, 493-4, 500, 519, 551-62; 6.116-9, 123].

Some of the names of Amora'im appear differently in Talmud Bavli than they do in Talmud Yerushalmi. For example: R.Abba - R.Ba; R.Yossi - R.Assi; R.Yehuda - R.Yudan; R.Avun - R.Bun [Dor.Har.5.459, 461-2, 6.114].

4112 / 352

Rava died (see 4098/338), and although there was no central Talmudic authority for a while (see 4131/371), R.Nachman II (bar Yitzchak) succeeded him as Rosh Metivta of Pumpedita. R.Pappa (and R.Huna Brei D.R.Yehoshua) opened a Metivta in the vicinity of Sura, in Naresh, and many Amora'im also studied in Neharde'a (where Ameimar had a central role), and in Pum Nahara (where R.Kahana had a central role). [There were as many as six Amora'im at various times named R.Kahana (see 3990/230)] [Sed.Had.2/Dor.Har.5.367, 373, 381, 481, 496-9, 505, 515-9, 228].

4119 / 359

Hillel II, who established the calendar, became Nassi.

R.Yehuda Nessia III died and was succeeded by his son Hillel II as Nassi of the Jewish remnants (see 4111/351) in Eretz Yisrael. Hillel II recognized that the monthly Jewish calendar-fixing system was in total jeopardy (see 4085/325, 4111/351) so he established (later) the Jewish calendar system (see 4121/361) [Ramban Sefer HaZechut Git.34b (Rif.18a)/Dor. Har.5.348, 393-8].

4121 / 361

Julian (called "the Apostate" because he rejected Christianity, see 4073/313) became the new emperor of Rome. In his letters to the Jews he encouraged the rebuilding of the Beit Hamikdash. During the 20-month respite of Julian's reign (see 4111/351, 4123/363), Hillel II, who was Nassi in Eretz Yisrael, called a session of the Talmud scholars and established the continuous calendar system that no longer required monthly moon sightings (see 4119/359). This system is still used today [Mmn.Kid.Hach.5.3/Ramban Sefer HaZechut Git.34b (Rif. 18a)/Dor.Har.5.24-5, 375-6, 348, 393-8].

4123 / 363

After the death of Emperor Julian (see 4121/361) (who may have died a natural death) while in battle, the Christians attacked the Jews of Eretz Yisrael.

4131 / 371

R.Pappa died, and R.Ashi became Rosh Metivta in the vicinity of Sura (see 4112/352) at Mata Mechassiya. He developed wider recognition and achieved the emergence (once again) of central Talmudic authority (see 4112/352, 4152/392) [Igg.R.Sher.G.per Dor.Har. 5.497-8/Dor.Har.5.498-9, 505, 507, 549, 593-4, 599].

4152 / 392

R.Ashi was the leading Talmudic authority.

R.Ashi, together with his colleague Ravina I (and all the senior Amora'im), undertook the editing of the Talmud of Bavel—gathering all the organized statements on the Mishna of the earlier Amora'im (see 4111/351), adding the clarifications of the later Amora'im (comparing them with the Talmud Yerushalmi of Eretz Yisrael, see 4111/351), deciding on issues that were still unresolved, and presenting it in a comprehensible logical style. This was called the Gemara (see 4187/427) [Tal.B.M.86a/Rif Eruv.-end(on Tal. Eruv.35b)/Dor.Har.5.526, 535-6, 539, 549-50, 551-62, 573, 589, 591; 6.102-13, 116-9, 123, 127].

Two sections (Masechtot) of the Mishna were not organized with the Gemara statements of the Amora'im (Zera'im and Taharot), but most of their concepts are explained elsewhere [Rashi Suk.14a (Mishum Hachi)].

4155 / 395

The Jews left Corinth (Greece) after the invasion of the Visigoths (a people of the Germanic group called Barbarians) from the vicinity of present-day Sweden (see 4215/455).

4174 / 414

The Jews were expelled from Alexandria by the Christian authorities.

4178 / 418

Many Jews of Minorca, a Mediterranean island, were killed, and the remaining 540 were forcibly baptized.

4181 / 421

Ravina I died (see 4152/392) [Sed.Had./Dor.Har.6.10, 85].

4187 / 427

R.Ashi died after the compilation of the Gemara.

R.Ashi died after almost sixty years of leadership in Mata Mechassiya, near Sura, during which time he presided over the complete compilation of the Gemara (the Talmud Bavli) into its final form (see 4152/392).

Many of the Amora'im in his Metivta (the central Talmudic authority) also lived long lives, and those that took part in his deliberations were still called Amora'im, though some of them lived on for many years (see 4235/475). Mareimar succeeded R.Ashi as the Rosh Metivta of Sura (although some scholars and students remained in Mata Mechassiya, see 4131/371) and the Amora'im continued to add minor editorial material to the Gemara (see 4236/476, 4320/560) [Igg.R.Sher.G./Dor.Har. 5.309, 498, 597-9, 600-2; 6.10,19-20, 21-2, 64-5].

4189 / 429

R.Gamliel VI had died, the Roman Emperor (Theodosius II) prohibited raising any more funds for the office of Nassi, and the office effectively ceased to exist.

4191 / 431

Mareimar died and was succeeded (as Rosh Metivta of Sura) by R.Iddi bar Avin (the second Amora with the same name, see 3990/230) [Sed.Had.4192/Dor.Har.6.89-91/Igg.R.Sher.G./Dor.,Har.5.598, 601; 6.7, 89-91].

4211 / 451

R.Iddi (bar Avin) died and was succeeded by R.Nachman III (bar Huna) as Rosh Metivta of Sura [Igg.R.Sher.G./Dor.Har.5.598, 601; 6.7, 89-91].

4214 / 454

R.Nachman III (bar Huna) died, and the elderly Mar (Tivyumi) bar Rav Ashi succeeded him as Rosh Metivta of Sura (at Mata Mechassiya) see 4187/427) [Tal.B.B.12b/Igg.R.Sher.G./Dor.Har.5.598; 6.7, 93].

4215 / 455

The Jews of Bavel (Persia) were prohibited, among other things, from keeping the Shabbat, by the king (Yesdegerd II), who was later killed by a snake [Igg.R.Sher.G./Dor.Har.5.598; 6.89, 93].

The Vandals (a people of the Germanic group called Barbarians and from the vicinity of present-day Norway) (see 4155/395) sacked and looted Rome and (some say) took utensils of the Beit Hamikdash (see 3829/69) to Africa, which they also conquered. This westward move of the Barbarians (see 4155/395) contributed to the fall of the Western Roman Empire some twenty years later.

4227 / 467

Mar (Tivyumi) bar Rav Ashi died on the 11th Tishrei (Motza'ei Yom Kippur) 4227/466, and was succeeded by Rabbah Tospha'a [Igg.R.Sher.G./Dor. Har.5.598].

4229 / 469

Three Jewish notables, R.Ameimar (bar Mar Yenuka), Huna (bar Mar Zutra) the Reish Galuta (Exilarch), and R.Mesharshiya (bar Pekod), were arrested in Bavel in Tevet, by orders of the king Firuz "the wicked"), the son of Yesdegerd (see 4215/455). R.Mesharshiya and Huna were killed on the 18th Tevet, and R.Ameimar was killed in Adar [Tal.Chul.62b/Igg.R.Sher.G./Dor.Har. 6.8, 73,99-100].

4234 / 474

Rabbah Tospha'a had died by this time and was succeeded by Ravina II (R.Avina, a nephew of Ravina I) as the Rosh Metivta of Sura [Tal.Ket.100b/ Igg.R.Sher.G./Dor.Har.6.9, 13-14, 100-1].

All the synagogues were closed in Babylon (later called Baghdad) and many Jewish children were handed over to the priests (see 3986/226, 4229/ 469) [Igg.R.Sher.G./Dor.Har.6.8, 22, 100-3]. Some say that these persecutions led to Jewish emigrations from

Bavel to other areas (Arabia, Egypt, North Africa, and Europe) (see 4285/525, 4397/637).

4235 / 475

The Talmud was complete when Ravina II died.

Ravina II (R.Avina), the last of the Amora'im who had taken part in R.Ashi's deliberations (see 4187/427), died on 13th Kislev very soon after Rabbah Tospha'a [Tal.B.M.86a/Igg.R.Sher.G. per Dor.Har.6. 7-9/Sef.Hak.q.Sed.Had.4134/Dor.Har.5.598, 602, 6.7-9, 15-7, 19, 22-3, 98].

The Talmud was complete at this stage (see 4187/427) and no further additions were made, except for the minimal editing undertaken by the (Rabbanan) Savurai (see 4236/476) [Igg.R.Sher.G./ Dor.Har.6.17, 19, 21-23].

The Talmud was henceforth not to be disputed, but logical deductions could be made from it (to cover new situations as they arose) [Mmn.Hakd.L'Yad].

CHAPTER 11

The Talmudic Academies of Bavel

The Rabbanan Savurai
The Ge'onim and Arabic Dominion

The eleventh chapter in Jewish history covers the period of time when the scholars of Bavel, the Savurai, and the Ge'onim were the focal point of the Jewish people. It concludes when this influential role of Bavel suffered a sharp decline.

THE TALMUDIC ACADEMIES OF BAVEL

The Rabbanan Savurai

Jewish Year		Secular Year
4311	Mar Zutra proclaimed Jewish self-rule in Babylonia.	551

The Ge'onim and Arabic Dominion

Jewish Year		Secular Year
4349	The Metivta of Pumpedita was reconstituted	589
4369	The Metivta of Sura was reconstituted	609
4374	The Persians conquered Eretz Yisrael:	614
4374	**JEWS WERE ALLOWED TO RETURN TO YERUSHALAYIM**	**614**
4389	The Byzantine (E.Roman) Empire reconquered Eretz Yisrael	629
4396	R.Yitzchak was the last Gaon of Neharde'a (Firuz-Shabur)	636
4397	**The Arabs conquered Eretz Yisrael**	**637**
4405	One of the *Takkanot HaGe'onim* was enacted	645
4515	R.Acha(i) Gaon left Bavel (Iraq) for Eretz Yisrael	755
4519	R.Yehudai became Gaon of Sura	759
4519	The *Halachot Gedolot* (BaHaG) was written at this time	759
4548	Another of the *Takkanot HaGe'onim* was enacted	788
4618	R.Amram (who wrote the Siddur) became Gaon of Sura	858
4688	Rbnu.Saadya was appointed Gaon of Sura	928
4715	Four Captives were ransomed at this time	955
4728	R.Sherira became Gaon of Pumpedita	968
4757	R.Hai became (the last) Gaon of Pumpedita	997
4798	**R.HAI GAON DIED AND THE ACADEMIES OF BAVEL DECLINED**	**1038**

4236 / 476

R.Yosef was the Rosh Metivta of Pumpedita at this time. He and his colleagues were called the (Rabbanan) Savurai (the generation of Talmud scholars immediately following the Amora'im). They added very minor editorial (and Halacha) clarifications to the Gemara (see 4187/427, 4320/560) wherever necessary. This first generation of Savurai included R.Rechumai, R.Tachana, a Mar Zutra, and two by the name of R.Achai (one of whom is mentioned in the Talmud [Zev.102b, see Tos.(where the words "She'assa She'iltot" appear to have been added later)/Dor.Har.6.56-9]) [Igg.R.Sher.G./Dor.Har.6.3, 6, 13, 21, 24-6, 28, 56-9].

Some say that it was this first generation of Savurai who actually recorded the Talmud in writing [Dor.Har.6.25-6].

4246 / 486

The persecutions of the Jews of Bavel (see 4229/ 469, 4234/474) lessened in intensity when Firuz died. New persecution arose under his successor who endorsed a religious cult, which all Babylonians were required to follow [Dor.Har.6.8, 61-3].

4280 / 520

R.Yosef had died by this time, and R.Simuna succeeded him as Rosh Metivta of Pumpedita. R.Eyna became Rosh Metivta of Sura for a while (there having been no successor since the death of Ravina II and the persecutions of Firuz) (see 4300/540) [Igg.R.Sher.G./Dor.Har.6.24-7, 30-3, 34, 61, 158]. Huna (bar Kahana), the Reish Galuta (Exilarch), and many of his family had died shortly after Huna had a political disagreement with his father-in-law R.Chinena (one of the leading Talmud scholars) and Huna punished the older scholar in a cruel demeaning way. Huna was survived by a posthumous son named Mar Zutra (I) (see 4298/538) [Sed.01.Zut.q.Dor.Har.6.38-46/Dor.Har. 6.38-46].

4285 / 525

Yussuf (a convert to Judaism) was king of the Hymarites, a nation in Southern Arabia (Yemen) which included many Jews (see 4234/474) and many more who had converted to Judaism. He was killed in battle when his country was conquered by the Ethiopians.

4295 / 535

Justinian I, emperor of the Byzantine (East Roman) Empire, ordered the closing of all synagogues among other repressive decrees against the Jews, and although it was not fully carried out, there were some forced conversions to Christianity. At this point, according to some, there was a decree against saying the Shma, so it was inserted in the Kedusha (prayer) of Mussaf as a camouflage.

4298 / 538

Through the representations of the elderly R.Chinena (see 4280/520), his 15-year-old grandson Mar Zutra (I) replaced the temporary Reish Galuta [Dor.Har.6.44].

4300 / 540

R.Simuna had died by this time and was succeeded as Rosh Metivta of Pumpedita by R.Reva'i (from Rov) who is mentioned in the Talmud [San.43a, Rbnu.Chananel].

R.Eyna (see 4280/520) had also died, but there was no successor to his position as Rosh Metivta of Sura because of local persecutions (see 4280/ 520, 4311/551) [Sef.Hak.q.Dor.Har.6.28/Igg.R.Sher.G./Sed. Had./Dor.Har.6.28-30, 34, 38-46, 106, 158].

4311 / 551

Mar Zutra (I) proclaimed Jewish self-rule.

During one of the local persecutions (see 4300/
540), R.Yitzchak, one of the great scholars of
Bavel, was killed. Mar Zutra (I), the Reish Galuta
(see 4298/538) staged a successful rebellion
against the local rulers (see 3986/226), and established a certain level of Jewish independence in his
area (see 4318/558) [Sef.Hak.q.Dor.Har.6.28/Sed.01.Zut.q.
Dor.Har.6.38-46/Igg.R.Sher.G./ Sed.Had./Dor.Har.6.28-30, 34, 38-
46].

4318 / 558

The Babylonian (Persian) forces overpowered the
forces of Mar Zutra (I). After seven years of Jewish
self-government, Mar Zutra (I) was hanged (together with his grandfather R.Chinena) in the city
of Mechuza (a suburb of the capital, Ctesiphon)
and the Jews of Bavel suffered increasing persecutions (see 4320/560). A son was born to Mar
Zutra at the time Mar Zutra was killed, and he
was named Mar Zutra (II) [Sed.01.Zut.q.Dor.Har.6.38-46/
Dor.Har.6.38-46].

4320 / 560

R.Reva'i (see 4300/540) had died at a very advanced age, and because of local persecutions (see
4246/486, 4318/558) the Metivta of Pumpedita
was later transferred to Firuz-Shabur (in the vicinity of Neharde'a) (see 4349/589).

The Talmud scholars of this period, the last of the
(Rabbanan) Savurai, including R.Giza and R.Sama
and some say R.Huna and R.Dimi Surgo, made
very minor editorial adjustments to the final version of the Gemara – such as placing subheadings
from the Mishna, where the Gemara begins a new
subject (see 4187/427, 4236/476). No new additions (or deletions) were made. (Some minor vari-
ations were later erroneously made by copier
scribes, particularly in the time of the Ge'onim [see
4349/589], whose explanations on the Talmud,
which were also in Aramaic, were sometimes
recorded in the margins of the text by their disciples [see 4519/759].) [Sed.Tan.VeAm.q. Dor.Har. 6.3, 21,
30, 35, 48-9/Igg.R.Sher.G./Mmn.Hil.Mal.VeLov.15.2/Sh.Mkbtzt.
B.M.13b (48b), 15b(55b)/Dor.Har.6.28-35, 36-8, 44-6, 55, 138-46,
166, 169, 198, 200, 227].

Some say the Savurai also compiled the smaller
secondary sections (*Masechtot Ketanot*) of the Talmud (*Sofrim, Smachot, Kalla,* and so on, printed at
the end of *Seder Nezikin* in standard versions of the
Talmud) from the sayings of Tanna'im and Amor-
a'im [Dor.Har.6.38].

4336 / 576

Five hundred Jews of Clermont-Ferrand in France
were forced to be baptized and the remainder fled
(see 4342/582).

4342 / 582

Frankish King Chilperic I forced many Jews to
become Christians (see 4336/576), but most of
them secretly remained Jewish.

4349 / 589

The Metivta of Pumpedita was reconstituted by R.Chanan.

The persecution of Jews in Bavel (see 4318/558) had lessened, and R.Chanan (from Ishkiya) returned to Pumpedita (see 4320/560) and he reconstituted the Metivta there, although the Metivta at Firuz-Shabur remained (more) active under R.Maari Surgo (the son of R.Dimi, see 4320/560). This ushered in the era of the Ge'onim. The "Gaon" was the head of a yeshiva (Rosh Metivta) in Bavel, an official position and title (see 3995/235) usually conferred on an elderly and suitable candidate [Igg.R.Sher.G./Dor.Har.6.35-6, 45-6, 54, 164, 166-7, 218]. Some say that greatly respected Talmud scholars everywhere in that period were given the title of Gaon [Mmn.Hakd.L'Yad].

During the four centuries of the Ge'onim, Bavel was considered the center of Jewish life; the Ge'onim received many questions on Halacha matters from many countries, which were discussed by the scholars of the Metivta. The answers (under the name of the presiding Gaon) were often very brief and did not reflect the internal discussions; they were written in the same language as the Talmud and in a similar style. The Metivta itself retained the same style developed at the time of the Amora'im (see 3995/235) [Igg.R.Sher.G./Dor.Har.6.154, 191, 215, 223, 245, 266-8].

At around this time Mar Zutra (II) (see 4318/558) left Bavel and settled in Eretz Yisrael, where he was accepted as a leader of the Talmud scholars and some say was given the title of "head of the Sanhedrin" (see 4189/429), which was passed on to his descendants [Sed.ol.Zut.q.Dor.Har.6.39/Dor.Har.6.47-8, 50].

4368 / 608

R.Chanan (from Ishkiya) died; R.Maari Surgo (see 4349/589) became the Gaon of Pumpedita, and was succeeded as Gaon of Firuz-Shabur by R.

Chanina (Min Bei Gihara) (Chanina I of Ge'onim) [Igg.R.Sher.G./Dor.Har.6.167, 172-3, 190].

4369 / 609

The Metivta of Sura was reconstituted.

The Metivta of Sura was reconstituted (see 4300/540), and R.Mar (bar R.Huna) became the Gaon (Rosh Metivta) [Igg.R.Sher.G./Dor.Har.6.172].

4372 / 612

The Jews of Spain were ordered to convert or leave (when the Christian Visigoths [see 4155/395] had gained complete control of the country). The order was apparently not strictly enforced, although many left, but it was reissued a number of times (see 4454/694), when some were forced to convert and some were expelled from certain locations.

4374 / 614

Jews were allowed to return to Yerushalayim.

The Persians captured Eretz Yisrael, including Yerushalayim, from the Byzantine Empire (see 4389/629), and the Jews were allowed to settle in Yerushalayim after almost 500 years (see 3893/133, 4389/629).

4380 / 620

At around this time R.Chana Gaon succeeded R.Maari Surgo as Gaon (Rosh Metivta) of Pumpedita, and R.Chanina (Chanina II of Ge'onim) succeeded R.Mar (bar R.Huna) as Gaon of Sura [Igg.R.Sher.G./Dor.Har.6.172-3].

4389 / 629

The Byzantine Empire reconquered Eretz Yisrael.

When the Byzantine Empire (Romans) reconquered Eretz Yisrael (see 4374/614), many

Jews were killed, many fled, and the rest were expelled from Yerushalayim again (see 4374/614 and 4397/637). The Byzantine emperor (Heraclius) later decreed unsuccessfully that all Jews in the empire should be forcibly baptized.

4392 / 632

A number of battles Muhammad fought in northern Arabia were against Jewish tribes who did not accept his new religion. He expelled many Jews from there, and many were expelled (under the claim of fulfilling his wishes) after he died in 4392, having become the strongest leader in Arabia. Since then, Jews have never been allowed to live in parts of Arabia.

4396 / 636

R.Yitzchak was the last Gaon of Neharde'a (Firuz-Shabur).

R.Yitzchak Gaon (Yitzchak I of Ge'onim) succeeded R.Chanina (I, Min Bei Gihara) as Gaon (Rosh Metivta) of Firuz-Shabur (see 4368/608). He was the last Gaon of the Metivta of Neharde'a (see 4420/660) [Igg.R.Sher.G./Dor.Har.6.164-8, 171, 173].

4397 / 637

The Arabs conquered Eretz Yisrael.

The Muslim Arabs conquered many countries at this time, including Babylonia from the Persian Empire, Eretz Yisrael from the Byzantine Empire, Syria, Egypt, North Africa, and (later) Spain. Communication became easier among the Jews of these countries (see 4234/474) and the Metivtot of Bavel (now Iraq).

4400 / 640

Around this time, Rava I of Ge'onim succeeded R.Chana as Gaon of Pumpedita (see 4380/620),

and R.Huna (Huna I of Ge'onim) succeeded R.Chanina (II) as Gaon of Sura (see 4380/620) [Igg.R.Sher.G./Dor.Har.6.173-5,177].

4405 / 645

One of the *Takkanot HaGe'onim* was enacted at this time.

R.Rava (I), Gaon of Pumpedita (see 4400/640), made a Takkana (enactment) together with R. Huna (I), Gaon of Sura (see 4400/640), that a woman should be given an immediate divorce if she refused to live with her husband. (This enactment was not unanimously accepted as part of Halacha.) [Igg.R.Sher.G./Rif Ket.27a(on Tal.Ket.63b), Shilt.Gib./ Mmn.Hil.Ish.14.14, Mag.Mish./Tur E.H.77/Dor.Har.6.173-5, 177, 215/see also Mmn.Hil.Mal.VeLov.2.2].

4410 / 650

R.Bustenai (Gaon) succeeded R.Rava (I) as Gaon of Pumpedita (see 4400/640), and R.Sheshna (Mesharshiya bar Tachlifa) succeeded R.Huna (I) of Sura (see 4400/640) [Igg.R.Sher.G./Dor.Har.175-7].

4420 / 660

Around this time R.Sheshna (see 4410/650) died, and for a number of years the Reish Galuta (Exilarch) was involved in political manipulation (see 4449/689) in the appointment of successors as Gaon of Sura [Igg.R.Sher.G./Dor.Har.6.152, 159, 176-7, 192].

Muhammad's son-in-law and a successor, Caliph Ali came to Bavel (Iraq) at around this time. R.Yitzchak (I) Gaon (see 4396/636) of Firuz-Shabur went out to meet him with a large contingent of the estimated 90,000 Jews of Neharde'a and its environs. He was accepted favorably [Igg.R.Sher.G./Dor.Har.6.166-8,178].

Bustenai, of whom many stories are told, was the first Reish Galuta (Exilarch) under the new Arab Islamic rule. A controversy later developed about he status of some of his children, who were said o be of an unconverted wife who came from the onquered Perisan royal family and was given to im by the caliph [Yuch.3.138/Sed.Had.4420/Dor.Har.6.169-71(3)].

4421 / 661

The new Muslim Arab caliph of Yerushalayim built a large wooden mosque on the site of the Beit Hamikdash. He also confiscated Jewish property in Eretz Yisrael and distributed it to Arab settlers.

4449 / 689

Mar R.Chanina(i) (Chanina III of Ge'onim) became Gaon of Sura, after many years of political manipulations by the Reish Galuta (see 4420/660). Mar R. Huna Mari (Huna II of Ge'onim) was Gaon of Pumpedita, having succeeded R.Bustenai (see 4410/650) [Igg.R.Sher.G./Dor.Har.6.176-7, 192, 233].

4454 / 694

The Jews of Spain were accused of plotting to overthrow the Christian Visigoth government, which had been continuously enacting laws to convert or expel them (see 4372/612). Many fled, some say to Morocco, but many were forcibly converted (see 4471/711).

4457 / 697

Mar R.Nahilai succeeded Mar R.Chanina(i) (III) as Gaon of Sura (see 4449/689) [Igg.R.Sher.G./Dor.Har.6.233].

4471 / 711

When the Moors (Muslims) invaded Spain, the Jews welcomed them (see 4454/694). Many Jews who had overtly converted to Christianity while

secretly observing Judaism, returned to their religion completely. The Jews became the invaders' indigenous allies, helped them to conquer and then to rule, and as a result Jewish life in Spain began to flourish.

4475 / 715

Mar R.Yaakov HaKohen (Yaakov I of Ge'onim) succeeded Mar R.Nahilai as Gaon of Sura (see 4457/697) [Igg.R.Sher.G./Dor.Har.6.233].

4479 / 719

Mar R.Chiya succeeded Mar R.Huna (II) Mari as Gaon of Pumpedita (see 4449/689), and Mar R.Rava (Rava II of Ge'onim) succeeded him. Around 4479, Mar R.Natrunai (Natrunai I of Ge'onim) succeeded Mar R.Rava (II) [Igg.R.Sher.G./Dor.Har.6.192, 233].

The son-in-law of Mar R.Natrunai (I) (Mar R.Yaneka) was a member of the (royal) family of the Reish Galuta. He wielded his influence (see 4449/689) and exercised harsh authority over the scholars of Pumpedita, which caused many to leave (for Sura) [Igg.R.Sher.G./Dor.Har.6.192].

4482 / 722

Many Jews were forced to accept Christianity in the Byzantine Empire, and many left Constantinople and other parts of the empire.

4493 / 733

Mar R.Shmuel (Shmuel I of Ge'onim) (the grandson of R.Rava I, see 4410/650) succeeded Mar. R.Yaakov (I) as Gaon of Sura (see 4475/715) [Igg.R.Sher.G./Dor.Har.6.233].

4499 / 739

R.Yehuda (Yehuda I of Ge'onim) had succeeded Mar R.Natrunai (I) as Gaon of Pumpedita (see

129

4479/719), and in 4499, R.Yosef (Yosef I of Ge'onim) succeeded him [Igg.R.Sher.G./Dor.Har.6.233].

4500 / 740

The Khazars, a people said to originate in the vicinity of Turkey, lived in a region between the Caspian and the Black Seas. Their king and many of his people converted to Judaism (see 4715/955) [Kuzari 1.1, 1.47].

4508 / 748

Many people died in an earthquake in Eretz Yisrael.

R.Shmuel (Shmuel II of Ge'onim) succeeded R.Yosef (I) as Gaon of Pumpedita (see 4499/739) [Igg.R.Sher.G./Dor.Har.6.233].

4511 / 751

R.Mari Kohen (Mari I of Ge'onim) succeeded Mar R.Shmuel (I) as Gaon of Sura (see 4493/733) [Igg.R.Sher.G./Dor.Har.6.233].

4515 / 755

R.Acha(i) Gaon left Bavel for Eretz Yisrael.

R.Natroy succeeded R.Shmuel (II) as Gaon of Pumpedita (see 4508/748) [Igg.R.Sher.G./Dor.Har.6.212, 233]. R.Acha(i) Gaon, who had written a work called She'iltot D'R.Acha(i) (Talmudic Halacha/ Agada on the order of the Chumash and in the style of the Talmud), was passed over in this appointment (due to the involvement of the Reish Galuta Shlomo bar Chisdai, see 4519/759). R.Acha(i) left Bavel and settled in Eretz Yisrael [Igg.R.Sher.G./Sef. Hak.q.Dor.Har.6.270/Yuch.3.139/Dor.Har.6.192-3, 212, 270].

4519 / 759

R.Yehudai became Gaon of Sura.

R.Avraham (Avraham I of Ge'onim) succeeded R.Natroy as Gaon of Pumpedita (see 4515/755) [Igg.R.Sher.G./Dor.Har.6.212, 233].

Mar R.Acha (Acha I of Ge'onim) succeeded R.Mari (I) Kohen for half a year (see 4617/857), as Gaon of Sura (see 4511/751). He was succeeded by R.Yehudai Gaon (Yehuda II of Ge'onim), who was brought to Sura by the Reish Galuta Shlomo bar Chisdai (a Talmud scholar) (see 4515/755) [Tsh.Hag.Zich.LeRi.183.q.Dor.Har.6.213/Igg.R.Sher.G./Dor.Har.6. 213-4, 233].

R.Yehudai Gaon (who was blind) was known for his lucid clarifications on the Talmud (some of which crept into the text because his disciples had written them in the margins, from where they were later mistakenly appended, see 4320/560) [Tos.B.K.53b, Rashal/Yuch.3.139/Sh.Mkbtzt.B.M.13b(48b), 15b (55b)/Dor.Har.6.139, 196-201].

The Halachot Gedolot (BaHaG) was written at this time.

R.Yehudai had already written many of his own Halachic decisions (see 4349/589). R.Shimon Kaira collected many of them (and also of the She'iltot of R.Acha(i), see 4515/755, and of other Ge'onim), and wrote the Halachot Gedolot (in the order of the Talmud), which is known as the BaHaG. It is probably the first work to have a hakdama (introduction) [Tsh.Hag.Zich.LeRi.376.q.Dor. Har. 6. 211/B. HaMa. Shab. 25b (Rif. 12a)/Sef. Hak./Sed. Had./Shem Hag.2.26/Dor.Har.6.191, 200-8, 211].

4521 / 761

R.Davidai (the brother of R.Yehudai (II) Gaon) (see 4519/759) succeeded R.Avraham (I) as Gaon of Pumpedita (see 4519/759) [Igg.R.Sher.G./Dor.Har.6.212, 233].

4523 / 763

Mar R.Achunai Kahana succeeded R.Yehudai (II) Gaon, as Gaon of Sura (see 4519/759) [Igg.R.Sher.G./ Dor.Har.6.230-1, 233].

Anan ben David founded a sect (of Jews), because he was passed over, some say, when his brother was appointed Reish Galuta. This sect later became known as (or merged with) the Kra'im (Kara'ites) (see 3628/−133) [Igg.R.Sher.G./Yuch.2.130; 3.139/Tzem.Dav.4515/Sed.Had.4515].

4524 / 764

R.Chanina (Chanina IV of Ge'onim) succeeded R.Davidai as Gaon (Rosh Metivta) of Pumpedita (see 4521/761) [Igg.R.Sher.G./Dor.Har.6.233].

4528 / 768

Mar R.Chanina Kahana (Chanina V of Ge'onim) succeeded Mar R.Achunai as Gaon (Rosh Metivta) of Sura (see 4523/763) [Igg.R.Sher.G./Dor.Har.6.230-1, 233].

4531 / 771

R.Malka (Malka I of Ge'onim) succeeded R.Chanina (IV) as Gaon (Rosh Metivta) of Pumpedita (see 4524/764) [Igg.R.Sher.G./Dor.Har.6.233].

At this time there was a controversial challenge (see 4577/817) to the leadership of the Reish Galuta (Exilarch), Zakkai bar Achunai, and when the challenger, Natrunai, was removed by the intervention of the Metivtot, he left Bavel (Iraq) for the west [Igg.R.Sher.G./Dor.Har.6.231-2].

4533 / 773

Mar R.Rava (Rava III of Ge'onim), the son of R.Davidai, succeeded R.Malka (I) as Gaon (Rosh Metivta) of Pumpedita (see 4531/771) [Igg.R.Sher.G./Dor.Har.6.233].

4536 / 776

Mar R.Mari HaLevi (Mari II of Ge'onim) succeeded Mar R.Chanina (V) Kahana as Gaon (Rosh Metivta) of Sura (see 4528/768) [Igg.R.Sher.G./Dor.Har.6.230-1, 233].

4540 / 780

Mar R.Bibi HaLevi succeeded Mar R.Mari (II) HaLevi as Gaon (Rosh Metivta) of Sura (see 4536/776) [Igg.R.Sher.G./Dor.Har.6.234].

4542 / 782

R.Shanui succeeded Mar R.Rava (III) as Gaon (Rosh Metivta) of Pumpedita (see 4533/773) [Igg.R.Sher.G./Dor.Har.6.233].

4543 / 783

R.Chanina Kahana (Chanina VI of Ge'onim), the son of R.Avraham (see 4521/761), succeeded R.Shanui as Gaon (Rosh Metivta) of Pumpedita (see 4542/782) [Igg.R.Sher.G./Dor.Har.6.234, 235].

4546 / 786

R.Chanina (VI) Kahana was removed from office by the Reish Galuta (Exilarch) and Mar R.Huna Mar HaLevi (Huna III of Ge'onim) succeeded him as Gaon (Rosh Metivta) of Pumpedita (see 4543/783) [Igg.R.Sher.G./Dor.Har.6.234, 270].

4548 / 788

Another of the *Takkanot HaGe'onim* was enacted at this time.

Mar R.Huna Mar HaLevi, Gaon of Pumpedita (see 4546/786), together with Mar R.Bibi HaLevi, Gaon of Sura (and R.Menasheh, who was to succeed Mar R.Huna, see 4549/789), made a *Takkana* enabling a widow to collect her ketuba and dowry (and enabling creditors to collect debts) from any of the husband's belongings, not only from real estate [Igg.R.Sher.G./Mmn.Hil.Ish.16.7, Mag.Mish./Dor.Har.6.232, 234].

4549 / 789

R.Menasheh (see 4548/788) succeeded Mar R.Huna Mar (III) HaLevi as Gaon (Rosh Metivta) of Pumpedita [Igg.R.Sher.G./Dor.Har.6.234].

4550 / 790

Mar R.Hilai (Hilai I of Ge'onim) succeeded Mar R:Bibi HaLevi as Gaon (Rosh Metivta) of Sura (see 4540/780) [Igg.R.Sher.G./Dor.Har.6.281].

4556 / 796

Mar R.Yeshayah HaLevi succeeded R.Menasheh as Gaon of Pumpedita (see 4549/789) [Igg.R.Sher.G./ Dor.Har.6.281].

4558 / 798

R.Yaakov HaKohen (Yaakov II of Ge'onim) succeeded R.Hilai (I) as Gaon of Sura (see 4550/790), and Mar. R.Yosef (Yosef II of Ge'onim) succeeded Mar R.Yeshayah HaLevi as Gaon of Pumpedita (see 4556/796) [Igg.R.Sher.G./Dor.Har.6.281].

4560 / 800

The caliph in Baghdad placed Yerushalayim under the protection of Charlemagne (the Frankish king, and newly proclaimed emperor of the reorganized [see 4215/455] Western Roman Empire). Charlemagne, who strengthened the power of the Church in his dominions, is said by some to have settled some Talmud scholars in Germany and France.

4565 / 805

Mar R.Kahana (the son of R.Chanina VI, see 4543/783) succeeded Mar R.Yosef (II) as Gaon of Pumpedita (see 4558/798) [Igg.R.Sher.G./Dor.Har.6.281].

4571 / 811

Mar R.Avimai (Ivumai, Avimai I of Ge'onim) succeeded Mar R.Kahana (his nephew, see 4565/805) as Gaon of Pumpedita (see 4565/805) [Igg.R.Sher.G./Dor.Har.235, 281].

4573 / 813

R.Avumai (Avumai II of Ge'onim) succeeded R.Yaakov (II), his nephew, as Gaon of Sura (see 4558/798) [Igg.R.Sher.G./Dor.Har.6.241-2, 281].

4575 / 815

Mar R.Yosef (Yosef III of Ge'onim) succeeded Mar R.Avimai (I) as Gaon of Pumpedita (see 4571/811) [Igg.R.Sher.G./Dor.Har.6.281].

4577 / 817

Mar R.Avraham (Avraham II of Ge'onim) succeeded Mar R.Yosef (III) as Gaon of Pumpedita (see 4575/815) [Igg.R.Sher.G./Dor.Har.6.281].

There was a challenge to the leadership of the Reish Galuta (Exilarch) (see 4531/771), and the challenger appointed another Gaon for Pumpedita (R.Yosef IV). The issue of Reish Galuta was resolved, and R.Yosef (IV) stepped aside (see 4588/828) when it became evident that the people were perturbed by the presence of two Ge'onim [Igg.R.Sher.G./Dor.Har.6.239].

4581 / 821

Mar R.Tzadok succeeded R.Avumai (II) as Gaon (Rosh Metivta) of Sura (see 4573/813) [Igg.R.Sher.G./ Dor.Har.6.281].

4583 / 823

R.Hilai (Hilai II of Ge'onim) succeeded Mar R.Tzadok as Gaon (Rosh Metivta) of Sura (see 4581/821) [Igg.R.Sher.G./Dor.Har.6.281].

4587 / 827

Mar R.Kiyumi (Kiyumi I of Ge'onim), who some say was a brother of R.Tzadok (see 4583/823), succeeded R.Hilai (II) as Gaon of Sura (see 4583/823) [Igg.R.Sher.G./Dor.Har.6.281].

4588 / 828

R.Yosef (Yosef IV of Ge'onim) (see 4577/817) succeeded Mar R.Avraham (II) as Gaon of Pumpedita (see 4577/817) [Igg.R.Sher.G./Dor.Har.6.281].

4590 / 830

R.Moshe (or R.Mesharshiya) (the son of R.Yaakov (II), see 4573/813) succeeded Mar R.Kiyumi (I) as Gaon of Sura (see 4587/827) [Igg.R.Sher.G./Sef.Hak.q.Dor.Har.6.242/Dor.Har.6.241-2].

4593 / 833

Mar R.Yitzchak (Yitzchak II of Ge'onim) succeeded R.Yosef (IV) as Gaon of Pumpedita (see 4588/828) [Igg.R.Sher.G./Dor.Har.6.240, 271, 281].

4598 / 838

Mar R.Yosef (Yosef V of Ge'onim), who had been passed over in the appointment of Mar R.Yitzchak (II) as Gaon of Pumpedita (see 4593/833), succeeded R.Yitzchak [Igg.R.Sher.G./Dor.Har.6.240, 271, 281].

4601 / 841

R.Paltui succeeded Mar R.Yosef (V) as Gaon of Pumpedita (see 4598/838) [Igg.R.Sher.G./Dor.Har.6.281]. R.Moshe (Mesharshiya) died (see 4590/830), and was not replaced as Gaon of Sura for two years [Igg.R.Sher.G./Dor.Har.6.281].

4603 / 843

R.Kohen Tzedek (Tzedek I of Ge'onim) (the son of R.Avumai II) became Gaon (Rosh Metivta) of Sura after the position was vacant for two years (see 4601/841) [Igg.R.Sher.G./Dor.Har.6.2859, 281].

The Reish Galuta (Exilarch) Ukva attempted to redirect some of the funds raised for the Metivta of Sura to his own advantage (see 4420/660), and R.Kohen Tzedek was instrumental in stopping this. Ukva was eventually expelled from his position and from the central Jewish areas of Bavel. Some infer that other serious matters were also involved. He later managed to have himself reinstated (by the caliph) (see 4613/853), but was expelled once again due to public outcry [Yuch.2.133./Dor.Har.6.257, 249-262].

4608 / 848

R.Sar Shalom succeeded R.Kohen Tzedek as Gaon of Sura (see 4603/843) [Dor.Har.6.241-6, 259 281].

4610 / 850

The Jews of Bavel (Iraq) were required by their Muslim Arab rulers to wear a yellow patch.

4613 / 853

R.Natrunai (Natrunai II of Ge'onim) (the son of R.Hilai (II), see 4587/827) succeeded R.Sar Shalom as Gaon of Sura (see 4608/848) [Dor.Har.6.241-6,259 281-2].

Some say that during the controversy with the Reish Galuta Ukva (see 4603/843), R.Amram was appointed (by Ukva) to be Gaon of Sura during the tenure of R.Natrunai II; but he did not exercise any of the rights or powers of that position [Igg.R.Sher.G./Dor.Har.6.259(34)].

4617 / 857

R.Acha (Acha II of Ge'onim) succeeded R.Paltui as Gaon of Pumpedita (see 4601/841) for half a year (see 4519/759) and was succeeded by R. Menachem (the son of R.Yosef IV, see 4593/833). Not all the scholars of the Metivta accepted the appointment of R.Menachem, and some followed R.Mattityahu (see 4619/859). This was the only documented case in four centuries of Ge'onim where there was open dissent among the scholars [see Dor.Har.6.240, 269-75] over the leadership of the Metivtot of Bavel/Iraq) [Igg.R.Sher.G./Dor.Har.6.240, 271-2, 282].

4618 / 858

R.Amram (who wrote the Siddur) became Gaon of Sura.

R.Amram Gaon succeeded R. Natrunai (II) as Gaon of Sura (see 4613/853). R.Amram had the system (Seder) of prayers committed to writing, and this was sent to the Jews of Spain (see 4471/711). This earliest known book of written prayers is now commonly called a Siddur (prayer book) [Tzem.Dav.4600/Shem.Hag.2.34a/Dor.Har.6.241-6, 259, 282].

4619 / 859

R.Mattityahu (see 4617/857), who some say was the brother of R.Yosef (V) (see 4598/838), succeeded R.Menachem as Gaon (Rosh Metivta) of Pumpedita (see 4617/857) [Igg.R.Sher.G./Dor.Har.6.240, 242-3, 282].

4628 / 868

R.Abba, a grandson of R.Shmuel II (see 4515/755) succeeded R.Mattityahu as Gaon of Pumpedita (see 4619/859) [Igg.R.Sher.G./Dor.Har.6.249, 282].

4631 / 871

R.Tzemach (Tzemach I of Ge'onim), the son of R.Paltui (see 4617/857), succeeded R.Abba as Gaon of Pumpedita (see 4628/868) [Igg.R.Sher.G./Dor.Har.6.282].

R.Tzemach was asked to rule on the validity of the Halachic opinions of Eldad HaDani, a traveler who claimed to be from the lost tribe of Dan (see 3205/-556) [Mord.Chul.2a/Sed.Had./Shem.Hag.2.110].

4636 / 876

R.Nachshon (the son of R.Tzadok, see 4583/823, 4587/827) succeeded R.Amram Gaon as Gaon of Sura (see 4618/858) [Igg.R.Sher.G./Dor.Har.6.282].

4640 / 880

R.Hai (Hai I) of Ge'onim succeeded R.Tzemach (I) as Gaon of Pumpedita (see 4631/871) [Igg.R.Sher.G./Sef.Hak.q.Dor.Har.6.241/Dor.Har.6.2410-1282].

4644 / 884

R.Tzemach (Tzemach II of Ge'onim) succeeded his (maternal) half-brother R.Nachson as Gaon of Sura (see 4636/876) [Igg.R.Sher.G./Dor.Har.6.282].

4648 / 888

Mar R.Kiyumi (Kiyumi II of Ge'onim), the son of R.Acha (II), see 4617/857) succeeded R.Hai (I) as Gaon of Pumpedita (see 4640/880) [Igg.R.Sher.G./Dor.Har.6.248, 282].

4652 / 892

R.Malka (Malka II of Ge'onim) succeeded R.Tzemach (II) as Gaon of Sura (see 4644/884) for only a few weeks, and was succeeded by Mar R.Hai II of Ge'onim, the son of R.Nachshon, see 4644/884). Many of the other elderly scholars of the Metivta of Sura died within a three-month period (see 4671/911) [Igg.R.Sher.G./Dor.Har.6.246-7, 263, 282].

4658 / 898

Mar R.Hilai (Hilai III of Ge'onim), the son of R.Natrunai (II), see 4618/858) succeeded Mar R.Hai (II) as Gaon of Sura (see 4652/892) [Igg.R. Sher.G./Dor.Har.6.248, 282].

4665 / 905

Mar R.Shalom succeeded Mar R.Hilai (III) as Gaon (Rosh Metivta) of Sura (see 4658/898) [Igg.R.Sher.G./Dor.Har.6.282].

4666 / 906

R.Yehuda (Yehuda III of Ge'onim) succeeded Mar R.Kiyumi (II) as Gaon of Pumpedita (see 4648/888) [Igg.R.Sher.G./Dor.Har.6.248, 282].

4671 / 911

R.Yaakov (Yaakov III) of Ge'onim succeeded Mar R.Shalom as Gaon of Sura (see 4665/905). At this time the number of scholars in this Metivta had decreased significantly, many of them having joined the Metivta of Pumpedita (see 4652/892) [Igg.R.Sher.G./Yuch.2.133/Dor.Har.6.247, 263, 283].

4677 / 917

R.Mevasser, the son of Mar. R.Kiyumi II, see 4648/888) was appointed by the scholars of the Metivta of Pumpedita to succeeded R.Yehuda (III) (see 4666/906) as Gaon. However, David (ben Zakkai), the Reish Galuta (Exilarch), sought to appoint Mar R.Kohen Tzedek (Kohen Tzedek II of Ge'onim) (see 4686/926); the disagreement continued for five years, after which R.Mevasser was recognized as Gaon by the Reish Galuta although some scholars remained with R.Kohen Tzedek (II) Kahana [Igg.R.Sher.G./Dor.Har.6.249, 251-2, 260, 271-2, 282].

4683 / 922

Aharon ben Meir, the Rosh Metivta in Eretz Yisrael, announced that Rosh HaShana of this year should be on a Tuesday, while the calculations of the Ge'onim in Bavel established it for Thursday. This created a serious division, and Rbnu.Saadya Gaon (of Egypt) took a prominent stand, in lucid and articulate communication, supporting the Ge'onim of Bavel, who eventually prevailed after a few years of serious disruption in the calendars of many local communities which had developed opposing factions. [See Otz.Hag.2.128-35].

4683 / 923

R.Yom Tov Kahana succeeded R.Yaakov (III) as Gaon of Sura (see 4671/911), although he had not been one of the full-time scholars of the Metivta (see 4671/911) [Igg.R.Sher.G./Dor.Har.6.263, 283].

4685 / 925

Some Jews were killed and many enslaved, when the city of Oria (southern Italy) was attacked by Arabs.

4686 / 926

Mar R.Kohen Tzedek Kahana (II) (see 4677/917) was accepted as the successor to R.Mevasser as Gaon of Pumpedita [Igg.R.Sher.G./Dor.Har.6.249, 251-2, 282].

4687 / 927

R.Yom Tov Kahana died (see 4683/923), and the remaining scholars of the Metivta of Sura considered disbanding and moving to Pumpedita. The Reish Galuta (Exilarch) (David ben Zakkai) appointed Mar R.Natan to become Gaon, but he died before he took office, and a suitable candidate was not immediately found (see 4688/928) [Igg.R.Sher.G./ Dor.Har.6.247, 263-4, 283].

4688 / 928

Rbnu.Saadya was appointed Gaon of Sura.

The Reish Galuta (Exilarch) David ben Zakkai appointed Rbnu.Saadya Gaon (see 4683/922) as Gaon of Sura (see 4687/927), with the hope – shared by the scholars of Pumpedita – of breathing new life into the Metivta [Igg.R.Sher.G./Yuch.2.134/ Dor.Har.6.159, 264-5, 283].

4690 / 930

Rbnu.Saadya, Gaon of Sura and author of *Emunot VeDeyot* (philosophy), questioned some official documents of judgment favoring David ben Zakkai, the Reish Galuta (Exilarch), and he refused to sign them. A severe (political) dispute broke out, during which time David appointed R.Yosef (who was not an outstanding scholar) as Gaon (Rosh Metivta) of Sura. Rbnu.Saadya appointed the brother of David ben Zakkai as Reish Galuta, and the strife spilled out into a wider circle, involving the need for the approval of the caliph for the Reish Galuta (see 3990/230) (and the accompanying monetary representations customary at that time).

The caliph endorsed David (who was of greater stature), and Rbnu.Saadya withdrew from public life until the dispute, in which many people had taken sides, had receded. (R.Yosef was nominal Gaon of Sura in his absence) [Igg.R.Sher.G./Yuch.2.134-5, 3.140/Dor.Har.6.159, 258, 261, 274-9].

Rbnu.Saadya wrote many works and was actively engaged in refuting the claims of the Kra'im (see 4523/763) who were very influential in Eretz Yisrael at this time.

4692 / 932

The Jews were forced to convert, in parts of Italy, and they were massacred in Bari. Some say that

Chisdai ibn Shaprut, a very influential (Jewish) statesman (see 4715/955), accomplished the withdrawal of an expulsion order.

4695 / 935

R.Tzemach (Tzemach III of Ge'onim) succeeded Mar R.Kohen Tzedek (II) as Gaon of Pumpedita (see 4686/926) [Igg.R.Sher.G./Dor.Har.6.265, 283].

4699 / 939

R.Chanina (Chanina VII of Ge'onim, the son of R.Yehuda III, see 4677/917) succeeded R.Tzemach (III) as Gaon of Pumpedita (see 4695/935), more than a year after R.Tzemach had died [Igg.R.Sher.G./Dor.Har.6.249, 283].

4702 / 942

Rbnu.Saadya Gaon died (some say he was only 50), and R.Yosef (see 4690/930) continued (unsuccessfully) as the Gaon of Sura. He lacked the scholarly stature for the position, and because of the bitterness over his involvement in the controversy (see 4690/930) against Rbnu.Saadya (which had been the most divisive in the recorded four centuries of the Ge'onim), he left Sura after a year or two, and the Metivta at Sura was disbanded [Igg.R.Sher.G./Yuch.3.140/Dor.Har.6.244, 274-5, 283].

4704 / 944

R.Aharon succeeded R.Chanina (VII) as Gaon of Pumpedita (see 4699/939) [Igg.R.Sher.G./Dor.Har.6.265-6, 283.

4705 / 945

A new fanatic dynasty took control of Bavel (Iraq), and the Jews suffered persecutions during its century of reign (see 4757/997).

4715 / 955

"Four Captives" were ransomed around this time.

Four great Talmudic scholars were said to have left Bari (Italy) on a journey across the Mediterranean (to collect money for charity), when they were captured by a Spanish warship.

One of them, R.Chushiel, was sold in North Africa and went to Kairou'an (Tunisia).

R.Moshe (who had traveled with his wife and young son) was sold with his son (R.Chanoch) in Spain, and arrived in Cordova where he was appointed head of the local yeshiva by Chisdai ibn Shaprut (see 4692/932). (His wife had taken her own life because of the pirates' intentions for her.)

R.Shemaryahu was sold in Alexandria and then went to Cairo.

These four scholars, each in his respective location, raised the level of scholarship and transformed the local style in a remarkable way. The Talmud scholars of Italy, from where they had come, were quite independent from the Ge'onim of Bavel (Iraq) (see 4098/338). Their style of scholarship was based on their own logical deductions from the Talmud (as distinct from the Babylonian adherence to directly transferred tradition). They also tended to rely on the scholars and the tradition (Nussach) of Eretz Yisrael, which was mostly under the same (Roman) government as Italy and most of Europe (Ashkenaz). [Sef.Hak.q. Dor.Har.6.283-4/Sef.Hay.619/Rosh R.H.(Caph.4) 35a(p.40a)/Yuch. 5.182/Sed.Had.4790/Dor.Har.6.234, 283-90, 293-4, 295-7, 298-300, 301-2].

[Recent archival findings pose questions for this account of how the scholars arrived in those places. However, the answer may lie in the fact that there seems to have been another R.Shemaryahu ben Elchanan (slightly later) (see Dor.Har.6.299[47], 299-300) and possibly another R. Chushiel.]

R.Menachem (ben Yaakov) ben Saruk, the Spanish author of a dictionary (*Machberet*) of Hebrew words, was secretary to Chisdai ibn Shaprut, who (some say) sent a letter to Joseph, the Jewish king of Khazars (see 4500/740).

R.Donash ben Lavrat of Baghdad, a disciple of R.Saadya Gaon, was a grammarian who disagreed with many things in R.Menachem's dictionary. He also wrote poems and *piyutim*.

4720 / 960

R.Nechemyah, son of Mar R.Kohen Tzedek (II) (see 4695/935) who had wanted to become Gaon (Rosh Metivta) of Pumpedita earlier, succeeded R.Aharon (see 4704/944) as Gaon, although not all the scholars (including R.Sherira) accepted his leadership (because it lacked scholarly stature) [Igg. R.Sher.G./Dor.Har.6.265-6, 279, 283].

4728 / 968

R.Sherira became Gaon of Pumpedita.

R.Sherira Gaon, the son of R.Chanina VII, (see 4704/944), a descendant of King David, succeeded R.Nechemyah as Gaon of Pumpedita (see 4720/ 960) [Igg.R.Sher.G./Dor.Har.6.47, 279-80].

4757 / 997

R.Hai became (the last) Gaon of Pumpedita.

R.Sherira Gaon wrote a famous detailed letter (Iggeret) in answer to some questions about the historical background of the Talmud tradition. This letter has served as a basis for the clear chronology of the Metivtot of Bavel (Babylonia, Persia/ Iraq) [Igg.R.Sher.G./Dor.Har.4.682(18); 6.28, 162-3, 166-7, 180].

R.Sherira lived until almost 100 years of age. Some say that he stepped aside, and his son R.Hai (Hai III of Ge'onim) succeeded him as Gaon of Pumpedita (see 4728/968).

R.Sherira was slandered to the caliph (see 4705/945), who arrested him and his son R.Hai (III) and confiscated their property. R.Hai (III) was released and R.Sherira was hanged [Igg.R.Sher.G./Yuch.3.141; 5.181/Sef.Hak.q.Dor.Har.6.279-80/Dor.Har.6.252, 279-80].

4764 / 1004

Some Jews in Eretz Yisrael were forced to convert by the Arab Muslim rulers. Synagogues were burned down, and the Jews of Egypt were required to wear a distinctive sign on their clothing.

4767 / 1007

Many Jews were killed and many were forced to convert to Christianity in riots throughout France. Most of the converts returned to Judaism a few years later, after the riots had ceased.

4772 / 1012

When a priest converted to Judaism in Mayence (Mainz, Germany), the Jews were forced to convert or leave. The expulsion order was withdrawn within the year.

At around this time, R.Amnon of Mayence, it is said, asked for three days to consider whether to convert or be put to death. Then, regretting having even asked for time, he pleaded for his tongue to be cut out. Other bodily parts, however, were hacked off for his refusal to convert,and he asked to be brought to the synagogue on Rosh HaShana on his deathbed, where he composed the prayer *Unetaneh Tokef* as he lay dying.

4773 / 1013

Many Jews were killed when the Berbers conquered Cordova (Spain), and divided Spain into many provinces. R.Shmuel HaNagid fled to Granada where he became very influential (see 4815/1055).

4785 / 1025

R.Chanoch, who had been one of the "Four Captives" (see 4715/955), died a few days after he fell in the synagogue on Simchat Torah, in Tishrei 4785/1024 (although some say 4775/1014) [Sef. Hak.q.Yuch.3.143/Dor.Har.6.301-2].

4795 / 1035

Thousands of Jews (6,000) were massacred in Fez (Morocco), some say in an invasion, at around this time.

4798 / 1038

R.Hai Gaon died.

The elderly R.Hai Gaon, son of R.Sherira Gaon, the last (and most influential) of the Ge'onim, died in Pumpedita on the 20th Nissan. He had maintained communication with an ever-increasing range of Jewish communities throughout the world, but after his death the influential role of the Metivtot of Bavel (Iraq) rapidly declined (see 4705/945, 4715/955, 4800/1040) [Yuch.3.141/Dor. Har.6.156, 304-5].

R.Hai (III) was succeeded by R.Chizkiyah (the grandson of David ben Zakkai) who was killed two years later (see 4705/945, 4800/1040).

Living in the Year 1040		
	b.	d.
Rbnu.Gershom Me'or Hagola	960?	1040?
Rbnu.Chananel	985?	1057?
R.Shmuel HaNagid	993	1056?
Rif (Alfasi)	1013	1103
Rashi	1040	1105

Universal Dispersion

CHAPTER 12

The Rishonim –
Early Scholars

The twelfth chapter in Jewish history begins with the emergence of great scholars in the regions of North Africa, Spain, Germany, and France, which developed into a new era of Torah scholarship.

This chapter covers the beginning of the codification of the laws of the Talmud (led by the Rif and the Rambam) and the great commentaries to the Talmud (led by Rashi and Tosaphot). The chapter concludes when the Jews were expelled from Spain, after having been expelled from England, France, and Austria, and having been decimated by persecutions and local expulsions in Germany, Bohemia, Moravia, Switzerland, and Italy.

THE RISHONIM – EARLY SCHOLARS

Early Rishonim, Tosaphot, and the Crusade Massacres

Jewish Year		Secular Year
4800	Rbnu.Gershom Me'or HaGolah died	1040
4848	The Rif arrived in Spain (from Morocco)	1088
4856	**THE FIRST CRUSADE DESTROYED JEWISH COMMUNITIES**	**1096**
4859	**Yerushalayim was captured by the Crusaders**	**1099**
4863	**The Rif died**	**1103**
4865	**RASHI DIED AND THE ERA OF THE TOSAPHOT BEGAN**	**1105**
4895	**THE RAMBAM (MAIMONIDES) WAS BORN**	**1135**
4904	**THE FIRST (RECORDED) BLOOD LIBEL TOOK PLACE**	**1144**
4907	**The Second Crusade attacked Jewish communities**	**1147**
4907	Rabbenu Tam was captured by the Crusaders	1147
4908	The Rambam's and the Radak's families left Cordova	1148
4925	The Rambam visited Eretz Yisrael	1165
4931	Rabbenu Tam died	1171
4935	The Rashbam died	1175
4944	The young son of the Ri was killed	1184
4948	**Jews were allowed to return to Yerushalayim**	**1187**
4949	R.Yaakov D'Orleans was killed in London	1189
4950	Jews were massacred in England in the Third Crusade	1190
4951	The Radak wrote his commentary	1191
4954	The Ramban (Nachmanides) was born	1194
4959	The Ra'avad died	1198
4965	The Rambam died	1204
4996	Rampaging mobs massacred Jews in France	1236
5002	**A massive burning of the Talmud took place in Paris**	**1242**
5004	Yerushalayim was sacked by Egyptians and Turks	1244
5012	The Inquisition began to use torture	1252
5027	**The Ramban (left Spain and) settled in Eretz Yisrael**	**1267**
5030	The Ramban (Nachmanides) died in Eretz Israel	1270
5046	**The Maharam MeRothenburg was imprisoned**	**1286**
5050	**THE ERA OF THE TOSAPHOT CONCLUDED AROUND THIS TIME**	**1290**

Later Rishonim, Persecutions, and Expulsions

Jewish Year		Secular Year
5050	**The Jews were expelled from England**	**1290**
5053	The Maharam MeRothenburg died in prison	1293
5058	**The Rindfleisch massacres began**	**1298**
5058	The Mordechai and Hagahot Maimoniyot were killed	1298
5065	The Rashba placed a limited ban on philosophy	1305
5065	The Rosh (and his son, the Tur) arrived in Spain	1305
5066	The Jews were expelled from France	1306
5070	The Rashba died	1310
5080	Jews were massacred by the Pastoureaux Crusaders	1320
5088	The Rosh died	1327
5096	Jews of Germany were massacred by the Armledder bands	1336
5098	The Ralbag wrote his commentary on the Bible	1338
5109	**THE BLACK DEATH MASSACRES SWEPT ACROSS EUROPE**	**1349**
5127	The Ran, Rivash, and other scholars 'were imprisoned	1367
5151	Jews of Spain were massacred — many became Marranos	1391
5151	The Rivash and Rashbatz left Spain	1391
5155	**The final expulsion of Jews from France**	**1394**
5173	R.Yosef Albo was in a forced debate with Christians	1413
5181	Jews of Austria massacred in the Wiener Gezera	1421
5235	**THE INVENTION OF PRINTING WAS USED FOR JEWISH BOOKS**	**1475**
5241	**The Inquisition was established in Spain**	**1481**
5248	R.Ovadya Bertinura settled in Yerushalayim	1488
5251	Columbus consulted R.Avraham Zacuto before his travels	1491
5252	**THE JEWS WERE EXPELLED FROM SPAIN AND SICILY**	**1492**

MAJOR RISHONIM

	Secular Year	
	Born	Died
Rbnu.Gershom Me'or Hagolah	960?	– 1070?
Rbnu.Chananel	985?	– 1057?
R.Shmuel HaNagid	993	– 1056?
Rif (Alfasi)	1013	– 1103
Rashi	1040	– 1105
Rashbam	1080?	– 1174?
R.Avrahim ibn Ezra	1089?	– 1164
Rabbenu Tam	1100?	– 1171
Ri (R.Yitzchak)	1120?	– 1200?
Ra'avad	1120?	– 1198
Ba'al Halttur	1120?	– 1193?
Ba'al Hama'or	1125?	– 1186
Rambam (Maimonides)	1135	– 1204
R.Yehuda HaChasid	1150?	– 1217
Roke'ach (R.Elazar)	1160?	– 1237?
Radak (Kimchi)	1160?	– 1235?
Rbnu.Yona (Gerondi)	1180?	– 1263
Ramban (Nachmanides)	1194?	– 1270?
Maharam MeRothenburg	1215?	– 1293
Rashba	1235?	– 1310?
Mordechai (Pirush)	1240?	– 1298
Hagahot Maimoniyot	1240?	– 1298
Me'iri (R.Menachem)	1249?	– 1315?
Rosh (R.Asher)	1250?	– 1327
Rbnu.Bachya II	1265?	– 1340?
Tur (R.Yaakov ben Asher)	1275?	– 1349?
Ralbag (Gersonides)	1288	– 1344
Ran (R.Nissim)	1290?	– 1380?
Rivash	1326	– 1408?
Maharil	1360?	– 1427
Rashbatz	1361?	– 1444

4800 / 1040

Rbnu. Gerhsom Me'or HaGolah died.

Rbnu. Gershom ben Yehuda Me'or HaGolah, a disciple of R. Yehuda Ben Meir HaKohen (Rbnu. Leontin), died in Mayence (Mainz, Germany) where he headed the first famous yeshiva in Europe. (Some say he died as many as thirty years later.) He was a prolific scribe who copied accurate versions of many works, and is remembered for his Ch'ramim (bans) and Takkanot (enactments) including the one for monogamy. R. Chizkiyah Gaon) (see 4798/1038) was slandered to the king, arrested, tortured, and killed.

4810 / 1050

Rbnu. Nissim Gaon died and Rbnu. Chananel (ben Rbnu. Chushiel), who wrote a Talmud commentary, died shortly thereafter (although some say he died ten years earlier). They both lived in Kairou'an (Tunisia) and were disciples of Rbnu. Chushiel and followers (through correspondence) of R.Hai Gaon.

4815 / 1055

R.Shmuel HaNagid died.

R.Shmuel HaNagid, a disciple of R.Chanoch and author of Mavoh LaTalmud (Introduction to the Talmud), was an influential statesman in the province of Granada and a prosperous, generous, Talmud scholar. He died in 4815/1055, and his son R.Yosef HaNagid (who was a son-in-law of R.Nissim Gaon) succeeded him (see 4827/1066). R.Shlomo ibn Gabirol, a grammarian and poet who lived (in Spain) at this time, wrote Tikkun Middot HaNefesh (Mussar) (see 4928/1167).

Moshe HaDarshan of Narbonne (France) also lived at this time (see 4866/1105).

4827 / 1066

Yosef ben Shmuel HaNagid of Granada (see 4815/1055) was killed at the gates of the city on Shabbat, 9th Tevet, and 4,000 Jews were killed in the massacre. The influential Jewish community of Granada ceased to exist for a time.

4848 / 1088

The Rif arrived in Spain.

The Rif, R.Yitzchak ben Yaakov Alfasi HaKohen (see 4863/1103), was (some say) a disciple of Rbnu.Chananel and Rbnu.Nissim Gaon. Some say he was called Alfasi because he lived in Fez (Morocco) (Al Fazi, Rif - R.Isaac Fazi) [see Hakd. SMaG]. He fled Morocco in 1088, because he was denounced; and he was appointed Rabbi in Alusina (Lucene) (which was a completely Jewish town) shortly after his arrival there.

4856 / 1096

The First Crusade destroyed Jewish communities in its path.

Pope Urban II declared a crusade to capture Yerushalayim, because of the way the Moslems were treating Christian pilgrims in Eretz Yisrael. The masses who gathered in Europe for the crusade attacked the Jews before they left.

The Jews of Speyer (Bavaria) were massacred in this First Crusade on Shabbat the 8th Iyar, and the Jews of Virmyze (Worms, Germany) on the 23rd. The Jews of Cologne (Germany) were saved, on the 25th Iyar (see Tammuz), when the crusaders could not enter the city because the bishop had ordered the gates closed. The Jews of Virmyze who took refuge in a castle (see Iyar). were massacred (during the prayer of Hallel for Rosh Chodesh) on the 1st Sivan. R.Klonymos of Rome (who had succeeded R.Yaakov ben Yakar [see 4865/1105] in Worms) was killed. One Jew (Simcha ben Yitzchak HaKohen) stabbed the bishop's nephew while being forced into baptism and was killed for this.

On the 2nd Sivan, crusaders massacred the Jews of Neuss (Prussia); 1000 Jews of Mayence (Mainz, Germany) were massacred on the 3rd; and the

Jews of Bachrach (Germany) were massacred Erev Shavu'ot (5th Sivan).

On the first day of Shavu'ot, some Jews in Cologne (see Iyar) chose to be killed rather than baptized, as was the case in many other cities during the crusade. On the 5th Tammuz, the Jews of Xanten (Germany) took their own lives, rather than be massacred or baptized. There were many other instances. The Jews of Mehr (Germany) were massacred on the 6th Tammuz; and Jews of Cologne were attacked on the 7th, although they escaped total destruction (see Iyar, Sivan).

The crusaders moving eastward also attacked Jews in the cities of Troyes and Metz (France), Regensburg (Germany), Prague, Pressburg, and in other towns and cities before the Hungarians put an end to their excesses when they arrived there. The dead numbered in the tens of thousands, according to some, and many were forced to baptize although most continued as secretly practicing Jews. Those who were baptized were allowed to openly return to Judaism one year later by Henry IV. Some German Jews moved eastward to Poland-Lithuania, taking their language, which later became Yiddish.

4859 / 1099

Yerushalayim was captured by the Crusaders.

When the crusaders reached Yerushalayim they laid siege to it on the 15th Sivan, and conquered it on the 23rd Tammuz. They forced all the Jews into a synagogue, which they then set on fire, killing almost all; very few escaped from the city. The Christian "Kingdom of Jerusalem" was established, in which Jews were not allowed to live (see 4948/1187 and 4389/629, 4925/1165).

Living in the Year 1100		
	b.	d.
Rif (Alfasi)	1013	1103
Rashi	1040	1105
Rashbam	1080?	1174?
R.Avraham ibn Ezra	1089?	1164
Rabbenu Tam	1100?	1171

4863 / 1103

The Rif died.

The Rif, R.Yitzchak Alfasi (see 4848/1088), died at the age of 90 in Alusina (Lucene, Spain) on the 11th Iyar. Some say he died in Nissan 1123. His major work *Halachot* follows the order (and is in the form of a summary) of the Talmud, and i similar in style to the works of the Ge'onim (see Figures F, G, pages 318, 319). The Ri Migash R.Yosef HaLevi ibn Migash, his young disciple succeeded the Rif in his position in Alusina.

4865 / 1105

Rashi died and the era of the Tosaphot began.

Rashi, R.Shlomo (Yarchi) ben Yitzchak (R Shlomo Yitzchaki), died on the 29th Tammuz in Troyes (France) where he was born. Rashi's commentaries on Bible and Talmud (see Figures A, D pages 313, 316) were in their simple clarity unique departure from the style which had prevailed until this time (see 4863/1103). Rashi (descendant of R.Yochanan HaSandlar) was the disciple of R.Yakkov ben Yakar (who was a disciple of Rbnu.Gershom Me'or HaGola) and of R.Yitzchak ben Asher I HaLevi, among others [Rash Bet.24b-end/Shem.Hag.35a-b].

Rashi's disciple R.Simcha, author of the *Machzo Vitry*, died in the same year.

Rashi was succeeded by the Rashbam, R.Shmue ben Meir, his grandson and disciple, who wrote (lengthier) commentary on Talmud and the *Chumash* (Bible) (see Figure A, page 312). R.Ye huda ben Natan, the Rivan, was a son-in-law o Rashi, and part of his commentary is printed around a section of the Talmud (*Makot*) in th place of Rashi, who had died. He is mentioned i *Tosaphot* [Tan.27b, Zev.96a, Bech.50b etc.].

At this time R.Yehuda HaLevi ben Shmuel disciple of the Rif and the Ri Migash), who wa renowned for his poetry, wrote (some say edite the *Kuzari* (see 4928/1167), a philosophy based on a dialogue with the king of the Khazars (see 4500/740).

R.Yitzchak ben Asher II, the Riva, was a disciple of Rashi and was one of the earliest scholars mentioned in *Tosaphot* [Nid.39b, etc].

Tosaphot were considered "additional" explanations to Rashi's commentary on the Talmud (see 5050/1290), and followed a new style of scholarship involving logical deductions from the Talmud [See Dor.Har.6.295].

4866 / 1105

The Ba'al HeAruch, R.Natan ben Yechi'el, who (some say) was a disciple of Rbnu.Chananel and R.Moshe HaDarshan, died in Rome in 4866/1105. There he wrote the *Sefer HeAruch,* a Talmudic Aramaic/Hebrew dictionary, which some say he finished one year before he died.

4885 / 1125

The Jews were expelled from Ghent and from the rest of the province of Flanders.

4886 / 1126

R.Baruch ben Yitzchak I, a disciple of the Rif, died in Elul 1126. His disciple (and nephew) was R.Avraham ben David (ibn Daud), Ra'avad I, author of *Sefer HaKabbala* (history), who was killed for refusing to convert to Christianity.

4895 / 1135

The Rambam (Maimonides) was born.

The Rambam, R.Moshe ben Maimon, a descendant of King David, was born on 14th Nissan, and was a child when he saw the Ri Migash (see 4863/1103), who blessed him. The Rambam then considered him as his teacher [Shem.Hag.1.49a/ Mmn.Hil.Sh.Up.5.6].

4901 / 1141

The Ri Migash (see 4895/1135) died on the 30th Nissan.

4904 / 1144

The first recorded blood libel took place.

On the second day of Pesach 1144, the Jews of Norwich (England) were accused of using Christian blood for ritual purposes (see Av 5050/1290).

4906 / 1146

R.Peter ben Yosef, a disciple of Rabbenu Tam (see 4950/1190), was killed, according to some, in Austria.

4907 / 1147

The Second Crusaders attacked Jewish communities in their path.

When the remnant of the First Crusaders lost some territory in the Middle East to the Turks, Pope Eugene III proclaimed a second Crusade, to restore Christian power in the area. These crusaders also massacred Jews in Europe (see 4856/1096) before leaving for the Middle East, where they failed. The Jews of Wurtzburg (Germany) were massacred on the 24th Adar, and the Jews of Cologne (Germany) were attacked on the 23rd Nissan, although many Jews fled to the safety of the mountains or castles. The Jews of Bachrach (Germany) were attacked on the 5th Sivan (Erev Shavu'ot).

Rabbenu Tam was captured by the crusaders.

Rabbenu Tam, R.Yaakov ben Meir (see 4931/1171), was a grandson of Rashi, and a son of R.Meir (who is mentioned in *Tosaphot* [Kid.59a, Shab.56a, etc.]. Rabbenu Tam, one of the leading Ba'alei *Tosaphot* (authors of *Tosaphot*, see 4865/1105, 5050/1290), was captured by the crusaders in Ramerupt (France) on the second day of Shavu'ot. They ransacked his home and tore his Sefer Torah scroll into pieces. He escaped the next day, with serious injuries, after being left in a field; some say he escaped with the help of a friendly knight.

Living in the Year 1160		
	b.	d.
Rashbam	1080	1174?
R.Avraham ibn Ezra	1089?	1164
Rabbenu Tam	1100?	1171
Ri (R.Yitzchak)	1120?	1200?
Ra'avad	1120?	1198
Ba'al Halttur	1120?	1193?
Ba'al Hama'or	1125?	1186
Rambam (Maimonides)	1135	1204
R.Yehuda HaChasid	1150?	1217
Roke'ach (R.Elazar)	1160?	1237?
Radak (Kimchi)	1160?	1235?

4908 / 1148

The Rambam's family and the Radak's father left Cordova.

The Jews of Cordova (Spain) were attacked by anti-Jewish rioters and many synagogues were destroyed on the 24th Tammuz 1148. When a fanatical Islamic sect took power there, the Jews were forced to convert (which some did while secretly retaining their Jewish religion). Many fled the country, including R.Maimon ben Yosef, father of the Rambam, and his family (see 4925/1165); R.Yosef Kimchi, father of the Radak (see 4951/1191), who settled in Narbonne (Provence); and R.Yehuda ibn Tibbon (see 4928/1167), who settled in Lunel (Provence).

4910 / 1150

R.Zerachyah (ben Yitzchak) HaLevi, called the RaZah and the Ba'al HaMa'or, was writing his work *HaMa'or* (comments on *Halachot* of the Rif) (see Figure F, page 318) in 1150 in Lunel (Provence). (The Rambam appears to have taken extreme exception to one of his Halacha rulings) [Mmn.Hil.Mam.4.1/HaMa'or HaKatan on Rif Pes.7a(Tal.Pes.28a), Ra'avad/TBY.O.C.443].

4919 / 1158

R.Avraham ibn Ezra wrote a letter about Shabbat in London on the 14th of Tevet.

4921 / 1161

Rbnu.Bachya I ben Yosef (ibn Paquda) (Rabbenu Bachaye) wrote Chovat HaLevavot (Mussar) in Arabic (see 4928/1167), around 1161 (in Spain). Some say it was written earlier. R.Eliezer ben Natan, the Ravan, a disciple of the Riva, wrote *Even HaEzer* (*Halacha*, customs) and corresponded with Rabbenu Tam and the Rashbam. He is mentioned in *Tosaphot* [Shev.26b, Shab.69b, etc./Shem.Hag.1.10b].

R.Eliezer of Metz (France) (R'EM, R.Eliezer Mi Metz) was a disciple of Rabbenu Tam and the Ri. He wrote the *Sefer Yere'im* (Halacha, Ethics), and is mentioned in *Tosaphot* [Shab.36a, 64a, Chul.26b, etc.].

4924 / 1164

R.Avraham ben Meir ibn Ezra, who wrote a commentary on the Bible (see Figure A, page 312), died on Rosh Chodesh Adar 1164 after his wife and children had all died (on separate occasions). There are other opinions as to when he died [Sed.Had.5934]. He had had discussions with Rabbenu Tam, on his many wanderings (see 4919/1158), and is mentioned in *Tosaphot* [R.H.13a, Tan.20b, Kid.37b]. He was a close contemporary of R.Yehuda HaLevi, (to whom many say he was related), and he is still known in the world of mathematics.

4925 / 1165

The Rambam visited Eretz Yisrael.

After fleeing Cordova (see 4908/1148) where he was born, the Rambam spent some time traveling before settling in Fez (Morocco) for some five years. Due to forced Islamic conversions (see 4958/1198), he left Fez with his family and sailed to Eretz Yisrael. His ship was threatened by a storm, but reached Acco (Acre) on the 3rd Sivan; six months later he visited Yerushalayim (see 4859/1099). He subsequently left Eretz Yisrael for Egypt and settled in Fostat (old Cairo), where he reversed the influence of the Kra'im (see 4523/763) that then prevailed [Mmn.Hil.Mel.5.7, Radvaz].

4928 / 1167

R.David ben Levi, of whom little is known, was killed in Virmyze (Worms, Germany) on the 21st Cheshvan, 4928/1167.

R.Yehuda ibn Tibbon (see 4908/1148) translated many works from Arabic into Hebrew including *Emunot VeDeyot* (see 4690/930), the *Kuzari* (see 4865/1105), *Tikkun Middot HaNefesh* (see 4815/1055), and *Chovat HaLevavot* (see 4921/1161).

There was a blood libel in Gloucester (England) in 1168 (see 4904/1144).

4931 / 1171

Rabbenu Tam died.

Fifty-one Jews were burned at the stake (because of a blood libel) in Blois (France) on the 20th Sivan; according to some, Rabbenu Tam (see 4907/1147) declared it a fast day, before his death (only two weeks later) on the 4th Tammuz. Rabbenu Tam was a brother of the Rashbam (see 4865/1105) (and his disciple) and of the Rivam (who had died young, leaving seven orphans). He wrote the *Sefer HaYashar* (*Pirush Sugiyot* and *Sh'elot UTeshuvot*), and his Bet Din was considered the leading Talmudic authority in his generation [Tos.Git.36b/Sed.Had.4930/Shem.Hag.]. Rabbenu Tam had eighty disciples before him when he lectured (see 4935/1175) [Yam.Sh.Sh.Hakd.].

4932 / 1172

The Ra'avad (III) was imprisoned (in Provence) for a short while on a false charge.

4933 / 1173

Binyamin ben Yona of Tudela (Spain) traveled extensively and recorded what he saw in *Masa'ot Binyamin* (or *Sefer HaMasa'ot*), a book that has served as a valuable record of Jewish communities of that time.

R.Petachyah of Regensburg also traveled extensively at this time, and a description of his travels appears in the book *Sivuv*.

4935 / 1175

The Rashbam died.

The Rashbam was very old when he died in 4935/1175 (see 4931/1171).

The Ri, or Ri HaZaken R.Yitzchak ben Shmuel of Dampierre (France), was one of the leading Ba'alei Tosaphot (see 4865/1105, 5050/1290). He was a grandson of R.Simcha (see 4865/1105), great grandson of Rashi, and a disciple of his uncle, Rabbenu Tam (see 4931/1171). He lectured to sixty disciples (see 4931/1171), each one of them thoroughly conversant in a different section (*Mesechta*) of the Talmud, which allowed them instant clarification of any issue.

4939 / 1179

The Ba'al HaIttur, R.Yitzchak ben Abba Mari of Marseilles, completed forty years of work on his encyclopedic Halacha *Sefer HaIttur*, in which he often mentions the *Sefer Yere'im* (see 4921/1161).

Living in the Year 1180		
	b.	d.
Ri (R.Yitzchak)	1120?	1200?
Ra'avad	1120?	1198
Ba'al Halttur	1120?	1193?
Ba'al Hama'or	1125?	1186
Rambam (Maimonides)	1135	1204
R.Yehuda HaChasid	1150?	1217
Roke'ach (R.Elazar)	1160?	1237?
Radak (Kimchi)	1160?	1235?
Rbnu.Yona (Gerondi)	1180?	1263

4941 / 1181

Jews were seized in Paris while attending services on Shabbat 25th Adar, and they were held for ransom.

There was a blood libel in Bury St. Edmunds (England) in 1181.

4942 / 1182

There was a blood libel in Saragossa (Spain) in 1182, and the Jews were expelled from part of France (see 4958/1198).

4944 / 1184

The son of the Ri was killed during his father's lifetime.

R.Elchanan, the son and disciple of the Ri (see 4935/1175), was killed in Dampierre (France) in 1184, while his father was still alive [Otz.Hag.2.155]. He is mentioned in Tosaphot [Zev.45b, Shev.25a, B.M. 111b, etc].

4948 / 1187

Jews were allowed to return to Yerushalayim.

Jews were allowed to return to Yerushalayim, when Saladin, Sultan of Egypt (whose personal physician was the Rambam) recaptured it from the Christians (see 4859/1099). Later, R.Shimshon ben Avraham of Shantz (Sens, France) emigrated to Eretz Yisrael (see 4962/1202, 4971/ 1211). He was one of the leading Ba'alei Tosaphot (see 5050/1290), is referred to in Tosaphot as "Rashba," and is also called Ish Yerushalayim. He was the author of Tosaphot Shantz and the Pirush Rash, a commentary on some Mishna (see Figure C, page 315). His older brother R.Yitzchak is referred to in Tosaphot as the Ritzba, "Ri Ha Bachur" (to distinguish him from "Ri HaZaken" [see 4939/1179]), and sometimes as the "Riva" [Otz.Hag.5.211a] (although Riva usually refers to R.Yitzchak ben Asher II, see 4865/1105) [Shem Hag.35a-b]. Both brothers were disciples of Rabbenu Tam and the Ri (see 4931/1171, 4935/1175).

4949 / 1189

R.Yaakov D'Orleans was killed in a massacre in London.

R.Yaakov of Orleans, a disciple of Rabbenu Tam, who is mentioned in Tosaphot [Ket.47a, Zev.55b, Nid.8a, etc.] and referred to sometimes as Rabbenu Tam, was killed with many other Jews in the anti-Jewish riots which took place in Elul in London at the coronation of Richard I (the Lion-Hearted). Richard later went on a crusade to recapture Yerushalayim (see 4948/1187).

4950 / 1190

Jews were massacred in England in the Third Crusade.

A crusading enthusiasm swept England (see 4949/1189, 4952/1192, 4956/1196). The Jews of Norwich were massacred on 28 Shvat (see 4904/1144), and the Jews of Stamfordfair were massacred on 27 Adar. The Jews of York refused to be baptized, and R.Eliyahu, a disciple of

Rabbenu Tam (see 4906/1146), was killed there; many Jews in York took their own lives on the 7th Nissan. On the 9th of Nissan, fifty-seven Jews were killed in Bury St. Edmunds, and in 1191 another disciple of Rabbenu Tam, R.Yom Tov, was killed in York (see 4951/1191).

One hundred Jews were burned to death in France by order of the king in 1190.

R.Shmuel ben Eli HaLevi was head of the vibrant Baghdad yeshiva which had been reconstituted by his father (a descendant of Shmuel HaNavi – the Prophet) from the old academies in Sura and Pumpedita. He was not completely successful in his attempt, in 1190, to have the position of Reish Galuta (Exilarch) abolished so that the funds could be diverted to the yeshiva. He had a Halacha disagreement with the Rambam. His very learned daughter gave Torah lectures (in a special arrangement, so that the yeshiva students could not see her).

4951 / 1191

The Radak wrote his commentary.

R.David ben Yosef Kimchi of Narbonne, the Radak, who was very young when his father died (see 4908/1148), wrote his commentary on the Bible around this time (see 4992/1232).

A disciple of Rabbenu Tam, R.Yom Tov, author of *Omnam Kein* (*piyut* said on Yom Kippur evening), was killed in York (see 4950/1190).

4952 / 1192

R.Yaakov of Corbeil, a disciple of Rabbenu Tam who is mentioned in *Tosaphot* [Shab.27a, Bet.6b, Ket.12b, etc.], was killed, some say in Corbeil (see 4950/1190, 4951/1191).

There was a blood libel in Winchester (England) in 4953/1193.

4954 / 1194

The Ramban was born.

R.Moshe ben Nachman, the Ramban (see 5030/1270), was born in Gerona (Spain) on the 12th Elul.

4956 / 1196

Fifteen Jews (including an adviser to the duke) were massacred in Vienna by participants in the Third Crusade (see 4950/1190).

R.Yitzchak ben Asher III (see 4948/1187), who was named after his grandfather, the Riva (see 4865/1105), was killed in Speyer (Germany) in 1196.

4957 / 1197

On the 6th Adar 1197, R.Shmuel ben Natrunai, a son-in-law and disciple of the Ravan, was tortured and then killed, with many other Jews, in Neuss (France).

4958 / 1197

R.Elazar ben Yehuda Roke'ach of Virmyze (Worms, Germany) (see 4998/1237), author of the *Roke'ach*, was wounded, some say by crusaders, who killed his wife and children on the 22nd Kislev.

4958 / 1198

Jews were allowed to return to the areas of expulsion in France in 1198 (see 4942/1182). The Jews of North Africa (even those who had openly converted to Islam, while secretly remaining Jews, see 4925/1165) were required to wear special dress (see 4610/850).

4959 / 1198

The Ra'avad died.

The Ra'avad (Ra'avad III), R.Avraham ben David of Posquieres (see 4932/1172), a son-in-law of Ra'avad II (R.Avraham ben Yitzchak Av Bet Din), died on the 26th Kislev. He was born in Narbonne, established a yeshiva in Posquieres (Provence) and wrote *Hasagot* – critical comments, sometimes acerbic – on the Rambam (see Figure H, page 320), on the Rif, and on HaMa'or (see 4910/1150).

Living in the Year 1200		
	b.	d.
Ri (R.Yitzchak)	1120?	1200?
Rambam (Maimonides)	1135	1204
R.Yehuda HaChasid	1150?	1217
Roke'ach (R.Elazar)	1160?	1237?
Radak (Kimchi)	1160?	1235?
Rbnu.Yona (Gerondi)	1180?	1263
Ramban (Nachmanides)	1194?	1270?

4962 / 1202

A letter was sent to the Torah scholars of Lunel, Provence by (the young) R.Meir ben Todros Abulafia HaLevi, the Ramah of Toledo (see 5004/1244), raising doubts about the philosophical views of the Rambam. He requested, unsuccessfully, that study of the Rambam's philosophical works be prohibited for students below a certain age (see 4992/1232). He also raised these doubts with the scholars in northern France. R.Shimshon (Ba'al Tosaphot Shantz, see 4948/1187) replied with respect and admiration for the Rambam, whose works he had apparently just seen.

4963 / 1203

R.Yaakov HaChasid (HaLevi) of Marvege (France) recorded an entry in his *Sh'elot UTeshuvot Min HaShamayim* (*Responsa from Heaven*) on the 29th Elul.

R.Baruch ben Yitzchak II, a disciple of the Ri, wrote the *Sefer HaTeruma*, and is mentioned in *Tosaphot* [A.Z.9b, 76a, Yom.46b.]. He later settled in Eretz Yisrael.

R.Avraham ben Natan HaYarchi, who had left Lunel (Provence) – hence the name HaYarchi, for "lunar" – and traveled through Germany and France and settled in Spain where he wrote his *Sefer HaManhig*.

4965 / 1204

The Rambam died.

The Rambam, R.Moshe ben Maimon (Maimonides), died on the 20th Tevet. R.Avraham, his 19-year-old son (and disciple) succeeded him. The Rambam's Halacha code, *Yad HaChazaka – Mishneh Torah* (see Figures H, I, pages 320, 321), an encyclopedic compilation (in Hebrew) of all Talmudic law in a brilliant, original systematic arrangement, which was a departure from previous works (see 4863/1103, 4865/1105), was quickly accepted as the final word in Jewish law in the Sephardic communities (see 4996/1236) [Tsh. Mhrm.Alashkar.96.p.260-end/etc.]. In a letter five years before his death, he had praised and encouraged R.Shmuel ben Yehuda ibn Tibbon (the son of a translator, see 4928/1167) for his work translating *Moreh Nevuchim* (*Guide for the Perplexed*) from Arabic into Hebrew. In addition to other works, the Rambam also wrote a commentary on Mishna (see 5070/1310) (see Figure C, page 315).

4966 / 1206

Some Jews were killed in Halle (Germany), and the rest were expelled.

4969 / 1209

Two hundred Jews were killed in a massacre in Beziers (Provence) on the 19th Av.

4971 / 1211

Jews were imprisoned (for ransom) in England by order of the king, on the 13th Cheshvan 4971/1210.

In 1211 a group of 300 Talmud scholars (from France and England) emigrated to Eretz Yisrael. This was after the emigration of R.Shimshon (Ba'al Tosaphot Shantz, see 4948/1187, 4962/1202). [See Encyl.Jud.14.778].

4977 / 1216

Pope Innocent III issued an order in Tevet for Jews to wear a badge in order to distinguish them from the rest of the population (see 4610/850, 4958/1198). (This was followed in various ways, and in different countries, for five centuries.) Many Jews in England paid to be exempted from wearing the badge (see Av 5050/1290), and Jews in Spain threatened to leave the Christian-controlled part of the country.

4977 / 1217

R.Yehuda HaChasid of Regensburg, a disciple of the Ri, and author of *Sefer HaChasidim* (Mussar, Halacha, Kabbala/Customs), died on the 13th Adar. He had learned his Kabbala concepts from his father, R.Shmuel ben Klonymos, who had received them from his ancestors (see 4998/1237). He is mentioned in *Tosaphot* [B.M.5b].

R.Eliezer ben Yoel HaLevi, the Raviyah, who was a disciple of (his grandfather) the Ravan, R.Yehuda HaChasid, and also of R.Eliezer of Metz, lived in Germany and was the author of *Avi HaEzri* and *Avi Assaf* (both Halacha). He is mentioned in *Tosaphot* [Tan.13a, Pes.100b, Chul.47b].

Living in the Year 1220		
	b.	d.
Roke'ach (R.Elazar)	1160?	1237?
Radak (Kimchi)	1160?	1235?
Rbnu.Yona (Gerondi)	1180?	1263
Ramban (Nachmanides)	1194?	1270?
Maharam MeRothenburg	1215?	1293

4981 / 1221

Many Jews were killed in Erfurt (Germany) in a massacre on the 25th Sivan, and some threw themselves into the flames of the burning synagogue.

The Jews of Sicily and Pisa were all ordered to wear blue badges, and the men ordered to grow beards (see 4977/1216).

4985 / 1225

The Jews were expelled from Cremona and Pavia (northern Italy), but within fifty years were resettling there.

4988 / 1227

R.Ezra (HaNavi) of Gerona (Spain), a disciple of R.Yitzchak Sagi Nahor (the blind son of the Ra'avad, who was extremely well versed in the Kabbala he had learned from his father), was a teacher of the Ramban and is mentioned in *Tosaphot* [Shev.25a, B.B.28a, Git.88a]. He died on the 9th Tevet.

R.Shmuel HaSardi of Spain was a contemporary and disciple of the Ramban, and he wrote *Sefer HaTerumot*.

4990 / 1230

Jews of Wiener-Neustadt (Austria) were attacked for eleven days by anti-Jewish rioters.

Many Jews were killed, and many were forced to convert to Christianity in Astorga (Spain).

4992 / 1232

The Jews were massacred in Marrakesh (Morocco).

R.Shlomo (ben Avraham, Min HaHar) of Montpellier, who was respected by his contemporaries, the Ramban and the Ramah, was concerned over the tendency toward the study of philosophy; he attempted to prohibit such studies (see 4962/1202), including the Rambam's works. This raised a controversy involving others (see 5024/1263), in which the Ramban (Nachmanides), a recognized leader, appeared to be a mediator, and the (elderly) Radak supported the Rambam's works. Nevertheless, the controversy passed into non-Jewish hands, and there was a burning of the Rambam's works (see 5002/1242).

4995 / 1235

Seven Jews were tortured and burned at the stake in Bischofsheim (Germany), on the 10th Shvat.

Thirty four Jews were killed in Fulda (Germany) in a blood libel on the 18th Tevet 4996/1235 (see 5007/1247).

4996 / 1236

R.Moshe ben Yaakov of Coucy (France) traveled through Provence and Spain, encouraging Jews in keeping *mitzvot* (particularly, *Tefillin*, and avoidance of intermarriage in Spain). He wrote the *Sefer Mitzvot Gadol* (*S'MaG*), which made use of the Rambam's work and received broad acceptance in the Ashkenazi communities (see 4965/1204). He is mentioned in *Tosaphot* [Me.16a, A.Z.13a, Ber.14b, etc.]. His brother-in-law was R.Shimshon, mentioned in *Tosaphot* as HaSar MiCoucy (the count of Coucy) [Me.9b, Ber.9a, 14a, etc.].

Rampaging mobs massacred Jews in France.

Over 2,500 Jews were killed in France by rampaging mobs, some say crusaders. The Jews of Narbonne (Provence) were saved, and they instituted a local Purim (which is the first recorded) on the 21st Adar, in commemoration of their salvation.

4998 / 1237

R.Avraham Maimuni HaNagid (only son of the Rambam) (see 4965/1204) died on the 18th Kislev. He was succeeded by his son R.David

HaNagid (see 5045/1285), who wrote *DeRashot R.David* (or *Midrash David*).

R.Elazar ben Yehuda Roke'ach (see 4958/1197) was a disciple of R.Yehuda HaChasid, and he wrote the *Sefer Roke'ach* (Halacha, Customs, Mussar) in which some of his teachings are attributed to direct transmission (through R.Yehuda Ha Chasid) all the way back to R.Shimon HaPakuli (see 3836/76, 4977/1217) [Shem.Hag.1.11a].

5000 / 1240

Pope Gregory IX ordered the confiscation of all copies of the Talmud and other Jewish books, on the 16th Tammuz 1239; and on the 7th Adar2 1240, all copies of the Talmud were confiscated in France. R.Yechi'el of Paris, who is mentioned in *Tosaphot* [Yom.18b] and was a disciple of R.Yehuda of Paris (who was a descendant of Rashi), was forced to debate (see 5014/1254) the *meshumad* (apostate) who had libeled the Talmud. R.Moshe of Coucy (see 4996/1236) also attended the debate, which began on the 4th Tammuz. Despite the eloquence of the defenders, the Talmud was burned two years later (see 5002/1242).

The Jews were expelled from Brittany (France) by the local duke, in Tammuz 1240.

Living in the Year 1240	b.	d.
Rbnu.Yona (Gerondi)	1180?	1263
Ramban (Nachmanides)	1194?	1270?
Maharam MeRothenburg	1215?	1293
Rashba	1235?	1310?
Mordechai (Pirush)	1240?	1298
Hagahot Maimoniyot	1240?	1298

5001 / 1241

Most of the Jews of Frankfurt Am Main were massacred and the Jewish quarter was destroyed on the 14th Sivan.

Many Jews were killed in Bohemia when the Tartars invaded the country.

The Jews in (Christian) Spain were forced to attend conversion sermons, by order of the king (James I of Aragon) issued in 1241 (see 5023/1263).

5002 / 1242

A massive burning of the Talmud took place in Paris.

Twenty-four wagon-loads of handwritten copies of the Talmud, as well as other Jewish books (made before the invention of printing), were burned during Tammuz as a result of the events two years earlier (see 5000/1240). That Erev Shabbat, Parshat Chukat was observed as a fast day for many generations to commemorate this monumental loss from which Torah scholarship in France never really recovered (see 5066/1306). Some say that this burning took place in Paris at the same place as had another burning nine years earlier (see 4992/1232).

5003 / 1243

Jews were burned to death in Belitz (Germany) in the first recorded libel of ritual desecration. (The charge, called "desecration of the host," was that Jews purposely desecrated one of the Christian sacraments.)

Eleven Jews were killed in a blood libel in Kitzingen (Germany).

5004 / 1244

Yerushalayim was sacked by Egyptians and Turks.

Most Jews fled from Yerushalayim, but some were massacred by the hordes who sacked the city, leaving almost no Jews there (see 4948/1187, 5027/1267).

On the 26th Adar, Pope Innocent IV ordered further burnings of the Talmud (see 5002/1242).

The Ramah of Toledo (Spain) (see 4962/1202), who was a close contemporary of the Ramban, well versed in Kabbala and the author of Yad Ramah (Chidushim), died on the 18th Nissan.

R.Yeshayahu HaZaken of Trani (Italy), who wrote Tosaphot Rid (R'Yeshayahu D'Trani), was the leading Torah scholar in Italy. He had great respect for his contemporary, R.Yitzchak (ben Moshe) of Vienna, who was a disciple of the Raviyah, R.Yehuda HaChasid, and of R.Yehuda of Paris. R.Yitzchak of Vienna wrote the Sefer Or Zaru'a, which was later abbreviated by his son, R.Chaim (Eliezer).

5007 / 1247

Many Jews were killed, and others were forcibly converted to Islam, in Meknes (Morocco), with the rise of a new government.

Emperor Frederick II had planned to kill all the Jews in his Holy Roman Empire if the blood libel in Fulda (see 4995/1235) were true. Upon much investigation, he concluded that blood libels were false; Pope Innocent IV, who had ordered the burning of the Talmud, (see 5004/1244) stated also, in 1247, that the blood libels were false. In that same year many Jews in Valreas (France) were tortured, some mutilated, others killed, and the rest imprisoned (with Jewish properties confiscated) in a blood libel. In 1248 Christians in France were forbidden to have contact with Jews.

5010 / 1250

The Jews of Tunisia were required by their Muslim rulers to wear a special badge (see 4610/850, 4977/1216).

A new government, which oppressed the Jews, began to rule in Egypt (and spread to surrounding countries). Conditions of Jewish life there declined significantly.

5012 / 1252

The Inquisition began to use torture.

The Inquisition was a series of local church courts empowered (by the central authority, the presiding pope) to investigate and judge Christian heretics who could be punished and killed. Jews were subsequently open to such charges of "heresy" (see 5038/1278). In 1252, Pope Innocent IV (see 5007/1247) allowed the use of torture during investigations of heresy. He also ordered the expulsion of the Jews from Vienne (France) in Av 1253.

5014 / 1254

A Jewish participant in a religious debate (see 5000/1240, 5023/1263) in Cluny (France) was killed by a Christian knight.

5015 / 1255

Many (prominent) Jews were killed in England, in the blood libel of Lincoln on the 24th Elul. In this same year R.Eliyahu Menachem ben Moshe was removed from his position of Chief Rabbi in London because he refused to force the Jews to pay a heavy tax.

5017 / 1257

The Jews of Rome were required to wear special badges in 1257 (see 4977/1216), and the Jews of Mayence (Mainz, Germany) were required to do so in 1259.

5020 / 1260

R.Yechi'el of Paris left France to settle in Eretz Yisrael (see 5000/1240, 5002/1242, and 4971/1211), which was under threat of invasion by the Mongols (who had conquered Syria and massacred Jews).

R.Tzidkiyah ben Avraham HaRofeh was a cousin and disciple of the Rivevan, R.Yehuda ben Binyamin, and he wrote the *Shibbolei HaLeket* (Customs, Halacha) in Italy.

Living in the Year 1260		
	b.	d.
Rbnu.Yona (Gerondi)	1180?	1263
Ramban (Nachmanides)	1194?	1270?
Maharam MeRothenburg	1215?	1293
Rashba	1235?	1310?
Mordechai (Pirush)	1240?	1298
Hagahot Maimoniyot	1240?	1298
Me'iri (R.Menachem)	1249?	1315?
Rosh (R.Asher)	1250?	1327

5023 / 1263

The Ramban was forced by King James I of Aragon (Spain) (see 5001/1241) to debate (see 5014/1254) a *meshumad* (apostate) on the 12th Av. Although he did so quite successfully, he had to leave Aragon because of the ensuing controversy. The king ordered that all references to (early) Christianity be removed from the Talmud.

5024 / 1263

Rbnu.Yona (HaChasid) (ben Avraham) Gerondi (Gerona, Spain), who was a disciple and supporter of R.Shlomo Montpellier (see 4992/1232), died in Cheshvan. He was a cousin and *mechutan* of the Ramban and the author of *Sha'arei Teshuva* (Mussar) and Chidushim.

5024 / 1264

Jews of Arnstadt (Germany) were attacked and massacred by anti-Jewish rioters on 11th Av.

5025 / 1265

Twenty Jews were killed in Koblenz (Germany).

5026 / 1266

R.Avraham, a Ger from Augsburg (Germany), was killed on the 22nd Kislev. Twelve Jews were killed in Cologne (Germany) in Tammuz. Jews were ordered to wear special hats in parts of Poland (see 5039/1278).

5027 / 1267

The Ramban settled in Eretz Yisrael.

The Ramban arrived in Eretz Yisrael (see 5023/1263 and 5020/1260), and when he visited Yerushalayim in Elul, he established a house for prayer for Rosh HaShana. He effectively renewed the Jewish settlement in Yerushalayim, after the city had been sacked (see 5004/1244).

The Jews of Poland, Austria, and Silesia (the region between Germany and Poland), were required to wear special hats (see 4977/1216), by an order issued in Shvat 1267.

5029 / 1269

The Jews of Spain were exempt from wearing the special badge, in 1268 (see 5027/1267, 4977/1216), but were required to wear a round cape in its stead. The Jews of France were ordered to wear a yellow badge in Tammuz 1269; they were expelled from Carpentras (Provence). They returned a few years later when that area (around Avignon) was ceded by the king to the Pope.

5030 / 1270

The Ramban died.

The Ramban, R.Moshe ben Nachman (Nachmanides) (see 4988/1227, 5027/1267), who wrote a commentary on the Bible (see Figure A, page 312), Chidushim, and many other works, died on the 11th Nissan.

The Me'iri, R.Menachem ben Shlomo Me'iri of Provence, author of *Beit HaBechira* (basic commentary on the Mishna/Talmud), corresponded with (and had great respect for) the Rashba (see 5065/1305, 5070/1310), who was a disciple of the Ramban, and Rabbi in Barcelona.

5031 / 1271

The Jews of Brabant (a province bordering the Netherlands and Belgium) were to be expelled under terms of the last will of the duke. However, his widow received a declaration from Thomas Aquinas, a famous Christian philosopher who was strongly influenced by the Rambam's philosophy, in which he indicated that heavy taxes should be extracted instead, and that the Jews should wear a special badge (see 5029/1269).

5035 / 1275

The Jews were expelled from Worcester (England) (see 5039/1278).

5037 / 1277

The Jews were attacked in an anti-Jewish riot in Pamplona (Spain), and their houses were destroyed.

5038 / 1278

R.Yitzchak Males, Rabbi of Toulouse (France), was burned at the stake on the 9th Shvat by the Inquisition (see 5012/1252), which was well established by this time in the central and western parts of Europe.

On the 14th Av, an order was issued by Pope Nicholas III that Jews must attend conversion sermons by Christian priests (see 5001/1241). The order was enforced in England shortly thereafter (see 5039/1278, Av 5050/1290), and sporadically at various times in various countries (see 4977/1216).

5039 / 1278

Over a number of years, the Jews of England were subject to very restrictive laws in business, restricted as to where they could live, and continuously forced to pay very high taxes (see 5015/1255, 5035/1275, 5038/1278). On the 10th Cheshvan, many were imprisoned and killed on charges of circulating counterfeit money. On the 18th Nissan 1279, a number of Jews were killed in London in a blood libel.

The Jews of Poland were required to wear a red badge (see 5026/1266).

5040 / 1280

The S'MaK, R.Yitzchak of Corbeil, France (also called R.Yitzchak Ba'al HaChotem), was author of *Sefer Mitzvot Katan* (S'MaK, or Amudei HaGola), and son-in-law and disciple of R.Yechi'el of Paris. He died in 1280 (some say in 1270). R.Avraham (ben Shmuel) Abulafia, a controversial personality from Spain [Tsh.Rashba.548/Shem.Hag.2.19a/Otz.Hag.2.33], traveled to Rome to convert Pope Nicholas III to Judaism; although a stake had been prepared for his immolation there,he did not turn back until he heard that the Pope had died.

Living in the Year 1280		
	b.	d.
Maharam MeRothenburg	1215?	1293
Rashba	1235?	1310?
Mordechai (Pirush)	1240?	1298
Hagahot Maimoniyot	1240?	1298
Me'iri (R.Menachem)	1249?	1315?
Rosh (R.Asher)	1250?	1327
Rbnu.Bachya II	1265?	1340?
Tur (R.Yaakov ben Asher)	1275?	1349?

5041 / 1281

Jews were killed in a blood libel in Mayence (Mainz, Germany), and the synagogue was burned (see 5043/1283).

5043 / 1283

There was another blood libel in Mayence (see 5041/1281) and one in Bachrach (Germany), and many Jews were killed in the ensuing massacres.

5045 / 1285

One hundred and eighty Jews were killed in a blood libel in Munich (see 5043/1283).

R.David ben Avraham HaNagid, the grandson of the Rambam (see 4998/1237), was removed (by the Sultan) from his position in Cairo and he left for Eretz Yisrael, where he defended the works of the Rambam (see 4992/1232, 5065/1305). He was asked to return to Cairo five years later (see 5050/1290).

5046 / 1286

The Maharam MeRothenburg was imprisoned.

Maharam MeRothenburg, R.Meir ben Baruch, a disciple of R.Yitzchak of Vienna and of R.Yechi'el of Paris, was the leading Halacha authority in Germany. He wrote thousands of *Sh'elot UTeshuvot*, as well as *Tosaphot* on Yoma, now printed as the standard *Tosaphot* (see 5050/1290). He intended leaving the country because of the continuing difficulties of the Jews (see 5043/1283), but was denounced by a *meshumad* (apostate), and imprisoned on the 4th Tammuz in the fortress at Ensisheim. A huge ransom was imposed for his release, but he refused (on Halacha grounds) to have it paid (so that a precedent not be set). The Maharam MeRothenburg continued his teaching in the fortress for seven years (see 5053/1293), and his disciple R.Shimon ben Tzadok visited him regularly and recorded his Halacha rulings in a work called *Tashbetz* [see 5168/1407].

On the same day that the Maharam Me Rothenburg was imprisoned, forty Jews were killed in a blood libel in Oberwesel (Germany) (see 5045/1285). This was followed by another massacre in Bachrach (Germany) in 1287 (see 5043/1283).

5048 / 1288

Thirteen Jews were burned at the stake by the Inquisition in Troyes (France) in a blood libel on 20th Iyar; others were killed in a blood libel in Neuchatel (Switzerland).

5050 / 1289

The Jews were expelled from Anjou and Le Mans (France).

5050 / 1290

Kabbala (Torah mysticism) was handed down orally (and discreetly) through the generations (see Adar 4977/1217, 4988/1227) (hence the name Kabbala – received teachings). R.Menachem (ben Binyamin) of Recanti (Italy) wrote a Kabbala commentary on the *Chumash* (Bible) and *Piskei Ha Recanti* (Halacha). R.Moshe de Leon (Spain), found (and copied) a Kabbala manuscript that has been accepted by Talmud scholars as the *Zohar*, composed by R.Shimon bar Yochai, the Tanna. R.Yosef ben Avraham Gikatilya (of Spain) wrote *Sha'arei Ora* (Kabbala).

The era of the Tosaphot concluded around this time.

R.Peretz ben Yitzchak of Corbeil (France), a disciple of R.Yechi'el of Paris, wrote one of the last *Tosaphot*, called *Tosaphot Rbnu.Peretz*, (part of) which

is now printed as the standard *Tosaphot* on a section of the Talmud (*Avoda Zara*).

R.Eliezer of Touques (France) also wrote one of the last *Tosaphot*, called *Tosaphot Tuch* (Touques), which is an abbreviated version of *Tosaphot Shantz* (see 4948/1187), and edited to include other *Tosaphot*.

Although *Tosaphot Tuch* is now the major part of the *Tosaphot* printed around the Talmud (see Figure D, page 316), many independent *Tosaphot* were written [Tos.Shev.35a, B.M.111a, M.K.20b, Yom.2b, Mrsha 'A"N N"L'/See 5004/1244, 5046/1286]. The authors, the *Ba'alei Tosaphot*, included more than 100 scholars of France and Germany, and extended over a period of almost 200 years (see 4865/1105).

It is, therefore, not certain which *Tosaphot* writings were included in the standard version now available (see 5046/1286) [Tos.A.Z.9b-end/Sh.Mkbtzt.Ket31b-end/Yam.Sh.Sh.Yev.4.34./Yad.Mlchi.Klly.HaTos.2.14/She.Hag.2. 54a-b].

Many earlier (and other) scholars are quoted in Tosaphot,including R.Yehudai Gaon [Pes.30a, B.K.53b, etc.], *Halachot Gedolot* (*BaHaG*) [Pes.30a, etc.], *She'iltot D'R.Acha*(i) [Pes.30a, etc.], R.Saadya Gaon [Git.2a, etc.], R.Tzemach Gaon [M.K.20b, etc.], *Shimusha Rabba* [Min.29b, 34b, Ber.60b], R.Hai Gaon [A.Z.58b, etc.], Rbnu.Gershom Me'or HaGola [Betz.24b, etc.], the Rif [Eruv.104a, etc.], (R.Natan Ba'al) HaAruch [Shab.27b, etc.], Machzor Vitry [Ber.14a, etc.], the Rambam [Min.42b, Ber.44a/see Yam.Sh.Sh.Hakd], the Ra'avad [Tem. 12b, etc.].

In 1290, R.David HaNagid was reinstated in Cairo (see 5045/1285).

[5050/1290 is continued in next section.]

5050/1290 is continued from previous section.]

The Jews were expelled from England.

England, the first European country to have a blood libel (see 4904/1144), was among the first to require Jews to wear special badges (see 4977/1216) and was the first to force Jews to attend conversion sermons (see 5038/1278). On Tisha B'Av in 1290, England became the first European country to completely expel the Jews from its borders (see 5416/1656). Sixteen thousand Jews left, and most settled in Germany and some provinces of France.

The Jews of Naples, Bari (see 4692/932), and other cities in southern Italy were massacred or underwent forced baptism (see 5071/1311), in a blood libel in 1290 and many left.

5051 / 1291

Rbnu.Bachya ben Asher, a disciple of the Rashba (in Spain) wrote *Midrash Rbnu.Bachya (Bachaye)*, a commentary on *Chumash* (Bible) which includes Kabbala from the *Zohar* (see 5050/1290).

A Jewish physician who had risen to a position of the highest power under the Mongol ruler of Persia (Arghun Khan), was assassinated by enemies on the 3rd Nissan; many other Jews were massacred.

The Sultan of Egypt conquered Acco (Acre) in 1291, killed many Jews and imprisoned others, including R.Yitzchak (ben Shmuel) of Acco a disciple of the Ramban (see 5027/1267) who was well versed in Kabbala. When released he went to Spain, and he wrote a commentary on the Ramban's Chumash (Bible) commentary, and an authentication of the Zohar (see 5050/1290 on p. 161).

5053 / 1293

The Maharam MeRothenburg died in prison.

The Maharam MeRothenburg died in the fortress of Ensisheim (Germany) (see 5046/1286) on the 19th Iyar, but his body was not released for burial for fourteen years (see 5067/1307).

R.Aharon HaLevi, the Ra'ah, a descendant of the Razah and disciple· of the Ramban, wrote Chidushim and also *Bedek HaBayit*, a critique on the Rashba's *Torat HaBayit* (see 5070/1310). They were both rabbis in Barcelona. The Rashba wrote *Mishmeret HaBayit* (anonymously at first) in reply.

Some Jews were forced to convert to Islam in Iraq.

5054 / 1294

Some Jews were killed in Berne (Switzerland) in a blood libel, and the rest were expelled. They were allowed to return after paying an enormous amount of money, and also agreeing that all debts to them be annulled. (The annullment of debts to Jews was not uncommon in Europe.)

5058 / 1298

The Rindfleisch massacres began.

A knight named Rindfleisch led a mob in a Jewish massacre, which began in Rottingen (Germany) on 7 Iyar, and spread out to some 150 Jewish communities within a few months, causing many thousands of deaths (as many as 100,000) in the course of a few years. The blood libel charges of previous years (see 5043/1283, 5046/1286, 5048/1288, 5054/1294) were still prominent in the minds of those who participated in these slaughters.

Jews were massacred in Wiener-Neustadt (Austria) on the 12th Tammuz and in Ifhauben (Austria) on the 13th; 250 Jews were killed in Rothenburg (Germany) on the 14th. The Jews of Morgentheim (Austria) were massacred on the 18th Tammuz, the Jews of Wurtzburg (Germany) on the 13th Av, and Jews of Bischofsheim (Germany) on the 14th.

The Mordechai was killed in the Rindfleisch massacres.

R.Mordechai (ben Hillel) (Ashkenazi), a disciple of Maharam MeRothenburg and author of the *Mordechai* (Halacha), was killed with his wife and five children on the 22nd Av, together with 728 other Jews of Nuremberg (Germany). R.Avraham ben Baruch, who some say was the brother of Maharam MeRothenburg, was killed with his wife and children in Mayence (Mainz, Germany) [Otz.Hag.2.101].

Ten Jews were killed in Korneuburg (Austria) in a ritual desecration libel (see 5003/1243).

5059 / 1298

The author of *Hagahot Maimoniyot* was killed in the Rindfleisch massacres.

R.Meir (ben Yekutiel) HaKohen, the author of *Hagahot Maimoniyot* (notes on the Rambam's *Yad HaChazaka*) (see Figure H, page 320), was a disciple of the Maharam MeRothenburg and R.Peretz of Corbeil (France). He was killed with his family in the Rindfleisch massacres. Two hundred Jews of Heilbronn (Germany) were killed on the 12th Cheshvan.

Living in the Year 1300		
	b.	d.
Rashba	1235?	1310?
Me'iri (R.Menachem)	1249?	1315?
Rosh (R.Asher)	1250?	1327
Rbnu.Bachya II	1265?	1340?
Tur (R.Yaakov ben Asher)	1275?	1349?
Ralbag (Gersonides)	1288	1344
Ran (R.Nissim)	1290?	1380?

5062 / 1301

The Jews of Renchen (Germany) were massacred in 1301, in a continuation of the Rindfleisch massacres (see 5058/1298).

5063 / 1303

The Jews of Barcelona were ordered (in Nissan 1302) to kneel when passing Christian priests.

The Jews of Gotha (Germany) were attacked in the Rindfleisch massacres (see 5062/1301), and the Jews of Weissensee (Germany) were massacred on the 7th Nissan.

Many Jews in Egypt were forced to convert to Islam (see 5010/1250), and all Jews were henceforth required to wear yellow turbans.

The Rosh (see 5088/1327), a disciple of Maharam MeRothenburg, was consulted (as a leading Halacha authority in Germany) on many questions arising from the Rindfleisch massacres (particularly on property where no inheritors survived) Concerned that he might be imprisoned for ransom, as was his teacher, the Maharam (see 5046/1286), he left Germany with his family as the Maharam had attempted to do (see 5065/1305).

R.Yitzchak (ben Meir) of Dura (Duren, Gemany), a disciple of Maharam MeRothenburg, wrote *Sha'arei Dura* (*She'arim Belssur VeHeter*, Dietary Halacha), which was widely accepted in Ashkenazi communities.

5065 / 1305

The Rashba placed a limited ban on the study of philosophy.

R.Abba Mari of Montpellier was concerned over the tendency of the young in Provence, to study philosophy. He appealed to the Rashba (see 5030/1270, 5070/1310), who was the leader of Spanish Jews and had great influence over all Jewish communities through his *Sh'elot UTeshuvot* (responsa), to prohibit the study of philosophy for those under 25 years of age (see 4962/1202, 4992/1232). The Rashba did prohibit such study although he endorsed the Rambam's integrity and greatness and allowed the study of medicine.

The Rosh arrived in Spain.

The Rosh arrived in Barcelona in 1305 (see 5063/1303), where he was warmly received by the Rashba (and agreed to the ban). He became Rabbi in Toledo (Spain) shortly thereafter, some say with the assistance of the Rashba, bringing (some say) the French-German *Tosaphot* style of Talmud analysis to Spain (see 5050/1290, 5088/1327). He was surprised to find that the Jewish courts in Spain were actually using the death sentence (under the imprimatur of the government) (see 3789/29) [Tsh.HaRosh.17.8/Mmn.Hil.Chov.UMaz.8.10, 11/See Sed.Had.5241].

5066 / 1306

The Jews were expelled from France.

The Jews of France were arrested, their property confiscated, and they were expelled on the day after Tisha B'Av. Although they were allowed to return nine years later (see 5075/1315), Talmud scholarship in France deteriorated (see 5002/1242). Among the refugees leaving France were Rbnu.Yerucham (see 5095/1334); R.Aharon the father of R.Menachem ibn Zerach (see 5088/1328); R.Shimshon ben Yitzchak of Chinon, author of the *Sefer Keritut* (principles of the Talmud); R.Aharon ben Yaakov HaKohen of Lunel, author of *Orchot Chayim* (Halacha); and R.Eshtori Ha-Parchi, a disciple of the Rosh and of R.Eliezer ben Yosef of Chinon (see 5082/1321), who traveled to Spain, Egypt, and then Eretz Yisrael and later wrote *Kaftor VaPherach*, a scholarly book on the geography of Eretz Yisrael in Halacha, which identifies many historical sites.

5067 / 1307

The body of the Maharam MeRothenburg was released for burial on the 4th Adar (see 5053/1293), through the efforts of R.Alexander ben Shlomo (Susskind) Wimpen, who was subsequently buried near him.

5069 / 1309

One hundred and ten Jews were killed by a mob in Born (the Netherlands), and many were killed (after refusing to be baptized) in neighboring Louvain (Belgium).

5070 / 1310

The Rashba died.

The Rashba, R.Shlomo ben Avraham ibn Aderet (see 5030/1270, 5065/1305), a disciple of the Ramban and Rbnu.Yona (Gerondi), wrote Chidushim, thousands of *Sh'elot UTeshuvot*, *Torat HaBayit* and *Avodat HaKodesh* (both Halacha), as well as *Mishmeret HaBayit* (see 5053/1293). He was instrumental in having the *Pirush HaMishna* of the Rambam translated into Hebrew (see 4965/1204). After the Rashba died in Barcelona, the Rosh became the leading Halacha authority, and students came to him in Toledo from as far away as Bohemia and Russia [Tsh.HaRosh.51.2-end].

5071 / 1311

Forced converts in southern Italy (see Av, 5050/1290) were severely punished for (secretly) returning to Judaism.

5072 / 1312

Many Jews were killed around this time in Fuerstenfeld and Judenberg (Styria, a province of Austria), in a ritual desecration libel (see 5003/1243) and a blood libel.

5075 / 1315

Jews were allowed to return to France (see 5066/1306) by the new king, Louis the Quarreller, son and successor to Philip the Fair who had expelled them.

5079 / 1319

The Ritva, R.Yom Tov ben Avraham (ibn Ash-vili), a disciple of the Rashba and the Ra'ah, wrote an exhaustive commentary on the Talmud (in Spain), which includes an overview of previous writings. He wrote many other works; some are attributed to others, and some attributed to him are by others.

The Inquisitor ordered the Talmud burned, in Toulouse and Perpignan (France), and several Jews were burned at the stake in Tudela (Spain).

5080 / 1320

Jews were massacred by the Pastoureaux Crusaders.

Forty thousand teenage shepherds (pastoureaux), marched on a crusade through France, from north to south, on their way to fight the Muslims in Spain. They attacked the Jews of 120 towns on their way, forcing conversions (which the Inquisition later insisted were valid, although they were forced), looting, and killing (including 500 Jews seeking refuge in Verdun).

The Jews were expelled from Milan (see 4985/1225). In 1320, an order for the expulsion of the Jews of Rome came from Avignon where the popes were residing at this time (see 5029/1269); the Jews were expelled before the news of a withdrawal of the order reached Rome.

Living in the Year 1320		
	b.	d.
Rosh (R.Asher)	1250?	1327
Rbnu.Bachya II	1265?	1340?
Tur (R.Yaakov ben Asher)	1275?	1349?
Ralbag (Gersonides)	1288	1344
Ran (R.Nissim	1290?	1380?

5082 / 1321

One hundred and sixty Jews were burned to death in France on the second day of Rosh HaShana on a charge of poisoning the wells (in conjunction with the local lepers), in Chinon and in Tours and in Vitry (see 5082/1322). Among those killed were R.Eliezer ben Yosef (see 5066/1306) (a brother-in-law of R.Peretz of Corbeil, see 5050/1290) and his two brothers.

5082 / 1322

The Jews were expelled from parts of France (see 4942/1182, 5066/1306, and 5082/1321).

The Talmud was burned in Rome.

5086 / 1326

Twenty-seven Jews were killed in a ritual desecration libel (see 5003/1243) in Constance (Germany).

5088 / 1327

The Rosh died.

R.Asher ben Yechi'el, the Rosh (see 5063/1303, 5065/1305, 5070/1310), who had eight sons, died in Cheshvan. He had written a Halacha commentary which like the Rif, follows the order of the Talmud, and is in contrast to the Rambam's system [Tsh.HaRosh.31.9] (see 4863/1103, 4965/1204, 5065/1305); and also *Sh'elot UTeshuvot*, and *Tosaphot HaRosh* (see 5065/1305). R.Yehuda, one of his younger sons (who had married his niece, the daughter of the Tur) succeeded his father.

5088 / 1328

Six thousand Jews of the province of Navarre (Spain) were killed in anti-Jewish riots; but in the town of Estella, R.Menachem ben Aharon ibn Zerach, author of *Tzeida LaDerech*, survived – some say he was rescued by a knight – after his parents and four brothers were killed (see 5066/1306). He went to Toledo to study and became a disciple of R.Yehuda, son of the Rosh.

The Tur (see 5100/1340), R.Yaakov ben Asher, son of the Rosh, encouraged Jews to leave Germany (as he had done with his father, see 5063/1303), because it was a dangerous place for them to live [Otz.Hag.5.75].

5092 / 1332

Three hundred Jews were killed in a blood libel in Uberlingen (Germany) when a mob set the synagogue on fire.

5095 / 1334

Rbnu.Yerucham (see 5066/1306), a disciple of the Rosh and of R.Avraham ben Ismael (who was a disciple of the Rashba), wrote *Meisharim* and *Adam VeChava* (Halacha) (in which there appear to be copying errors).

The Jews of Poland received renewed promises of certain rights in Cheshvan.

5096 / 1336

Jews of Germany were massacred by the Armledder Bands.

Bands of peasants (who wore leather arm bands - *armledder*) roamed through Germany and Alsace (a region between France and Germany) for three years, killing Jews and ravaging 120 communities. Fifteen hundred Jews were killed in Ribeuville, and all the Jews of Deggendorf were killed because of a ritual desecration libel there (see 5003/1243).

R.Shem Tov ben Avraham ibn Gaon, a disciple of the Rashba who emigrated to Eretz Yisrael, wrote *Migdal Oz* a (somewhat controversial) commentary on the Rambam's *Yad HaChazaka* (see Figures H, I, pages 320, 321) [Yam.Sh.Sh.Hakd./Shach Chosh.Mish. Hil.Ed.36.S.K.6-end].

5097 / 1337

Many Jews were killed in massacres in Bohemia.

5098 / 1338

The Ralbag wrote his commentary on the Bible.

The Ralbag, R.Levi ben Gershom (Gersonides) of France, a descendant of the Ramban, wrote a commentary on the Bible; he also wrote *Milchamot HaShem* (philosophy) for which he was criticized [see Mhrl.MiPrg.Hakd.Gevrt.HaSh.], although his stature as a Talmud scholar was undiminished. He wrote works on mathematics, and invented the Jacob Staff (an instrument used in astronomy). (A crater on the moon has been named "Rabbi Levi" after him.)

Jews were burned at the stake in Pulkau (Austria) in a ritual desecration libel in 1338 (see 5003/1243), and the massacre spread to twenty-seven towns.

Living in the Year 1340		
	b.	d.
Rbnu.Bachya II	1265?	1340?
Tur (R.Yaakov ben Asher)	1275?	1349?
Ralbag (Gersonides)	1288	1344
Ran (R.Nissim)	1290?	1380?
Rivash	1326	1408?

5100 / 1340

R.Yaakov ben Asher (see 5088/1328) wrote the *Tur* (the *Arba'a Turim*), an encyclopedic compilation of Halacha (quoting most of the preceding Halacha works) in the systematic arrangement of daily life (see 5088/1327). This system later became the basis for the *Shulchan Aruch* (see 5323/1563). The Tur also wrote a commentary on the *Chumash* (Bible), some of which is printed (as *Ba'al HaTurim*) (see Figure A, page 313). He died on the 12th Tammuz (some say in 1348), in Toledo (Spain) [Otz.Hag5.75].

5102 / 1342

R.David (ben Yosef) Abudraham, a disciple of the Tur, wrote the *Abudraham* (guide and commentary to prayer).

R.Shimon, the eighth son of the Rosh, died in a plague on the 12th Elul.

5104 / 1344

The Ralbag (Gersonides) (see 5098/1338) died on the 6th Iyar.

R.Vidal di Tolose (Spain), also called AnVidal (for Adon Vidal), wrote the *Maggid Mishneh* commentary on the Yad HaChazaka of the Rambam (see Figures H, I, pages 320, 321). He was a colleague of the Ran, R.Nissim ben Reuven (see 5127/1367), who wrote a commentary on the Rif and on (parts of) the Talmud (see Figure G, page 319).

5109 / 1349

The Black Death massacres swept across Europe.

An epidemic of plague, with a very high death rate moved slowly across Europe, killing as many as half of the total population (75,000,000) in three years. On the 23rd Kislev it was announced in Lausanne (Switzerland) that Jews had confessed to poisoning the wells, and the rumor spread throughout Europe. The Jews were savagely attacked and massacred by sometimes hysterical mobs, who were encouraged by the rumors of Jewish confessions to the crime. In some towns the Jews were expelled, and in others they were massacred before the plague had even arrived. Some confessions were extracted through torture. The killings continued despite statements from Pope Clement VI that the Jews were innocent, and despite the fact that Jews were dying [see Tammuz] in the same plague. More than three-quarters of the Jews of Saragossa (Spain) died, and

the Jewish cemetery in Vienna (where there were no massacres) was extended because of the large number dying of the disease.

The Jews of Berne (Switzerland) were burned to death as soon as the alleged confessions in Lausanne became known, and they were accused of sending the poison on to Basel (see Shvat). The Jews of Colmar (Alsace) were imprisoned on the 8th Shvat, for well poisoning and burned to death seven months later. Six hundred Jews of Basel were burned to death on the 19th Shvat in a specially constructed house on the Rhine, and 140 children were forcibly baptized. The Jews of Speyer (Bavaria) perished on the 2nd Adar1, when they set their own houses afire, rather than face destruction by mob violence. The Jews of Freiburg (Germany) were killed in the Black Death massacres on the 10th Adar1, and the Jews of Uberlingen (Switzerland) were massacred on the 22nd. Two thousand Jews were burned to death in Strasbourg (Alsace) on the 25th; The Jews were expelled from Burgsdorf (Switzerland) on the 27th; and Jews of Zurich were burned (and some expelled) on 2nd Adar2 (see 4th Nissan). The Jews of Virmyze (Worms, Germany) set fire to their own homes and perished on the 10th Adar2.

Some Jews of Zurich were burned to death (see 2nd Adar2), and the rest were expelled on the 4th Nissan. The Jews of Muehlhausen (Germany) and 3,000 Jews in Erfurt (Germany) were killed Erev Pesach. Some say that R.Alexander Zisslin, a disciple of R.Yitzchak of Dura, and author of the *Aguda* (Halacha), was killed in Erfurt. Sixty Jews were killed in Breslau (Silesia) on the 10th Sivan, in the riots that followed a disastrous fire.

R.Yehuda, the son of the Rosh (see 5088/1327), died of the plague (as did some of his family) on the 17th Tammuz 1349. The Jews of Frankfort were massacred on Erev Tisha B'Av (8th Av), and 300 Jews were killed in Tarrega (Spain) on the 10th Av. Some Jews of Mayence (Mainz, Germany) were killed fighting a rioting mob; many others – 6,000 – set fire to their homes and died in the flames on the 7th Elul. The Jews of Cologne did the same two days later.

5110 / 1349

The Jews of Krems (Austria) were massacred in the Black Death riots on the 16th Tishrei, the Jews in Augsburg (Germany) on the 17th Kislev; 560 Jews of Nuremberg (Germany) were killed and burned on the 23rd, and Jews were massacred in Hanover and in Brussels on the 24th.

R.Peretz (ben Yitzchak) HaKohen left Provence because of the Black Death massacres and settled in Barcelona, where he became a Rabbi at the same time as the Ran (see 5127/1367).

5110 / 1350

Over 300 Jewish communities were completely destroyed by the Black Death massacres and expulsions, particularly in Germany. Jewish communities of Provence (France) also suffered severe destruction, while other regions of France, Belgium, the Netherlands, and Spain were less severely affected. Many Jews moved east, to Poland-Lithuania (see 4856/1096), which were the only countries (besides Austria) where the Jews had not suffered an irreversible setback, economically and in Torah scholarship (see 5195/1435).

The Jews of Cheb (Eger), Bohemia were all massacred in 1350.

5115 / 1355

Twelve hundred Jews were killed in a Christian and Moslem mob attack on the Jewish section of Toledo (Spain) on the 25th Iyar.

5118 / 1358

Hundreds of Jews were killed in Catalonia (a province of Spain) on the day after Tisha B'Av.

Living in the Year 1360		
	b.	d.
Ran (R.Nissim)	1290?	1380?
Rivash	1326	1408?
Maharil	1360?	1427

5120 / 1360

Many Jews of Breslau (Silesia) were killed, in anti-Jewish riots following a fire, and the rest were expelled. The Jews were expelled from Hungary, but were allowed to return a short while later.

Shmuel ben Meir HaLevi Abulafia, a wealthy and genrous Jew in Castille, was arrested, tortured to death, and his enormous wealth was confiscated.

5123 / 1363

R.Mattityahu ben Yosef Treves, a descendant of Rashi, who studied in Spain and returned to Paris to open a yeshiva, was appointed Chief Rabbi by the king of France.

5127 / 1367

The Ran, Rivash, and other scholars were imprisoned.

The Jews of Barcelona were accused of a ritual desecration (see 5003/1243); three Jews were killed, and all the Jews were held prisoner in the synagogue for three days.

The Ran (see 5104/1344) was imprisoned on what may have been a related charge, together with R.Chisdai Crescas I (ben Yehuda) and his young grandson R.Chisdai Crescas II (ben Avraham ibn/ben Yehuda), and his young disciple, the Rivash (see 5151/1391), as well as others [Tsh.Rivash 373, 376]. They were released after a short period.

5130 / 1370

Many Jews were killed as a result of a civil war in Castille; R.Menachem ben Zerach lost all his belongings (see 5088/1328) and moved (back) to Toledo where 8,000 Jews had been killed.

Hundreds of Jews were burned alive in a ritual desecration libel (see 5003/1243) in Brussels, and the remainder were expelled, in 1370.

5137 / 1377

Some Jews of Huesca (Spain) were tortured and burned to death in a ritual desecration libel (see 5003/1243).

5141 / 1380

Jews of Paris were killed by anti-Jewish rioters in Kislev.

R.Yisrael of Krems (Austria) wrote *Hagahot Ashri* on the Talmud commentary of the Rosh.

5148 / 1388

After the devastation of German Jewry (see 5109/1349), R.Meir ben Baruch HaLevi (Maharam Levi) of Vienna introduced *Semicha* for rabbis, to ensure minimum qualifications for those officiating in marriages and divorces. He empowered R.Yeshayahu ben Abba Mari of France to be Chief Rabbi there, and to confer the *Semicha* on suitable rabbis. This led to a dispute with R.Yochanan Treves who had succeeded his father (see 5123/1363). R.Yochanan consulted the Rivash and R.Chisdai Crescas II (in Spain), but the matter ended when the Jews were expelled from France (see 5155/1394) [Tsh.Rivash.369-372].

5149 / 1389

Three thousand Jews were killed in Prague on the day after Pesach, their houses were burned, and the cemetery was desecrated.

R.Yitzchak Abohab I wrote *Menorat HaMa'or* (Mussar) [Otz.Hag.5.222].

5151 / 1391

The Jews of Spain were massacred and many became Marranos.

Four thousand Jews of Seville (more than half) were killed on the 1st Tammuz, in a massacre that spread throughout Spain and Portugal, killing a total of 50,000 Jews. Women and children were sold as slaves to Muslims, and many synagogues were forcibly converted into churches. Many Jews (mostly the wealthy) who saved their lives by openly converting to Christianity while remaining secretly Jewish, were called *Anussim* ("the forced ones"), Marranos, or Conversos. They numbered about 200,000 in Aragon and Castille (provinces of Spain).

Four thousand Jews were killed in Ja'en and Toledo on the 17th Tammuz, and the Jewish community of Valencia was destroyed on the 7th Av. Jews were massacred in Barcelona and in the whole of Catalonia on the 22nd Av; in Palma (Majorca) on the 1st Elul; and in Gerona on the 9th. The Jews of Perpignan, France (near the Spanish border) were also attacked.

The Rivash and Rashbatz left Spain.

The Rivash, R.Yitzchak ben Sheshet Perfet (see 5127/1367), a disciple of the Ran and of R.Peretz HaKohen (see 5110/1349), fled the massacres of Spain (some say he lost two sons in Majorca on his way to North Africa, see 1st Elul); he went on to Algiers where he was appointed rabbi of the community.

Some say R.Vidal Ephrayim Gerondi, also a disciple of the Ran, was killed in the massacres. His disciple, the Rashbatz, also fled to Algiers, and R.Ephrayim ben Yisrael AlNakava fled to North Africa after his father was killed.

Although his son was killed, R.Chisdai Crescas II stayed in Spain and tried to rebuild the Jewish communities, which no longer included the wealthy and influential Jews. He wrote *Or HaShem* (philosophy) and *Bitul Ikarey HaNotzrim* (answering Christianity). R.Yitzchak (R.Profiat) ben Moshe HaLevi Duran (HaEphodi), his disciple who was affected by the persecution before he left Spain [Sed.Had.5154], also wrote works in answer to Christianity, *Kelimat HaGoyim* and *Al Tehi Ke Avotecha* (satire).

5152 / 1392

A Jew was burned alive in Damascus, and other Jews were tortured after being accused of setting fire to a mosque.

5153 / 1393

The Nimukei Yosef, R.Yosef Chaviva, wrote a commentary on the Halacha of the Rif in Spain (see Figure F, page 318). R.Shalom (ben Yitzchak) of Vienna, a disciple of R.Yisrael of Krems, was a prominent rabbi in Wiener-Neustadt (Austria).

Almost all the Jews fled Baghdad when the Tartars conquered the city (see 5160/1400).

The Jews of Venice were required to wear yellow badges (see 4977/1216).

5155 / 1394

The final expulsion of Jews from France occurred.

The Jews of Paris were attacked on Yom Kippur, and seven Jews were imprisoned on the charge that they had captured a *meshumad* (apostate) to force him to return to Judaism. Shortly thereafter, the Jews were expelled from all of France (see 5082/1322) except for Narbonne, Montpellier, and other parts of Provence (see 5261/1501).

5157 / 1397

The Jews were expelled from Basel (Switzerland).

5159 / 1399

Eighty Jews were killed in Prague, because a *meshumad* (apostate) accused them of denigrating Christianity (see 5160/1400). R.Yom Tov Lipman (ben Shlomo) Millhousen of Prague, author of the sought-after *Sefer HaNitzachon* (a brilliant collection of answers to Christianity which was discreetly circulated), was imprisoned with other Jews. He managed to escape, and the book was eventually published (in Latin, by a priest who added counterrefutations). The pope forbade the Jews to own the book, and it was the subject of many later Christian refutations (known as anti-Lipmanniana).

Living in the Year 1400		
	b.	d.
Rivash	1326	1408?
Maharil	1360?	1427
Rashbatz	1361?	1444?

5160 / 1400

The Jews were massacred in Syria when the Tartars conquered the country (see 5153/1393).

Seventy-seven Jews were killed in anti-Jewish riots in Prague in Elul (see 5159/1399).

5161 / 1401

Thirty Jews were burned at the stake in a blood libel in Schaffhausen (Switzerland) on the 14th Tammuz (see 5157/1397).

5164 / 1404

Many Jews were killed in Salzburg (Austria) in a ritual desecration libel (see 5003/1243). The rest were expelled, but returned a few years later.

5166 / 1406

The Jews on the island of Corfu were required to wear special badges.

5168 / 1407

The Jews of Cracow were attacked by riotous mobs (in a blood libel) on the 25th Cheshvan. One Jew was publicly tortured and burned at the stake on a charge of counterfeiting, and some Jews were forcibly converted.

The Rashbatz, R.Shimon ben Tzemach Duran, who was a physician, was appointed Rabbi in Algiers after the death of the Rivash (see 5151/1391). He refused (on principle) to accept any confirmation of the appointment by the government (in contrast to his predecessor), although he maintained that a rabbi should be paid by the comunity in order to allow total devotion to his rabbinical work. He wrote many *Sh'elot UTeshuvot* [collected in Tashbatz, see 5046/1286], and *Magen Avot* (philosophical/ideological, with commentary on *Pirkei Avot*, and answers to Christianity, see 5151/1391).

5172 / 1412

A *meshumad* (apostate) who had become bishop of Burgos (Spain) and an advisor to the king of Castille, instigated anti-Jewish laws which seriously affected the economic position of the Jews, who had already lost their wealth and influence (see 5151/1391). They were also required to wear red badges, distinctive clothing, and long hair and long beards (see 4977/1216, 5029/1269).

5173 / 1413

R.Yosef Albo was forced to debate with Christians.

R.Yosef Albo, a disciple of R.Chisdai Crescas II and author of *Sefer Halkkarim* (religious principles),

was a leader of those Jews who were forced to debate a *meshumad* (apostate, in this case a follower of the bishop in Burgos, see 5172/1412) in Tortosa (Spain), under very intimidating circumstances. The twenty-one-month debate, which was presided over by [one of a few who claimed to be] Pope Benedict XII, resulted in Jews being forced to convert, and an order that all anti-Christian statements (as defined by the *meshumad*) be removed from the Talmud (see 5023/1263).

5178 / 1418

The Jews were expelled from Koblenz and Cochem (Germany).

Jewish women in Salzburg (Austria) were ordered to wear bells on their dresses (see 4977/1216).

5181 / 1421

The Jews of Austria were massacred in the Wiener Gezera.

The Jews of Austria were imprisoned and their possessions confiscated on the 10th Sivan 1420, after a ritual desecration libel (see 5003/1243) in Enns, in which the accused were tortured. Many children were forcibly baptized, and many Jews took their own lives rather than accept Christianity. Later, on the 9th Nissan 1421, 212 Jews were burned at the stake, and R.Aharon (Blumlein) of Neustadt was also killed. He was a disciple of R.Shalom of Vienna (whose son, R.Yona, was killed) and author of *Hilchot Nida*. His disciple and nephew, R.Yisrael Isserlein (see 5220/1460), fled after his mother was killed.

Fifty-eight Jews of Styria were burned on the 10th Sivan, and the rest of the Jews in (most of) Austria were expelled after many had been killed in the war of the Hussites (a new Christian sect the Jews were accused of supporting) against the Catholics.

The Jews of Chomutov (Bohemia) were massacred by the Hussites, and the Jews of Cheb (Eger) (then Bohemia) (see 5110/1350, 5190/1430) and glau (Bohemia) (see 5186/1426) were expelled or allegedly supporting the Hussites.

5184 / 1424

The Jews were expelled from Cologne (Germany).

5186 / 1426

The Jews were expelled again from Iglau (Bohemia) (see 5181/1421, 5195/1435).

5187 / 1427

The Jews were expelled from Berne (Switzerland) on the 13th Iyar (see 5054/1294, 5157/1397).

The Maharil, R.Yaakov (ben Moshe) HaLevi Moellin of Mayence (Mainz, Germany), a disciple of R.Shalom of Vienna (see 5181/1421), was a leading Rabbi in Germany. He died on the 21st of Elul and his opinions are recorded in *Minhagey Maharil* (customs and ritual) and *Sh'elot UTeshuvot.*

5188 / 1428

The Jews were expelled from Fribourg (Switzerland) (see 5187/1427).

On the 18th of Shvat the Jews of Sicily were ordered to attend conversion sermons.

5190 / 1430

Fifteen Jews were burned to death in a blood libel in Constance, Lindau, and Ravensburg (Germany), and the rest were expelled. The Jews were also expelled from Miessen and Thuringa in Germany, and again from Cheb (Eger), Bohemia see 5181/1421, 5195/1435).

5195 / 1435

Two hundred Jews were forcibly converted in Majorca in 1435 (after a blood libel in 1432), and the rest fled to North Africa.

In Augsburg (Germany) in 1434, Jewish men were required to wear yellow badges and women to wear yellow pointed veils (see 4977/1216).

Since the Jewish community in Speyer (Germany) had been rebuilt after the Black Death massacres (see 5109/1349), the Jews were expelled twice (in 1405 – returning in 1421, and in 1430 – returning in 1434). On 6th Iyar 1435 the Jews were expelled once again, and were not allowed to return until thirty years later. This was similar to the pattern of settlement in many communities after the devastation of the Black Death massacres (See 5120/1360, 5130/1370, 5155/1394, 5181/1421, 5184/1424, 5211/1450, 5233/1473, 5251/1491).

5196 / 1436

The Jews were expelled from Zurich (see 5188/1428).

Living in the Year 1440		
	b.	d.
Rashbatz	1361?	1444
R.Yitzchak Abarbanel	1437	1508
Yuchasin	1440?	1515

5202 / 1442

The Jews were expelled from Upper Bavaria (province of Germany) (see 5211/1450, 5311/1551).

5204 / 1444

The Rashbatz (see 5168/1407) died in 1444, and was succeeded by his son R.Shlomo ben Shimon Duran, as Rabbi in Algiers.

5206 / 1446

The Jews were expelled from Berlin and the whole province of Brandenburg (Germany) (see 5202/1442), but they were permitted to return in 1447 (see 5195/1435).

5209 / 1449

Many Jews were killed in an attack in Lisbon and many houses were destroyed.

5211 / 1450

On the 29th of Tishrei, the Jews were expelled from forty cities in Lower Bavaria (see 5202/1442, 5206/1446, 5238/1478) after paying a huge ransom (see 5195/1435).

5211 / 1451

R.Yaakov (ben Yehuda) Weil, the Mahariv, a disciple of the Maharil (see 5187/1427), was a leading Rabbi in Germany. He wrote Shechitot UBedikot (Halacha of meat) which was printed with Sh'elot UTeshuvot Mahariv, and has been reprinted over seventy times.

Jews were forbidden to have social contact with non-Jews by order of Pope Nicholas V on 24th Adar (see 5007/1247). The Jews were ordered to wear special badges (see 4977/1216) in Hanover (Germany) and also on the 25th Tishrei 5212/1451, in Arnhem (Holland).

5213 / 1453

Forty-one Jews were burned at the stake in Breslau (Silesia) on the 28th Tammuz; the rest of the Jews were expelled (see Iyar 5195/1435, 5120/1360, 5509/1749) in a ritual desecration libel (see 5003/1243), to which some had confessed after being tortured. The libel was instigated by a traveling Italian priest, who made an identical charge in Schweidnitz (Silesia) in which seventeen Jews were burned at the stake – including, some say, R.David, who taught R.Yisrael Brunna (see 5214/1454) – on the 8th Elul 1453; the rest of the Jews were expelled from there and from some of the surrounding towns.

The Jews were invited to settle in the Turkish (Ottoman) Empire (see Av 5252/1492), after the Turks had conquered Constantinople (later called Istanbul).

5214 / 1454

Many Jews were killed in anti-Jewish riots in Cracow after the Italian priest (see 5213/1453) visited in 1454; and the Jews were expelled from Brno and other cities of Moravia on the 28th Av 1454, after he visited there. R.Yisrael (ben Chaim) Brunna of Brno (see 5234/1474), a disciple of the Maharay (see 5220/1460) and the Mahariv (see 5211/1451), moved to Regensburg (Germany) some say before the expulsion.

5216 / 1456

R.Yisrael Brunna (see 5214/1454) was arrested in Regensburg over the Jewish community's refusal to pay an exorbitant tax.

5217 / 1457

The Jews were expelled from Hildesheim (Germany).

5218 / 1458

The Jews were expelled from Erfurt (Germany).

5219 / 1459

Sixty Jews were killed in anti-Jewish riots in Carpentras (France).

5220 / 1460

The Jews were expelled from Mayence (Mainz, Germany) (see 5195/1435, 5233/1473), and the Rabbi, R.Moshe (Maharam Mintz I), a disciple of the Mahariv (see 5211/1451), eventually settled in Posen (Poznan, Poland).

R.Yisrael (ben Petachyah) Isserlein (Maharay) (see 5181/1421), a leading Rabbi who wrote *Terumat HaDeshen,* died in Austria.

Living in the Year 1460		
	b.	d.
R.Yitzchak Abarbanel	1437	1508
Yuchasin	1440?	1515
R.Ovadya Bertinura	1445?	1524?
Eyn Yaakov		
(R.Yaakov ibn Chaviv)	1445?	1516?
R.Yaakov Pollak	1460?	1530?

5223 / 1463

R.Yitzchak (ben Yaakov) Kanpanton was over 100 years old when he died in Spain.

5224 / 1464

The Jews were attacked in Seville (Spain) in anti-Jewish riots on the 27th Nissan, and thirty Jews were killed in anti-Jewish riots in Cracow on 4 Iyar (see 5214/1454).

5225 / 1465

The Jews were massacred in a revolt in Fez (Morocco).

5226 / 1466

Some Jews were killed in Arnstadt (Germany), and the rest were expelled.

The Jews of Rome were forced to run humiliating races before jeering crowds in the Christian carnival (a period of festivity preceding Lent). These humiliating performances became an annual event over the next two centuries (see 5427/1667).

5227 / 1467

Eighteen Jews were burned to death in a blood libel in Nuremberg (Germany).

R.Shlomo ben Shimon Duran died, and his sons R.Shimon Duran and R.Tzemach Duran succeeded him as Rabbis in Algiers. Together they wrote *Yachin UBo'az* (*Sh'elot Uteshuvot*).

5229 / 1468

The Jews of Landau (Germany) were forced to wear yellow badges in Cheshvan (see 4977/1216).

5230 / 1470

R.Eliyahu and his two brothers (see 5290/1530) were killed in a blood libel in Endingen (Germany), and the Jews were subsequently expelled from the whole province of Baden.

5232 / 1472

The Jews were expelled from Schaffhausen (Switzerland) (see 5196/1436). The Jews of Muehlhausen (Germany) were required to wear yellow badges (see 4977/1216) and were forbidden to enter non-Jewish houses.

5233 / 1473

The Jews were allowed to return to Mayence (Mainz, Germany) (see 5220/1460, 5195/1435). Jews were massacred in Cordova on Purim (see 5224/1464, 5234/1474).

5234 / 1474

Three hundred sixty Jews were killed in a massacre in Sicily. The Jews were also massacred in Segovia (Spain) on the 29th Iyar.

R.Yisrael Brunna (see 5214/1454) was arrested in Regensburg (Germany) in a blood libel, instigated by a *meshumad* (apostate) who later confessed.

5235 / 1475

The new invention of printing was used for Jewish books.

Less than thirty-five years after the invention in Germany of movable type for printing, Rashi's commentary on *Chumash* (Bible) was printed in Reggio di Calabria (Italy) on the 10th Adar. It was the first Jewish book to be (dated and) printed. The *Tur* (see 5100/1340) was printed on 28th Tammuz, in Piove Di Sacco (Italy).

Many Jews of Trent (Italy) were tortured and killed in a blood libel in 1475, some were forcibly baptized, and the rest were expelled.

5237 / 1477

The Jews were expelled from Tuebingen (Germany) and from Nancy and the whole Duchy of Lorraine (France).

5238 / 1478

Ten Jews were killed in a ritual desecration libel (see 5003/1243) in Passau (Bavaria), and the rest were expelled (see 5211/1450). The Jews were expelled from Bamberg (Germany), and there was a blood libel in Mantua (Italy).

5239 / 1479

The Jews were expelled from Shlettstadt (Selestat, Germany) (see 5238/1478).

5240 / 1480

R.Yosef (ben Shlomo) Kolon, the Maharik, died in Italy, and three Jews were burned at the stake in a blood libel in Venice.

Living in the Year 1480	b.	d.
R.Yitzchak Abarbanel	1437	1508
Yuchasin	1440?	1515
R.Ovadya Bertinura	1445?	1524?
Eyn Yaakov (R.Yaakov ibn Chaviv)	1445?	1516?
R.Yaakov Pollak	1460?	1530?
Radvaz	1463?	1573?
R.Yosef Yoselman	1478?	1555?

5241 / 1481

The Inquisition was established in Spain.

The Spanish Inquisition, established with the intention of exposing secret Jews – Anussim or Marranos – began to function in 1481. It devoted its efforts to anti-Jewish activity to a greater extent than any previous (localized) inquisition (see 5012/1252). The first public sentencing and burning (*auto da fe*) by the Spanish Inquisition, was held at Seville on the 7th Adar. On the 4th Sivan, Pope Sixtus IV instructed all his local bishops to return to Spain all those Jews who had fled the Inquisition there.

5243 / 1483

Tomas de Torquemada was appointed head of the Spanish Inquisition in Cheshvan 5244/1483, and the persecutions grew worse (see 5241/1481). The Jews were expelled from Andalusia, a province that included Seville and Cordova, making it easier for the Inquisition to isolate the Anussim (Marranos) who remained (see 5241/1481).

The Jews were also expelled from Warsaw, and from Mayence (Mainz, Germany) (see 5233/1473, 5239/1479).

R.Yitzchak Abarbanel fled from Portugal to Spain.

Don Yitzchak Abarbanel (see 5269/1508), member of a wealthy aristocratic family who were descendants of King David, succeeded his father as treasurer to the king of Portugal. He fled to Spain in 1483 when he was suspected of being in a conspiracy against a new king, and he subsequently became important in the court of the Spanish king (see 5252/1492). Some say that his grandfather originally had been a royal treasurer in Spain, but left for Portugal to revert to open Judaism, after having been forcibly converted (see 5151/1391).

5245 / 1485

The Jews were attacked in anti-Jewish riots in many towns of Provence (France) in 1484 and again in 1485, and many were killed.

The Spanish Inquisition burned twenty-two Anussim (Marranos) in Perpignan, France (near the Spanish border) (see 5151/1391) in 1485.

The Jews were expelled from Perugia in 1485 (see 5235/1475), and then from Gubbio and Vicenza (Italy) in 1486.

5247 / 1487

R.Yaakov (ben Yehuda) Landau, a German Talmud scholar residing in Naples, wrote *Sefer HaAgur* (Halacha) which was printed in Naples in 1487. This was probably the first book to be printed during the life of the author (see 5235/1475), and the first work to be published with *Haskamot* (approbations), a practice which later included warnings of copyright to extend over a number of years.

5248 / 1488

R.Ovadya Bertinura settled in Yerushalayim.

R.Ovadya Bertinura, a disciple of the Maharik, arrived in Yerushalayim on the 13th Nissan after two years of travel from Italy via Egypt. He became the leading Rabbi in Yerushalayim (which was suffering extreme poverty). He subsequently finished his popular commentary to the Mishna (see Figure B, page 314).

R.Yosef Karo (see 5335/1575) was born.

Sixteen Jews were burned at the stake in Toledo (Spain) on 22nd Av. Forty Anussim (Marranos) were burned in Toledo during this year (see 5250/1490), and over 100 bodies were exhumed and also burned. By this time, the Spanish Inquisition had burned over 700 Anussim (see 5241/1481).

5249 / 1489

The Jews were attacked in parts of Provence (France), some were forcibly converted, and the rest ordered to leave. The expulsion was enforced only later (see 5261/1501). The Jews were expelled from Lucca (Italy) (see 5245/1485).

5250 / 1490

Four hundred and twenty-two Anussim were burned in Toledo (see 5248/1488).

The Jews were expelled from Geneva (see 5232/1472), and (for the third or fourth time) from Heilbronn (Germany).

5251 / 1491

The Jews were expelled from Thurgau (Switzerland), leaving almost no Jews in Switzerland (see 5250/1490). Jews were expelled from Ravenna (Italy) and the synagogue was burned (see 5249/1489).

5252 / 1491

A Jew was burned at the stake in Avila (Spain) on a blood libel in the month of Kislev, and another was stoned to death by an angry mob. In the same month, the Jews of Granada were given permission to depart peacefully, before the Castilian (Christian) forces took control from the Moors (Muslims) and completed Christian control over all of Spain.

Columbus consulted R.Avraham Zacuto before beginning his travels.

Christopher Columbus – who may have been of Jewish origin – consulted (and was encouraged by) R.Avraham Zacuto (see 5264/1504), a disciple of the Maharyah (see 5252/1492). He was famous for his knowledge of astrology, achievements in astronomy, and his refinement of the astrolabe (an instrument for navigation). Columbus used R.Avraham's improved astronomical tables, which once saved the lives of the whole expedition. (A menacing native tribe was pacified by Columbus when he threatened to take away the light of the moon – which he knew was going to be eclipsed.)

5252 / 1492

The Jews were expelled from Spain and Sicily.

It is estimated that 100,000 to 300,000 Jews were expelled from Spain, and many became Marranos (Anussim). This added to the large number of Marranos already existing (see 5151/1391), 13,000 of whom had been exposed by the Inquisition (see 5241/1481).

R.Yitzchak Abarbanel (see 5243/1483) attempted to use his (wealth and) influence to have the Spanish expulsion order withdrawn.

Most of the Jews, who had all left Spain by the 9th Av, settled in Turkey (where they were welcomed, see 5213/1453) North Africa, and Italy (see 5253/1493, 5249/1489). Many, some say 150,000, went to Portugal where R.Yitzchak Abohab II, the Maharyah (see 5253/1493) and the leading Talmud scholar in Castile, convinced the king of Portugal to allow some Jews to settle. The Jews were forced to pay a tax for temporary residence in Portugal, and 700 young Jews were forcibly sent to populate an island off the coast of central Africa. The Jews were also expelled from Sicily and Sardinia, which were under Spanish rule, and an estimated 37,000 to 100,00 Jews left.

Among the refugees leaving Spain were the Maharyah (see 5253/1493) and his disciples, R.Yaakov ibn Chaviv (see 5276/1516) and R.Yaakov Bei Rav (see 5298/1538) who was not yet 18; R.Avraham Zacuto (see 5257/1496); R.Yitzchak Abarbanel (see 5253/1493); Maharam Alashkar (see 5270/1510); R.Ephrayim Karo with his family (including his 4-year-old son, Yosef) (see 5282/1522); R.Yosef Saragossi and his disciple the Radvaz (see 5277/1517) who was not yet 13 (though some say the Radvaz left Spain earlier); and R.Meir ibn Gabbai, who was almost 13, and would later write the *Avodat HaKodesh* and other Kabbala works.

5253 / 1492

Twenty-seven Jews were burned in Mecklenburg (a region of Germany) in a ritual desecration libel (see 5003/1243), and the rest were expelled on the 3rd Cheshvan. The Jews had also been expelled from Olesnica, Silesia, between Germany and Poland.

CHAPTER 13

The Kov'im, Torah Consolidation, and the Shulchan Áruch

The thirteenth chapter in Jewish history begins with the expulsion from Spain, and ends with the massacre of the Jews of Poland during the Chmielnitzki-led Cossack uprising. This era is notable for the ultimate development of the Halacha (in the form of the Shulchan Aruch) and other aspects of Torah study, and for the caliber of the Torah scholars living at that time. So great was the effect of this era that it represents a chapter all of its own. (See Appendix D.)

THE KOV'IM, TORAH CONSOLIDATION, AND THE SHULCHAN ARUCH

Jewish Year		Secular Year
5253	R.Yitzchak Abarbanel arrived in Naples from Spain	1493
5257	**The Jews were expelled from Portugal**	**1496**
5276	The *Eyn Yaakov* was printed	1516
5276	The Turks (Ottoman Empire) conquered Eretz Yisrael	1516
5285	R.Yosef Yoselman saved Jews during the Peasants War	1525
5314	A mass burning of Jewish books took place in Rome	1553
5323	**The Shulchan Aruch was completed by R.Yosef Karo**	**1563**
5330	**SHULCHAN ARUCH PUBLISHED WITH SUPPLEMENTS OF RAMO**	**1570**
5332	**The Ari'zal died in Tzfat (Safed)**	**1572**
5333	The Maharal came to Prague	1573
5334	The Maharshal died	1573
5335	R.Yosef Karo died in Tzfat	1575
5359	The Maharal returned to Prague again	1599
5374	The Maharsha became Rabbi in Lublin	1614
5377	The Tosaphot Yom Tov commentary was concluded	1616
5382	The Shaloh arrived in Eretz Yisrael	1621
5389	R.Yom Tov Lipman Heller was imprisoned in Prague	1629
5400	R.Yoel Sirkes, the Bach, died	1640
5406	**The Shach and Taz (on Shulchan Aruch) were printed**	**1646**
5408	**THE JEWS WERE MASSACRED BY CHMIELNITZKI'S FORCES**	**1648**

5253 / 1493

R.Yitzchak Abarbanel arrived in Naples from Spain.

The overcrowded ships arriving with Jewish refugees from Spain had been allowed to land in Genoa (northern Italy) for three days only. At the beginning of 1493, this permission was withdrawn. R.Yitzchak Abohab II (see 5252/1492), a disciple of R.Yitzchak Kanpanton, died in Portugal in 1493; and R.Yitzchak Abarbanel, who had studied under him, arrived in Naples (see 5254/1494).

The Jews (including refugees from Spain) were expelled from Perpignan, France near the Spanish border (see 5254/1485) on Yom Kippur 5254/1493.

As many as 20,000 Spanish Jews died in Morocco of attacks, disease, and famine, and some returned to Spain (and converted).

5254 / 1494

Sixteen Jews were killed in Tyrnau (Slovakia) in a blood libel (see 5297/1537). The Jews were expelled from Camp S. Pietro and Brescia in Italy (see 5251/1491), and from Arles (France) (see 5261/1501).

R.Yitzchak Abarbanel's home (see 5253/1493) was looted by invading French troops, and he moved to the island of Corfu for a while, before returning after the French left (see 5269/1508).

5255 / 1495

The Jews were expelled from Lithuania in 1495 and allowed to return eight years later (see 5263/1503).

Most of the Jews of Cosenza (Italy) were forced to become baptized.

5256 / 1496

The Jews, who had been allowed to return to parts of Austria (see 5181/1421), were again expelled (see Iyar 5195/1435) from the provinces of Carinthia and Styria in the month of Adar.

5257 / 1496

The Jews were expelled from Portugal.

An expulsion order was issued in the month of Tevet giving all the Jews living in Portugal (see 5252/1492) one year to either convert or to leave the country. Many Jews resisted the force, including torture, that was used to try to convert them (see 5257/1497). Among the refugees leaving was R.Avraham Zacuto (see 5252/1492, 5264/1504), who had been consulted on astronomy and navigation (see 5252/1491) by the explorer Vasco da Gama before a trip to India (where, some say, he captured a traveling Jew and forced him to be baptized).

R.Yitzchak Karo (an uncle of R.Yosef Karo, who had settled in Portugal before the Spanish expulsion) left Portugal for Istanbul (Constantinople).

5257 / 1497

From the first day of Pesach, many Jewish children aged 4 through 14 were captured and forcibly baptized in Portugal (see 5257/1496), which led to some of the parents converting in order to remain in the country with their children. The government of Portugal also connivingly brought 20,000 Jews to a Lisbon palace, where they denied them food and water and forcibly baptized them. These became the Anussim (Marranos) of Portugal.

5258 / 1498

The Jews (including refugees from Spain) were expelled from Navarre (a province on the Spanish-French border) (see 5253/1493) and from the island of Rhodes. The Jews were expelled from Nuremberg in Tammuz (see 5211/1450, 5311/1551), although some settled in the surrounding villages. The Jews were again expelled (see 5164/1404) from Salzburg (Austria).

5259 / 1499

Seventy-five Anussim (Marranos) were burned at the stake in Avila (Spain), and the bones of twenty-six Jews exhumed and burned.

5260 / 1500

R.(Asher) Lemlein predicted that the Mashiach (Messiah) was about to come, and he propelled a movement of Teshuva (repentance) which spread to many communities in Europe. R.Zeligman Gans (grandfather of the author of Tzemach David) destroyed his special matza-baking oven, because he expected that next year he would be in Eretz Yisrael [Tzem.Dav.5260]. There was disappointment when R.Lemlein died, but no documented negative movements [see Encpd.Jud.11.11].

Living in the Year 1500		
	b.	d.
R.Yitzchak Abarbanel	1437	1508
Yuchasin	1440?	1515
R.Ovadya Bertinura	1445?	1524?
Eyn Yaakov		
(R.Yaakov ibn Chaviv)	1445?	1516?
R.Yaakov Pollak	1460?	1530?
Radvaz	1463?	1573?
R.Yosef Yoselman	1478?	1555?
Beit Yosef		
(R.Yosef Karo)	1488	1575

5261 / 1501

The Jews were expelled from Provence (France) in 1501 (see 5155/1394) except for that part which

belonged to the pope's court (see 5029/1269, 5080/1320, 5329/1569).

5262 / 1502

A number of Jews (refugees from Spain) were burned at the stake in Dubrovnik (Yugoslavia).

5263 / 1503

R.Yaakov Pollak was a leading rabbi who established a yeshiva in Cracow after he had left Prague, and it was there that he introduced his sharp (and somewhat controversial) style of Talmud scholarship (Chilukim) into Poland-Lithuania [Mrsha.B.M. 85a"DeLishtakach", Tzem.Dav.5290, Chav.Yair.152].

The Jews were permitted to return to Lithuania (see 5255/1495).

5264 / 1504

R.Avraham Zacuto (see 5257/1496) had settled in Tunisia (see 5270/1510) after the expulsion from Portugal (he was twice taken prisoner on his journey). He concluded his Sefer Yuchasin (history) in 1504, and later traveled to Turkey, Damascus, and some say Eretz Yisrael.

The Jews were expelled from Pilsen (Bohemia) in a ritual desecration libel (see 5003/1243).

5265 / 1505

The Jews were expelled from Orange (France) (see 5261/1501).

5266 / 1506

Two thousand Anussim (Marranos) were killed in Lisbon in 1506 (see 5257/1497), and in Venice a Jew was stoned to death by an angry crowd in a blood libel.

5269 / 1508

R. Yitzchak Abarbanel (see 5243/1483) died (some say in the month of Tishrei 5269/1508) in Venice where he had settled in 1503 (see 5254/1494), and he was buried in Padua. He wrote a commentary to the Bible as well as other works.

5270 / 1510

R. Chaim ben Yitzchak Katz (of whom little is known) was killed in Prague, in a libel on the 28th Tishrei 5270/1509. The Jews were expelled from Colmar (Alsace) in Shvat from Coltbus (Germany) and also from Naples, but some of the wealthy were allowed to remain.

Jewish books were confiscated in Frankfurt am Main at the instigation of a *meshumad* (apostate); they were returned in Sivan, less than two months later.

Thirty-eight Jews were burned at the stake in Berlin in Av, in a ritual desecration libel (see 5003/1243), and the rest were expelled from the whole province of Brandenburg (see 5206/1446 and 5303/1543).

R. Moshe (ben Yitzchak), the Maharam Alashkar, who had settled in Tunisia after the expulsion from Spain (see 5252/1492), left in 1510 when Spanish forces landed in parts of North Africa and imprisoned some Jews. He settled in Greece for a while and then moved to Cairo, where he remained for an extended time and wrote many *Sh'elot UTeshuvot*. He went to Eretz Yisrael shortly before he died.

5275 / 1515

The Jews were expelled from Laibach (Slovenia) in Tevet (see 5256/1496); and from Genoa (see 5253/1493), where they were allowed to return a short while later (see 5310/1550).

5276 / 1516

The *Eyn Yaakov* was printed.

After leaving Spain, R. Yaakov (ben Shlomo) ibn Chaviv (see 5252/1492) settled in Salonika; (some say he went to Portugal first). He wrote and began printing the *Eyn Yaakov* (collection of Agada quotes from the Talmud, with his compiled commentary), which was completed (after his death) by his son R. Levi who later settled in Yerushalayim (see 5298/1538).

The Ottoman Turks conquered Eretz Yisrael.

Eretz Yisrael was conquered by the Turks and became part of their rapidly expanding empire.

In the month of Iyar, the Jews of Venice were ordered to move from the city to a restricted area where there had previously been a foundry ("getto" in Italian). It is assumed that this is the origin of the term although there were many earlier cases of Jews being forced into separate but perhaps not so remote living areas. The popular *Chumash Mikra'ot Gedolot* (with commentaries) (see Figure A, pages 312, 313), was printed in Venice a year later, in Kislev 5278/1517.

The Jews were expelled from Lowicz (Poland).

5277 / 1517

The Radvaz, R. David (ben Shlomo) ibn (Avi) Zimra, settled in Egypt, having been in Tzfat (Safed) and some say also in Fez (Morocco), after leaving Spain (see 5252/1492). When the Turks conquered Egypt in 1517, and the system of Jewish communal structure changed, the Radvaz became the leader of the Egyptian Jews (see 5313/1553). He formally ended the *Minyan Shtarot* (see 3449/−313) which was still being used there, and he was consulted on Halacha questions from many countries [Radvaz Hil.Mel.5.7]. Much Jewish property was destroyed when the Turks conquered Tlemcen (Algeria), and the Jews were required to wear a yellow patch on their headgear.

5278 / 1518

The Jews of Hevron were attacked. Many were killed and many fled.

5279 / 1519

The Jews were expelled from the region of Wuertemberg (Germany) and from Regensburg (Bavaria) (see 5211/1450, 5311/1551).

Living in the Year 1520		
	b.	d.
R.Ovadya Bertinura	1445?	1524?
R.Yaakov Pollak	1460?	1530?
Radvaz	1463?	1573?
R.Yosef Yoselman	1478?	1555?
Beit Yosef		
(R.Yosef Karo)	1488	1575
Maharshal	1510?	1573
Maharal of Prague	1512?	1609
Shitta Mekubetzet		
(R.Betz.Ashkenazi)	1520?	1594?

5282 / 1521

The Jews of Yerushalayim were blamed for a severe water shortage during the month of Kislev and were required to pay heavy fines.

5282 / 1522

R.Yosef Karo settled with his father in Istanbul (Constantinople) after the expulsion from Spain; some say they were in Portugal until the expulsion from there. He became the disciple of his uncle R.Yitzchak Karo (see 5257/1496) after his father (R.Ephrayim) died. He moved to Adrianople (Turkey) where, in 1522, he began writing the *Beit Yosef* (a thorough study of the development of Halacha, written as a commentary on the *Tur*). From there he moved to Nikopol (Bulgaria).

Between 2,000 and 3,000 Jews had been captured and brought to the island of Rhodes (see 5258/1498) as slaves. In 1522 these Jewish slaves helped the Turks conquer Rhodes, which subsequently became a vibrant Jewish center.

5283 / 1523

Most of the Jews left Cranganore (India) when the Portuguese conquered the territory. Many settled in Cochin (India), where the Jews were granted certain protections by the local rajah.

5284 / 1524

The Jews of Cairo were to be massacred, unless they paid an exorbitant tax. On the day the money was to be paid, the local ruler was killed in a counter rebellion, and the Jews instituted *Purim Mitzrayim*, on the 28th Adar, to commemorate the event.

5285 / 1525

R. Yosef Yoselman saved Jews during the Peasants War.

R.Eliyahu Mizrachi, leading rabbi in Turkey and author of a famous work on Rashi's *Chumash* (Bible) commentary, died in Istanbul (Constantinople).

The Jews of Carpentras (France), part of the papal territory (see 5080/1320, 5261/1501), were ordered by Pope Clement VII to wear yellow hats, in Sivan 1525 (see 4977/1216).

R.Yosef Yoselman, the *shtadlan* (see 5290/1530), saved the Jews of Alsace during the bloody Peasants War (revolt), through brave negotiations.

5287 / 1526

The Jews were expelled from Hungary in the month of Kislev (see 5120/1360), as the Ottoman

Turks invaded the country. Many crossed to the Balkan countries, which were under Turkish rule, although some continued to live in small towns (see 5289/1529), and some returned to the larger towns a few years later (see 5120/1360).

5288 / 1528

Although the Spanish government required settlers in Mexico to prove that they had been Christian for four generations, many Anussim (Marranos) managed to emigrate there (see 5310/1550). Some were burned at the stake in 1528.

5289 / 1529

Thirty Jews were burned to death in Poesing (Slovakia) in a blood libel in Sivan 1529; the rest were expelled from there (see 5287/1526) and from a number of other towns.

5290 / 1530

R.Yosef Yoselman of Rosheim (eastern France) (see 5285/1525, 5303/1543) was a great scholar, *shtadlan*–an advocate and negotiator for Jewish causes–whose great-uncles had been killed in a blood libel (see 5230/1470). He was forced to debate a *meshumad* (apostate) on the Rosh Chodesh Av 1530, and the *meshumad* was subsequently expelled from Augsburg (Germany). He also succeeded in convincing the emperor that Jews were not spying for the Turks. R.Yosef was outstanding in the broad sphere of influence he managed to maintain and in the number of times he interceded for Jewish causes.

The Jews of Germany were required to wear a yellow badge in 1530 (see 4977/1216).

5293 / 1532

Shlomo Molcho was an Anuss (Marrano) from Portugal who returned to open Jewish practice under the influence of David Re'uveni (as did many), when David came to Portugal to involve the king in a war against the growing Ottoman Turkish empire (see 5276/1516, 5277/1517, 5287/1526). David's plan (which he skillfully succeeded in making credible) was that the Jews would take Eretz Yisrael, and that this would be the advent of Mashiach (the Messiah). Shlomo left Portugal with David (who was forced to leave), and after many journeys he took up David's mission, apparently indicating that he himself was Mashiach. They both traveled to Regensburg (see 5279/1519), where the emperor had them arrested and imprisoned, and where Shlomo was burned at the stake in Kislev 5293/1532 for refusing to convert to Christianity. David Re'uveni (whose country of origin was unclear, but believed to be Africa or Arabia) died in prison (some say he was burned at the stake).

5293 / 1533

The Jews were expelled from Constance (Germany).

5294 / 1534

Many Jews were massacred in Tlemcen (Algeria) when the Spanish conquered the town (see 5270/1510, 5277/1517), and 1,500 were enslaved (see 5295/1535).

5295 / 1535

Many Jews were killed in Tunis, and many were captured and sold as slaves, when invaders (see 5270/1510, 5294/1534) ransacked the city.

5296 / 1536

R.Yosef Karo (see 5282/1522) moved to Eretz Yisrael after his three children (and first wife) died; some say he had spent three years in Salonika and that they died there. He settled in Tzfat (Safed), where he considered himself a disciple of R. Yaakov Bei Rav (see 5298/1538) whom he may have studied under during a previous stay in Egypt.

5297 / 1537

When the brothers who had established the first Jewish printing press in Poland (Cracow) converted to Christianity, the Jews there boycotted their books until the king issued an order in Nissan 1537 which broke the boycott [see Ency.Jud.5.1037, 7.1189].

Jews were killed in Tyrnau (Slovakia), on a blood libel (see 5299/1539).

5298 / 1538

R.Yaakov Bei Rav was a (very young) rabbi in Fez (Morocco) after he left Spain (see 5252/1492). He then left Morocco and traveled (on business matters) to Egypt and Syria before settling in Tzfat (Safed), where he was accepted as a leader by such scholars as R.Yosef Karo (see 5296/1536). R.Yaakov attempted to use the Rambam's Halacha to re-introduce the original *Semicha* ordination for ruling and judging on all matters, including capital punishment. Although he was supported by the scholars of Tzfat, he was vigorously opposed by R.Levi ibn Chaviv (see 5276/1516) and other rabbis.

5299 / 1539

The Jews were expelled from Tyrnau (Slovakia) in Adar after a blood libel two years earlier (see 5297/1537, and 5254/1494).

5301 / 1540

The Portuguese Inquisition began to function (see 5012/1252, 5241/1481), with the intention of seeking out Anussim (Marranos) (see 5257/1497), and some were burned to death in Lisbon on the

19th Tishrei. Eventually 1,200 Anussim were burned to death (see 5266/1506).

Living in the Year 1540		
	b.	d.
Radvaz	1463?	1573?
R.Yosef Yoselman	1478?	1555?
Beit Yosef		
(R.Yosef Karo)	1488	1575
Maharshal	1510?	1573
Maharal of Prague	1512?	1609
Shitta Mekubetzet		
(R.Betz.Ashkenazi)	1520?	1594?
Ramak (Cordovero)	1522?	1570
Ramo (R.Moshe Isserles)	1525?	1573?
R.Mordechai Yaffe (Levush)	1530	1612
Ari'zal (R.Yitzchak Luria)	1534	1572
Sma (R.Yehoshua Falk)	1540?	1614

5301 / 1541

The Jews were massacred in Bohemia after an order was issued expelling them from the country (see 5317/1557). All the Jews who had resettled in Naples were expelled again (see 5270/1510).

5302 / 1542

R.Yosef Karo finished his *Beit Yosef* (commentary on the *Tur,* see 5282/1522) on the 11th Elul, and it brought him great respect among leading Talmud scholars of the time.

R.Ovadya Seforno of Italy, wrote a commentary on the Bible (see Figure A, page 312).

The Jews of Kalisch (Poland) were attacked in anti-Jewish riots.

5303 / 1543

The Jews were expelled from Muehlhausen (Germany) (see 5232/1472) and other towns of the province through the influence of Martin Luther

(German Christian reformer) who had turned against the Jews (some say in disappointment because they did not accept his form of [less "paganistic"] Christianity).

R.Yosef Yoselman (see 5290/1530) unsuccessfully tried to intercede, although through his representations the Jews were allowed to return to Brandenburg (see 5270/1510, 5333/1573). Some say that R.Yosef is the Jew with whom John Calvin (French Christian reformer) debated (recorded in Calvin's writings).

5305 / 1545

Two hundred Jews were killed and 5,000 houses destroyed in a fire in Salonika on the 4th of Av.

5307 / 1547

Many Jews were killed in Treviso (Italy) in anti-Jewish riots, and the rest left the town.

5310 / 1550

The Jews were expelled from Genoa (see 5275/1515).

Some say that in Mexico City at this point, there were more Anussim (Marranos) than there were Christians (see 5288/1528).

5311 / 1551

The Jews of Bratslav (Poland) were attacked by the Tartars who invaded the town.

The Jews in Austria were required to wear a yellow badge (see 4977/1216). The last Jews of Bavaria were expelled (see 5211/1450, 5238/1478, 5258/1498, 5279/1519).

5313 / 1553

The elderly Radvaz (see 5277/1517) settled in Eretz Yisrael, in Yerushalayim at first and then in Tzfat (Safed), where he lived for some twenty years. He wrote many Sh'elot UTeshuvot, and a commentary on some of the Rambam's Yad HaChazaka (see Figure I, page 321).

He was succeeded in Egypt by his disciple, R.Betzalel Ashkenazi, author of the Shitta Me Kubetzet (a selection of unpublished commentaries and Tosaphot [see 5050/1290] of early scholars on the Talmud). Later, R.Betzalel also went to Eretz Yisrael, where some say he had been born.

R.Yitzchak Luria Ashkenazi, the Ari'zal (see 5330/1570) who was born in Yerushalayim, was brought to Cairo by his mother (after his father died), to her wealthy brother who later became his father-in-law. He was a disciple of the Radvaz, and also of R.Betzalel, although R.Betzalel and the Ari'zal later wrote the Shitta MeKubetzet on Zevachim together [Shem.Hag.1.37a].

5314 / 1553

A mass burning of Jewish books took place in Rome.

A Ger Tzedek (convert to Judaism) who had previously been a monk was burned alive in Elul in Rome.

Pope Julius III ordered the burning of the Talmud (and the cessation of its printing) because of its alleged anti-Christian content (see 5002/1242, 5023/1263). On the first day of Rosh HaShana the Inquisition staged a massive burning of the Talmud and other Jewish books in Rome, and Jewish books were subsequently burned in many cities in Italy (see 5319/1559 and 5361/1601). In Venice, over 1,000 copies of the Talmud and 500 copies of the Rif were burned on the 13th Cheshvan.

Doña Gracia (Mendes) Nassi, a distinguished Jewish stateswoman who used her vast wealth and aristrocratic contacts to conduct a network to aid her fellow Anussim (Marranos) to leave Portugal, left Ferrara, Italy (see 5343/1583) and settled in Istanbul (Constantinople). She was born into a family of Anussim in Portugal (see 5257/1497), had left Portugal after her husband's (untimely) death, and later openly declared herself Jewish. In Constantinople she extended her financial support to assist Jewish study and Jewish causes.

5315 / 1555

The Jews of Rome (and other cities) were ordered by Pope Paul IV (see 5316/1556) to live in ghettos, and to lock the ghetto doors at night. Men were to wear yellow hats and women yellow kerchiefs, and they were severely restricted economically (see 5558/1798).

5316 / 1556

Twenty-six Portuguese Anussim (Marranos) who had openly returned to Judaism were burned to death in Ancona (Italy) on the 3rd of Iyar, by order of Pope Paul IV (see 5315/1555).

Three Jews were killed in Sochatchev (Poland) in a ritual desecration libel (see 5003/1243).

5317 / 1557

The Jews of Bohemia who had returned after the last expulsion (see 5301/1541) were expelled again from the major cities (although they were allowed to return a short while later); a few Jews were allowed to remain in Prague. Among those leaving Prague was R.Mordechai Yaffe (see 5352/1592), a disciple of the Ramo and the Maharshal and author of the *Levushim*, known as *Levush* (Halacha). He lived in Italy for approximately ten years, before becoming Rabbi in Grodno (Lublin), Lithuania and then Kremeniec (Poland). He participated in the *Va'ad Arba Aratzot* (see 5340/1580).

5318 / 1558

Seventy-five hundred Jews (many of them exiles from Portugal and Spain) died in a cholera epidemic in Marrakesh (Morocco) (see 5253/1493).

5319 / 1559

Ten thousand Jewish books were burned in Cremona (Italy) under the instructions of the Inquisition (see 5314/1553). However, the *Zohar* was printed there in the same year by a recently established press of non-Jewish ownership, which also published a *Chumash* (Bible) with Yiddish translation in the following year.

Living in the Year 1560		
	b.	d.
Radvaz	1463?	1573?
Beit Yosef		
(R.Yosef Karo)	1488	1575
Maharshal	1510?	1573
Maharal of Prague	1512?	1609
Shitta Mekubetzet		
(R.Betz.Ashkenazi)	1520?	1594?
Ramak (Cordovero)	1522?	1570
Ramo (R.Moshe Isserles)	1525?	1573?
R.Mordechai Yaffe (Levush)	1530	1612
Ari'zal (R.Yitzchak Luria)	1534	1572
Sma (R.Yehoshua Falk)	1540?	1614
R.Chaim Vital	1542?	1620
Lechem Mishneh		
(R.Avraham di Boton)	1545?	1588
Kli Yakar		
(R.Shlomo Ephrayim)	1550?	1619
Maharsha (R.Shmuel Edels)	1555	1631
Bach (R.Yoel Sirkes)	1560?	1640
Shaloh		
(R.Yeshayahu Horowitz)	1560?	1630

5323 / 1563

The *Shulchan Aruch* was completed by R.Yosef Karo.

R.Yosef Karo, who was already greatly respected by most Talmud scholars (see 5302/1542), finished writing the *Shulchan Aruch* (code of law, which was an abbreviated extension of his commentary, the *Beit Yosef*, see 5282/1522), on the 17th Adar. He corresponded with the Ramo, who later supplemented R.Yosef's Sephardi-oriented *Shulchan Aruch* with Ashkenazi rulings and customs. This helped consolidate the eventual role of the *Shulchan Aruch* as the ultimate word in Halacha.

The Jews were expelled from Neutitschein (Moravia) in Elul.

5324 / 1563

Thirty Jews of Polotzk (Lithuania) were drowned (on the 25th Kislev) in the Dvina (Daugava) River, for refusing to be baptized, when Ivan the Terrible captured the city.

5325 / 1565

The Maharam Padua, R.Meir (ben Yitzchak) Katzenellenbogen, a disciple of R.Yaakov Pollak and R.Yehuda of Mintz (Mahari Mintz, whose granddaughter he married), died on the 10th Shvat.

5326 / 1566

Jewish men were required to wear yellow hats in Lithuania, and the women were required to wear yellow kerchiefs.

5327 / 1567

Jews were expelled from the rest of the province of Genoa (see 5310/1550), although they returned after a short while.

5329 / 1568

R.Yisrael (ben Yeshayahu) HaLevi Horowitz, a great-uncle of the Shaloh and of R.Pinchas (see 5345/1585), was burned to death with his son-in-law, R.Moshe ben Yoel, in Prague on 27th Kislev.

5329 / 1569

The Jews were expelled from the Papal States (most of central Italy, including Bologna and Recanti) in Adar, by Pope Pius V. The expulsion excluded Rome and Ancona, but included Carpentras (France) (see 5261/1501).

5330 / 1570

The *Shulchan Aruch* was published with the supplements of the Ramo.

The Ramo, R.Moshe Isserles (ben Yisrael – Isserel), a disciple (and son-in-law) of R.Shalom Shachna (who was a disciple of R.Yaakov Pollak, see 5263/1503), wrote *Darkei Moshe* (supplement to the *Beit Yosef* on the *Tur*) and then *Hagahot* (supplementary comments to the *Shulchan Aruch*) (see 5323/1563). These supplements (see Figures J, K, L, M, pages 322–325), which included Ashkenazi Halacha decisions and customs, helped consolidate the eventual role of the *Shulchan Aruch* as the ultimate word in Halacha (see 5374/1614). The Ramo (see 5334/1573) wrote many other works, although he died very young; opinions vary down from 47 to 33 years of age [Shem.-Hag.1.46b].

With the establishment of an investigatory tribunal in Peru in Shvat, the Inquisition became official in South America (see 5310/1550).

The Ari'zal (see 5313/1553, 5332/1572), who had spent many years in secluded study near Cairo, settled in Tzfat (Safed) not long before R.Moshe Cordovero, the Ramak (from whom he was eager to learn) died, on the 23rd Tammuz. The Ramak, author of *Pardes Rimmonim* (Kabbala) and a commentary on the *Zohar*, among other works, was a disciple of R.Yosef Karo and of his own brother-in-law, R.Shlomo HaLevi Alkabetz (author of the *Piyut Lecha Dodi*).

R.Menachem Azaryah of Fano (Italy), the Rama MiFano, who was the author of many works of Kabbala, as well *Alfasi Zuta* (summary of the Rif), helped the Ramak (financially) in publishing his works.

5331 / 1571

Anti-Jewish riots began in Berlin, because of accusations that a court Jew, whose name, recorded as Lippold, had (wrongly) exploited his power as a royal administrator (see 5333/1573).

5332 / 1572

The Ari'zal died in Tzfat (Safed).

The great Kabbala scholar, the Ari'zal (see 5330/1570, 5334/1573), R.Yitzchak Luria, who had attracted as many as thirty disciples in the approximately two years that he lived in Tzfat, died on the 5th Av, at the very youthful age of 38 during an epidemic. He had earned his living (it appears) as a merchant, and his daughter married the son of R.Yosef Karo. His teachings, which he transmitted orally, gave a new dimension to the study of Kabbala. R.Chaim Vital, his major disciple, who was approximately 29, had previously been a disciple of the Ramak and was also a disciple of R.Moshe Alshich. R.Chaim recorded the Ari'zal's Kabbala in notes, and the other disciples agreed to the superior authenticity of these notes; some say the Ari'zal had instructed only him to take notes. He lived almost 50 years longer and wrote many works, including *Etz Chaim* and *Pri Etz Chaim*.

5333 / 1573

The Maharal came to Prague.

R.Yehuda Liva (Loew, Leib) (ben Betzalel), a descendant of King David, known as the Maharal (of Prague), left Mikulov (Nikolsburg) where he had been Rabbi of the province of Moravia for twenty years, and settled in Prague (for eleven years, see 5317/1557, 5352/1592). There he opened a yeshiva called the Klaus.

Lippold (see 5331/1571) was executed in Berlin in Shvat when he refused to convert, and (consequently) the Jews were expelled from Berlin and the whole province of Brandenburg (see 5303/1543, 5430/1670).

5334 / 1573.

The Maharshal died.

The Maharshal, R.Shlomo Luria (a descendant of Rashi, who was also related to the Ramo and the Ari'zal), died in Lublin, on the 12th Kislev. He wrote (among other works) *Yam Shel Shlomo,* on the Talmud, and *Chochmat Shlomo,* (now printed at the end of standard editions of the Talmud) (see Figure N, page 326).

5335 / 1575

R.Yosef died in Tzfat.

R.Avraham di Boton, a disciple of R.Shmuel de Medina (Maharashdam) in Salonika, was writing *Lechem Mishneh,* a commentary on the Rambam's *Yad HaChazaka* (see Figures H, I, pages 320, 321), when he saw on the 5th Adar the *Kesef Mishneh* of R.Yosef Karo, which was a similar work (see Figures J, K, L, M, pages 322–325) [Lech.Mish. Hil.Tef.11.15].

R.Eliyahu de Vidas, a disciple of the Ramak (see 5330/1570), completed writing *Reishis Chochma* (Mussar) in Tzfat (Safed), on the 18th Adar2.

R.Yosef Karo died in Tzfat (Safed) on the 13th Nissan, shortly after the sixth edition of the *Shulchan Aruch* (see 5323/1563), and his *Kesef Mishneh,* were printed.

R.Moshe Alshich, his disciple, was also a rabbi in Tzfat. He wrote *Torat Moshe Alshich* (comments and homilies on the Bible).

R.Shmuel Uceda (Uzida), a disciple of the Ari'zal, wrote *Midrash Shmuel* (commentary on *Pirkei Avot*).

R.Gedalyah ibn Yachya left Italy and settled in Alexandria. He was author of the chronicle *Shalshelet HaKabbala,* which attracted much criticism from scholars [Shem.Hag.1.(2al-b, 3–4), 1.85-end, etc./Dor. Har.5.267/Otz.Hag.3.75].

5337 / 1577

Twenty Jews were killed in anti-Jewish riots in Posen (Poznan, Poland). Jews of Rome and Ancona (see 5329/1569) were ordered by Pope Gregory XIII to attend conversion sermons in churches (see 5038/1278). He designed the Gregorian calendar.

5340 / 1580

The *Va'ad Arba Aratzot* (Council of Four Lands–provinces of Poland) was formed. It was an autonomous Jewish body which served as the leadership of Polish Jews for some 200 years (see 5524/1764), administering the social (welfare), monetary (taxes), and legal (Halacha) matters of Polish Jews. Many of the great rabbis participated in the *Va'ad* (see 5317/1557, 5374/1614, 5400/1640, 5414/1654). Meetings usually took place in an appointed city at the time of a fair, and its Bet Din would (also) sit in judgment. The Council used its powers to implement the decisions it had made.

5343 / 1583

Yosef Saralvo, one of the Portuguese Anussim (Marranos, see 5257/1497) who returned to Judaism, was arrested in Ferrara (Italy), a city that had served as a refuge for oppressed Jews. He was burned at the stake in Rome on the 27th Shvat, with other Jews of similar background. He had claimed to have returned 800 Anussim to Judaism.

5344 / 1584

R.Yissachar Ber (ben Naftali) HaKohen (known as Berman Ashkenazi) who, some say, was a disciple of the Ramo, finished writing *Matanot Kehuna* (commentary on *Midrash Rabba*) in Poland.

At this time, R.Shmuel (ben Yitzchak) Yaffe Ashkenazi, Rabbi of the Ashkenazi community in Istanbul (Constantinople) was writing *Yefei To'ar* (commentary on *Midrash Rabba*).

5345 / 1585

R.Pinchas HaLevi Horowitz (see 5329/1568), a Talmud scholar from Prague, who married the sister of the Ramo (Miriam Beilla, famous for her scholarship and piety) was living in Cracow when he became the head of the *Va'ad Arba Aratzot* (see 5340/1580).

5349 / 1589

The Jews who returned to Cochem (Germany) (see 5178/1418) were again expelled. At around this time the Jews were also expelled from a number of German provinces.

5350 / 1590

Seventy-six Jews died in a fire in Posen (Poland) on the 9th Sivan, and eighty Torah scrolls were burned. The Jewish section there was abandoned for two years (see 5380/1620).

The Jews were expelled from Petrokov (Poland) after a blood libel.

5352 / 1592

The Maharal of Prague, who had left Prague for four years (see 5333/1573) before returning in 1588, left again four years later to become Rabbi in Posen (Poland) (see 5350/1590). R.Mordechai Yaffe, the Levush, became Rabbi in Prague (see 5317/1557, 5359/1599).

R.Elazar Azkiri (Azikri) wrote the *Sefer Charedim* (Mussar) in Tzfat (Safed).

The Jews of Vilna were attacked and their houses and shops were plundered (see 5395/1635).

5354 / 1593

Many Jews were massacred in Bucharest on the 28th Cheshvan when the local residents revolted against the Ottoman Turkish rule.

In 1594 Rodrigo de Castro, a physician from Lisbon, and an Anuss (Marrano), settled in Hamburg where he became a physician to royalty. He became openly Jewish at the persuasion of a fellow physician, Shmuel Cohen, who had also been one of the Portuguese Anussim.

5355 / 1595

The Jews of Patras (Greece) were murdered and their properties plundered by sailors from Naples and Sicily.

5357 / 1597

The Jews were expelled from the Italian province of Milan (although there were no longer any Jews living in the city of Milan, see 5080/1320).

5359 / 1599

The Maharal returned to Prague again.

The Maharal returned to Prague again (see 5352/1592), and R.Mordechai Yaffe, the Levush, took his position in Posen (Poland). The Maharal wrote many works, including *Gur Aryeh,* a commentary on Rashi's commentary on the *Chumash* (Bible), but he is most famous for the *Golem of Prague.*

R.Yeshayahu Menachem, who was Rabbi in Cracow and a leading participant in the *Va'ad Arba Aratzot* (see 5340/1580), was the originator of the *Heter Iska* (a document to circumvent paying direct interest on loans). He died on the 25th Av.

Living in the Year 1600		
	b.	d.
Maharal of Prague	1512?	1609
R.Mordechai Yaffe (Levush)	1530	1612
Sma (R.Yehoshua Falk)	1540?	1614
R.Chaim Vital	1542?	1620
Kli Yakar		
(R.Shlomo Ephrayim)	1550?	1619
Maharsha (R.Shmuel Edels)	1555	1631
Bach (R.Yoel Sirkes)	1560?	1640
Shaloh		
(R.Yeshayahu Horowitz)	1560?	1630
Tosaphot Yom Tov		
(Lipman Heller)	1579	1654
Taz (R.David ben Shmuel)	1586	1667

5361 / 1601

Mordechai (ben Shmuel) Meisel, a wealthy philanthropist, died in Prague. Although he left huge sums of money for charity under the Maharal of Prague, the emperor seized all his properties, and the inheritors (he had no children) were tortured to force them declare any other properties.

The Church authorities in Rome confiscated and burned Jewish holy books in the month of Shvat (see 5314/1553).

5362 / 1602

Seven Jews were hanged in Mantua (Italy).

5365 / 1605

The Jews of Bisenz (Moravia) were massacred in Iyar.

A Jew was killed in a desecration libel (see 5003/1243) in Bochnia (Poland).

5369 / 1609

The Maharal of Prague (see 5333/1573) 5359/1599) died on the 18th Elul at the age of at least 83. R.Shlomo Ephrayim Lunshitz (see 5379/1619) had been a rabbi in Prague since 1604 (see 5375/1615).

5373 / 1613

The Tzemach David, R.David Gans, a disciple of the Ramo and author of *Tzemach David* (historical chronology), died in Prague in Elul. Ten days later, R.Yitzchak Chayes, author of *Appey Ravreve* (Halacha in verse), also died there.

5374 / 1614

The Maharsha became Rabbi in Lublin.

The Maharsha, R.Shmuel HaLevi Edels, who wrote a commentary on Talmud, Rashi, and Tosaphot (which is now printed in standard editions of the Talmud) (see Figure N, page 326), became Rabbi in Lublin (Poland), where he stayed eleven years (see 5392/1631). He had previously been Rabbi in Chelm (Poland) for nine years, after the death of his mother-in-law (Edel) who had supported him and his disciples for twenty years. R.Yehoshua Falk HaKohen (Katz), known as the Sma for his commentary on the *Shulchan Aruch* called *Sefer Me'irat Enayim* (printed in standard editions on the *Choshen Mishpat* section) (see Figure M, page 325), died on the 19th of Nissan. The importance he placed on every word of the *Shulchan Aruch* further consolidated its acceptance as the ultimate authority on Halacha (see 5406/1646). The Sma, who participated in the *Va'ad Arba Aratzot* (see 5340/1580), was a disciple of the Ramo and the Maharshal, and he also wrote the *Derisha* and *Perisha* (commentaries on the *Tur*). His wife Beilla, who was known for her scholarship and great piety, contributed to two Halacha decisions [See Hakd.LeDerisha/Mag.Av.O.C.263.12, Caf.HaChym. 43, etc.].

The Jews of Virmyze (Worms, Germany) repelled an attack on the Jewish quarter on Erev Tisha B'Av. The Jews of Frankfurt am Main were attacked in the month of Elul and forced to leave the city for awhile.

5375 / 1615

The Shaloh (see 5382/1621), who had been the Rabbi in Frankfort for eight years after having previously been Rabbi in a number of towns, became a Rabbi in Prague (see 5369/1609, 5379/1619).

5376 / 1616

R.Meir (ben Gedalyah), Maharam Lublin, had been Rosh Yeshiva in Lublin at a very early age. Then he was Rabbi and Rosh Yeshiva in Lvov and later in Cracow (Poland), before returning to Lublin, where he died in the month of Iyar. He wrote *Me'ir Eynei Chachamim* (now printed at the end of standard editions of the Talmud, as the "Maharam") (see Figure N, page 326).

5377 / 1616

The *Tosaphot Yom Tov* commentary was concluded.

R.Yom Tov Lipman Heller (see 5400/1640) had become a *dayan* at the age of 18 in Prague, where he was a disciple of the Maharal of Prague and R.Shlomo Ephrayim (see 5369/1609). He finished his *Tosaphot Yom Tov* commentary on the Mishna (see Figure B, page 314), on the 22nd Cheshvan at the age of 38. He later became Rabbi in Vienna but subsequently returned to Prague (see 5389/1629).

5379 / 1619

A Jew was killed in Sochatchev (Poland) in a blood libel. R.Shlomo Ephrayim of Lunshitz, a disciple of the Maharshal, and author of *Kli Yakar* (commentary on the *Chumash*) (see Figure A, page 313) and *Ollelot Ephrayim* (homiletic Mussar), died on the 7th of Adar, in Prague where he was Rabbi (see 5369/1609) at the same time as the Shaloh (see 5375/1615).

The Bach (see 5400/1640) became Rabbi in Cracow, after having previously been Rabbi in six or seven other towns.

5380 / 1620

The Jews of Posen (Poland) were expelled from a temporary area of settlement outside of the city (in which they had settled after their second fire in 1613, see 5350/1590).

Living in the Year 1620	b.	d.
R.Chaim Vital	1542?	1620
Maharsha (R.Shmuel Edels)	1555	1631
Bach (R.Yoel Sirkes)	1560?	1640
Shaloh (R.Yeshayahu Horowitz)	1560?	1630
Tosaphot Yom Tov (Lipman Heller)	1579	1654
Taz (R.David ben Shmuel)	1586	1667
Chelkat Mechokek (R.Moshe Lima)	1605?	1658

5382 / 1621

The Shaloh arrived in Eretz Yisrael.

The Shaloh (HaKadosh), R.Yeshayahu (ben Avra-ham) HaLevi Horowitz, left Prague (see 5375/1615) when his wife died, and arrived in Yerushalayim in Kislev 5382/1621, where he wrote *Shnei Luchot HaBrit* (SHaLoH) (Kabbala/Mussar).

5382 / 1622

The (third edition of) *Tzena URena* (a simple Yiddish Midrashic work, intended for women) by R.Yaakov Ashkenazi, was published.

5385 / 1625

Fifteen scholars, including the Shaloh (see 5382/1621), were arrested in Yerushalayim on Shabbat the 11th Elul and released after a ransom was paid. The Shaloh first settled in Tzfat (Safed) and later in Teverya (Tiberius), where he died.

When the Portuguese recaptured Bahia (Brazil) from the Dutch, they allowed all the Dutch to leave (including the Jews), but five Portuguese Anussim (Marranos) who had become openly Jewish under Dutch rule, were captured and killed (see 5407/1647).

5389 / 1629

R.Yom Tov Lipman Heller was imprisoned.

R.Yom Tov Lipman Heller, the Tosaphot Yom Tov (see 5377/1616), was slandered (by some people who had considered the tax assessments for the Thirty-Year War [see 5409/1648] between the Catholics and the Protestants, to be unfair – he was one of the assessors). He was imprisoned on the 5th Tammuz for a short while, but was released on the revised and relatively lenient conditions that he was forbidden to be Rabbi in Prague, and that the slandered parts of his books were censored (after the entire books had originally been banned).

5390 / 1630

Moshe Shmuler was killed in Przemysl (Poland) in a ritual desecration libel (see 5003/1243).

Invading German troops expelled the Jews of Mantua (Italy) after confiscating their possessions.

Eighteen Jewish children were forcibly baptized, in Reggio Emilia (Italy).

The Jews of Venice and of Prague were forced to attend Christian conversion sermons (see 5337/1577).

Jews were permitted to live in Recife (Brazil) after the Dutch had conquered the area from the Portuguese, and many Anussim (Marranos) became openly Jewish there (see 5385/1625, 5407/1647, 5414/1654). The Jews prospered in Recife, which was the only town in colonial South America to allow openly Jewish life at that time. A whole military company made up of Jewish soldiers was exempt from guard duty on Shabbat, and at one point the Jews were in the majority (see 5310/1550).

5392 / 1631

R.Meir Schiff, the Maharam Schiff, finished his Chidushim on Talmud *Bava Kama,* in Cheshvan 5391/1630.

The Maharsha (see 5374/1614) died on the 5th Kislev 5392/1631, in Ostraha (Poland) where he had been Rabbi during the last seven years of his life.

5395 / 1635

The Jews of Vilna were attacked, and their houses were ransacked (see 5352/1592, 5448/1687).

5396 / 1636

R.Fliyahu ben Moshe Loanz, who was called R.Eliyahu Ba'al Shem of Virmyze (Worms, Germany), died on the 21st Tammuz. He was a grandson of R.Yosef Yoselman the *shtadlan,* and the author of *Michlal Yofi,* commentary on *Kohelet* (Ecclesiastes).

There were at least two other people called R. Eliyahu Ba'al Shem, who lived around the same time [Otz.Hag.2.183, 184/Great Maggid, N.Y.1974.p.31].

The Jews of Lublin were attacked and some killed after a blood libel trial. The Jews of Brisk (Brest-Litovsk) were attacked in an anti-Jewish riot.

5399 / 1639

Twenty Jews were arrested and tortured in a blood libel in Lunshitz (Poland). Two were later publicly killed in front of the synagogue and their bodies mutilated.

Living in the Year 1640		
	b.	d.
Bach (R.Yoel Sirkes)	1560?	1640
Tosaphot Yom Tov		
(Lipman Heller)	1579	1654
Taz (R.David ben Shmuel)	1586	1667
Chelkat Mechokek		
(R.Moshe Lima)	1605?	1658
Shach (R.Shabbetai Kohen)	1621	1663?
Beit Shmuel (R.Shmuel)	1630?	1700?
Magen Avraham		
(R.Avr.Abele Gombiner)	1637?	1683

5400 / 1640

R.Yoel Sirkes, the Bach, died.

The Bach, R.Yoel Sirkes, who wrote a commentary on the Tur (Bayit Chadash – BaCH) and Hagahot notations) on the Talmud (see Figure D, F, pages 316, 318), died in Cracow (see 5379/1619) on the 20th Adar. He was succeeded (a few years later) by the Tosaphot Yom Tov (see 5377/1616) who had moved from place to place, participated in the Va'ad Arba Aratzot (see 5340/1580) (and was the victim of further hatred), after he was forced to leave Prague (see 5389/1629).

R.Yehoshua (ben Yosef) Falk, the author of Meginei Shlomo (defending Rashi on the questions posed by the Tosaphot) and of Sh'elot UTeshuvot Pnei Yehoshua I, was a disciple of the Maharam Lublin and the Sma. He became Rosh Yeshiva in Cracow in 1640, upon the death of R.Natan Shapiro (author of Megaleh Amukot), after having previously been Rabbi in a number of communities. His greatest disciple, the Shach (see 5406/1646, 5415/1655), moved to Cracow with him. Another disciple of the Meginei Shlomo, R. Moshe Lima (see 5415/1655), author of Chelkat Mechokek (commentary on the Even HaEzer section of the Shulchan Aruch, now printed in standard editions) (see Figure L, page 324), was Rabbi in Slonim (Poland). He later became Rabbi in Vilna.

5402 / 1642

R.Yitzchak Abohab III da Fonseca was born in Portugal to a family of Anussim (Marranos) who escaped (when he was a child) and raised him openly as a Jew in Amsterdam. In 1641 he left his position as a rabbi in Amsterdam and arrived in Recife (Brazil) in 1642 to become the first rabbi in the Western Hemisphere (see 5390/1630).

5404 / 1644

A Spanish nobleman (Lopa de Vera y Alarcon) decided to convert to Judaism (after studying the Bible) and was arrested and tried by the Inquisition. In prison he circumcised himself and changed his name to Yehuda HaMa'amin (the believer). He refused to renounce Judaism, despite torture, and his death at the stake in Tammuz left a deep impression on the Anussim (Marranos) of Spain (see 5407/1647).

5405 / 1645

The Jews of Mogilev (Poland) were attacked by rioters (including the mayor) during Tashlich on Rosh HaShana.

5406 / 1646

The *Shach* and *Taz* (on *Shulchan Aruch*) were printed.

R.David (ben Shmuel) HaLevi, the Taz (see 5414/1654), was a disciple of the Bach, whose scholarly daughter, Rivka, he married. He had previously been Rabbi in Posen (Poland) for twenty years, before he became Rabbi in Ostraha (Poland). There, in the course of some five years, he wrote and then published (in 1646) *Turei Zahav* (*TaZ*) on the *Yoreh Deya* section of the *Shulchan Aruch*. He later wrote on other sections as well as other works.

R.Shabbetai (ben Meir) HaKohen, the Shach (see 5400/1640), wrote and published *Siftei Kohen* (*ShaCh*) on *Yoreh Deya*, although he was not yet 25; he later wrote on the section of *Choshen Mishpat*. The writings of both the Taz and the Shach are printed in standard editions of the *Shulchan Aruch* (see Figure K, page 323), and they further consolidated its acceptance as the ultimate word in Halacha (see 5374/1614).

5407 / 1647

R.Yitzchak de Castro (Tartas) was burned alive in Lisbon for teaching Judaism to Anussim (Marranos) in Portuguese Brazil (see 5385/1625). His cries of "Shma Yisrael" at his death made a deep impression on the Anussim of Portugal (see 5404/1644).

5408 / 1648

The Jews were massacred by Chmielnitzki's Cossack forces.

The Cossacks rebelled (against Polish rule) under the leadership of Bogdan Chmielnitzki (who had also gained some military assistance from the Tartar rulers of Crimea), and they attempted to establish an independent Ukraine. Whenever they could, these rebellious forces attacked the Jews.

They tortured many, forcibly converted some, massacred tens of thousands, and mutilated their remains. Three hundred Jewish communities were destroyed, and between 100,000 and 300,000 Jews were killed in the massacres, which became known as *Gezerot Tach VeTat* (for the years 5408, and 5409. Many had expected 5408 to be the year the Mashiach [Messiah] would come [Or HaChama (Ramak) Sh.(2).10].).

Poland-Lithuania, which had been a haven for Jews for many years (see 5110/1350), became a scene of massive Jewish devastation. On the 20th Sivan, 6,000 Jews of Nemirov (Poland) were killed, and that day was later declared a fast day (see 4931/1171, 5410/1650), to mark the beginning of the massacres. A thousand Jews were tortured and then killed on the 4th Tammuz, in Tulchin (Poland); 10,000 were killed in Polonnoye (Poland) on the 3rd Av, including R.Shimshon of Ostropole (a maggid and writer of Kabbala); and 3,000 Jews were killed in Staro-Konstantinov (Poland) on Tisha B'Av (including those who had taken refuge in the city).

5409 / 1648

R.Naftali (son of Yitzchak HaKohen Katz who was the son-in-law of the Maharal of Prague) was killed on the 5th Tishrei by Chmielnitzki's forces. Four thousand Jews of Dubno (Poland) were killed on the 15th, when the Poles would not allow them to seek refuge in a fortress; 12,000 Jews in Narol (Poland) were drowned, or killed in the synagogue (which was then set afire on the 17th of Cheshvan); and the 40,000 Jews who had fled from other parts of the country, seeking refuge in the vicinity of Narol, were all massacred. The Jews of Medzibuzh (Poland) were saved from Chmielnitzki's troops by a man called Mordechai and his wife Esther. The 12th of Tevet was instituted as Mordechai Purim, in commemoration of this event.

The parents of R.Avraham Abele Gombiner, the Magen Avraham (see 5433/1673), were killed in the massacres; and the Taz (see 5406/1646) left Ostraha (Poland) and took refuge in a fortress (see 5414/1654).

Many Jews moved to other countries, but Germany was also in a state of ruin at the conclusion of the Thirty-Year War (see 5389/1629, 5415/1655).

The Jews of Prague were presented with a banner in recognition of their defense of the city against Swedish invaders.

KOV'IM			
	Secular Year		
	Born		Died
R.Yitzchak Abarbanel	1437	–	1508
Yuchasin	1440?	–	1515
R.Ovadya Bertinura	1445?	–	1524?
Eyn Yaakov (R.Yaakov ibn Chaviv)	1445?	–	1516?
R.Yaakov Pollak	1460?	–	1530?
Radvaz	1463?	–	1573?
Beit Yosef (R.Yosef Karo)	1488	–	1575
Maharshal	1510?	–	1573
Maharal of Prague	1512?	–	1609
Shittah Mekubetzet (R.Betz.Ashkenazi)	1520?	–	1594?
Ramak (Cordovero)	1522?	–	1570
Ramo (R.Moshe Isserles)	1525?	–	1573?
R.Mordechai Yaffe (Levush)	1530	–	1612
Ari'zal (R.Yitzchak Luria)	1534	–	1572
Sma (R.Yehoshua Falk)	1540?	–	1614
R.Chaim Vital	1542?	–	1620
Lechem Mishneh (A.Avraham di Boton)	1545?	–	1588
Kli Yakar (R.Shlomo Ephrayim)	1550?	–	1619
Maharsha (R.Shmuel Edels)	1555	–	1631
Bach (R.Yoel Sirkes)	1560?	–	1640
Shaloh (R.Yeshayahu Horowitz)	1560?	–	1630
Tosaphot Yom Tov (Lipman Heller)	1579	–	1654
Taz (R.David ben Shmuel)	1586	–	1667
Chelkat Mechokek (R.Moshe Lima)	1605?	–	1658
Shach (R.Shabbetai Kohen)	1621	–	1663?

CHAPTER 14

The Acharonim –
Later Scholars

Acharonim and Early Chasidim
Later Acharonim and Changing Society

The fourteenth chapter in Jewish history begins after the devastating massacres brought about by the Cossack uprisings and ends with the devastation of European Jewry by the Nazi Holocaust. This period of time includes the Acharonim and the development of the Chasidic movement as a dynamic force among observant Jews that provided leadership against the many eroding factors of the industrial and social revolutions.

During this time, the Jewish people were rocked by the disruptive influence of the false Messiahs. The social emancipation of the Jews gave rise to the Haskala and the Reform movements. The persistent persecutions in Eastern Europe led to massive emigrations to the United States and to the emergence of Zionism as a strong nationalistic force.

THE ACHARONIM – LATER SCHOLARS

Jewish Year		Secular Year
5414	The first Jews settled in New Amsterdam (New York)	1654
5415	Jews killed in Russian and Swedish invasions of Poland	1655
5416	Jews were permitted to live in England	1656
5416	Baruch Spinoza was excommunicated	1656
5433	The Magen Avraham (on Shulchan Aruch) was completed	1673
5437	**SHABBETAI TZVI DIED AS A MUSLIM**	**1676**
5449	The Beit Shmuel (on the Shulchan Aruch) was printed	1689
5458	**THE BA'AL SHEM TOV WAS BORN**	**1698**
5463	The Pnei Yehoshua's family was killed in an explosion	1702
5472	The Siftei Chachamim was arrested	1712
5484	R.Yaakov Culi (Me'am Lo'ez) arrived in Constantinople	1724
5487	The Mishneh LeMelech died	1727
5494	**Jews were massacred by the Haidamack bands**	**1734**

Acharonim and Early Chasidim

Jewish Year		Secular Year
5501	The Or HaChayim arrived in Eretz Yisrael	1741
5507	R.Moshe Chaim Luzzatto (Ramchal) died in Acco (Acre)	1747
5510	R.Yonatan Eybeshutz became Rabbi in Hamburg	1750
5515	The Noda BiYehuda became Rabbi in Prague	1754
5518	**The Frankists instigated mass burnings of the Talmud**	**1757**
5519	Frankists supported blood libel charges against Jews	1759
5520	**The Ba'al Shem Tov died**	**1760**
5524	The Va'ad Arba Aratzot was discontinued	1764
5528	**The Haidamacks massacred thousands of Jews**	**1768**
5532	The Maggid of Mezeritsch died	1772
5542	R.Natan Adler and Chassam Sofer visited the Noda BiYehuda	1782
5546	R.Elimelech of Lizensk died	1786
5551	**The Pale of Settlement was established in Russia**	**1791**
5553	Jews suffered in the Reign of Terror of the French Revolution	1793
5558	The Vilna Gaon died	1797

Jewish Year		Secular Year
5559	The Ba'al HaTanya was released from first imprisonment	1798
5559	Napoleon led an army expedition through Eretz Yisrael	1799
5566	The Chida (R.Chaim Yosef David Azulai) died	1806
5566	The Chassam Sofer became Rabbi in Pressburg	1806
5570	R.Levi Yitzchak of Berditchev died	1809
5571	R.Nachman of Bratslav died	1810
5574	R.Akiva Eger became Rabbi in Posen	1814
5575	Kozhnitzer Maggid and Yehudi of Pershisskha both died	1814
5575	Chozeh of Lublin and R.Mendel of Rymanov died	1815
5579	Anti-Jewish (Hep! Hep!) riots spread throughout Germany	1819
5587	**Russia began conscripting Jewish children into the army**	**1827**
5600	Adm.R.Yisrael of Ruzhin was released from imprisonment	1840

Later Acharonim and Changing Society

5603	The Tzemach Tzedek was arrested in Russia	1843
5606	Sir Moshe Montefiore visited Russia to help the Jews	1846
5609	R.Yisrael Salanter left Vilna	1848
5611	R.Shimshon Rapha'el Hirsch became Rabbi in Frankfurt am Main	1851
5619	R.Menachem Mendel of Kotzk died	1859
5624	The Malbim was imprisoned and expelled from Rumania	1864
5626	The Chidushei HaRim died	1866
5633	The *Chafetz Chaim* was published	1873
5634	The Minchat Chinuch died	1874
5638	Petach Tikva agricultural settlement was established	1878
5641	**MANY JEWS BEGAN LEAVING RUSSIA AFTER A WAVE OF POGROMS**	**1881**
5646	R.Shlomo Ganzfried (Kitzur Shulchan Aruch) died	1886
5652	R.Chaim (Brisker) became Rabbi in Brisk	1892
5665	The Sfass Emess died	1905
5665	**Many Jews were killed in (official) Russian pogroms**	**1905**
5671	*Chazon Ish* was published	1911
5674	**Over 500,000 Jewish soldiers fought in World War I**	**1914**
5678	**Over 60,000 Jews were killed during Russian Revolution**	**1918**
5684	*Daf HaYomi* study cycle commenced	1923
5687	The Lubavitcher Rebbe was released from Soviet prison	1927
5699	Jews were attacked in Kristallnacht pogrom in Germany	1938

MAJOR ACHARONIM

	Secular Year Born		Died
Beit Shmuel (R.Shmuel)	1630?	–	1700?
Magen Avraham (R.Avr.Abele Gombiner)	1637?	–	1683
Siftei Chachamim (R.Shabbetai Bass)	1641	–	1718
Mishneh LeMelech (R.Yehuda Rosannes)	1657?	–	1727
Pnei Yehoshua (R.Yaakov Yehoshua Falk)	1680	–	1756
R.Yaakov Culi (Me'am Lo'ez)	1689?	–	1732
R.Yonatan Eybeshutz	1690?	–	1764
Sha'agat Aryeh (R.Aryeh Leib Gunzberg)	1695?	–	1785
Or HaChayim (R.Chaim (ib)n Attar)	1696	–	1743
R.Yaakov Emden	1697?	–	1776
Korban HaEida (R.David Frankel)	1707	–	1762
Pnei Moshe (R.Moshe Margolis)	1710?	–	1781
Noda BiYehuda (R.Yechezk'el Landau)	1713	–	1793
Vilna Gaon	1720	–	1797
Chida (Azulai)	1724	–	1806
Pri Megadim (R.Yosef Te'omim)	1727?	–	1792
R.Shneur Zalman (Rav of Lyady)	1745	–	1813
Ketzot HaChoshen (R.Aryeh Leib Heller)	1745?	–	1813
Chayei Adam (R.Avraham Danziger)	1748	–	1820
Yismach Moshe (R.Moshe Teitelbaum)	1759	–	1841
Chavat Da'at (R.Yakv.of .Lissa/Netivot)	1759?	–	1832
R.Ephrayim Zalman Margolis	1760	–	1828
R.Akiva Eger	1761	–	1837
Chassam Sofer	1762	–	1839
Tiferet Yisrael (R.Yisrael Lipshutz)	1782	–	1860
Tzemach Tzedek (of Lubavitch)	1789	–	1866
Divrei Chaim (of Tzanz)	1793	–	1876
Chidushei HaRim (of Gur)	1799	–	1866
Minchat Cinuch (R.Yosef Babad)	1800?	–	1874
Kitzur Shulchan Aruch (R.Shl.Ganzfried)	1804	–	1886
Malbim (R.Meir Leib(ush))	1808?	–	1879
Pitchei Teshuva (R.Avraham Tzvi Hirsch)	1813	–	1868
Aruch HaShulchan (R.Yechi'el Epstein)	1829	–	1908
Sdei Chemed (R.Chaim Chizkiyah Medini)	1832?	–	1904
Ben Ish Chai (R.Yosef Chaim Al-Chakkam)	1833?	–	1909
Chafetz Chaim (R.Yisrael Meir Kagan)	1838	–	1933
Darkei Teshuva (R.Tzvi Hirsch Shapira)	1845?	–	1913
Sfass Emess (of Gur)	1847	–	1905
R.Chaim Brisker	1853	–	1918
Rogatchover Gaon (R.Yosef Rozin)	1858	–	1936
Torah Temima (R.Baruch Epstein)	1860	–	1942

MAJOR ADMURIM AND CHASIDIC LEADERS

	Secular Year Born		Died
Ba'al Shem Tov	1698	–	1760
Maggid of Mezeritsch (R.Dov Ber)	1698?	–	1772
R.Avraham Gershon of Kitev	1701?	–	1761
R.Nachman of Horodenka	1705?	–	1765
R.Elimelech of Lizensk	1717?	–	1786
R.Zushya of Annopol	1718?	–	1800
R.Yechi'el Michel of Zlotchov	1721?	–	1786?
R.Yaakov Yosef of Polannoe	1724?	–	1784?
The Shpoler Zeideh	1725	–	1812
R.Shmelke of Nikolsburg	1726?	–	1778?
R.Pinchas of Koretz	1728	–	1790
R.Menachem Mendel of Vitebsk	1730?	–	1788
R.Nachum of Chernobyl	1730	–	1797
R.Pinchas Horowitz	1730	–	1805
R.Yisrael (Maggid) of Kozhnitz	1733?	–	1814
R.Aharon of Karlin	1736	–	1772
R.Shlomo of Karlin	1738	–	1792
R.Levi Yitzchak of Berditchev	1740	–	1810
R.Avraham of Kalisk	1741	–	1809
Adm.R.Yitzchak Aisik of Kalliv	1744?	–	1821
R.Shneur Zalman (Rav of Lyady)	1745	–	1813
Chozeh of Lublin	1745?	–	1815
R.Baruch of Medzibuzh	1753?	–	1811
Adm.R.Avraham Yehoshua Heschel of Apta	1755	–	1825
Adm.R.Menachem Mendel of Rymanov	1755?	–	1815
Yismach Moshe (R.Moshe Teitelbaum)	1759	–	1841
Adm.R.Meir of Apta	1760	–	1827
Adm.R.Naftali Tzvi of Ropshytz	1760	–	1827
Adm.R.Klonymos Kalman of Cracow	1763?	–	1823
Adm.R.Asher of Stolin	1765	–	1826
The Yehudi of Pershisskha	1766	–	1814
Adm.R.Simcha Bunim of Pershisskha	1767	–	1827
Adm.R.Mordechai of Chernobyl	1770	–	1837
R.Nachman of Bratslav	1772	–	1811

MAJOR ADMURIM AND CHASIDIC LEADERS (cont'd.)

	Secular Year Born		Died
Adm.R.Dov Ber of Lubavitch	1774	–	1827
Adm.R.Shalom of Belz	1779	–	1855
Adm.R.Meir(el) Premishlaner	1780?	–	1850
Bnei Yissachar (of Dynov)	1783?	–	1841
Adm.R.Elazar Nissan Teitelbaum	1786?	–	1856
R.Mendel of Kotzk	1787	–	1859
Tzemach Tzedek (of Lubavitch)	1789	–	1866
Divrei Chaim (of Tzanz)	1793	–	1876
R.Yisrael of Ruzhin	1797	–	1850
Chidushei HaRim (of Gur)	1799	–	1866
Adm.R.Shlomo of Radomsk	1803	–	1866
Adm.R.Aisik of Komarno	1806	–	1874
Adm.R.Yekutiel Yehuda of Sighet	1808	–	1883
Divrei Yechezk'el (of Shinev)	1811?	–	1899
Adm.R.Yitzchak of Skvira	1812	–	1885
Adm.R.Menachem Mendel of Vizhnitz	1830	–	1884
Adm.R.Shmuel of Lubavitch	1834	–	1882
Adm.R.Chananyah Yom Tov Lipa of Sighet	1836	–	1904
Adm.R.Avraham of Sochatchev	1839	–	1910
Darkei Teshuva (of Munkatch)	1845?	–	1913
Sfass Emess (of Gur)	1847	–	1905
Adm.R.Shlomo of Bobov	1848	–	1906
Adm.R.Sholom DovBer of Lubavitch	1860	–	1920
Adm.R.Avraham Mordechai of Gur	1866	–	1948
Adm.R.Chaim Elazar of Munkatch	1871?	–	1937
Adm.R.Aharon of Belz	1880	–	1957
Adm.R.Chaim Tzvi Teitelbaum of Sighet	1880?	–	1926
Adm.R.Yosef Yitzchak of Lubavitch	1880	–	1950
Adm.R.Yoel(ish) of Satmar	1888	–	1979
Adm.R.Yisrael of Gur	1894	–	1977
Adm.R.Simcha Bunim of Gur	1896	–	1992
Adm.R.Menachem Mendel Schneersohn	1902	–	
Adm.R.Moshe of Sighet	1915	–	
Adm.R.Pinchas Menachem of Gur	1925	–	

5409 / 1649

Ninety-six Marranos were burned to death in Mexico (see 5288/1528, 5310/1550).

5410 / 1650

Many Jews were killed in Jassy (Moldavia) by the Cossacks (see 5413/1652).

The *Va'ad Arba Aratzot* proclaimed the 20th Sivan as a fast day in commemoration of the Chmielnitzki massacres (see 20th Sivan 5408/1648). *Va'ad Medinat Lita* (Council of Lithuania, similar to *Va'ad Arba Aratzot*, see 5340/1580) instituted three years of memorial mourning (forbidding such things as music at weddings).

A Jew was killed in a blood libel in Kadan (Bohemia), and the rest of the Jews were expelled.

5411 / 1651

Many Jews were killed in Bar (Ukraine) by the Cossacks and the Tartars (see 5408/1648).

5413 / 1652

David ben Chaim (of whom little else is known) was burned to death in Podhayetz (Poland) on the 7th Kislev. Manuel Fernandes de Villareal, a Poruguese diplomat, was discovered to be secretly Jewish. He was executed by the Inquisition during Chanuka in Lisbon, and (subsequently) some of his relatives became openly Jewish in Livorno (Leghorn) (Italy).

Many Jews were killed in Jassy (Moldavia) by invading Cossacks (see 5410/1650).

5414 / 1654

After the Chmielnitzki massacres, the Taz (see 5409/1648) traveled around for a few years (spending a few days in the house of the Shach), and he became a rabbi in Lemberg (Lvov) (Poland)

in 1654 (see 5424/1664). He participated in the *Va'ad Arba Aratzot* (see 5340/1580).

R.Yom Tov Lipman Heller, the Tosaphot Yom Tov (see 5400/1640), died in the month of Elul and was succeeded as Rabbi in Cracow by the Rebbe R.Heschel, R.Yehoshua Heschel, who had previously been Rosh Yeshiva and Rabbi in Lublin.

The first Jews settled in New Amsterdam.

Recife (Brazil) was reconquered by the Portuguese (see 5390/1630, 5407/1647), and the Jews fled, most (including the Rabbi, see 5402/1642) to Holland. Twenty-three of them settled in New Amsterdam – the first Jews in what later became New York – where they were not readily accepted by Governor Peter Stuyvesant.

5415 / 1655

Avraham Nunez Bernal, a leader of Spanish Anussim (Marranos), was burned at the stake in Cordova in the month of Nissan; his open proclamation of allegiance to Judaism aroused many other Anussim. His nephew was also burned within a few months.

Jews were killed in Russian and Swedish invasions of Poland.

Jews (some say as many as 25,000) were killed when Vilna was attacked by invading Russian forces on the 23rd Tammuz (see 5416/1655, 5420/1659). The Shach (see 5406/1646, 5416/1655), who was part of the Vilna Beit Din of R.Moshe Lima (the Chelkat Mechokek, see 5400/1640), fled from the city (see 5416/1655).

Another who fled was R.Moshe Rivkes, the author of *Be'er HaGola,* (a bibliography of the *Shulchan Aruch*) (see Figures J, K, L, M, pages 322–325) which was published in Amsterdam where he was allowed to settle for a while. (He was not sent on to Germany with other refugees, because of the influence R.Shaul Levi Morteira and R.Yitzchak Abohab III [see 5416/1656] exercised on his behalf.)

209

R.Ephrayim HaKohen, a disciple of R.Moshe Lima, and author of *Sha'ar Ephrayim (Sh'elot UTeshuvot),* also left Vilna (see 5420/1660); his son-in-law R.Yaakov Sak (see 5420/1660), who had been left for dead inthe fighting also managed to escape.

R.Hillel, author of *Beit Hillel (on Shulchan Aruch),* and some say a nephew of R.Yehoshua Heschel (see 5414/1654) was also a member of the *Beit Din* of R.Moshe Lima.

Cracow was captured by the Swedes, and many Jews fled (including some who had sought refuge there from Chmielnitzki's forces and from the Thirty-Year War in Germany, see 5409/1648). Those remaining suffered under the two-year Swedish occupation,and under Stefan Czarnetzki, the Polish resistance leader (see 5416/1656, 5419/1659).

One hundred and fifty Jews of Chmielnick (Poland) were accused of helping the Swedes and were killed by the Polish resistance forces. The parents of the Siftei Chachamim, R.Shabbetai (Meshorer) Bass (see 5449/1689), were both killed by the Polish in Kalisch (Poland) (see 5419/1659).

5416 / 1655

The Jews of Mogilev (then part of Poland), who had been living under the occupying Russian forces (see 5414/1655), were massacred early in Tishrei when Polish forces approached the town to counterattack. On the 14th Tishrei, thousands of Jews were killed in Lublin where the Shach had fled (see 5415/1655). He fled once again, this time to Moravia where he became a Rabbi in Holeschau (Holesov) until his death (at the early age of 41 or 42).

R.Aharon Shmuel Kaidanover (Maharshak, author of *Birkat HaZevach*) also fled after his two young daughters were killed at Lublin. He later became Rabbi in Nikolsburg (Moravia).

Most of the Jews of Sandomierz and Tarnobrzeg (Poland) were killed, and the rest were expelled.

5416 / 1656

Jews were permitted to live in England.

Jews were permitted to live in England (see 5050/1290) under the rule of Oliver Cromwell after repeated written and personal representations by Menasheh ben Yisrael. He was a scholar from Amsterdam, whose father had escaped from Portugal after being captured as a Marrano. Menasheh (who was personally close to Rembrandt) had established a Jewish printing press, and wrote a number of works including a code of Jewish law for returning Anussim (Marranos).

Three hundred and fifty Jewish families were killed in Krotoszyn (Poland) by the Polish resistance in the war against Sweden (see 5415/1655, 5416/1655). Two hundred families were killed in Apta, 100 families in Brest Kuyavsk, 50 families in Cheshanov, 40 families in Brzeziny; and 150 Jews were killed in Checiny, all towns in Poland.

Baruch Spinoza was excommunicated.

R.Shaul Levi Morteira (see 5415/1655, 5458/1697), R.Yitzchak Abohab III (see 5402/1642, 5414/1654, 5415/1655), and other rabbis of Amsterdam placed 24-year-old Baruch Spinoza in *cherem* (excommunication) when he did not retract his views (which included questioning the authenticity of the Bible).

5417 / 1656

Three thousand Jews were killed when the Polish recaptured Lunshitz (Poland) from the Swedes (see 5416/1656), and some say that 600 Torah scrolls were burned.

5418 / 1658

Three Jews were killed in Cracow on Erev Shavu'ot (see 5415/1655).

5419 / 1659

Hundreds of Jews were killed in Kalisch (Poland) (see 5415/1655, 5468/1708) at the end of the war with Sweden. Eight Jews were killed in Przemysl (Poland) in Nissan of this year.

5420 / 1659

R.Yisrael ben Shalom and R.Tuvyah Bachrach were killed in Ruzhany (Poland) on Rosh Ha-hana in a blood libel.

Three hundred Jews were killed in Bichov (Poland-Lithuania) when the Russians captured the town in the month of Tevet (see 5415/1655, 5416/1655).

5420 / 1660

When the Shach was in Kalisch (Poland) (see 5419/1659) he met R.Avraham Abele, the Magen Avraham (see 5433/1673).

R.Ephrayim HaKohen (see 5415/1655) became Rabbi in Budapest, where he was accompanied by his son-in-law R.Yaakov Sak (see 5415/1655) and his newborn grandson, who grew up to become the Chacham Tzvi (see 5446/1686).

Living in the Year 1660		
	b.	d.
Taz (R.David ben Shmuel)	1586	1667
Shach (R.Shabbetai Kohen)	1621	1663?
Beit Shmuel (R.Shmuel)	1630?	1700?
Magen Avraham (R.Avr.Abele Gombiner)	1637?	1683
Siftei Chachamim (R.Shabbetai Bass)	1641	1718
Mishneh LeMelech (R.Yehuda Rosannes)	1657?	1727
Chacham Tzvi (R.Tzvi Ashkenazi)	1660	1718
Seder HaDorot (R.Yechi'el Heilprin)	1660?	1747?

5421 / 1661

R.Menachem Mendel Krochmal, a disciple of the Bach and author of *Tzemach Tzedek I (Sh'elot UTeshuvot)* died on the 2nd Shvat, in Nikolsburg (Moravia), where he was Rabbi of that province (see 5333/1573).

Many Jews of Persia had been forced to convert to Islam over the previous twenty years although they remained secretly Jewish. In 1661, they were allowed to openly return to Judaism.

5422 / 1662

The Jews fled Cochin (India) when the Portuguese rulers (see 5283/1523) attacked them and plundered their property, blaming them after the unsuccessful Dutch attempt to conquer the territory. The Jews returned a year later, when the Dutch had successfully conquered it (see 5385/1625).

5424 / 1663

Mattityahu Kalahora, a physician, was dismembered and burned in Cracow on the 14th Kislev (see 5516/1755), after being accused of cursing Christianity.

5424 / 1664

Many Jews were massacred in Bratslav (Poland), in a Cossack invasion. R.Mordechai and R. Shlomo (sons of the Taz) were killed, together with many other Jews, in anti-Jewish riots in Lvov (Lemberg) during the month of Iyar. The Taz died three years later.

5425 / 1665

Shabbetai Tzvi publicly proclaimed himself as the Mashiach (Messiah) while in Eretz Yisrael in the month of Sivan, with the strong support of a follower (Natan of Gaza) who claimed to be a prophet and was well versed in Kabbala.

Word of the proclamation of Shabbetai Tzvi as the "Mashiach" spread with exceptional speed and was sometimes preceded by apparently unasso-ciated rumors that the ten lost tribes were march-ing toward Eretz Yisrael. This was despite the fact that Shabbetai Tzvi had previously been banished by various rabbis from cities where he had lived (Izmir, Salonika, Istanbul) for unusual and unac-ceptable behavior, and transgression of Halacha (for which he made a blessing ". . . he who permits the forbidden").

Many stories about "miracles" he had (supposed-ly) performed were circulated, and "proofs" from Torah and Kabbala were discovered, which strengthened his acceptance.

Jews, including rabbis, from virtually every coun-try in the world were electrified with anticipation and enthusiasm; the countries included Algeria, Bohemia, Moravia, Egypt, England, Germany, Greece, Holland, Kurdistan, Morocco, Persia, Poland-Lithuania, Russia, Tripoli, Turkey, and Yemen. Many rabbis raised their voices on the issue with opinions ranging from doubt to out-right opposition, and he was banished from Yerushalayim, a fact which was apparently not publicized.

He traveled to his home town of Izmir (Turkey) where he whipped up much excitement through his charismatic speeches and feverish prayer style, which, some say, included ecstatic (and hysterical) congregational chanting of the "Shem HaMe-phorash" (the complete and Holy name) and fe-male participation in the Torah-reading ceremo-nies. The exciting atmosphere he created gained him many supporters, who rallied in masses against those who would question or disbelieve in the fulfillment of one of the principal beliefs of Judaism, the coming of the Mashiach.

It appears that, aside from those who were sub-jected to this pressure, some Rabbis who met him at times of subdued behavior found him to be a dignified scholar with a touch of nobility, and consequently considered his case seriously. It was reported that the Taz (see 5424/1664) sent his son and stepson from Poland to investigate. They were suitably impressed, and Shabbetai Tzvi sent a silk garment to honor the Taz. However, those

who witnessed his state of euphoria saw a strange (although extremely charismatic behavior, and hi flouting of Halacha (which he claimed was no longer valid). Yet it seems that some Rabbis may have been swept along by the charisma and excite ment.

He was arrested by the Turkish authorities when he traveled to Istanbul (Constantinople), but wa treated more leniently (see 5426/1666) than someone who was leading a revolt. (Eretz Yisrael over which he was to be king, was part of the Turkish-Ottoman empire at that time, see 5276/1516.)

5426 / 1666

In Nissan, a Jew from Tunis disrupted proceeding at his forced baptism in Rome by committing suicide.

Shabbetai Tzvi (see 5425/1665) managed to use his detainment in the Turkish fortress of Gallipol as if it were a royal court, receiving followers and delegations from all over; this posture while in captivity increased his stature and following. In the month of Elul, however, he was brought be fore the Sultan in Adrianople (Turkey) and wa given the choice of death or conversion to Islam He chose Islam, and some of his followers also converted (see 5443/1683).

The rest of the Jewish world remained stunned in disbelief and confused for generations. Many fol lowers persisted with interpretations of his ac tions, developing a new mystical style (pseudo Kabbala) that continued along the lines of Shabbetai Tzvi's own divergence from Kabbal (see 5437/1676).

5427 / 1667

The Jews of Podhayetz (Poland) were massacre when the Tartars invaded the town.

The Jews "performed" their annual humiliating races at the Carnival in Rome for the last time (se 5226/1466).

5428 / 1668

Some Jews were expelled from parts of Morocco.

5430 / 1670

R.Raphael Levi was burned to death at the beginning of 1670, on a blood libel charge in Metz (France).

The Jews were expelled from Austria (see 5256/1496), including Jews who had settled there after the Chmielnitzki massacres in Poland, and the last Jews left Vienna on Tisha B'Av. They were allowed to return twenty-three years later. Fifty (wealthy) families were permitted to settle in the province of Brandenburg, and some of them subsequently settled in Berlin (see 5333/1573). Among those leaving Vienna was the Rabbi, R.Gershon Ashkenazi (Olif), who then became Rabbi in Metz. He was a disciple of the Bach, of the Meginei Shlomo, and of his father-in-law, R.Menachem Mendel Krochmal (see 5421/1661); and he was author of *Avodat HaGershuni (Sh'elot JTeshuvot)* among other works.

5433 / 1673

The *Magen Avraham* (on *Shulchan Aruch*) was completed.

R.Avraham Abele HaLevi Gombiner, Rabbi in Kalisch (Poland), completed writing his major work, *Magen Avraham,* a commentary on the Orach Chayim section of the *Shulchan Aruch* (now printed in standard editions) (see Figure J, page 422). However, although he had *haskamot* (approbations), he did not succeed in having his work (Ner Yisrael) printed during his lifetime. His son later printed it as *Magen Avraham N"Y.*

R.Reuven Katz of Prague, author of the *Yalkut Re'uveni* (collected sayings on the *Chumash*) died.

R.Chaim Benveniste, author of *Knesset HaGedola* (supplements to the *Shulchan Aruch),* died on the 9th Elul in Izmir (Turkey) where he was Rabbi.

5437 / 1676

Shabbetai Tzvi died as a Muslim.

Shabbetai Tzvi, the self-proclaimed Messiah who had converted to Islam (see 5426/1666), died on Yom Kippur in Dulcigno (Albania), where he had been exiled by the Turkish authorities because of his unacceptable behavior (see 5425/1665). Some claimed to be his successor, and many of his followers continued the movement he had begun (as sects, mostly secret, called Shabbateans), for many more generations, particularly in Turkey, Italy, and Poland-Lithuania (see 5443/1683, 5478/1718, 5490/1730, 5518/1757, and 5461/1700, 5490/1730) .

5437 / 1677

Four Jews were killed in Cracow, and 1,000 died of plague (see 5440/1680) in Kazmierz (part of Cracow).

5438 / 1678

The Jews were expelled from Yemen where many synagogues had previously been demolished. They were allowed to return a year later after the general population suffered from the loss, but many communities were not re-established.

Living in the Year 1680		
	b.	d.
Beit Shmuel (R.Shmuel)	1630?	1700?
Magen Avraham (R.Avr.Abele Gombiner)	1637?	1683
Siftei Chachamim (R.Shabbetai Bass)	1641	1718
Mishneh LeMelech (R.Yehuda Rosannes)	1657?	1727
Chacham Tzvi (R.Tzvi Ashkenazi)	1660	1718
Seder HaDorot (R.Yechi'el Heilprin)	1660?	1747?
Pnei Yehoshua (R.Yaakov Yehoshua Falk)	1680	1756

5440 / 1680

More than 3,000 Jews died of plague (see 5437/1677) in Prague.

5442 / 1682

Many Jews were killed in Cracow in Adar, in anti-Jewish riots (see 5437/1677).

5443 / 1683

All the Jews of Uhersky Brod (Moravia) were killed including R.Natan Nata Hanover, who had chronicled the Chmielnitzki massacres in his book, *Yeven Metzula*. He was killed in the attack during his prayers, some say by Hungarian rebels (see 5464/1704).

Three hundred followers of Shabbetai Tzvi converted to Islam in Salonika (Greece), in emulation of their leader (see 5426/1666), and most of them (secretly) maintained their Shabbatean beliefs (as a group).

5446 / 1686

Many Jews were killed during the Austrian siege of Budapest, including the wife and baby daughter of the ChachamTzvi (see 5420/1660, 5470/1710), who had returned to Budapest after studying in Salonika (Greece) and becoming a Chacham (Sephardi Rabbi). He had also been to Belgrade and had adopted the name Ashkenazi. When the Austrian forces later captured the city, they plundered the Jewish section and burned the Torah scrolls.

5448 / 1687

Although the Jews of Posen (Poland) fought a successful three-day battle in the month of Kislev to defend themselves from anti-Jewish rioters, they suffered heavy losses.

The Jews of Vilna were attacked and their property damaged in anti-Jewish riots (see 5395/1635, 5415/1655).

5449 / 1689

The *Beit Shmuel* on the *Shulchan Aruch* was printed.

R.Shmuel ben Uri Shraga Faivish, a disciple of R.Yehoshua Heschel (see 5414/1654), was Rabbi in Szydlowiec (Poland) where he wrote *Beit Shmuel*, commentary on the *Even HaEzer* section of the *Shulchan Aruch* which is now printed in standard editions (see Figure L, page 324). It was printed two years before he became Rabbi in the prestigious community of Fuerth-Fiyorda (Germany).

The *Beit Shmuel* was the first book printed on the new printing press of the Siftei Chachamim, R.Shabbetai (Meshorer) Bass (see 5415/1655, 5472/1712), author of *Siftei Chachamim* (a commentary on Rashi) (see Figure A, page 313) and *Siftei Yesheinim* (bibliography).

R.Ya'ir Chaim Bacharach, author of *Chavat Ya'ir* (*Sh'elot UTeshuvot*), fled to Metz (France) when the French army occupied Virmyze (Worms, Germany) in 1689. He was the son of (the previous Rabbi of Virmyze) R.Moshe Shimshon (who was the son of Chava, the learned daughter of R.Yitzchak Katz, see 5409/1648). R.Ya'ir Chaim returned to Worms ten years later, to become Rabbi (three years before he died). He intended the name of his *Sh'elot UTeshuvot*, "Chaves Yo'ir," to memorialize his grandmother Chava, who herself had written comments on Torah.

R.Menachem Mendel Auerbach, a disciple of the Bach and author of *Ateret Zekeinim* (on the *Shulchan Aruch*, printed in standard versions), died on the 20th Tammuz in Krotoszyn (Poland) where he was Rabbi.

R.Yosef Shmuel of Cracow, who wrote *Hagahot HaShas* (annotations on the Talmud) and edited *Mesorat HaShas* (bibliography of the Talmud) (see Figure D, page 316), became Rabbi of Frankfurt four years before he died.

Three hundred Jewish houses and eleven synagogues were destroyed in a fire in Prague (see 5440/1680).

5450 / 1690

R.Aharon (ben Moshe) Te'omim, author of *Matteh Aharon* (commentary on the Hagada), had just become the Rabbi of Cracow (Poland), having previously been Rabbi in Virmyze (Worms, Germany). He was arrested on Shabbat, while away from Cracow (for a meeting of the *Va'ad Arba Aratzot*, see 5340/1580), and died on the 2nd Av before he reached prison. Some say he was brutally killed.

5451 / 1691

Glikl (Glueckel) of Hameln (Germany) began writing her memoirs, which give a rich description of Jewish life in Germany when her (first) husband died leaving her with twelve children.

5452 / 1692

R.Chizkiyah ben David da Silva printed his work, *Pri Chadash* (on the *Shulchan Aruch*) in Amsterdam, when he was there on a mission from Eretz Yisrael, only a few years before he died at a very early age.

5456 / 1696

The Jewish section of Brody (Russia) was destroyed by fire.

5458 / 1697

R.Moshe Zacuto, the RaMaZ (or ReMeZ), who had been a disciple of R.Shaul Levi Morteira (in Amsterdam, see 5416/1656, before he went to Poland-Lithuania to study), was outstanding in Kabbala (in which he was a disciple of the elderly R.Binyamin HaLevi, a follower of the Ari'zal). He wrote many works, and died on the second day of Sukkot 5458/1697 in Mantua (Italy), where he had been Rabbi for approximately twenty-four years (after being Rabbi in Venice for approximately twenty-eight years).

5458 / 1698

The Ba'al Shem Tov was born.

R.Yisrael ben Eliezer, the Ba'al Shem Tov (see 5494/1734), was born on the 18th Elul. Both of his parents died when he was a young child.

Living in the Year 1700	b.	d.
Beit Shmuel (R.Shmuel)	1630?	1700?
Siftei Chachamim		
(R.Shabbetai Bass)	1641	1718
Chacham Tzvi		
(R.Tzvi Ashkenazi)	1660	1718
Seder HaDorot		
(R.Yechi'el Heilprin)	1660?	1747?
Pnei Yehoshua		
(R.Yaakov Yehoshua Falk)	1680	1756
R.Yaakov Culi		
(Me'am Lo'ez)	1689?	1732
R.Yonatan Eybeshutz	1690?	1764
Sha'agat Aryeh		
(R.Aryeh Leib Gunzberg)	1695	1785
Or HaChayim		
(R.Chaim (ib)n Attar)	1696	1743
R.Yaakov Emden	1697?	1776
Ba'al Shem Tov	1698	1760
Maggid of Mezeritsch		
(R.Dov Ber)	1698?	1772

5461 / 1700

R.Yehuda Chasid (Segal), an extremely pious scholar, traveled around Europe encouraging Jews to repentance because the Mashiach (Messiah) was about to arrive. He emigrated to Eretz Yisrael with a large group of followers, but only a fraction of them reached their destination, and R.Yehuda died a few days after arriving in Yerushalayim in Cheshvan. Further problems developed, as some of the group were suspected Shabbateans (see 5437/1676) (and their leader's reputation was subsequently also questioned, see 5490/1730).

5463 / 1702

The Pnei Yehoshua's family was killed in an explosion.

R.Yaakov Yehoshua Falk (see 5478/1718), author of *Pnei Yehoshua* and a grandson of R.Yehoshua Falk (the Meginei Shlomo and Pnei Yehoshua I), was living in Lvov (Lemberg) Poland. As he describes in his *hakdama,* he was teaching his disciples on the 3rd Kislev when a gunpowder storehouse exploded. Thirty-six Jews were killed, including his wife, daughter, and mother-in-law, but he survived although he had been buried under the rubble.

5464 / 1703

The Jews of Belaya Tzerkov (then Poland) were attacked at the start of the Haidamack massacres (see 5496/1736).

5464 / 1704

Many Jews were killed and many more were displaced (see 5443/1683, 5474/1714), during the (unsuccessful) Hungarian revolution at this time. The Jews of Krotoszyn (Poland) were attacked and their property looted in anti-Jewish riots.

5466 / 1706

Forty-five Jews were killed in a fire in Kalisch (Poland) (see 5468/1708).

The Jews of Lissa (Poland) were attacked and plundered by invading Russian soldiers, and the whole Jewish section of the town was burned (see 5469/1709).

5468 / 1708

Four hundred fifty Jews died in a plague in Kalisch (Poland) (see 5419/1659, 5466/1706).

A fire destroyed the Jewish section of Vitebsk (then Poland).

5469 / 1709

The Jews of Lissa (Poland) (see 5466/1706) were accused of spreading plague and were expelled. They were allowed to return when the plague was over.

5470 / 1710

The Jews were expelled from Groningen (Netherlands).

R.Tzvi Ashkenazi, the Chacham Tzvi, had spent eighteen years as a Rosh Yeshiva in Altona (Hamburg, Germany), until he succeeded R.Meshulam Zalman, the father of his second wife (see 5446/1686), as Rabbi there. However, he returned to his studies after a short while because of a Halacha dispute with another rabbi, and in 1710 he became the rabbi of the relatively new Ashkenazi community in Amsterdam (see 5478/1718).

Adel (the daughter of Moshe Kikinish of Lvov [Lemberg], Poland)–a wealthy descendant of Yona HaNavi), was killed on the 26th Elul, when she confessed to a blood libel to save the lives of other Jews.

5471 / 1711

R.Yechi'el Heilprin, the author of *Seder HaDorot,* a biographical, chronological history, was Rabbi

216

in Minsk (then Poland) until he died some thirty-six years later.

A fire broke out in the house of R.Naftali Katz, the Rabbi of Frankfurt, which destroyed the whole Jewish section. R.Naftali, a great scholar (especially in Kabbala), was maliciously maligned; some accused him of preventing the flames from being extinguished so that he could test his *Kameyot* (amulets) for fire extinguishing. Although he was cleared of any charges, he was compelled to leave Frankfurt.

5472 / 1712

The Siftei Chachamim was arrested.

R.Shabbetai (Meshorer) Bass, the author of *Siftei Chachamim* (see 5449/1689), was arrested on the charge that his press in Dyhernfurth (Silesia) was printing books that were spreading hatred against Christians. He was later released.

R.Eliyahu Shapiro of Prague (see 5514/1754), a disciple of the Magen Avraham, and a brother-in-law of the Chok Yaakov (see 5494/1733), was author of *Eliyahu Rabba* and *Zuta* (Halacha, on the *Levushim*). He died on the 8th Nissan.

5474 / 1713

R.Yoel Ba'al Shem (ben Yitzchak Halpern), a grandson of R.Yoel (also a Ba'al Shem), and author of *Toldot Adam* (Kabbala), died on the 4th Tishrei.

5474 / 1714

R.Meir Eisenstadt, known as the Maharam Esh (or Ash)–an abbreviation of Eisenstadt, became Rabbi in Eisenstadt, which had just recovered from the Hungarian revolution (see 5464/1704). He wrote *Panim Me'irot* (*Chidushim* and *Sh'elot Uteshuvot*).

5475 / 1715

Eight hundred ninety-two Jews died in a plague in Boskowitz (Moravia).

5476 / 1716

The Jews of Posen (Poland) were attacked, a few years after an epidemic (of ergot disease) had decimated the community. Many Jews subsequently left the town (see 5496/1736).

5478 / 1718

The Chacham Tzvi left Amsterdam after four years (see 5470/1710), due to a controversy (involving differences with the older Portuguese Sephardi congregation) following his *cherem* (excommunication) of a prominent Shabbatean (see 5437/1676). He had traveled to England, Germany, and Poland, before becoming Rabbi in Lvov (Lemberg) Poland shortly before he died, on Rosh Chodesh Iyar 1718. He was succeeded by the Pnei Yehoshua (see 5490/1730), who had previously left Lvov after losing his family (see 5463/1702), and had since then been the Rabbi in a number of towns.

5479 / 1719

The whole Jewish section of Nikolsburg (Moravia) was completely destroyed by fire. Shimshon Wertheimer, an extremely wealthy *shtadlan* from Vienna (who was a scholar, and supported other scholars in addition to his many activities on behalf of Jews throughout Europe), organized the raising of funds to rebuild the community.

5480 / 1720

The Jews of Budapest were attacked and their homes plundered.

Living in the Year 1720

	b.	d.
Mishneh LeMelech		
(R.Yehuda Rosannes)	1657?	1727
Seder HaDorot		
(R.Yechi'el Heilprin)	1660?	1747?
Pnei Yehoshua		
(R.Yaakov Yehoshua Falk)	1680	1756
R.Yaakov Culi		
(Me'am Lo'ez)	1689?	1732
R.Yonatan Eybeshutz	1690?	1764
Sha'agat Aryet		
(R.Aryeh Leib Gunzberg)	1695?	1785
Or HaChayim		
(R.Chaim (ib)n Attar)	1696	1743
R.Yaakov Emden	1697?	1776
Ba'al Shem Tov	1698	1760
Maggid of Mezeritsch		
(R.Dov Ber)	1698?	1772
Ramchal (Luzzatto)	1707	1747
Korban HaEida		
(R.David Frankel)	1707	1762
Pnei Moshe		
(R.Moshe Margolid)	1710?	1781
Noda BiYehuda		
(R.Yechezk'el Landau)	1713	1793
R.Elimelech of Lizensk	1717?	1786
R.Zushya of Annopol	1718?	1800
Vilna Gaon	1720	1797

5481 / 1720

Arabs broke into the Ashkenazi synagogue in Yerushalayim, which had been built in honor of R.Yehuda Chasid (see 5461/1700) and burned the Torah scrolls on 8th Cheshvan. The Ashkenazi Jews had to flee (they could not return), and the synagogue remained in disrepair for many years (see 5597/1837), thus attracting the name Churvat R.Yehuda Chasid.

5483 / 1723

R.Yeshayahu (ben Avraham) HaLevi, grandson of the Taz and author of the first *Ba'er Heitev* (1) a summary of commentaries on the *Orach Chayim* section of *Shulchan Aruch,* was burned to death (see 5424/1664) with his wife and daughter in a fire in Mogilev (then Poland), on their way to Eretz Yisrael.

R.Yehuda ben Shimon of Tiktin (Poland) wrote *Ba'er Heitev* (2) (a commentary on all sections of the *Shulchan Aruch*). However, only his *Ba'er Heitev* on the *Orach Chayim* and *Even HaEzer* sections are now printed in standard editions of the *Shulchan Aruch* (see Figures J, K, L, M, pages 322–325).

R.Zecharyah Mendel, of Belz (Poland), also wrote a *Ba'er Heitev* (3) (summary of commentaries) which is printed (in standard editions of the *Shulchan Aruch*) on the sections of *Yoreh Deya* and *Choshen Mishpat* (see Figures K, M, pages 323, 325).

R.Moshe (ben Shimon) Frankfurter, also wrote a *Ba'er Heitev* (4) (summary of commentaries) on the *Choshen Mishpat* section of *Shulchan Aruch*.

5484 / 1724

R.Yaakov Culi (Me'am Lo'ez) arrived in Istanbul (Constantinople).

R.Yaakov Culi came to Istanbul (Constantinople) to print the works of a his grandfather (R.Moshe ibn Chaviv), and there he became a disciple of R.Yehuda Rosannes. He later edited the *Mishneh LeMelech* (after R.Yehuda died, see 5487/1727) and wrote *Me'am Lo'ez* (extensive basic commentary and homily) on *Bereshit* and *Shmot* (*Chumash,* Bible) in Ladino (a Judeo-Spanish language, similar in concept to Yiddish). After he died (at an early age), further volumes of the *Me'am Lo'ez* were written by others, who continued his work (partly from manuscript he had left). This popular work played an important role in the Torah re-orientation of the Sephardi Jews, after the confusion left by Shabbetai Tzvi (see 5426/1666, 5437/1676, 5494/1734).

5486 / 1726

The Jews were attacked in Jassy (Moldavia) after a blood libel, and the synagogues were desecrated.

5487 / 1727

The Mishneh LeMelech died.

R.Yehuda Rosannes of Istanbul (Constantinople), author of the *Mishneh LeMelech* (commentary on the Rambam's *Yad HaChazaka*) (see Figures H, I, pages 320, 321) (see 5484/1724), died on the 22nd Nissan which was Acharon Shel Pesach (the last day of Pesach).

5488 / 1728

Two brothers, a rabbi, R.Chaim, and R.Yehoshua Reitzes, a Rosh Yeshiva, were tortured and then burned in Lvov (Lemberg) Poland on Erev Shavu'ot. Some say R.Yehoshua took his own life in prison, and that his body was mutilated and burned. The charge against them was that they had attempted to convince a *meshumad* (apostate) to return to Judaism, and that they had "profaned Christian symbols."

5490 / 1730

The Pnei Yehoshua (see 5478/1718, 5494/1733) had left Lvov (Lemberg) Poland because of a controversy over his public *cherem* (excommunication) of the Shabbateans (see 5437/1676, 5478/1718), and he had not settled elsewhere until he became Rabbi in Berlin in 1730 (see 5430/1670).

R.Moshe Chaim Luzzatto, the Ramchal (see 5507/1747) of Italy, a brilliant young scholar, was suspected of being influenced by the Shabbateans because of his personal mystical style and his Kabbala writings (which he subsequently undertook to cease). He later left Italy and settled in Amsterdam for a while (see 5507/1747).

The Kabbala, and its transference through the generations (see 5050/1290), is not as strictly defined as the Talmud and Halacha, and does not have the same clear structure. It can be possible for "analysts" to assume that the origins of some works were Shabbatean, when they may have been from other (discreet) sources. It is also possible, within the unstructured nature of transference of the Kabbala tradition, that some scholars may (mistakenly) accept the authenticity of Kabbala works which were in fact influenced by Shabbetai Tzvi's divergence from Kabbala (see 5426/1666).

5494 / 1733

R.Yaakov Reisher, author of *Shvut Yaakov, Minchat Yaakov,* and *Chok Yaakov* (Halacha), died on the 10th Tevet 5494/1733. A year later he was succeeded as Rabbi of Metz (France) by the Pnei Yehoshua (see 5490/1730), who was remarried (see 5463/1702) to a scholarly woman.

R.Alexander Sender (ben Ephrayim Zalman) Schorr published *Simla Chadasha* (Halacha of Shechita) with his own commentary, called *Tevu'ot Shor,* four years before he died.

5494 / 1734

Jews were massacred by the Haidamack bands.

Twenty-seven Jews were massacred in Korsun (Poland) by the roaming Haidamack bands (see 5464/1703, 5496/1736).

For a number of years, the Ba'al Shem Tov had kept company with the itinerant "Tzadikim Nistarim" (see 5546/1786) (who secretly worked to alleviate the massive economic and spiritual plight of the Jews in and around Poland-Lithuania, after the Chmielnitzki massacres and the confusion left by Shabbetai Tzvi, see 5408/1648, 5426/1666,

5437/1676). The Ba'al Shem Tov became a leader in their clandestine society and began teaching his concepts of Chasidut publicly in 1734, at the age of 36.

5496 / 1736

The Haidamacks, roving bands of armed peasants and their assorted colleagues, attacked travelers and the smaller towns (see 5464/1703, 5494/1734, 5528/1768), in Polish Ukraine. In 1736 they massacred thirty-five Jews in Pavoloch, and fourteen Jews in Pogrebishche.

Many Jews were imprisoned and tortured in a blood libel in Posen (Poland), and the community deteriorated further (see 5476/1716, 5516/1755).

5497 / 1737

Some Jews were tortured and killed in a blood libel in Yaroslav (Poland).

5498 / 1738

Baruch Leibov and a Russian naval officer (Alexander Vosnitsyn), whom he had introduced to Judaism, were both tortured and burned at the stake in St. Petersburg.

5500 / 1740

The *Zohar* (see 5050/1290) had predicted [Zoh. 1.117a] that the "gates of wisdom" would be opened in the "sixth hundred year of the sixth (thousand)," or 5500. This coincides with the increased development of the new sciences and technologies of the Industrial Revolution, which ushered in a new era in the history of mankind.

Living in the Year 1740		
	b.	d.
Seder HaDorot		
(R.Yechi'el Heilprin)	1660?	1747?
Pnei Yehoshua		
(R.Yaakov Yehoshua Falk)	1680	1756
R.Yonatan Eybeshutz	1690?	1764
Sha'agat Aryeh		
(R.Aryeh Leib Gunzberg)	1695?	1785
Or HaChayim		
(R.Chaim (ib)n Attar)	1696	1743
R.Yaakov Emden	1697?	1776
Ba'al Shem Tov	1698	1760
Maggid of Mezeritsch		
(R.Dov Ber)	1698?	1772
Ramchal (Luzzatto)	1707	1747
Korban HaEida		
(R.David Frankel)	1707	1762
Pnei Moshe		
(R.Moshe Margolis)	1710?	1781
Noda BiYehuda		
(R.Yechezk'el Landau)	1713	1793
R.Elimelech of Lizensk	1717?	1786
R.Zushya of Annopol	1718?	1800
Vilna Gaon	1720	1797
Chida (Azulai)	1724	1806
Pri Megadim		
(R.Yosef Te'omim)	1727?	1792
R.Levi Yitzchak		
of Berditchev	1740	1810

5501 / 1741

The Or HaChayim arrived in Eretz Yisrael.

R.Chaim (ib)n Attar, author of *Or HaChayim,* commentary on *Chumash* (Bible) (see Figure A, page 313) and other works, left his birthplace Morocco, because of persecutions and famine. He traveled via Algiers to Italy, where he sought to publish his works. His popular reception there inspired him to seek (financial) support for his proposed yeshiva in Yerushalayim (some disciples had followed him). After more than a year in Italy, he sailed (with 30 people) to Eretz Yisrael, arriving in 1741. He stayed in Acco for a year, because of a plague (see 5507/1747) in Yerushalayim, where he finally arrived and lived for one year before his death at 47.

R.Yonatan Eybeshutz (see 5510/1750), an orphan who was raised by the Maharam Esh, was the author of *Creti UPeleti* and *Urim VeTumim* (pilpul – fine and sharp distinctions – on Halacha). He was appointed Rabbi in Metz (France) in 1741, when the Pnei Yehoshua left (see 5494/1733, 5514/1754). The French army had attacked Prague (see 5505/1745) before R.Yonatan had a chance to leave, but they permitted him to leave for Metz. The (defending) Austrian government confiscated his belongings for this "treason."

5502 / 1742

The Jews were expelled from most of what was then Russia (see 5532/ 1772).

5503 / 1743

R.David Frankel (Mirels), author of *Korban Ha-Eida* (commentary on Talmud Yerushalmi, now printed in standard editions) (see Figure E, page 317) was appointed Rabbi of Berlin.

5505 / 1745

Some Jews were massacred in Roudnice (Bohemia). The Jews were expelled from Prague (see 5501/1741) in a decree issued in 1744 by Maria Theresa, empress of Austria (see 5506/1746, 5534/1774). They were allowed to return three years later.

R.Shneur Zalman (see 5530/1770), the son of R.Baruch (a direct descendant of the Maharal of

Prague), was born on the 18th Elul (see 5369/1609, 5458/1698). His mother, Rivka, was a scholarly woman who held daily *shi'urim* (study sessions).

5506 / 1746

The Jews were expelled (by Empress Maria Theresa, see 5505/1745) from Buda (Budapest).

5507 / 1747

R. Moshe Chaim Luzzatto (Ramchal) died in Acco (Acre).

R.Moshe Chaim Luzzatto (see 5490/1730), author of *Mesilat Yesharim* (Mussar), left Amsterdam and settled in Eretz Yisrael, where he died four years later in a plague (see 5501/1741) in Acco (Acre) on the 26th Iyar. Many Jews in Tzfat (Safed) also died of a plague (see 5520/1759).

Five Jews were killed in a blood libel in Izyaslav (Poland).

R.Avraham Gershon of Kitev (Poland), a Torah scholar (who was respected by R.Yonatan Eybeshutz and the Noda BiYehuda), left Europe to settle in Eretz Yisrael at the request of his brother-in-law, the Ba'al Shem Tov, whose follower he was.

5509 / 1749

The Jews of Breslau (Silesia), who had recently returned (see 5213/1453), were killed in riots that followed the explosion of a gunpowder storehouse.

5510 / 1750

R.Yonatan Eybeshutz became Rabbi in Hamburg.

R.Yonatan Eybeshutz (see 5501/1741) became Rabbi in the combined communities of Hamburg Altona and Wandsbek, where R. Yaakov Emden, the son of the Chacham Tzvi (see 5470/1710), was living (after having been Rabbi in Emden,

Germany, for a few years). When R.Yonatan arrived, there was an "epidemic" in which many women died at childbirth, and the community turned to the new Rabbi who was renowned for his expertise in (practical) Kabbala. R.Yonatan wrote *Kameyot* (amulets), which were later opened, and interpreted by R.Yaakov Emden to be of Shabbatean content (see 5490/1730).

Although R.Yonatan had been a participant in a *cherem* (excommunication) of the Shabbateans (see 5437/1676) in Prague in 1725, and restated his position regarding them; nevertheless, a prolonged and widespread (see 5514/1753, 5514/1754) controversy ensued (which also extended outside the Jewish communities). R.Yaakov Emden (see 5536/1776) maintained his accusations (from Amsterdam, after he had to leave Hamburg), and R. Yonatan presented explanations for his *Kameyot*.

5513 / 1753

Eleven Jews were (skinned alive and) killed, and thirteen were forced to convert to Christianity in a blood libel in Zhitomir (then Poland).

5514 / 1753

R.Yonatan Eybeshutz was cleared of suspicion (see 5510/1750) by the scholars of the *Va'ad Arba Aratzot* in Yaroslav, on the 3rd Cheshvan.

5514 / 1754

R.Yechezk'el Landau (Noda BiYehuda) became Rabbi in Prague.

R.Yechezk'el Landau was author of *Noda BiYehuda* (*Sh'elot UTeshuvot*) and other works. He became Rabbi of Prague (see 5505/1745) and all of Bohemia two years after his proclamation of mediation allowing both sides in the Emden–Eybeshutz controversy a dignified retreat (see 5510/1750). The Noda BiYehuda was not kind in his (later) statements about the Chasidim.

The Pnei Yehoshua (see 5501/1741) had left Metz (France), and then been Rabbi in Frankfurt am Main for ten years. He left there after becoming involved in the Emden–Eybeshutz controversy (see 5510/1750) in favor of R.Yaakov Emden (see 5490/1730). He was living in Virmyze (Worms, Germany) when the Chida (see 5566/1806) visited him while on his travels as an emissary for Eretz Yisrael, (somewhat over a year) before the Pnei Yehoshua died.

Most of the Jewish section of Prague was destroyed by a fire (in which many writings of R.Eliyahu Shapiro, see 5472/1712, were burned).

5515 / 1755

Hertzl Levi was killed in Colmar (Alsace) after a (libel) trial.

5516 / 1755

R.Aryeh Leib ben Yosef Kalahora, the *Darshan* (preacher) was killed (see 5424/1663) on the 18th Kislev, only a few weeks after Yaakov ben Pinchas (a community trustee) and Wolf Winkler were killed in a blood libel in Posen (Poland) (see 5496/1736).

5517 / 1756

R.Yitzchak (Chizkiyah) Lampronti, author of the monumental Talmudic encyclopedia *Pachad Yitzchak,* died in the month of Cheshvan (at 78) in Ferrara (Italy), where he had served as Rabbi, Rosh Yeshiva, and doctor. His burial place is unknown, because the Inquisition (see 5012/1252) had forbidden Jews to erect tombstones.

5518 / 1757

The Frankists instigated mass burnings of the Talmud.

Jacob Frank, who had spent many years in Turkey with members of Shabbatean sects (see 5437/

1676), had returned to Poland (where, some say, he was called "frenk" for his acquired Sephardi style, and therefore subsequently adopted the name "Frank"). He became a leader (see 5519/-1759) among the mostly secret Shabbatean followers in Europe, and began to encourage them to express their beliefs openly. A *cherem* (excommunication) was proclaimed in Brody (then Russia), against the now identifiable Shabbatean followers of Frank (who were later called *Frankists*). The *cherem* included a ban against the study of Kabbala for anyone under the age of 40.

The Frankists had begun developing close relations with the bishop of Kaminetz-Podolski (then Poland), who subsequently organized a debate in his city between the Shabbatean Frankists and leaders of the traditional Jews. At the debate, the Frankists degraded the Talmud, and as a result the bishop declared that all copies were to be confiscated and burned (see 5314/1553). A mass burning took place in Kaminetz-Podolski in Kislev-Cheshvan 5518/1757 (and the bishop died at this time , a miracle attributed to the Ba'al Shem Tov). Jewish books were also burned in other towns in Poland and Russia, including Lvov (Lemberg) and Brody.

5519 / 1759

Frankists supported blood libel charges in public debate.

Jacob Frank (see 5518/1757) had drawn his Shabbatean followers closer to Christianity. After the debate of 1757 he was involved with Christians in organizing another debate with the traditional Jews, in which he and his followers were to prove (among other things) that Jews did use non-Jewish blood for ritual purposes. It was also understood that, after the debate, he and his followers would participate in a mass conversion to Christianity (although they secretly intended to retain their Shabbatean beliefs, see 5443/1683).

R. Chaim HaKohen Rappaport, the distinguished Rabbi of Lvov (Lemberg), Poland (and a secret follower of the Ba'al Shem Tov), was the leading spokesman for the traditional Jews; (some say the Ba'al Shem Tov was not among those present) in the highly charged (but inconclusive) debate that took place in 1759 in Lvov (Lemberg).

There were no resultant burnings of the Talmud (see 5518/1757), but Jacob Frank led many of his followers (some say thousands) to baptism after the debate (he himself was baptized again, later). However, many of his followers did not convert, yet remained devoted to him without following his (stated) "path through the religions, to a world higher than any religious order." Frank was arrested a short while later because of Christian suspicions about his ("heretic" personal Messianic) ambitions and intentions, and because of the scandalous nature of some of the pseudo-religious orgies that the Shabbateans indulged in. He remained imprisoned in the fortress at Czestochowa (Poland) for thirteen years (see 5532/1772).

5520 / 1759

Two hundred Jews died in an earthquake in Tzfat (Safed) in the month of Cheshvan, and most of the survivors began leaving the town (see 5507/1747, 5597/1837).

5520 / 1760

The Ba'al Shem Tov (Besht) died.

The Ba'al Shem Tov (Besht) (see 5494/1734), the founder of the movement of Chasidim, died on Wednesday, the first day of *Shavu'ot*. He had attracted thousands of followers (some of them secret, see 5494/1734, 5519/1759, 5543/1783), called *Chasidim,* to his joyous "new" expression of Judaism (based in Kabbala), in which the "quality" of spiritual dedication in the heart was considered as important as the "quantity" of intellectual (Torah) information in the mind, and in which the ability to feel close to the Creator (love) became as important as the need to stand distant (fear, respect). He also stressed the need to love all fellow Jews (Ahavat Yisrael), regardless of status and background.

A veritable literature of stories, tales, and legends has evolved about his miraculous healing of both bodies and souls, and about rescues and other wondrous accomplishments.

This personal charismatic centrality in the role of "Tzadik," or Rebbe, was one of the contributing factors to the serious suspicions that this new movement was yet another group of Shabbatei Tzvi'niks (Shabbateans) (see 5437/1676, 5518/1757, and the *Va'ad Arba Aratzot* threatened to make a cherem (excommunication).

The other contributing factor to this suspicion was the "new" emotional and expressive style of Chasidim in prayer, mitzvot, and life in general, a style accompanied by the (spiritual) desire to be unobtrusive and often secretive in the fulfillment of good deeds, thus removing many of the finer aspects of the movement from the eye of casual observation.

Chasidim became known by many as 'the sect' (HaCat), particularly in the circles of the scholars, whose suspicions were intensified because of the Ba'al Shem Tov's "people orientation" (even the unlearned could participate in the dedication of the heart, and were in fact encouraged to do so, with Ahavat Yisrael). This stood in stark contrast to their own 'subject orientation' (with an elitist emphasis on accumulated knowledge and intellectual skills). These suspicions (see 5532/1772), and their often harsh social consequences, increased the incidence of secret followers of the new movement, a fact which probably further increased the suspicion.

The Ba'al Shem Tov, who lived in Medzibuzh (then Poland), had begun a mass re-orientation among the Jews of Poland and Eastern Europe who had not recovered (economically or spiritually, see 5494/1734) from the decimation of the Chmielnitzki massacres (see 5408/1648), and from the confusion left in the wake of Shabbatei Tzvi (see 5426/1666, 5484/1724, 5518/1757).

R.Dov Ber (see 5533/1772), the Maggid of Mezeritsch (Poland), succeeded the Ba'al Shem Tov as the leader of the movement. However, some of the other major disciples (see 5507/1747, 5524/

1764), including R.Pinchas of Koretz, R.Yechi'el Michel of Zlotchov, and R. Yaakov Yosef of Polonnoye (Poland), author of *Toldot Yaakov Yosef* (see 5541/1781), had many followers (chasidim) of their own.

The Jews were expelled from the region of Courland (Latvia).

Living in the Year 1760		
	b.	d.
R.Yonatan Eybeshutz	1690?	1764
Sha'agat Aryeh		
(R.Aryeh Leib Gunzberg)	1695?	1785
R.Yaakov Emden	1697?	1776
Ba'al Shem Tov	1698	1760
Maggid of Mezeritsch		
(R.Dov Ber)	1698?	1772
Korban HaEida		
(R.David Frankel)	1707	1762
Pnei Moshe		
(R.Moshe Margolis)	1710?	1781
Noda BiYehuda		
(R.Yechezk'el Landau)	1713	1793
R.Elimelech of Lizensk	1717?	1786
R.Zushya of Annopol	1718?	1800
Vilna Gaon	1720	1797
Chida (Azulai)	1724	1806
Pri Megadim		
(R.Yosef Te'omim)	1727?	1792
R.Levi Yitzchak		
of Berditchev	1740	1810
R.Shneur Zalman		
(Rav of Lyady)	1745	1813
Ketzot HaChoshen		
(R.Aryeh Leib Heller)	1745?	1813
Chozeh of Lublin	1745?	1815
Chayei Adam		
(R.Avraham Danziger)	1748	1820
R.Chaim Volozhiner	1749	1821
Yismach Moshe		
(R.Moshe Teitelbaum)	1759	1841
Chavat Da'at		
(R.Yakv. of Lissa/Netivot)	1759?	1832
R.Ephrayim Zalman Margolis	1760	1828

5522 / 1761

Many Jews were killed in Mogilev-Podolski (then Poland) and some Jews of Wojslawice (Poland) were killed in a blood libel supported by the Frankists (see 5519/1759).

5522 / 1762

The Jews of Emden (Germany) were attacked in anti-Jewish riots in the month of Sivan.

5523 / ˙1763

Four Jews were killed in Kalisch (Poland) in a blood libel.

5524 / 1764

The *Va'ad Arba Aratzot* was discontinued.

The *Va'ad Arba Aratzot* (see 5340/1580) was dissolved by the government of Poland, which sought to end Jewish autonomy and devised another method of collecting Jewish taxes.

R.Yonatan Eybeshutz (see 5501/1741) died on the 21st Elul, and R.Yitzchak Horowitz was appointed Rabbi in Hamburg (with the approval of R.Yaakov Emden). R.Yitzchak, known as "Reb Itzikel MeHamburg," eventually managed to restore dignity to both sides in the Emden–Eybeshutz controversy (see 5510/1750).

R.Nachman of Horodenka (Poland) settled in Eretz Yisrael (see 5507/1747) together with some other disciples of the Ba'al Shem Tov.

5527 / 1767

Twenty Jews were killed when a fire destroyed the whole Jewish section of Lissa (Poland).

R.Malachi (ben Yaakov) HaKohen published *Yad Malachi* (principles and methods of Talmud and Halacha study).

5528 / 1768

The Haidamacks massacred thousands of Jews.

The Haidamacks (see 5496/1736) brutally killed many Jews in the Polish-Ukrainian towns of Fastov, Lysyanka, Zhabotin, Kanyev, Tetiyev, Korsun (see 5494/1734), and Balta (where some had come to seek refuge). Many fled to the fortified city of Uman (then Poland), where, on the 5th Tammuz, many Jews fought the attackers until they were overwhelmed. Thousands of Jews in Uman were massacred in the synagogues, which were subsequently burned together with the desecrated Torah scrolls.

5529 / 1769

R.Netanel Weil of Prague, descendant of the Mahariv, and author of *Korban Netanel* (on the Rosh), died in Karlsruhe (Germany) where he was succeeded by his son as Rabbi.

5530 / 1770

R.Yechi'el Hillel Altshuler completed and printed his father's commentaries on the *T'nach* (Bible), *Metzudat David* and *Metzudat Tzion*.

R.Shneur Zalman (see 5532/1772, 5559/1798), a disciple of the Maggid of Mezeritsch, had been appointed Maggid in 1767 in his hometown of Liozhna (then Poland-Lithuania). Three years later he began to write an edition of the *Shulchan Aruch* (based on the original) that includes all the important opinions on Halacha since the *Shulchan Aruch* of R.Yosef Karo and the Ramo, in one synthesized

(descriptive) text, later commonly called *Shulchan Aruch HaRav*. This task was assigned to him by the Maggid of Mezeritsch, who treated him as one of his favored disciples (even though he was probably the youngest).

Eight hundred Jews died in a plague in Zholkva (Poland).

5532 / 1772

A public debate was held in Shklov (then Poland-Lithuania) on the "movement of Chasidim" (see 5520/1760), by their opponents (called *Mitnagdim*). The Chasidim were represented by two disciples of the Maggid of Mezeritsch, R.Shneur Zalman (see 5530/1770), the Ba'al HaTanya VeShulchan Aruch, and R.Avraham of Kalisk (who, some say, was a former disciple of the Vilna Gaon).

Although the Chasidim demonstrated that they were great scholars, and that they were not diverging from Halacha (as had the Shabbateans, to whom they had been compared, see 5520/1760) the questioners concentrated on the issue of some of the excesses of R.Avraham's disciples (which included public levity in the disparaging of intellectual elitists, see 5520/1760).

The meeting did not end with a peaceful result and in the month of Nissan, a *cherem* (excommunication) was proclaimed by the Bet Din in Vilna (and included the signature of the Vilna Gaon) against the Chasidim (see 5541/1781). Letters (of the cherem) were circulated to many communities, which resulted in harsh persecutions of Chasidim. (The Chasidim were the subject of many *ch'ramim* [excommunications] in many locations, over an extended time, and they sometimes reciprocated in kind.)

R.Shneur Zalman, and R.Menachem Mendel of Vitebsk (Poland-Lithuania), the disciples of the Maggid of Mezeritsch who had many followers.

in the regions of Lithuania, later (unsuccessfully) attempted to meet the Vilna Gaon to explain the direction of the new movement (he left town until they had departed).

In 1772, Austria, Prussia, and Russia all partitioned large sections of Polish territory, and incorporated these sections into their own empires. The Russians freed Jacob Frank (see 5519/1759) from prison, which was in the territory they had annexed, and the Austrian (Hapsburg) Empire now contained the largest Jewish population in Europe.

5533 / 1772

The Maggid of Mezeritsch died.

The Mezeritscher Maggid, R.Dov Ber (the Rebbe R.Ber), the disciple and successor of the Ba'al Shem Tov (see 5520/1760) (who, some say, was previously a disciple of the Pnei Yehoshua), died on the 19th Kislev.

His major disciples had included: (see 5537/1777) his son R.Avraham; R.Aharon of Karlin (then Poland-Lithuania), who had died a half year earlier at 35); R.Elimelech (see 5546/1786) of Lizensk (Poland) and his brother R.Zushya of Annopol (Poland); R.Yisrael (the Maggid) of Kozhnitz (see 5575/1814); R.Levi Yitzchak (see 5570/1809) of Berditchev (Poland); R.Menachem Mendel of Horodok (see 5537/1777) and Vitebsk (then Poland-Lithuania); R.Pinchas Horowitz of Frankfurt (see 5542/1782) and his (older) brother R. Shmuel Shmelke of Nikolsburg (Moravia); R. Shlomo of Karlin (see 5552/1792); R.Nachum (see 5558/1797) of Chernobyl (then Poland); and R.Shneur Zalman (see 5559/1798) of Liozhna and Lyady (then Poland-Lithuania). Most of them were leaders in their own towns and regions, where they developed their own followings.

5533 / 1773

R.Meir (ben Yosef) Te'omim died in Lvov–Lemberg (then Austrian Poland); his son, R.Yosef,

author of the *Pri Megadim,* came from Berlin to succeed him, until he left for Frankfurt an der Oder some eight years later.

Some followers of Jacob Frank (see 5532/1772) converted to Christianity in Prossnitz (Moravia).

5534 / 1774

The Jews were expelled from Hodonin (Moravia) by Maria Theresa of the Austro-Hungarian Empire (see 5505/1745).

5536 / 1776

R.Yaakov Emden (see 5510/1750) (Yavetz– Yaakov ben Tzvi), author of *She'ilat Yavetz (Sh'elot UTeshuvot)* and *Siddur Yavetz* (with commentary), among other works, died on Rosh Chodesh Iyar.

Many Jewish people (who were in favor of the American Revolution) fled from New York during the British occupation of that city.

5537 / 1777

R.Menachem Mendel of Vitebsk (Poland-Lithuania) led a group of more than 300 Chasidim (including R.Avraham of Kalisk, see 5532/1772), to settle in Eretz Yisrael.

R.Shalom Shar'abi, a Rabbi and Rosh Yeshiva renowned for his knowledge and experience in Kabbala, died in Yerushalayim.

5538 / 1778

The Jews were expelled from Kitzingen (Germany).

Living in the Year 1780		
	b.	d.
Sha'agat Aryeh		
(R.Aryeh Leib Gunzberg)	1695?	1785
Pnei Moshe		
(R.Moshe Margolis)	1710?	1781
Noda BiYehuda		
(R.Yechezk'el Landau)	1713	1793
R.Elimelech of Lizensk	1717?	1786
R.Zushya of Annopol	1718?	1800
Vilna Gaon	1720	1797
Chida (Azulai)	1724	1806
Pri Megadim		
(R.Yosef Te'omim)	1727?	1792
R.Levi Yitzchak		
of Berditchev	1740	1810
R.Shneur Zalman		
Rav of Lyady)	1745	1813
Ketzot HaChoshen		
(R.Aryeh Leib Heller)	1745?	1813
Chozeh of Lublin	1745?	1815
Chayei Adam		
(R.Avraham Danziger)	1748	1820
R.Chaim Volozhiner	1749	1821
Yismach Moshe		
(R.Moshe Teitelbaum)	1759	1841
Chavat Da'at		
(R.Yakv. of Lissa/Netivot)	1759?	1832
R.Ephrayim		
Zalman Margolis	1760	1828
R.Akiva Eger	1761	1837
Chassam Sofer	1762	1839
R.Nachman of Bratslav	1772	1811

5540 / 1780

R.Elchanan (ben Shmuel) Ashkenazi, author of
Sidrei Tahara, and Rabbi in Shottland, a suburb of
Danzig (Gdansk), Poland, died there in the month
of Elul.

5541 / 1781

R.Moshe (ben Shimon) Margolis, author of *Pnei
Moshe* (commentary on Talmud Yerushalmi, now

printed in standard editions) (see Figure E, page
317), died in Brody (then Austria) while traveling
in search of the means to continue printing his
work.

The Kalliver Rebbe, Adm.R.Yitzchak Aisik
(Taub), a disciple of R.Shmelke of Nikolsburg and
R.Elimelech of Lizensk, became Rabbi in Kalliv
(Hungary) where he lived for forty years.

A new *cherem* (excommunication) was proclaimed
in Vilna against the Chasidim (see 5532/1772)
(which again included the signature of the Vilna
Gaon), and as a result, the book *Toldot Yaakov Yosef*
(see 5520/1760) was publicly burned. (It was the
first book published by Chasidim, and a probably
objective contemporary Sephardi observer, the
Chida, praised it.) The *cherem* brought further per
secutions of Chasidim, and some of the leaders
had to leave their towns. R.Yechi'el Michel of
Zlotchov left Brody, R.Shlomo left Karlin (then
Russia), and R.Levi Yitzchak of Berditchev left his
position as Rabbi in Pinsk (Russia).

5542 / 1782

**R.Natan Adler and the Chassam Sofer visited
the Noda BiYehuda.**

R.Natan Adler (HaKohen) left Frankfurt, where
he had been a Rosh Yeshiva, to become Rabbi in
Boskowitz (Moravia) after a controversy with the
"official" congregation (including Rabbi R.Pinchas
Horowitz, see 5543/1783). The controversy was
a result of his separate (private) congregation in
which he followed the *Nussach* (liturgy) of the
Ari'zal (which R.Pinchas followed secretly), and
other practical Kabbala-oriented ritual. He was
well received by the Noda BiYehuda, when he
passed through Prague with the Chassam Sofer
(see 5566/1806) who was one of his disciples, as
was R.Yitzchak (Ai) Sekel Wormser, later known
as the Ba'al Shem of Michelstadt. R.Natan re
turned to Frankfurt a few years later, but the *cherem*
(excommunication) against him was not removed
until Elul 1800, a few weeks before he died.

Some restrictions on the Jews were abolished in
(expanded) Austria (see 5532/1772). However

they were directed to open German-language schools for their children or to send them to general schools, and they were forbidden to use Hebrew or Yiddish in business and communal records (see 5547/1787). The measures that increased the assimilation (see 5547/1787) of Austrian Jews, as (some say) they were designed to do (see 5580/1820); were opposed by the Noda BiYehuda, Rabbi of Prague, which was then part of the Austrio-Hungarian Empire (see 5514/1754).

5543 / 1783

Moshe Mendelssohn (Moses of Dessau) (who previously had been a disciple of the Korban HaEida, R.David Frankel) became a rationalist philosopher of the "Enlightenment." He believed in Jewish integration into the surrounding society – opposing, for example, the use of Yiddish (see 5542/1782), and insisting on German – as a necessary preparation for being recognized as equal (social emancipation, see 5547/1787); and he supported an increased emphasis on secular studies among Jews. This ideology became the foundation of the Haskala movement (Jewish "Enlightenment").

Mendelssohn, who had previously been criticized by R.Yaakov Emden for some advice he had given a Jewish community, published a German translation and commentary (Bi'ur) on the Bible in 1783. This was severely criticized by the Noda BiYehuda and by R.Pinchas Horowitz, the Rabbi of Frankfurt, author of Sefer Hafla'a (Halacha-Pilpul), and a disciple (some say secret) of the Maggid of Mezeritsch (see 5533/1772). (The Bi'ur was later tacitly approved by the scholars of Vilna.)

Although it appears that Mendelssohn's personal lifestyle conformed to Halacha, four of his six children converted to Christianity, as did at least one of the remaining Jewish grandchildren.

The Haskala rapidly spread its ideology, particularly by opening schools for Jewish children (such a school had been in existence in Berlin since 1778).

5545 / 1785

The Sha'agas Aryeh, R.Aryeh Leib (ben Asher) Gunzberg, author of Sha'agat Aryeh (Sh'elot UTeshuvot) and other works, died in Metz (France), where he had been Rabbi for approximately twenty years.

5546 / 1786

R.Elimelech of Lizensk died.

R.Elimelech of Lizensk (Poland), author of No'am Elimelech, (who had previously been an "itinerant Tzadik," see 5494/1734), was the most influential disciple of the Maggid of Mezeritsch in Galicia (then Austria). His many disciples continued to gain Chasidim (followers) in the region, after he died on the 21st Adar.

5547 / 1787

The Constitution of the (newly independent) United States of America gave the Jews full equality with other citizens (social emancipation). This concept spread with time to other countries (see 5542/1782, 5549/1789, 5550/1790, 5570/1810, 5629/1869), allowing the Jews to integrate and then assimilate into the society around them (see 5570/1810). Society was also changing (see 5500/1740), and many non-Jews were leaving their religious beliefs and practices, which gave Jews the new alternative of assimilating with non-Jews without having to accept other religions.

The Jews of Austria were forced (see 5542/1782) to choose German-sounding names, from a prepared list.

5548 / 1788

R.Aryeh Leib HaKohen Heller, respected author of Ketzot HaChoshen and Avnei Millu'im (commentaries on the Choshen Mishpat and Even HaEzer sections of Shulchan Aruch, see Figures L, M, pages 324, 325), as well as other works, became Rabbi in Stryj (Poland).

5549 / 1789

Jews slowly returned to France (see 5155/1394), particularly to Alsace. The Declaration of the Rights of Man at the beginning of the ten-year long French Revolution implied that Jews were to be equal to all citizens (see 5547/1787). Equality (social emancipation) was fully granted two years later (see 5553/1793).

5550 / 1790

A Jew was killed in Grodno (Lithuania) in a blood libel.

The Jews of Warsaw were attacked by anti-Jewish rioters in the month of Sivan, and the Jews of Florence were attacked by mobs who were angry because the Jews had been granted some civil rights (see 5547/1787).

5551 / 1791

The Pale of Settlement was established in Russia.

The government of Russia restricted the residence of the many thousands of Jews in its newly annexed territories (see 5532/1772) into an area that later became known as the Pale of Settlement (see 5613/1853, 5677/1917). The area covered the regions (in what had previously been Poland) where the Jews were already living. It also included the steppes of southern Russia, which the government wished to populate (see 5564/1804).

5552 / 1792

R.Shlomo of Karlin (Russia), who had succeeded R.Aharon (see 5533/1772), was killed during prayers on the 22nd Tammuz in the Polish rebellion (see 5554/1794). He was succeeded by his disciple, R.Asher (son of R.Aharon), who settled near Karlin in Stolin.

5553 / 1792

Fifty Jews of Ofran (Morocco) chose to be burned alive on the 17th Tishrei rather than convert to Islam. The rest of the Jews left the city.

5553 / 1793

Although the Jews had been granted equality in France (see 5549/1789), some Jews were imprisoned and many synagogues were closed during the Reign of Terror, a period of the 10-year French Revolution. All Jewish books in Strasbourg were confiscated to be burned, and the yeshiva in Metz was closed (see 5501/1741, 5545/1785).

5554 / 1794

When the Poles (under the leadership of Kosciuszko, who had fought against the British in the American Revolution) rebelled against the occupying Russian and Prussian forces (see 5532/1772), many Jews were killed (see 5552/1792, 5555/1795). Yosef Shmuel Zbitkower, a wealthy government contractor, paid large sums of money (through his excellent political connections), to rescue Jews from the fighting.

5555 / 1795

Jews were killed by rioters in Vilna, following the Polish rebellion (see 5554/1794), and many Jews were killed in Warsaw in a similar incident.

5558 / 1797

The Vilna Gaon died.

The Vilna Gaon, the "Gra" (for Gaon R.Eliyahu) who had become a living legend of scholarship in Talmud (and Kabbala), died on the 19th Tishrei (Chol HaMo'ed Sukkot). Many of his teachings and annotations were published by his disciples after his death, from the notes they had recorded (see Figures D, J, pages 316, 322).

R.Nachum of Chernobyl (Russia) died on the 11th Cheshvan, and his 28-year old son, R.Mordechai (R.Mottel), succeeded him (see 5597/1837).

5558 / 1798

When Napoleon invaded Italy, conditions for the Jews (see 5315/1555) generally improved in the occupied areas. The Jews of Ancona had been attacked by rioters, as had the Jews of Rome (before the French occupation), and, later, the Jews of Siena. After Napoleon's army withdrew, the Jews of Pesaro were attacked, many were killed, and the two synagogues were plundered. The Jews of Senigallia were later attacked as well.

5559 / 1798

The Ba'al HaTanya was released from his first imprisonment.

After the death of the Vilna Gaon (who had reaffirmed his opposition to Chasidim one year before his death, see 5558/1797), the Mitnagdim (opponents of Chasidim) in Lithuania denounced, to the Russian government, the Rav (of Lyady, the Ba'al HaTanya VeShulchan Aruch); his Tanya–a major, intellectually presented treatise on the teachings of the Ba'al Shem Tov–had recently been published. He was arrested together with twenty-two other Chasidim who were directly released, including Adm.R.Asher of Stolin and Adm.R. Mordechai of Lechevitch (both in Russia). The Rav was cleared of the charges (including treason, for sending money to Turkish-dominated Eretz Yisrael), and was released from prison (after fifty-three days) on the 19th Kislev 5559/1798 (see 5533/1772). He subsequently continued to expound his particular, intellectually oriented (Chabad) style of Chasidut.

5559 / 1799

Napoleon led an army expedition through Eretz Yisrael.

Napoleon led a successful army expedition to Egypt; from there he moved northeastward through Eretz Yisrael (see 5571/1810) until Acco (Acre) where his advance was halted. (He subsequently retreated to Egypt.) It was reported that Napoleon had issued a proclamation in Eretz Yisrael promising that the Jews would be returned to their country.

Living in the Year 1800		
	b.	d.
R.Zushya of Annopol	1718?	1800
Chida (Azulai)	1724	1806
R.Levi Yitzchak		
of Berditchev	1740	1810
R.Shneur Zalman		
(Rav of Lyady)	1745	1813
Ketzot HaChoshen		
(R.Aryeh Leib Heller)	1745?	1813
Chozeh of Lublin	1745?	1815
Chayei Adam		
(R.Avraham Danziger)	1748	1820
R.Chaim Volozhiner	1749	1821
Yismach Moshe		
(R.Moshe Teitelbaum)	1759	1841
Chavat Da'at		
(R.Yakv. of Lissa/Netivot)	1759?	1832
R.Ephrayim		
Zalman Margolis	1760	1828
R.Akiva Eger	1761	1837
Chassam Sofer	1762	1839
R.Nachman of Bratslav	1772	1811
Tiferet Yisrael		
(R.Yisrael Lipshutz)	1782	1860
Bnei Yissachar		
(R.Tzvi Elmlch. of Dynov)	1783?	1841
R.Mendel of Kotzk	1787	1859
Tzemach Tzedek		
(of Lubavitch)	1789	1866
Divrei Chaim (of Tzanz)	1793	1876
R.Yisrael of Ruzhin	1797	1850
Chidushei HaRim (of Gur)	1799	1866
Minchat Chinuch		
(R.Yosef Babad)	1800?	1874

5561 / 1800

Exactly two years after his first arrest, the Rav (of Lyady) (see 5559/1798) was requested to report to the Russian capital on renewed charges (due to further denunciations by mitnagdim). He was released from this second imprisonment but was required to remain in the capital (outside of the Pale of Settlement) until a further investigation was concluded. He was subsequently granted total freedom (in the second document signed by Czar Alexander I, after the assassination of Czar Paul), and he decided to settle in Lyady (then Russia).

5561 / 1801

One hundred twenty-eight Jews were killed in anti-Jewish riots in Bucharest after a blood libel.

5564 / 1804

A Russian edict prohibited Jews from living in villages (and among other things, forbade them from selling alcohol to the peasants). Although this amounted to a major expulsion as many Jews were living in the numerous villages (shtetlach), it was not fully enforced, partly because of problems with resettlement (some of which was to be in the steppes, see 5551/1791). Expulsions from the villages were resumed later (see 5582/1822, 5642/1882).

5565 / 1804

The Maggid of Dubno, R.Yaakov Krantz, who was famous for his meshalim (parables), died on the 17th Tevet.

5565 / 1805

Naftali Busnach, an extremely wealthy (generous and pious) Jewish statesman (who unofficially controlled the Algerian government), was assassinated in Algiers by dissatisfied Turkish soldiers. The Jewish community was attacked and 200 to 500 Jews were killed in the massacre. Naftali was succeeded (as head of the Jewish community) by his relative and business partner, David Bakri (see 5571/1811).

5566 / 1806

The Chida (R.Chaim Yosef David Azulai) died.

The Chida, R.Chaim Yosef David Azulai, author of *Machazik Bracha, Birkei Yosef* (Halacha), and *Shem HaGedolim* (biography and bibliography), died on the 11th Adar in Livorno (Leghorn), Italy where he had lived for the last eight years of his life (after leaving Eretz Yisrael, his birthplace).

The Chassam Sofer became Rabbi in Pressburg.

The Chassam Sofer, R.Moshe Sofer, a disciple of R.Natan Adler and R.Pinchas Horowitz (see 5542/1782) (and later, with his second marriage, a son-in-law of R.Akiva Eger), became the Rabbi of Pressburg, then the most important community in Hungary. He established a famous yeshiva there, became the leading Rabbi in the effort to stop reforms (see 5570/1810), and wrote many *Sh'elot UTeshuvot*.

5567 / 1807

Napoleon convened an assembly of Jews (many of whom were rabbis) to approve certain "religious" regulations, which a previous assembly (of laymen) had already approved. This assembly, called the "French Sanhedrin," met in the month of Adar and approved a number of "regulations" designed to blur the religious distinction between Jews and non-Jews in a freer and more socially emancipated society.

Many Jews were killed during the British bombardment of Copenhagen in the month of Av.

The *Machatzit HaShekel* (commentary on the Orach Chayim section of *Shulchan Aruch,* now printed in standard editions) (see Figure J, page 322) was published; (some say) that the author,

R.Shmuel (ben Natan) HaLevi Kelin of Kolin, (Bohemia), died in the same year.

5568 / 1808

The Yismach Moshe, Adm.R.Moshe Teitelbaum of Uhel (Hungary), a disciple of the Chozeh of Lublin, and author of *Yismach Moshe* (commentary on the Bible) and *Heshiv Moshe* (Sh'elot UTeshuvot), became Rabbi (and Rebbe, Admur) in Uhel (Hungary).

5669 / 1809

The Chavat Da'at, R.Yaakov (Lorberbaum of) Lissa, a disciple of his relative the Pri Megadim (who raised him, because his father had died before he was born), became Rabbi in Lissa (then Prussia) (see 5582/1822). His work *Chavat Da'at* (on the *Yoreh Deya* section of Shulchan Aruch) had previously been published anonymously (gaining him a great reputation). He later wrote *Netivot HaMishpat* (commentary on the *Choshen Mishpat* section of Shulchan Aruch) (see Figure M, page 325) among other works.

R.Menachem Mendel of Shklov, a disciple of the Vilna Gaon, who had been instrumental in publishing his works (see 5558/1797), arrived in Tzfat (Safed) to settle with a group of (some say 70) people. R.Yisrael of Shklov, another disciple of the Vilna Gaon, also emigrated to Eretz Yisrael where he wrote *Pe'at HaShulchan* (Halacha of Eretz Yisrael).

5570 / 1809

R.Levi Yitzchak of Berditchev died.

R.Levi Yitzchak of Berditchev (see 5533/1772, 5541/1781) was author of *Kedushat Levi,* and a disciple of the Maggid of Mezeritsch (some say he had previously studied with the Pri Megadim). R.Levi had a strong personal following, and was famous for his ability to see only the good in his fellow Jews (and to intercede on their behalf). He

died on the 25th Tishrei. Another disciple of the Maggid, R.Avraham of Kalisk (see 5537/1777), died on the 4th Shvat.

5570 / 1810

R.Avraham Danziger, a disciple of the Noda BiYehuda, who was an (honorary) dayan in Vilna, published his *Chayei Adam* (a clear and simple [layman's] presentation of the laws in the *Orach Chayim* section of the *Shulchan Aruch*). He later wrote other similar works.

After Napoleon gained control of much of (western) Germany, and equal rights (social emancipation) (see 5549/1789) were granted to the Jews, the Reform movement in Judaism started. Laymen made changes in the prayer services to reflect the general society in which Jews could now mix. Later, suitably secular-oriented scholars were attracted to function as leaders of these transformed congregations (see 5578/1817) (many of which split, when reforms were introduced, see 5614/1854).

The first introduction (in 1810) of the organ into synagogue services, probably the most controversial of these changes, was made by Israel Jacobson, who had founded in 1801 (and supported) a school that emphasized modern and vocational subjects in Seesen (Germany). Jacobson conducted an inaugural service in part of the school (which, by then, also had some non-Jewish children). He was dressed in the robes of a Protestant clergyman, sang hymns in German, and was accompanied by the organ. (Most of Jacobson's ten children eventually had themselves baptized.)

5571 / 1810

R.Nachman of Bratslav died.

R.Nachman of Bratslav (Russia), a great-grandson of the Ba'al Shem Tov, grandson of R.Nachman of Horodenka, and author of *Likuetei MoHoran,*

233

died during Sukkot on the 18th Tishrei. He had visited Eretz Yisrael in 1798 (and spent Rosh HaShana in the newly rebuilt village of Haifa), but left when Napoleon invaded the country (see 5559/1799). He later became involved in controversies with his peers over some of his teachings. His followers (chasidim) are unique in that they have never appointed a successor.

5571 / 1811

David Bakri (see 5565/1805) was beheaded by the government of Algeria (see 5575/1815); he was replaced as leader of the Jewish community by David Duran (of a rival family, see 5575/1815), who was also killed the same year. Joseph Bakri (father of David) then became leader of the community.

5572 / 1811

R.Aryeh Leib, "Der Shpoler Zeideh," was considered a disciple of the Ba'al Shem Tov, and had a strong following among the common people (see 5520/1760) because of his extreme warmth and emotional piety. He died on the 6th Tishrei (at the age of 85).

R.Baruch of Medzibuzh (Russia), a grandson of the Ba'al Shem Tov, who had thousands of followers and considered himself the rightful heir of (all) Chasidic leadership, died on the 18th Kislev.

5572 / 1812

The Jews were attacked, and several synagogues were burned by Greek revolutionaries (see 5581/1821) in Galati (Rumania).

5573 / 1812

Napoleon's conquest of Eastern Europe was seen by many Jews as fulfillment of the prophecies of

wars before the arrival of Mashiach (Messiah), particularly in light of statements he had reportedly made in Eretz Yisrael (see 5559/1799). R.Mendel of Rymanov felt that the conquests would be beneficial for the Jews, but others (including the Maggid of Kozhnitz and Adm. R.Naftali of Ropshytz, a disciple of R.Mendel) felt that this would have negative effects on the Jews of Poland and Russia.

The Rav of Lyady (see 5561/1800), R.Shneur Zalman, had strong convictions that a victory for Napoleon would be detrimental to the Jews, and he even rendered assistance to the Russian war effort. When Napoleon's army advanced toward Lyady, he (hastily) left the town and spent five months traveling (even after Napoleon's defeat). He died on the 24th Tevet 5573/1812, while in a small village, and was succeeded by his son, Adm.R.Dov Ber, who settled in Lubavitch (Russia).

5574 / 1814

R.Akiva Eger became Rabbi in Posen.

R.Akiva Eger, author of *Sh'elot UTeshuvot, Chidushim,* and many other works, became Rabbi in Posen (then Prussia), despite strong opposition from the *maskilim* (see 5581/1821).

5575 / 1814

The Kozhnitzer Maggid and the Yehudi of Pershisskha died.

R.Yisrael, the Maggid of Kozhnitz (Galicia), a disciple of the Maggid of Mezeritsch, R.Shmelke of Nikolsburg, and R.Elimelech of Lizensk, was among those who brought the teachings of the Ba'al Shem Tov to Poland. He was author of a number of works on Talmud, Halacha, and

Kabbala. He died on the 14th Tishrei (Erev Sukkot) when he was, some say, over 80 years of age.

Adm.R.Yaakov Yitzchak of Pershisskha (Galicia), a leading disciple of the Chozeh of Lublin, was called HaYehudi HaKadosh (the Holy Jew). (Some say that the other disciples of the Chozeh did not want to call him by name, because his first names were identical with those of the Chozeh, so they gave him an appropriate pseudonym.) Although he died (before he was 49) on the 19th Tishrei (Chol HaMo'ed Sukkot) ten months before the Chozeh, he had already established his own following to a variation of the current Polish/Galician style of Chasidim. He placed a different emphasis on the role of the Rebbe (Admur, "Tzadik"), as being more of a spiritual guide and inspiration for honest introspective devotion in prayer, and in the study of Torah, rather than being a "miracle worker." He demanded higher standards in Torah study and in prayer from his followers (chasidim). This difference of style caused friction between him and other disciples of the Chozeh, and eventually with the Chozeh himself. He was succeeded primarily by his leading disciple, Adm.R.Simcha Bunim of Pershisskha.

5575 / 1815

The Chozeh of Lublin and R.Mendel of Rymanov died.

Adm.R. (Menachem) Mendel of Rymanov (Galicia), a disciple of R.Elimelech of Lizensk, died on the 19th Iyar.

The Chozeh of Lublin, R.Yaakov Yitzchak Horowitz, a follower (chasid) of the Maggid of Mezeritsch, and a disciple of R.Elimelech of Lizensk, died on Tisha B'Av. He was the leading Rebbe (Admur, "Tzadik") in Poland and Galicia and many of his disciples were the leading Admurim in these regions. He was called the

Chozeh (seer) by his followers (after his death, according to some), because of his reputation for predicting personalities and events.

R.Yitzchak Albuker, the Rabbi of Algiers, was killed with seven other Jewish leaders when internal Jewish (family) rivalries (see 5571/1811) spilled out into the wider community.

5578 / 1817

The first congregation established initially on a Reform basis in Germany (see 5570/1810) was opened in Hamburg in the month of Tishrei (despite the vehement opposition of R.Mordechai Benet); a prayer book with a significant ideological changes was printed there a year later.

5579 / 1819

Anti-Jewish "Hep! Hep!" riots spread throughout Germany.

An anti-Jewish riot broke out in Wurtzburg with the attacking mobs using the cry of "Hep! Hep!" and similar riots quickly spread to many towns. (The maskilim and the reformers refrained from reporting details on these destructive incidents in their periodicals, lest they change the attitude of Jews to their non-Jewish neighbors.)

5580 / 1820

R.Shlomo Kluger, a disciple of the Maggid of Dubno, became Rabbi in Brody (then part of Austria) where he remained for fifty years until his death.

A law was issued in Austria that required all Rabbis to study philosophy and to preach in the local language, and also required Jewish children to attend Christian schools (see 5542/1782). These laws were instituted after the lobbying by one of the maskilim (see 5605/1844) who had also proposed that beards and traditional Jewish dress be outlawed, and that many traditional Jewish writings (including the Talmud) be banned and censored.

Living in the Year 1820	b.	d.
Chayei Adam		
(R.Avraham Danziger)	1748	1820
R.Chaim Volozhiner	1749	1821
Yismach Moshe		
(R.Moshe Teitelbaum)	1759	1841
Chavat Da'at		
(R.Yakv. of Lissa/Netivot)	1759?	1832
R.Ephrayim		
Zalman Margolis	1760	1828
R.Akiva Eger	1761	1837
Chassam Sofer	1762	1839
Tiferet Yisrael		
(R.Yisrael Lipshutz)	1782	1860
Bnei Yissachar		
(R.Tzvi Elmlch. of Dynov)	1783?	1841
R.Mendel of Kotzk	1787	1859
Tzemach Tzedek		
(of Lubavitch)	1789	1866
Divrei Chaim (of Tzanz)	1793	1876
R.Yisrael of Ruzhin	1797	1850
Chidushei HaRim (of Gur)	1799	1866
Minchat Chinuch		
(R.Yosef Babad)	1800?	1874
Kitzur Shulchan Aruch		
(R.Shl.Ganzfried)	1804	1886
R.Shimshon Raphael Hirsch	1808	1888
Malbim (R.Meir Leib(ush)	1808?	1879
R.Yisrael Salanter	1810	1883
Divrei Yechezk'el		
(of Shinev)	1811?	1899
Pitchei Teshuva		
(R.Avraham Tzvi Hirsch)	1813	1868

5581 / 1821

R.Chaim Volozhiner died in the month of Sivan. He was a disciple of the Vilna Gaon and (some say) of the Sha'agat Aryeh, founder of the famous Yeshiva of Volozhin (Lithuania) and author of *Nefesh HaChayim* (Mussar).

R.Shlomo Zalman Lifshitz, author of *Chemdat Shlomo (Sh'elot UTeshuvot)*, became Rabbi of War-saw (where R.Akiva Eger once visited him at the same time as the Chavat Da'at was visiting, the Chidushei HaRim also being present). R.Shlomo had previously declined to return (as Rabbi) (to his native Posen (then Prussia), because he wanted to protect his children from the influence of the Haskala which was prevalent there (see 5574/1814 and 5496/1736).

Hundreds of Jews were killed in Jassy (Moldavia), in a Greek revolt against the Turkish Empire (see 5582/1822 and 5572/1812); some say that as many as 5,000 Jews were killed in Greece during the revolt.

The Jews were attacked in anti-Jewish riots in Odessa (Russia).

5582 / 1822

The Chavat Da'at left his position as Rabbi in Lissa (then Prussia), because of a rift with a large part of the community due to his strong stand against the reformers (see 5570/1810). He declined to become Rabbi in any community until eight years later when he became rabbi in Stryj (Austrian Poland).

The expulsion of Jews from Russian villages (see 5564/1804, 5585/1825) was resumed.

Sixty Jews were killed in Bucharest on Purim by Turkish soldiers suppressing the Greek revolution (see 5581/1821).

The Jewish section of Schaffa (Moravia) was destroyed by a fire on the 24th Sivan.

5583 / 1823

Adm.R.Klonymos Kalman of Cracow died on the 1st Tammuz. He was a disciple of R.Elimelech of Lizensk, and of the Chozeh of Lublin, author of *Ma'or VaShemesh* (commentary, Chasidut on Chumash) and had attracted many followers (chasidim) in Cracow and Galicia (then Austria).

5584 / 1824

A group of Jews seceded from the congregation in Charleston, (South Carolina), when the reforms they wanted to introduce (see 5570/1810) were not accepted. They established the first Reform group (later congregation) in the United States.

5585 / 1825

The Jews were expelled from the villages around Mogilev and Vitebsk (Russia), and removed to the cities (see 5582/1822).

The Apta Rav, Adm.R.Avraham Yehoshua Heschel of Opatow (Austrian Galicia), was a disciple of R.Elimelech of Lizensk, who is remembered by the sole epitaph (some say) he requested: "Oheiv Yisrael." The Apta Rav declared a fast day when the order for expulsion from the villages was received, and he died on the 5th of Nissan in Medzibuzh (then Russia), where he had lived for his last years (during which time he was regarded as the "elder statesman" of Polish-Galician Chasidim, being the last of the leading disciples of R.Elimelech).

Adm.R.Dov Ber of Lubavitch visited R.Akiva Eger when passing through Posen in 1825 (see 5574/1814).

5587 / 1827

Adm.R.Naftali Tzvi of Ropshytz (Austrian Galicia), a disciple of R.Elimelech of Lizensk, and (later) of the Chozeh of Lublin, the Maggid of Kozhnitz, and of Adm.R.Mendel of Rymanov (see 5575/1815), died on the 11th Iyar.

Adm.R.Meir of Apta (Austrian Galicia), a leading disciple of the Chozeh of Lublin, died on the 25th Tammuz.

Many Jews were killed by a fire in the Jewish section of Jassy (Moldavia).

Moshe Montefiore (later Sir Moses) visited Eretz Yisrael for the first time and recommitted himself to Jewish religious (Halacha) observance (he later took a shochet – ritual meat slaughterer – with him on his travels). A tall man who lived for over 100 years, he commanded respect in many circles and was a great *shtadlan* (advocate and negotiator for Jewish causes) (see 5600/1840, 5606/1846, 5618/1858, 5624/1864, 5627/1867). He supported Jewish scholars, Eretz Yisrael (which he visited seven times), and was a major force in confining the spread of reform in England.

Isaac (Adolphe) Cremieux, an assimilated Jew who rose to high positions in the French government and was an active advocate and negotiator for Jewish causes, was instrumental in the abolition of the humiliating "oath more judaico" which Jews were often required to take (in various forms and in various situations) for many centuries in Europe.

Adm.R.Simcha Bunim of Pershisskha (Austrian Galicia), who some say had previously studied under R.Mordechai Benet, was a disciple of the Chozeh of Lublin, and also of the Yehudi of Pershisskha whom he succeeded. He continued to develop the Pershisskha style (see 5575/1814), and his followers included many outstanding scholars. He died on the 12th Elul, and was succeeded (primarily) by Adm.R.Mendel of Kotzk (Austrian Galicia).

Russia began conscripting Jewish children into the army.

Czar Nicholas I of Russia issued a decree (during Elul) that male Jews between the ages of 12 and 25 were to be drafted into military service. Local communal leaders were held personally responsible for delivering their quotas of conscripts (which were high), and because there were virtually no volunteers for this military service, "chappers" (kidnappers) grabbed children as young as 8 and 9 (mostly from the poor).

Children younger than 18 years of age were "trained" in the cantonments (barracks that were established for military children), and there was strong pressure (including torture) to convert the Jewish children to Christianity. When they turned 18, they had to serve twenty-five years in the army. It is estimated that 30,000 to 100,000 Jewish Cantonists were "drafted" under this decree (which remained in force until 1856 see 5613/1853). There were many stories of bravery among them; but (some say) that at least half were eventually baptized (see 5588/1827).

5588 / 1827

Adm.R.Dov Ber of Lubavitch (Russia), author of many works (of Chasidut), was denounced to the government and detained for questioning, but was totally exonerated on the 10th Kislev 5587/1826. Exactly one year less a day later, on the 9th Kislev (his birthday) in 5588/1827, he died; he was succeeded by his son-in-law, the Tzemach Tzedek, Adm.R.Menachem Mendel, a grandson of the Rav (of Lyady).

The Tzemach Tzedek (who was 38 at this time) had been raised from the age of 2 (when his mother died) by his (maternal) grandfather the Rav, whose disciple he was. Thus he directly received the teachings from (the inner circle of) the Maggid of Mezeritsch (see 5530/1770), which was unique at this stage (see Nissan 5585/1825).

He immediately organized a clandestine group of followers (chasidim) to combat the Cantonist conscription law (see 5587/1827). They assisted communities to negotiate for lower quotas, they paid (illegal) ransoms for conscripted children, and they sent people to comfort the children at assembly points, and to encourage them to be loyal to Judaism. (Some of the organizers were later imprisoned for their efforts.)

He also organized visiting rabbis for the new agricultural colonies (see 5564/1804), and later bought land, and negotiated government assistance, to help resettle Jews on the land (see 5585/1825).

5588 / 1828

R.Ephrayim Zalman Margolis, a scholar and businessman from Brody (then Austria) died. He was the author of *Beit Ephrayim (Sh'elot UTeshuvot)*, *Yad Ephrayim* (on *Shulchan Aruch*), and *Matteh Ephrayim* (Halacha), among other works; he also edited the work of his brother, R.Chaim Mordechai, called *Darkei Teshuva* (on the *Orach Chayim* section of *Shulchan Aruch,* a collection of additional updated Halacha notes, see 5616/1856).

5590 / 1829

The Jews were ordered expelled from Kiev and later from the Russian port cities of Nikolayev and Sevastopol in Cheshvan 5590/1829, although none of these expulsion orders were immediately enforced.

5590 / 1830

The Divrei Chaim, Adm.R.Chaim Halberstam, a disciple of Adm.R.Naftali Tzvi of Ropshytz and Adm.R.Tzvi Hirsch of Zydachov (Austrian Galicia), and son-in-law of R.Baruch Frankel (author of *Baruch Ta'am),* was appointed Rabbi of Tzanz (Austrian Galicia). There he became Rebbe (Admur, "Tzadik") and attracted many followers (chasidim).

Adherents to the Reform movement gained control of the Jewish communal administration in Fuerth (Fiyorda), Germany, and closed the yeshiva of R.Avraham Binyamin (Wolf) Hamburg, expelling over 100 students (with the help of local police) (see 5641/1881).

5591 / 1831

Many Jews were killed in Oshmyany (Lithuania) when the Russian soldiers started a fire after a Polish rebellion.

R.Moshe Mintz (Muenz, Maharam Mintz II), the highly respected Rabbi of O-Buda (Hungary), died in the month of Elul.

5596 / 1836

R.Tzvi Hirsch Kalischer, a disciple of the Chavat Da'at and R.Akiva Eger, met Mayer Anschel Rothschild (an extremely wealthy and observant

Jew) and suggested that he involve himself in bringing about the Mashiach (Messiah) by creating facilities for a "return to Zion" and Eretz Yisrael. R.Tzvi Hirsch was suggesting he attempt to buy Eretz Yisrael (at least Yerushalayim) from the Turkish sultan.

5597 / 1837

R.Yisrael Lipshutz, author of *Tiferet Yisrael* (commentary on Mishna) (see Figure B, page 314), became Rabbi in Danzig (Gdansk) where he lived for the rest of his life.

Adm.R.Mordechai of Chernobyl (Russia) (see 5558/1797) died on the 20th Iyar and was succeeded as Admur (Rebbe, "Tzadik") by all of his eight sons (each in his own location), including Adm.R.Yitzchak of Skvira (then Russia).

Four thousand Jews died in an earthquake in Tzfat (Safed) (see 5520/1759) on the 24th Tevet, and 700–1000 died in Teverya (Tiberius) in the same earthquake. Many of the survivors eventually moved; among them was a group of (Lubavitch) Chasidim, who joined the Chabad settlement in Hevron (established ten years earlier by Adm.R. Dov Ber) and rejuvenated the community there.

The Churvat R.Yehuda Chasid synagogue (see 5481/1720) was reopened in Yerushalayim at the end of Tevet, after it had been reconstructed.

5598 / 1838

R.David Luria, Rabbi of Bichov (Russia) and author of *Chidushei HaRadal* (on Midrash Rabba), was released from prison when the evidence supporting his denunciation was found to be forged. R.David was an active leader against the (local) maskilim and the reformers.

Hundreds of Jews were arrested and tortured in Russia on a charge of being involved in an affair in which two Jews were (allegedly) killed by other Jews (for informing and illegal exploitation). Many died from the effects of their (hard labor) sentence.

5599 / 1839

The Chassam Sofer died, and was succeeded as Rabbi in Pressburg (Hungary) by his oldest son, R.Avraham Shmuel Binyamin (Zev), the Ktav Sofer (see 5629/1869).

Many Jews of Meshed (Persia) were killed in an anti-Jewish attack, and the remainder were forced to convert to Islam, although they remained secretly Jewish (see 5421/1661). Most of them eventually migrated to other places where they could be openly Jewish.

Living in the Year 1840		
	b.	d.
Yismach Moshe (R.Moshe Teitelbaum)	1759	1841
Tiferet Yisrael (R.Yisrael Lipshutz)	1782	1860
Bnei Yissachar (R.Tzvi Elmlch. of Dynov)	1783?	1841
R.Mendel of Kotzk	1787	1859
Tzemach Tzedek (of Lubavitch)	1789	1866
Divrei Chaim (of Tzanz)	1793	1876
R.Yisrael of Ruzhin	1797	1850
Chidushei HaRim (of Gur)	1799	1866
Minchat Chinuch (R.Yosef Babad)	1800?	1874
Kitzur Shulchan Aruch (R.Shl.Ganzfried)	1804	1886
R.Shimshon Raphael Hirsch	1808	1888
Malbim (R.Meir Leib(ush)	1808?	1879
R.Yisrael Salanter	1810	1883
Divrei Yechezk'el (of Shinev)	1811?	1899
Pitchei Teshuva R.Avraham Tzvi Hirsch)	1813	1868
Aruch HaShulchan (R.Yechi'el Epstein)	1829	1908
Sdei Chemed (R.Chaim Chizkiyah Medini)	1832?	1904
Ben Ish Chai (R.Yosef Chaim Al-Chakkam)	1833?	1909
Chafetz Chaim (R.Yisrael Meir Kagan)	1838	1933

5600 / 1840

Adm.R.Yisrael of Ruzhin was released from imprisonment.

Adm.R.Yisrael of Ruzhin (Russia), a great-grandson of the Maggid of Mezeritsch, and a grandson of R.Nachum of Chernobyl (Russia), was released from prison after almost two years. He had been charged with having (revolutionary) ambitions to be ruler of the Jews (his regal life-style being cited as evidence) and was also accused of implication in the informers' affair (see 5598/1838). He was under continuous surveillance even after his release. He subsequently left Russia and settled in Sadgora (Austrian Bukovina), where he continued his regal lifestyle which created controversy with other Chasidim in the region.

Many Jews were arrested in a notorious blood libel in Damascus (known as the Damascus Affair), including over sixty children (in order to extract a confession from their mothers). Two Jews died of torture, a number confessed, and one converted to Islam. It became in international affair involving the governments of Turkey, Egypt, France, and Austria. The Rabbi and leading Jewish people on the island of Rhodes were also arrested (by the Turks). The release of all the Jews was negotiated by a delegation of international Jewish notables including Sir Moshe Montefiore (see 5587/1827).

This act of successful international Jewish cooperation spurred the eventual formation of the Alliance Israelite Universelle (see 5620/1860).

5601 / 1841

R.Avraham David of Buczacz (Austrian Galicia), a disciple of R.Levi Yitzchak of Berditchev, and author of *Da'at Kedoshim* (Halacha) among other works, died on Erev Rosh Chodesh Cheshvan 5601/1840.

The Bnei Yissachar, Adm.R.Tzvi Elimelech of Dynov, a disciple of the Maggid of Kozhnitz, the Chozeh of Lublin, and R.Menachem Mendel of Rymanov, was Rabbi and Rebbe (Admur, "Tzadik") in many towns, including Dynov (Austrian Hungary) and Munkatch (Austrian Galicia). He wrote *Bnei Yissachar*, among many other works, and he died on the 18th Tevet.

The Yismach Moshe, Adm.R.Moshe Teitelbaum (see 5568/1808), died on the 28th Tammuz, in Uhel (Hungary). He was succeeded as Rebbe by his only son, Adm.R.Elazar Nissan, who was Rabbi of Drahavitsch (Austrian Galicia), and by his grandson (and disciple) Adm.R.Yekutiel Yehuda of Sighet (see 5618/1858), who became Rabbi of Uhel until he was forced to leave by the Mitnagdim (opponents to Chasidim).

5603 / 1843

The Tzemach Tzedek was arrested.

The Russian government convened a commission, which included the Tzemach Tzedek (representing Chasidim) and R.Yitzchak (son of R.Chaim) of Volozhin (Mitnagdim), a businessman, and a secularly oriented scholar, to discuss many Jewish issues, particularly the issue of secular education for Jewish children, which Max Lilienthal, a German-Jewish maskil and educator, had been lobbying for in government circles (see 5580/1820), and had been heavily promoting among the Jews (see 5543/1783).

The Tzemach Tzedek was detained for his outspoken views twenty-two times during the course of the conference, and although the immediate outcome (see 5605/1844) of the commission was unclear, the government did repeal the 1836 ban on publication and importation of certain Jewish books (essentially Kabbala and Chasidut, which the maskilim viewed as particularly irksome). The government also suspended the expulsion of Jews from the villages (see 5582/1822, 5642/1882).

5605 / 1844

The government of Czar Nicholas I (see 5587/1827) ordered the establishment of state schools for Jewish children (conceived by Lilienthal, see 5603/1843), and a secret clause in the decree indicated that the purpose was to attract Jews to Christianity. The government also ordered the establishment of "rabbinical seminaries" in the style of the maskilim, with secular education (see 5639/1879), the abolition of the older-style Jewish community structure, and the introduction of "government-appointed rabbis" (graduates of the government's "rabbinical seminaries").

Although many of these decrees were difficult to enforce, and these rabbis rarely had serious influence in the Jewish communities (but primarily served as clerks for recording births, marriages, etc.), the Jewish communal structure lost much of its power, including the power to control the establishment of new institutions in the community. This presented the maskilim with the opportunity to openly disseminate their views on Jewish life in the vast number of East European communities of Russia and Poland, as they had already done in the freer countries of Western Europe. They also encouraged parents to send their children to the government schools, which leaders of both Chasidim and Mitnagdim were discouraging. The maskilim claimed that all such children would be exempt from the conscription laws (see 5587/1827).

Lilienthal (see 5603/1843), who became very unpopular (even among the maskilim, for political reasons), left Russia amid a controversy over alleged misappropriation of funds, and settled in the United States. There he was later active in the Reform movement, together with his friend Isaac Mayer Wise who spread the Reform ideology throughout the United States (see 5641/1881) in his frequent travels, particularly to scattered communities.

5606 / 1846

Sir Moshe Montefiore (see 5587/1827) visited Russia in an attempt to intercede for the Jews and to negotiate a relaxation of the harsh and discriminatory decrees (see 5582/1822, 5587/1827, 5605/1844, 5613/1853). He met with the Chidushei HaRim (in Warsaw), R.Yitzchak Volozhiner, and R.David Luria, among other Jewish leaders and government officials.

5609 / 1848

R.Yisrael Salanter left Vilna.

ManyJews died in a cholera epidemic in Vilna. R.Yisrael Salanter (Lipkin), who was the original propounder of a new movement (in Lithuania) to study and practice Mussar (ethics), was very active in helping the sick. When doctors claimed that in order to maintain a healthy resistance to the disease, Jews should not fast on that Yom Kippur, R.Yisrael set a public example by eating in the synagogue. In the same year, he was asked to head the new government-sponsored rabbinical seminary in Vilna (see 5605/1844). He refused (although encouraged to do so by R.Yitzchak Volozhiner). He was consequently compelled to leave Vilna, and he settled in Kovno (Lithuania) for nine years (see 5617/1857).

5610 / 1850

Adm.R.Meir(el) Premishlaner, a popular Rebbe (Admur, "Tzadik") of Chasidim who had developed a wide reputation as a miracle worker, died on the 29th Iyar.

5611 / 1851

R.Shimshon Rapha'el Hirsch became Rabbi in Frankfurt am Main.

R.Shimshon Rapha'el Hirsch had already been Rabbi in a number of towns, and had already

written some of his major works, setting out his ideology. This ideology was based on traditional Judaism, but reflected the new cultural environment of the nineteenth century. It did not change the structure of Jewish law, as the Reform movement (in Germany) had done a few years earlier when they formally rejected sections of the Halacha, including dietary prohibitions. He had attracted the friendship of such people as Abraham Geiger (a leading Reform scholar), and Heinrich Graetz (a Reform scholar and historian, who had even spent some time studying under R.Shimshon Rapha'el), although both their relationships with him eventually cooled.

In 1851 he became Rabbi in Frankfurt am Main, where he established his ideology on a congregational basis, in which other congregations in Germany joined. He also founded Jewish schools, which offered a traditional Jewish education yet included secular studies.

R.Shimshon Rapha'el Hirsch was instrumental in consolidating and enhancing the position of the Halacha observant (Orthodox) Jews of Germany (see 5629/1869) at a time when the Reform movement, the Haskala, and outright assimilation had jeopardized their continued existence, and almost eliminated practical Halacha observance in many cities (including Frankfurt).

5613 / 1853

The government of Czar Nicholas I increased the quota of Jewish conscripts (and cantonists, see 5587/1827) during the Crimean War with England, France, and Turkey, which started with a dispute over control of Christian holy places in Yerushalayim.

The Russian government also issued decrees restricting the Jewish style of dress, and classifying Jews into various discriminatory economic classes. (The ancient settlement of Kra'im [Kara'ites] in the Crimea was later exempt from anti-Jewish laws [see Nissan 5702/1942].)

The decree of the Cantonists was repealed some three years later after the death of Czar Nicholas I, and (among other things) the right was granted for some (upper-economic-class) Jews to live outside the Pale of Settlement.

5614 / 1854

A group of people broke away from the synagogue in Mainz (Germany) when an organ was installed (see 5570/1810), and they formed their own (Orthodox) congregation. Meir (Marcus) Lehman, who wrote many historical novels, became their Rabbi.

5615 / 1855

Adm.R.Shalom of Belz (Austrian Galicia), a disciple of the Chozeh of Lublin and the Apta Rav, died on the 27th Elul. He was succeeded as Rebbe (Admur, "Tzadik") by his son, Adm.R.Yehoshua.

5616 / 1856

R.Avraham Tzvi Hirsch Eisenstadt, author of *Pitchei Teshuva* on the Shulchan Aruch (except the Orach Chayim section) (see Figure K, page 323), a collection of additional (updated) Halacha notes (see 5588/1828), left Grodno (Lithuania) to become Rabbi in Uttina (Lithuania).

5617 / 1857

R.Yosef Shaul Nathanson, author of *Sho'el UMeshiv (Sh'elot UTeshuvot)*, became Rabbi of Lemberg Lvov (Austria). He permitted the use of machines to bake matza,which created a widespread Halacha controversy, and he was active in combatting the introductin of the new education of the maskilim (see 5543/1783).

R.Yisrael Salanter (see 5609/1848, 5643/1883), who left Lithuania and went to Germany for medical reasons, remained there for a few years

and attracted Jewish university students to lectures (shi'urim) on Bible, Talmud, and Mussar (ethics), which he (dressed in German fashion) gave in German. He later settled in the town of Memel on the German-Lithuanian border.

A Jew was attacked by a mob in Tunisia and later killed for (allegedly) insulting Islam.

5618 / 1858

Adm.R.Yekutiel Yehuda Teitelbaum (see 5601/1841), author of *Yetev Lev*, became Rabbi of Sighet (Rumania); he was also Rebbe (Admur, "Tzadik"), succeeding his father (see 5601/1841) who had died two years earlier.

R.Meir Leib(ush) benYechi'el Michel, the Malbim, famous for his commentary on the Bible, became Rabbi in Bucharest, where he faced strong opposition from the reformers (see 5624/1864).

Edgardo Mortara, a 6-year-old Jewish boy, was forcibly taken from his parents in Bologna (Italy) by church authorities, and the baptized child was raised as a Christian, despite an international outcry (which included the intervention of Francis Joseph I, the Austrian emperor who had very friendly relations with the Jews, and of England's Sir Moshe Montefiore). The boy later became a church dignitary and theologian.

5619 / 1859

R.Menachem Mendel of Kotzk died.

Adm.R.Menachem Mendel of Kotzk (Poland), a disciple of the Chozeh of Lublin, the Yehudi of Pershisskha, and Adm.R.Simcha Bunim of Pershisskha (whom he succeeded), died on the 22nd Shvat, after having spent almost twenty years in the seclusion of his room. He was succeeded (primarily) by the Chidushei HaRim, Adm.R. Yitzchak Meir (who lived in Warsaw, but subsequently moved to Gur). The Chidushei HaRim maintained R.Mendel's high demands of his followers (chasidim) in regard to depth of Torah study, but reduced the intense pressure his predecessor had exerted and instilled in them, by his demands and search for absolute truth.

Many Jews were killed in an attack by rioters in Galati (Rumania), and the Jews were also attacked in Odessa (Russia).

Living in the Year 1860		
	b.	d.
Tiferet Yisrael		
(R.Yisrael Lipshutz)	1782	1860
Tzemach Tzedek		
(of Lubavitch)	1789	1866
Divrei Chaim (of Tzanz)	1793	1876
Chidushei HaRim (of Gur)	1799	1866
Minchat Chinuch		
(R.Yosef Babad)	1800?	1874
Kitzur Shulchan Aruch		
(R.Shl.Ganzfried)	1804	1886
R.Shimshon Raphael Hirsch	1808	1888
Malbim (R.Meir Leib(ush)	1808?	1879
R.Yisrael Salanter	1810	1883
Divrei Yechezk'el		
(of Shinev)	1811?	1899
Pitchei Teshuva		
R.Avraham Tzvi Hirsch)	1813	1868
Aruch HaShulchan		
(R.Yechi'el Epstein)	1829	1908
Sdei Chemed (R.Chaim		
Chizkiyah Medini)	1832	1904
Ben Ish Chai (R.Yosef		
Chaim Al-Chakkam)	1833?	1909
Chafetz Chaim		
(R.Yisrael Meir Kagan)	1838	1933
Darkei Teshuva		
(R.Tzvi Hirsch Shapira)	1845?	1913
Sfass Emess (of Gur)	1847	1905
R.Chaim Brisker	1853	1918
Rogatchover Gaon		
(R.Yosef Rozin)	1858	1942
Torah Temima		
(R.Baruch Epstein)	1860	1942

5620 / 1860

When the Spanish attacked, many Jews fled Morocco (some taking refuge in Gibraltar), and the Jews of Tetuan (Morocco) were massacred. Some Moroccan Jews subsequently settled in Eretz Yisrael.

The Alliance Israelite Universelle was established (see 5600/1840) as an organization through which Jews living in countries of more fortunate circumstances could help those in poorer conditions. The organization eventually undertook diplomatic activities, emigration assistance, and also educational programs. The education included French language and culture, which became a major factor in the organization's decline – in some places, because of its challenge to traditional Jewish education and culture (see 5543/1783) – and elsewhere because of the rise of local nationalism.

5621 / 1861

R.Moshe Schick, the Maharam Schick, a disciple of the Chassam Sofer and author of *Sh'elot UTeshuvot Maharam Schick,* became Rabbi in Chust (Hungary) where he developed the Jewish community (in the eighteen years until he died) into the most important in northern Hungary. He was vehemently opposed to the reformers (see 5629/1869), yet he maintained that it was permissible (where necessary) for a rabbi to preach in the local language.

R.Yisrael Zev Horowitz, a disciple of the Chassam Sofer and a direct descendant of R.Pinchas Horowitz (see 5345/1585), was a Rabbi in Uhel (Hungary) (see 5601/1841), before he settled in Eretz Yisrael. He died in Teverya (Tiberius) on the 18th Sivan.

5623 / 1862

General Ulysses S. Grant approved an order expelling Jews from Tennessee (the United States) in Kislev 5623/1862 less than two weeks before

Pres. Abraham Lincoln's Emancipation Proclamation, during the U.S. Civil War; he was instructed three weeks later by Pres. Lincoln to revoke the order.

5624 / 1864

The Malbim was imprisoned and then expelled from Rumania.

The Malbim (see 5618/1858) was arrested, after being denounced by the assimilationist Reform Jews of Bucharest. He was released on the condition that he leave Rumania (after personal representations on his behalf by Sir Moshe Montefiore). He was subsequently Rabbi in a number of towns, but was persecuted by the reformers and maskilim, and he did not find favor with the Chasidim.

5625 / 1864

Jews of many cities in North Africa, including Tunis and Tripoli, were massacred on Yom Kippur by insurgent tribes.

5626 / 1866

Chidushei HaRim, Tiferet Shlomo, and the Tzemach Tzedek, died.

The Chidushei HaRim, Adm.R.Yitzchak Meir of Gur (Poland), a disciple of the Maggid of Kozhnitz and of Adm.R.Simcha Bunim of Pershisskha, and author of Chidushei HaRim (on Talmud and Shulchan Aruch), died on the 23rd Adar. All his (thirteen) sons had died in his lifetime, and he was succeeded (four years later) by his young grandson and disciple), the Sfass Emess.

Adm.R.Shlomo HaKohen of Radomsk (Poland), a disciple of Adm.R.Meir of Apta, and author of Tiferet Shlomo (Chasidut on Chumash), died Erev Rosh Chodesh Nissan.

The Tzemach Tzedek (see 5603/1843), Adm. R.Menahem Mendel of Lubavitch, author of Tzemach Tzedekll (Sh'elot UTeshuvot, and Halacha notes) among other works, died on the 13th Nissan. He was succeeded in Lubavitch by his youngest son, Adm.R.Shmuel. All four other sons except for the oldest became Rebbe (Admur, "Tzadik") in their own towns.

5627 / 1867

The Jews were expelled from many villages in Rumania (some drowned in the Danube in their flight). The remainder were harassed with discriminatory laws, which Sir Moshe Montefiore (in a personal visit) attempted to have repealed.

5629 / 1869

When the Hungarian reformers (Neologs) rejected demands that the communal regulations be subject to the authority of the Shulchan Aruch (at a congress held one year after Hungary had granted the Jews equal rights), most of the Orthodox (observant) Jews split from the central communal structure. The Ktav Sofer (see 5599/1839) was an active organizer of the Orthodox, who subsequently established their own separate communal structure with the support of the Maharam Schick (see 5621/1861), and this structure was later recognized by the government.

R.Shimshon Rapha'el Hirsch followed the example of Hungarian Orthodoxy, and subsequently established German Orthodoxy on a separate basis.

R.Azriel Hildesheimer was Rabbi in Eisenstadt (Austrian Hungary), and had disagreed with the establishment of the separate Orthodox communal structure. This created friction between him and many other rabbis in Hungary, and in 1869 he left to become Rabbi in Berlin, where in many ways he followed the style of R.Shimshon Rapha'el Hirsch.

R.Yosef Chaim (ben Eliyahu) Al-Chakkam of Baghdad, a Halacha authority whose *piyutim* have been incorporated in the Iraqi liturgy, was author of the very popluar *Ben Ish Chai* (homily with Halacha and Kabbala), among many other (unpublished) works. He visited Eretz Yisrael in 1869.

5631 / 1871

The Jews were attacked in anti-Jewish riots in Odessa (Russia) during Pesach.

5632 / 1872

R.Shmuel Strashun of Vilna, a disciple of the Chayei Adam and author of *Hagahot HaRaShash* (notes on Talmud), died.

5633 / 1873

The *Chafetz Chaim* was published.

R.Yisrael Meir HaKohen (Kagan) (see 5672/ 1912) (anonymously) published his work *Chafetz Chaim* (Halacha of slander/gossip, etc.). He later became known as the Chafetz Chaim, and wrote the popular *Mishna Berura* (commentary on the *Orach Chayim* section of *Shulchan Aruch*).

5634 / 1874

Adm.R.Yitzchak Yehuda Yechi'el of Komarno (Austrian Galicia), known as R.Aisik (el) Komarno, who was a nephew of Adm.R.Tzvi Hirsch of Zydachov (a disciple of the Chozeh of Lublin) and was a prolific writer, died on the 10th Iyar.

The Minchat Chinuch died.

R.Yosef Babad, author of *Minchat Chinuch* (commentary on *Sefer HaChinuch*) and Rabbi of Tarnopol (then Austria), died, some say on the 25th Elul.

R.Yechi'el Michel Epstein, author of *Aruch Ha Shulchan* (Halacha update based on *Shulchan Aruch*),

became Rabbi in Novogrodek (Russia) where he remained until he died. His son (and disciple) was R.Baruch, author of Torah Temima (collection of Talmud statements on the *Chumash*.

5636 / 1876

The Divrei Chaim, Adm.R.Chaim (Halberstam) of Tzanz, died on the 25th Nissan. He was succeeded as Rebbe (Admur, "Tzadik") by his six sons, including Adm.R.Yechezk'el Shraga of Shinev (Austrian Galicia), known as the Divrei Yechezk'el, who later visited Eretz Yisrael and, some say, later considered settling in the United States. The Divrei Chaim was also succeeded by his grandson, Adm.R.Shlomo of Bobov (Austrian Galicia).

5638 / 1878

Petach Tikva agricultural settlement was established.

The agricultural village of Petach Tikva was established in Eretz Yisrael by a group of observant Jews from Yerushalayim and (recent immigrants) from Hungary. This was the first such settlement in Eretz Yisrael in almost 2,000 years, and the settlers faced the problems of malaria and of Arab attacks – problems which the many subsequent settlements (primarily secular Zionist) also faced. This was also probably the first time that some Jews from Yerushalayim sought their economic independence, rather than subsisting on the *Chaluka* (charity funds collected overseas), as had been the custom for centuries.

5639 / 1879

R.Shimon Sofer (son of the Chassam Sofer), was Rabbi in Cracow and together with Adm. R.Yehoshua of Belz (both in Austrian Galicia), he founded an organization (Machazikei HaDat) to counter the activities of the maskilim, who were well organized. The maskilim already held three seats in the Austrian parliament (see 5580/1820) and were planning to open a rabbinical seminary (see 5605/1844). Machazikei HaDat had four candidates for the next parliamentary election, and R.Shimon was (the only one) elected.

5640 / 1880

R.Yaakov AbiChatzira of Morocco, who was the author of many works and renowned for his expertise in practical Kabbala, with a wide reputation for miraculous deeds, died in Egypt on his way to Eretz Yisrael on the 20th Tevet.

Living in the Year 1880		
	b.	d.
Kitzur Shulchan Aruch		
(R.Shl.Ganzfried)	1804	1886
R.Shimshon Raphael Hirsch	1808	1888
R.Yisrael Salanter	1810	1883
Divrei Yechezk'el		
(of Shinev)	1811?	1899
Aruch HaShulchan		
(R.Yechi'el Epstein)	1829	1908
Sdei Chemed (R.Chaim		
Chizkiyah Medini)	1832	1904
Ben Ish Chai (R.Yosef		
Chaim Al-Chakkam)	1833?	1909
Chafetz Chaim		
(R.Yisrael Meir Kagan)	1838	1933
Darkei Teshuva		
(R.Tzvi Hirsch Shapira)	1845?	1913
Sfass Emess (of Gur)	1847	1905
R.Chaim Brisker	1853	1918
Rogatchover Gaon		
(R.Yosef Rozin)	1858	1936
Torah Temima		
(R.Baruch Epstein)	1860	1942

5641 / 1881

Many Jews began leaving Russia after a wave of pogroms.

Czar Alexander II, who had made many (mild) changes in Russia, was nevertheless assassinated by revolutionaries, and the Jews were blamed.

Pogroms (anti-Jewish riots) broke out in southern Russia (see 5642/1882) in Adar, and swept across the whole country (often with the open encouragement of local officials). The pogroms continued sporadically over the next three years, resulting in many injuries, enormous damage to Jewish property (including synagogues), and the desecration of Torah scrolls.

Maskilim were disillusioned by the attitude of non-Jewish intellectuals, who often demonstrated open support for the rioters; assimilationist Jews were disillusioned by the expressions of rejection from all strata of the Russian society (into which they believed they had successfully assimilated).

Many such Jews saw Jewish nationalism as an alternative ideology, and this gave momentum to the developing secular nationalistic concept of "the Return to Zion" (see 5655/1895). Many small groups were formed to discuss emigration (aliya) to Eretz Yisrael, and they were supported and joined by some Rabbis (see 5653/1893, 5655/1895, 5656/1896).

Many Jews decided to leave Russia, and 2 million left in the next thirty-two years. Most of them went to the economically appealing United States, where approximately 280,000 Jews were living (see 5660/1900, 5685/1925), and some say 200 synagogues, only twelve of which were not Reform already existed (see 5605/1844). A vast majority of the Jews arriving in the United States gave up some of their religious observances, particularly Shabbat because workers were required to work on Saturday (see 5698/1938), yet retained their Jewishness as a culture, and an ethnic identity.

Some idealistic groups emigrated to Eretz Yisrael, where there were over 20,000 Jews at this time (see 5675/1915), living under harsh economic conditions. These groups were small (the influential Bilu group numbered only fifty-three immigrants, and a number of them left for the United States or returned to Russia).

The yeshiva (of Chabad) in Starodub (Russia) was closed by the government, after a denunciation by one of the local maskilim (see 5590/1830).

5642 / 1882

The Jews were attacked in Algiers and other cities of Algeria, in sporadic anti-Jewish rioting over the course of the next few years (see 5657/1897). Many Jews were killed, some synagogues were plundered, and Torah scrolls were desecrated.

An enquiry by the Russian goverment into the pogroms of 1881 decided that the Jews themselves were to blame, because of their "economic exploitation" of other citizens. Consequently, the goverment passed the series of May Laws in which, among other discriminatory provisions, the Jews were expelled from all villages and rural settlements and were allowed to live only in the towns (see 5603/1843, 5651/1891).

Some Jews were accused in a blood libel in Tisza Eszlar (Hungary) and although they were later acquitted, the accusation led to many anti-Jewish riots throughout the country.

5643 / 1882

Adm.R.Shmuel Schneersohn of Lubavitch had traveled to Western Europe a number of times, and attempted to influence the large bankers there to withhold much-needed loans to the Russian government, if a change of policy toward the Jews was not forthcoming (see 5641/1881, 5642/1882). He died on 13th Tishrei and was succeeded by his (22-year-old second) son Adm.R.Shalom Dov Ber.

5643 / 1883

R.Yisrael Salanter lived in Paris for two years (see 5617/1857) before returning to Germany, where he died on the 25th Shvat.

The Yetev Lev, Adm.R.Yekutiel Yehuda Teitelbaum (see 5618/1858), died on the 6th Elul, and was succeeded by his son Adm.R.Chananyah

Yom Tov Lipa, as Rabbi and Rebbe (Admur "Tzadik") in Sighet (Rumania).

R.Shmuel Ehrenfeld died. He was a grandson of the Chassam Sofer, author of Chatan Sofer (Halacha), and Rabbi in Mattesdorf (Austria).

5645 / 1884

Adm.R.Menachem Mendel of Vizhnitz, a grandson of Adm.R.Menachem Mendel of Kossov (then Austria), and a son-in-law of Adm.R.Yisrael of Rushin, was the Rabbi and Rebbe (Admur, "Tzadik") of Vizhnitz (then Austria), and author of Tzemach Tzadik (Chasidut). He died on Erev Rosh Chodesh Cheshvan and was succeeded by his son Adm.R.Baruch.

Adm.R.Avraham (ben Yitzchak Mattityahu), a disciple of Adm.R.Moshe of Kobrin (who was a disciple of R.Mordechai of Lechevitch), was Rebbe in Slonim. He died on the 11th Cheshvan.

5645 / 1885

The Reform movement in the United States (see 5641/1881), at a conference in Pittsburgh, adopted a platform of principles that denied the current validity of Jewish law (Halacha) (see 5611/1851). A reaction developed against this extreme position, and many of the more traditional (although not fully Halacha-observant) scholars and laymen developed what came to be known as the Conservative movement.

5646 / 1886

R.Shlomo Ganzfried (author of *Kitzur Shulchan Aruch*) died.

R.Shlomo Ganzfried, author of the *Kitzur Shulchan Aruch* (Halacha) and *Kesset HaSofer* (Halacha for scribes), among other works, was Rabbi in Ungvar (Hungary). The *Kitzur* (abridged) *Shulchan Aruch* was already so popular during his lifetime that it had gone through fourteen editions, and had sold almost 250,000 copies, by the time he died in Tammuz 1886.

R.Chaim Yeshayahu Halbesberg had already written *Misgeret HaShulchan* (a commentary on the *Kitzur Shulchan Aruch*), which was later printed in an edition of the *Kitzur Shulchan Aruch* that included a number of his editorial refinements.

5648 / 1888

R.Meir Simcha HaKohen, author of *Or Same'ach* (commentary on the Rambam's Yad HaChazaka), became a rabbi in Dvinsk (Latvia), where he remained for almost forty years until his death.

There were already some 130 Orthodox synagogues in New York at this point (see 5641/1881). Many congregational rabbis, as well as self-proclaimed immigrant rabbis, were acting as independent Halacha authorities, particularly in the financially rewarding area of kashrut supervision. One of the largest congregations had (in association with other congregations) brought R.Yaakov Yosef from Vilna in 1888, to become their Rabbi and also the Chief Rabbi of New York.

Although R.Yaakov Yosef had some initial success in consolidating a structure of central religious authority, there were powerful (and ruthless) self-interest groups that resisted. By 1902 (when he died at 59 in poverty and almost forgotten) there were already 250 synagogues with increased petty rivalries stemming primarily from the different origins of the people. The Jewish "community" of New York had settled into irreversible anarchy.

5649 / 1889

R.Yosef Rozin, the Rogatchover Gaon, a great Talmud scholar of a caliber unknown for many generations, wrote a number of works all entitled *Tzaphnat Pane'ach*, which are often only cryptic notes (without the aid of commentary). In 1889 he

became Rabbi of the Chasidic community in Dvinsk (Latvia) (see 5648/1888).

5650 / 1890

A committee was established in Eretz Yisrael, to make Hebrew a language of daily use.

5651 / 1891

The Jews were expelled from Moscow (see 5642/1882), and 30,000 were forced to sell their properties and leave. Some wealthy merchants, and some Cantonists who had completed their full military service (see 5587/1827), were permitted to stay.

5652 / 1892

R.Chaim (Brisker) became Rabbi in Brisk.

R.Chaim Solovetchik, who had been a lecturer in the Volozhin Yeshiva (see 5653/1893), succeeded his father, R.Yosef Ber Solovetchik (who had previously been a Rosh Yeshiva in Volozhin) as Rabbi in Brisk (Brest-Litovsk). R.Chaim Brisker was known for introducing an analytical style of Talmud study.

5653 / 1893

R.Naftali Tzvi Yehuda Berlin, the Netziv, was a son-in-law of R.Yitzchak Volozhiner, and succeeded him as Rosh Yeshiva in Volozhin (see 5581/1821, 5603/1843). The Russian government had demanded that secular studies be taught at the yeshiva, and the number of students be reduced. The Netziv failed to fully accomplish either demand, although, some say, lectures in Russian were introduced, and so the yeshiva was closed. The Netziv left Volozhin, with the hope of settling in Eretz Yisrael, an ideal he supported (see 5641/1881), but he died in Warsaw in 1893, eighteen months after the yeshiva closed.

5655 / 1895

A Jewish captain in the French army (Alfred Dreyfus) was falsely convicted of spying in 1895, which aroused much anti-Jewish expression throughout the country. A newspaper reporter from Vienna, Theodore Herzl (a Hungarian Jew from an assimilated family), was profoundly moved by this wave of anti-Jewish sentiment, which sparked a Jewish identity crisis in him. He consequently developed the idea of creating a Jewish state (with its own political self-rule), and he became obsessed with the idea, meeting with wealthy Jews, as well as with statesmen and politicians, to promote the scheme. He persevered, despite the ridicule he received and within two years convened a congress of all the various groups that were promoting a return to Eretz Yisrael (see 5641/1881). He established the Zionist movement, which developed into a powerful (if controversial) political force under his leadership.

Many rabbis and virtually all Admurim (Chasidic "Tzadikim") strongly opposed the Zionist movement because of its secular orientation, which (ironically) was blended with a messianic undertone. There were also rabbis who were strong proponents of religious Zionism, which led to the later establishment of Mizrachi (from "MerkaZ RuCHanI"), in Vilna (in 1902), as a religious faction within the Zionist movement.

5656 / 1896

R.Yitzchak Elchanan Spektor, Rabbi of Kovno (Lithuania), who was very involved in Russian communal affairs and supported the new enthusiasm for settling in Eretz Yisrael (see 5641/1881), died in Adar.

Solomon Schechter, a conservative-progressive scholar (see 5645/1885) who was later responsible for the formal organization of the Conservative movement in the United States, extracted a large collection of (approximately 100,000) ancient Jewish manuscripts from Cairo and took them to Cambridge University in England. The "geniza"

was in the attic of the very old Ezra Synagogue (built in 4642/882, in Fostat, Old Cairo, where it is said the Rambam had taught). The existence of the books and documents (more of which were subsequently taken by other large libraries) had been known for a long time, but they had remained untouched because of local fears and beliefs.

5657 / 1897

Jews were attacked by anti-Jewish rioters in Mostaganem (Algeria) (see 5642/1882).

5658 / 1897

A general Jewish socialist workers union (Bund) was founded at a secret meeting in Vilna. The Bund later became involved in Russian revolutionary activity (in alliance with the Communists) and was at the forefront of a movement which promoted Yiddish as the basis of a secular culture (see 5680/1920).

Jews were attacked in a pogrom in Bucharest in Kislev.

5659 / 1899

R.Chaim Chizkiyah Medini, author of *Sdei Chemed* (Halacha encyclopedia), was Rabbi in the Crimea for over thirty years, after having lived in (Istanbul) Constantinople for fourteen years. In 1899 he returned to Yerushalayim, where he was born,and though he declined to become Sephardi Chief Rabbi (Rishon LeTziyon), he did become Rabbi in Hevron.

Leopold Hilsner, a Jew, was sentenced to death in Bohemia in a blood libel, which aroused strong anti-Jewish expressions in the press. His sentence was later reduced to life imprisonment.

5660 / 1900

There were now 50,000 Jews in Eretz Yisrael (see 5641/1881, 5675/1915), and 1,000,000 Jews in the United States (see 5641/1881, 5675/1915, and 5648/1888).

Living in the Year 1900		
	b.	d.
Aruch HaShulchan		
(R.Yechi'el Epstein)	1829	1908
Sdei Chemed (R.Chaim		
Chizkiyah Medini)	1832	1904
Ben Ish Chai (R.Yosef		
Chaim Al-Chakkam)	1833?	1909
Chafetz Chaim		
(R.Yisrael Meir Kagan)	1838	1933
Darkei Teshuva		
(R.Tzvi Hirsch Shapira)	1845?	1913
Sfass Emess (of Gur)	1847	1905
R.Chaim Brisker	1853	1918
Rogatchover Gaon		
(R.Yosef Rozin)	1858	1936
Torah Temima		
(R.Baruch Epstein)	1860	1942

5663 / 1903

Forty-nine Jews were killed and 500 were injured in Kishinev (Russia), in a pogrom in the month of Nissan (see 5668/1907) which had begun with a blood libel, and was further incited by newspaper attacks. Russian officials openly supported the pogrom, in order to divert public attention from the fermenting revolution (see 5641/1881, 5665/1905).

Eight Jews were killed in Homel (Russia) in a pogrom in the month of Elul and thirty-six of the Jews who fought in self-defense were charged with committing a pogrom against Russian citizens.

5664 / 1903

Marcus Jastrow, a Polish conservative-progressive scholar (see 5645/1885) and the author of an Aramaic–English dictionary (popular among English-speaking Talmud students), died in the month of Tishrei in the United States.

5664 / 1904

Adm.R.Chananyah Yom Tov Lipa Teitelbaum (see 5643/1883) died in the month of Shvat, and was succeeded by his sons – Adm.R.Chaim Tzvi, author of a number of works called *Atzei Chayim*, who was Rabbi and Rebbe (Admur, "Tzadik") in Sighet (Rumania); and Adm.R.Yoel(ish), who later (see 5688/1928) became Rabbi and Rebbe in Satmar (Satu Mare Rumania).

R.Yaakow Chaim (Sofer) of Baghdad, author of *Caf HaChayim* (on Shulchan Aruch), settled in Eretz Yisrael.

5665 / 1905

The Sfass Emess died.

The Sfass Emess, Adm.R.Yehuda Leib Alter of Gur, author of *Sfat Emet* (Chasidic thought, Chidushim) had maintained regular (Torah) contact with Chasidim fighting at the front in the Russo-Japanese War. He died on the 5th Shvat, and was succeeded by his son, Adm.R.Avraham Mordechai.

Many Jews were killed in (official) Russian pogroms.

After losing the war with Japan, Russia was stirring with revolutionary agitation (the Czar was forced to establish a parliament), and government officials and Czarist supporters sought to divert the attention of the masses with anti-Jewish incitement (see 5663/1903). As a result almost 700 (sanctioned) pogroms were carried out against the Jews, and more than 800 Jews were killed over the course of less than two years (see 5666/1906).

Twenty-five Jews were killed in Zhitomir in the month of Nissan (including ten who were killed on their way from another town to help with the fighting). One hundred and twenty Jews were killed in Yekaterinoslav (Dnepropetrovsk) in the month of Tishrei 5666/1905; forty were killed in Simferopol (Crimea); fifty in Rechitsa; and 300 in Odessa.

5666 / 1906

Seventy Jews were killed (and seventy seriously injured) in a pogrom (see 5665/1905) in Bialystok (Russia) in the month of Sivan, and thirty Jews were killed in Siedlice (Russia) in Elul.

R.Yosef Engel, who wrote many works on Halacha and Kabbala, became Rabbi in Cracow.

5668 / 1907

Thirty Jews were killed (and 250 women and children were abducted) in tribal riots in Casablanca (Morocco).

Nineteen Jews were killed in a pogrom (see 5665/1905) in Kishinev (Russia) in Cheshvan (see 5663/1903).

5669 / 1909

R.Shmuel Salant, Chief Rabbi of the Ashkenazi community in Yerushalayim (where he had lived for almost 70 of his 93 years), died in the month of Av and was succeeded by R.Chaim Berlin. Since R.Shmuel's arrival in Yerushalayim in 1841, he had seen the Jewish community grow from 500 people to 30,000 (see 5660/1900, 5675/1915).

The city of Tel Aviv was founded as a suburb of Yaffo (Jaffa) in 1909.

5670 / 1910

Adm.R.Avraham of Sochatchev (Poland), the son-in-law of R.Mendel of Kotzk, and author of *Eglei Tal* and *Avnei Nezer* (Halacha, *Sh'elot UTeshuvot*), died on the 11th AdarI.

5671 / 1911

Chazon Ish was published.

The Chazon Ish, R.Avraham Yeshayahu Karelitz (see 5714/1953), anonymously published the first volume of *Chazon Ish* (on *Shulchan Aruch*).

Menachem Mendel Beilis was accused of murder (on extremely weak evidence) in a blood libel in Kiev (Russia) in 1911, and was imprisoned for two years. The case raised an international outcry; he was later tried (in 1913) and subsequently freed.

5672 / 1912

An organization (political in nature) was formed to maintain and strenthen the adherence to Halacha among Jews (see 5639/1879), because of the eroding influences of the reformers, assimilationists, and socialist/Yiddishists (see 5658/1897). The organization, Agudat Yisrael, was founded in the month of Sivan at a conference in Kattowitz (Silesia) and included the Orthodox communities of Germany and Hungary, as well as the religious Jews of Poland, Russia, and Lithuania. The conference was opened by the Chafetz Chaim (a revered Torah leader), and was supported by (see 5674/1914) such notables as R.Chaim Brisker and the Admur (Rebbe "Tzadik") of Gur (see 5674/1913).

5674 / 1913

Adm.R.Tzvi Hirsch Shapira, a great-grandson of the Bnei Yissachar and a disciple of the Divrei Chaim (Tzanzer), was Rabbi and Rebbe (Admur, "Tzadik") in Munkatch (Austrian Hungary). He was author of *Darkei Teshuva* (commentary and update on the *Yoreh Deya* section of *Shulchan Aruch*) and *Be'er LaChay Ro'i* (commentary on *Tikkunei Zohar*), and was opposed to Hungarian religious Jews joining the Agudat Yisrael (see 5672/1912) (because they would be influenced by the modernity of the participating German Jews). He died on the 16th Tishrei (second day of Sukkot) and was succeeded by his son Adm.R.Chaim Elazar, who was vehemently opposed to the recent settlement of Eretz Yisrael, and was involved in many controversies, including some with other Chasidic Rebbes (Admurim).

5674 / 1914

R.Yitzchak HaLevi Rabinowitz (of Lithuania), was Rabbi of Hamburg and author of *Dorot HaRishonim* (an exhaustively erudite – if cumbersome and emotive – defense of classical-traditional Jewish history). He had been one of the motivators for the formation of Agudat Yisrael (see 5672/1912), and he died on the 20th Iyar.

Over 500,000 Jewish soldiers fought in World War I.

Germany declared war on Russia on Tisha B'Av, which marked the opening of the Eastern European front in World War I, during which some 400,000 Russian Jews and over 100,000 German Jews were drafted. Some 12,000 Jewish German soldiers were killed during the four-year war, and many more Russian Jews were killed in the upheavals that rocked that country over the next seven years (see 5677/1917, 5678/1918, 5680/1920).

Fifty thousand Jews served as soldiers in the English armies, suffering heavy (10,000) casualties.

When the Russians suffered defeat and losses, they sought to blame the Jews (as the front lines passed through densely Jewish-populated areas). Many Jews were accused of treason and espionage, and tens of thousands were sent to the Russian interior. The Jews were expelled from towns near the front line, and printing in Hebrew characters (which included Yiddish) was prohibited, silencing the Yiddish newspapers and blacking out vital precautionary information on military clashes near populated areas.

Germany and Austria conquered territory with a total Jewish population of over 2,250,000.

Thirty-three Jews were killed when the invading German army set fire to the Jewish section of Kalisch (Poland).

5675 / 1915

Of the 85,000 Jews living in Eretz Yisrael (under Turkish rule) at this time (see 5660/1900, 5685/1925), thousands died of starvation during the war, and many left.

At this point there were approximately 3,250,000 Jews in the United States (see 5660/1900, 5685/1925) who raised very substantial sums of money to assist the Jews in Russia and in the occupied areas of the war as well as Eretz Yisrael.

A Jew, Leo Frank, who had been charged with murder based on flimsy evidence, was lynched by an anti-Semitic mob, in Georgia (the United States) in the month of Elul.

5677 / 1917

Widespread strikes and street demonstrations in Russia crippled the authority of Czar Nicholas II who was forced to resign, and the country was ruled (for a few months) by a provisional government which abolished most of the discriminatory restrictions against the Jews, including the Pale of Settlement (see 5551/1791). This government failed to gain full control, and the communist Bolsheviks seized power, plunging Russia into a civil war (which lasted until 1921) in which the Jews suffered many attacks (see 5678/1918, 5679/1918, 5679/1919, 5680/1920).

5678 / 1917

Sarah Schenirer started a small school in Cracow to teach traditional Jewish studies to girls. The school (Beit Yaakov) grew rapidly, and became the beginning of a new direction in the traditional education of women and girls.

The British (who were also fighting on the Middle Eastern front during World War I) announced in the Balfour Declaration that they supported the Zionist concept of a national country (see 5655/ 1895) for the Jews in Eretz Yisrael. They captured Tel Aviv and Yaffo (Jaffa) from the Turkish Empire (see 5276/1516) at the beginning of Kislev 5678/1917, and the Jews,who has been expelled by the Turks, returned. The British then captured Yerushalayim.

Fifty thousand Greek Jews were left homeless, (according to some) when a fire destroyed much of Salonika. This, along with subsequent government restrictions and other hardships caused many of them to leave the country.

5678 / 1918

Over 60,000 Jews were killed during the Russian Revolution.

The Ukrainians (under Simon Petlyura, see Tammuz 7 5701/1941) established their independence from Russia (which was in the throes of a civil war), and the Jews were massacred for over two years in pogroms originating from all sides (army forces, nationalists, and peasant bands). Over 525 communities were attacked, 60,000 Jews were killed, and many times that number were wounded (see 5679/1919, 5680/1920).

Ninety Jews were killed in the month of Nissan, in Novgorod-Seversk (Ukraine), in an anti-Jewish attack by the "Red" Russianarmy retreating from the Germans.

5679 / 1918

Seventy Jews were killed in Lvov (Lemberg) Poland in a pogrom by Polish soldiers in the month of Kislev. The soldiers were fighting the Ukrainians (see 5678/1918) for control of eastern Galicia.

5679 / 1919

Seventeen hundred Jews were killed in the month of Adar by the Ukrainian Nationalists (see 5678/

1918) in a four-hour pogrom in Proskurov and eighty Jews were killed in Zhitomir (Ukraine).

Thirty-five Jews were executed by the Polish in Pinsk (then Poland) on dubious allegations, in the month of Nissan; two Jews were killed in a pogrom in Kalisch (Poland).

Seven hundred Jews of Cherkassy (Ukraine) were killed by Cossacks in pogroms in the month of Iyar, and 250 were later killed by the Russian "White Army" in Av.

Four hundred Jews were killed by peasant bands in a pogrom in Trostyanets (Ukraine) in the month of Iyar (see 5678/1918); 317 were killed in another pogrom in Zhitomir (Ukraine), and 170 in Tulchin (Ukraine); and 80 Jews were killed by Polish troops in Vilna (then Poland).

Forty Jews were massacred in Bugoslav (Ukraine) by the Russian "White Army" on the 30th Av.

Thirty-six Jews of Kiev were executed by Petlyura's Ukrainian army in the month of Elul, and 1,500 Jews were killed by the Russian "White" army in a pogrom in Fastov (Ukraine).

5680 / 1919

Adm.R.David (benYitzchak) of Skvira (see 5597/1837) died on the 15th Kislev in Kiev (where he had moved with his whole family because of the pogroms and unrest in other parts of the Ukraine), and many of his family died the same year.

5680 / 1920

Arab nationalists attacked many of the new Jewish settlements in northern Eretz Yisrael in the month of Adar (see 5638/1878), and a number of defenders were killed (eight of them at Tel Chai, including Yosef Trumpeldor, a decorated Jewish Russian officer who had come to asist in the defense). Five Jews were killed during Pesach, in an Arab attack in Yerushalayim.

Although there was a high proportion of Jews in the early leadership of communist Russia (see 5658/1897) (and almost half of the "Red Army" officers were Jewish), there was an ideological commitment among many of these leaders to eradicate the distinctiveness of the Jews. A special government "Jewish section" had been established (the Yevesektzia) which used the assistance of the police and the dreaded internal security forces to close down synagogues and all places of Jewish learning. Religious observance was singled out for particularly cruel and venomous suppression, and rabbis, schochtim (ritual slaughterers), and teachers risked their lives to fulfill their communal religious obligations (see 5684/1924, 5687/1927, 5693/1933, Av 5704/1944).

Adm.R.Shalom Dov Ber of Lubavitch (see 5643/1882) established a yeshiva (in 1911) in Hevron in the particular Chasidic style of the yeshiva he had established earlier (in 1897) in Lubavitch (Russia), which he had left late in 1915, before settling in Rostov (Russia). He died on the 2nd Nissan and was succeeded by his (only) son, Adm.R.Yosef Yitzchak, who immediately expanded his father's activities in assisting the Jews of Russia at a time of desperate religious and economic need.

The British took formal control of Eretz Yisrael in the month of Iyar (see 5678/1917), under the authority of the internationally endorsed Palestine Mandate.

A newly established council (Rabbanut) of Yerushalayim invited R.Avraham Yitzchak Kook (who was returning to Eretz Yisrael after the war) to be Av Bet Din, and (the first) Ashkenazi Chief Rabbi of Eretz Yisrael. This council was opposed by R.Yosef Chaim Sonnenfeld (a disciple of the Ktav Sofer) and R.Yitzchak Yerucham Diskin (because secular Zionists were involved in its formation), and they established their own council, which became known as Eda HaCharedit.

Four thousand Jews were killed by armed bands in a pogram in Tetiyev (Ukraine).

R.David AbiChatzira was killed by a cannon shot in Morocco.

Living in the Year 1920		
	b.	d.
Chafetz Chaim		
(R.Yisrael Meir Kagan)	1838	1933
Rogatchover Gaon		
(R.Yosef Rozin)	1858	1936
Torah Temima		
(R.Baruch Epstein)	1860	1942

5681 / 1921

Forty-seven Jews were killed in Arab riots in Yaffo (Jaffa) in Nissan (see Adar 5680/1920), and four Jews were killed while defending Petach Tikva from an Arab attack.

R.Shraga Faivel Mendelovitz, who had settled in the United States in 1913, became Rosh Yeshiva in New York where he was active in attempts to reassert the traditional study of Torah in the United States.

5684 / 1923

Daf HaYomi study cycle commenced.

R.Meir Shapira, who was a leading Rabbi in Poland known as the Lubliner Rav, and a member (for a while) of the Polish parliament, instituted the practice of Daf HaYomi (one page of Talmud study per day) which began on Rosh HaShana 5684/1923.

5684 / 1924

Adm.R.Yosef Yitzchak of Lubavitch organized a mass underground network of Jewish religious institutions in Russia (see 5680/1920), and when any melamed (teacher), shochet (ritual slaughterer), or rabbi was arrested for this work, the Lubavitcher rebbe's followers (chasidim) were prepared to replace them at great personal risk. He was forced by the internal security forces to leave Rostov at the instigation of the Yevesektzia (see

5680/1920), and he moved to Leningrad where he secretly continued his work (see 5687/1927).

5685 / 1925

There were now approximately 120,000 Jews in Eretz Yisrael (see 5675/1915, 5689/1929), and 4,500,000 Jews in the United States (see 5675/1915), the largest Jewish community in the world and the largest single ethnic group in the United States.

R.Menachem Kasher, a disciple of the Adm.R. Avraham of Sochatchev and author of *Torah Sheleima* an encyclopedic collection of Talmud and Midrash statements on passages of the *Chumash* (Bible), among other encyclopedic works, settled in Yerushalayim, where he was Rosh Yeshiva in the yeshiva established by Adm.R.Avraham Mordechai of Gur.

The (original) yeshiva of Slobodka (Russia) was transferred to Hevron.

R.Isser Zalman Meltzer, a disciple of R.Chaim Brisker and the Chafetz Chaim, and author of *Even HaEzel* (on *Yad HaChazaka* of the Rambam), was Rosh Yeshiva in Slutzk (Russia). He settled in Eretz Yisrael, and became a Rosh Yeshiva in Yerushalayim.

5687 / 1927

The Lubavitcher Rebbe was released from Soviet prison.

Adm.R.Yosef Yitzchak of Lubavitch was arrested on the 15th Sivan by the communist regime of Russia, for his underground organizing of religious activity (see 5684/1924). He was abused, tortured (see 5710/1950), and sentenced to death without a trial which caused an international outcry. He was given notice of release on the 12th Tammuz (his 47th birthday), and expelled from Soviet Russia. He settled in Riga (Latvia) before visiting Eretz Yisrael and the United States, and he later settled in Warsaw.

5688 / 1928

Adm.R.Yoel Teitelbaum (see 5664/1904) was appointed Rabbi (amid opposition) in Satmar (Rumania). A conflict ensued, but his supporters eventually prevailed after six years.

5689 / 1929

There were 150,000 Jews in Eretz Yisrael at this time (see 5685/1925, 5699/1939). Many were killed in an Arab pogrom (see 5681/1921), including sixty in Hevron where the community was virtually destroyed (see 5696/1936), and from which most of the survivors moved to Yerushalayim (see 5680/1920, 5685/1925).

After seven years of paralysis, Franz Rosenzweig, a German Jew who had become interested in Judaism after almost converting to Christianity, died (at the age of 43). He had come to the full observance of Halacha, after a fifteen-year search for Jewish expression, and his work in those years had a major impact on (German) secular-oriented scholars.

5693 / 1933

R.Yechezk'el Abramsky, author of *Chazon Yechezk'el* (on Tosephta), had been released in Soviet Russia from his sentence of hard labor (see 5680/1920) after two years. Allowed to leave Russia, he settled in London and became a very influential rabbi.

The Nazis (a virulently anti-Jewish, extreme right-wing political party led by Adolf Hitler) came to power in Germany on the 3rd Shvat, and the 500,000 Jews of Germany (see 5699/1939) began to suffer immediate hardships (economic sanctions, arrests, torture, and in some cases, murder).

The Chafetz Chaim, R.Yisrael Meir Kagan, died on the 24th Elul.

5694 / 1934

Twenty-five Jews were killed and many were wounded, in attacks by the (French-incited) Muslim population of Constantine (Algeria). The attacks ceased when the Jews organized a resistance.

5695 / 1935

R.Avraham Yitzchak Kook (see 5680/1920), an author of many works, who was also considered a philosopher and a mystic, died in 1935. He had narrowed the sphere of his influence as Ashkenazi Chief Rabbi of Yerushalayim (and Eretz Yisrael), by some of his politically unpopular opinions.

5696 / 1936

Eighteen Jews were killed in Arab riots in Tel Aviv in the month of Nissan (see 5689/1929), and strikes, terror, and unrest continued for three years in what was called "the Arab Revolt" against increased Jewish immigration (see 5699/1939). A total of almost 500 Jews were killed (despite well-organized Jewish defense [Hagana] units), and the Jewish community of Hevron which had recently been resettled (see 5689/1929) ceased to exist because of the upheavals. Nevertheless some 60,000 Jews entered Eretz Yisrael (legally and illegally) during those three years (164,000 had arrived in the previous three years).

Three Jews were killed and sixty wounded in a pogrom in Przytyk (Poland).

Two Jews were killed in a bomb attack in Temesvar (Rumania).

5698 / 1938

The Jews were attacked in many cities of Poland during this year.

The five-day (forty-hour) work week was introduced in the United States (other Western countries followed later), and this eventually allowed

for an increased level of Shabbat observance in industrialized Western countries (see 5641/1881).

All Jews of foreign origin were expelled from Italy in the month of Elul (by the extreme right-wing government of Mussolini, who had been in power since 1922).

5699 / 1938

Jews were attacked in the Kristallnacht pogrom in Germany.

The Nazi government of Germany incited a massive country-wide pogrom, which swept through Germany and Austria on the night of the 16th Cheshvan. Thirty-six Jews were killed (and many hundreds took their own lives); 30,000 were arrested and sent to concentration (prison) camps; 300 synagogues (and over 1,000 private Jewish properties) were completely destroyed; hundreds of Torah scolls were desecrated and destroyed (over sixty in the cities of Bamberg and Darmstadt alone); and many Jewish cemeteries were ruined. The pogrom was called Kristallnacht because of all the broken glass.

5699 / 1939

Hitler indicated in Shvat that there would be a war, and that the Jews of Europe would be exterminated.

There were over 400,000 Jews in Eretz Yisrael at this time (see 5689/1929, 5696/1936, 5709/1949).

The British Government announced their new policies for Eretz Yisrael (in what was called the White Paper), which restricted Jewish immigration (see 5696/1936) to 10,000 a year, and also restricted the possibility for Jews to buy land there.

A German ship arrived in Cuba with 1,000 Jews fleeing Europe, but they were not permitted to disembark, and no country would agree to accept them. They eventually returned to Europe; only 287 survived World War II.

By the time German troops invaded Poland on the 17th Elul (which started World War II), over 300,000 German Jews had left the country since the Nazi rise to power (see 5693/1933); 55,000 of them had gone to Eretz Yisrael, 70,000 to England and France, and 65,000 to the United States.

Over 100,000 Jews had left Austria since the Nazi annexation in Adar2 1938; 10,000 had gone to Eretz Yisrael, 30,000 to England, 28,000 to the United States, and 66,000 remained.

[5699/1939 continued in Chapter 15]

CHAPTER 15

The Holocaust, the Independent State of Israel, and the Current Era

THE HOLOCAUST, THE INDEPENDENT STATE OF ISRAEL, AND THE CURRENT ERA

The Holocaust

Jewish Year		Secular Year
5699	Germany started World War II and mass killing of Jews	1939
5701	**200,000 Jews were killed at Babi Yar and Ponary**	**1941**
5702	**400,000 Jews of Warsaw were sent to death camps**	**1942**
5703	**THE REMAINING JEWS IN WARSAW STAGED A MASSIVE UPRISING**	**1943**
5703	Jewish uprisings at Treblinka, Sobibor, and Bialystok	1943
5704	**300,000 Hungarian Jews were killed in three months**	**1944**
5705	Uprising in Auschwitz death camp just before freedom	1944
5705	Nazi Germany was conquered and World War II ended	1945
5705	**6,000,000 JEWS WERE KILLED BY THE NAZIS DURING THE WAR**	**1945**

The Independent State of Israel and the Current Era

Jewish Year		Secular Year
5707	Publication of the Talmud Encyclopedia was commenced. It hasn't been completed YET.	1947
5708	The United Nations divided Eretz Yisrael	1947
5708	Arabs attacked in Eretz Yisrael to gain territory	1947
5708	**THE STATE OF ISRAEL WAS ESTABLISHED IN ERETZ YISRAEL**	**1948**
5708	**Eretz Yisrael was invaded by many Arab countries**	**1948**
5709	**The War of Independence (in Eretz Yisrael) ended**	**1949**
5710	The Jews left the ancient Jewish community of Iraq	1950
5710	The Jews of Yemen emigrated to Eretz Yisrael	1950
5717	Jewish forces invaded Egypt and conquered the Sinai	1956
5727	**YERUSHALAYIM REUNITED UNDER JEWISH RULE IN SIX DAY WAR**	**1967**
5734	2,500 Jewish soldiers were killed in Yom Kippur war	1973
5742	Massive enemy arsenals were discovered in Lebanon	1982

5699/1939 is continued from Chapter 14.]

The following chronology is not comprehensive, but only a list of major incidents, incidents that serve to illustrate, and incidents that can be placed in a chronological context.

Germany started World War II and the mass killings of Jews.

The Germans started World War II by invading Poland on the 17th **Elul**, and they massacred Jews in their conquests. In Czestochowa (see Tammuz 5703/1943), they killed several hundred Jews on the 19th Elul. On the 25th Elul they set afire a synagogue in Bendin (Bedzin); the fire spread to the whole Jewish section, and no Jews were permitted to escape alive. Several hundred perished in the fire (as was the case in similar incidents elsewhere).

This was the start of a campaign to kill all the Jews in Europe (see Shvat 5699/1930). An estimated 6 million were eventually killed during the six years of World War II; many died of disease and starvation. The Jews were treated in the most hideous ways, many of which almost defy adequate description.

Russia annexed the eastern part of Poland in accord with a secret agreement with Germany (see 27th Sivan 5701/1941), and many Jews in those parts of Poland fled eastward into Russia. The Soviet Russians prohibited most (organized) Jewish activity (see 5680/1920), and many Jews were transported further east to work camps. In fact a larger proportion of Polish Jews who were in Russia during the war managed to survive. Among them was R.Dov Ber Wiedenfeld of Tschebin (Galicia), author of *Dovev Meisharim* (*Sh'elot UTeshuvot*), who settled in Yerushalayim after the war.

5700 / 1939

Five hundred Jews were killed in Przemysl (Poland) after the Germans captured the town on Rosh HaShana.

Ostrov Mazovyetzka (Poland) became a border town between the German and Russian armies

(see Elul 5699/1939), and the 560 Jews (out of 7,000) who did not escape to the Russian side, were killed by the Nazi German troops on the 29th **Tishrei**.

On the 13th **Cheshvan** the Nazis began to use Polish Jews for slave labor.

The Nazis forced the Jews of Petrokov (Poland) into a ghetto on the 15th Cheshvan. This was the beginning of the campaign in which they eventually crowded most of Polish Jewry into ghettos (mainly in Warsaw, Cracow, and Lublin), where as many as 30 percent died of disease and starvation under the resulting intolerable conditions.

5700 / 1940

After spending the first months of the war in Nazi-occupied Warsaw, Adm.R.Yosef Yitzchak of Lubavitch traveled a dangerous route (via Berlin) to Latvia (see 5687/1927) and then directly to the United States. He was met at the port by thousands of Jews on the 9th **Adar2**, and within days of his arrival he had established a yeshiva and embarked on a massive educational program, which included publications (in English and Yiddish), shi'urim (study sessions), and Jewish schools in towns outside of New York.

Although 1,750,000 Jews in the United States (see 5675/1915, 5685/1925) spoke Yiddish at home [U.S. 1940 census], there was a prevailing notion that "things were different in America" as compared with the religious observances in their native countries (see 5641/1881); it was this attitude that he consciously (and conscientiously) set out to fight.

He was joined fifteen months later by his son-in-law Adm.R.Menachem Mendel Schneersohn (who had been in Paris).

The Nazis transported Jews from villages and towns mostly to ghettos in larger cities and camps (where they instituted systematic killing). They opened the largest death camp on the 8th **Sivan** at Auschwitz (Oswiecim) Poland. This camp eventually covered an area of forty square kilometers, and could hold 140,000 prisoners. Two-and-a-half million Jews were killed there and half a million died of starvation and disease during its five-year existence.

By the 16th Sivan the Germans had also conquered Denmark, Norway, Holland, Belgium, and France.

5701 / 1940

Several thousand Jews had arrived "illegally" in Eretz Yisrael from Rumania, and the British decided to deport them (see 5699/1939). Seventeen hundred were placed on the steamer "Patria," which sank on the 24th **Cheshvan** (through miscalculated Jewish political sabotage) while still in the port of Haifa, and 250 Jews died.

Government representatives looked on as armed bands of Macedonian refugees confiscated Jewish businesses in Constanta (Rumania) on the 13th **Kislev**, and those who resisted disappeared. The city nevertheless served as an escape port for Jews fleeing Europe.

Eighteen hundred Jews of Chelm (Poland) were taken on a "death march" on the 19th Kislev and 1,400 were shot on the way.

The Imrey Emess, Adm.R.Avraham Mordechai of Gur, who (some say) had 250,000 followers (chasidim) and was the recognized leader of Polish religious Jewry, escaped from Warsaw and arrived in Eretz Yisrael (see 5685/1925) (where he had property bought on previous visits).

5701 / 1941

Many Jews (120) were killed in pogroms in Bucharest in the month of **Tevet**.

Many Jews (120–180) were killed in a massacre in Baghdad on the first day of Shavu'ot.

The Germans had already conquered Yugoslavia and Greece by this time.

On the 9th **Sivan**, Jewish property was confiscated by the Republic of Croatia (which joined Nazi Germany, together with Rumania, Hungary, and Bulgaria), and Jews were ordered to wear yellow badges.

35,000 Jews of Vilna were massacred and buried at Ponary.

On the 27th Sivan, the Germans suddenly attacked Russia with whom they had previously signed a peace agreement (see Elul 5699/1939), and they were welcomed with flowers by many non-Jewish Lithuanians when they entered Vilna. The Nazis immediately rounded up and began killing 35,000 Jews in the forest of Ponary, and 100,000 were eventually killed there. A thousand Jewish men of Augustow (Poland) were killed by the Nazis on the 27th Sivan.

When the Nazis conquered Lithuania within one week, the great yeshivot of Lithuania were closed, and some students escaped eastward (through Russia) to Shanghai. Some of the great Lithuanian Talmud scholars were killed by the Nazis, including R.Elchanan Wasserman (Rosh Yeshiva of Baranowice), R.Avraham Yitzchak Bloch, and R.Azriel Rabinovitz (Roshei Yeshiva in Telz).

R.Shimon Shkop (Rosh Yeshiva in Grodno) had died a year earlier, and R.Boruch Ber Leibovitz (the Kaminetzer Rosh Yeshiva) and R.Chaim Ozer Grodzinski (Rabbi in Vilna, and author of *Achi'ezer* (Sh'elot UTeshuvot) both died in this same year. R.Aharon Kotler (Rosh Yeshiva in Kletzk) escaped (via Japan) to the United States and established a new yeshiva in Lakewood, New Jersey. R.Yosef Kahaneman (Rabbi and Rosh Yeshiva in Ponevitch [Lithuania]) had been overseas when the war broke out, and he settled in Eretz Yisrael where he later established the Ponevitcher Yeshiva in Bnei Brak. R.Eliezer Yehuda Finkel (Rosh Yeshiva of Mir) escaped from war-torn Europe to Yerushalayim, where he established a yeshiva (called Mir); and the Mir Yeshiva which operated in Shanghai during the war years was later transferred to New York (two years after the war). The Yeshiva of Telz opened in Cleveland,

Ohio less than half a year after the original yeshiva was closed in Lithuania.

The Jews of Kovno (Lithuania) were massacred by Lithuanian Nazi sympathizers on the 1st Tammuz (see Av 5701/1941); 800 Jews were killed by invading Rumanian troops in Novoselitsa (Bessarabia, Russia) on the 2nd Tammuz; and the Germans killed over 6,000 Jews of Kovno in the ten days following the 3rd Tammuz. Twelve thousand Jews were killed in Jassy (Rumania) by German and Rumanian soldiers in a two-day massacre that started on the 3rd Tammuz; 1,000 Jews were burned in a synagogue in Bialystok (Poland) on the 3rd (see Av 5703/1943), and 3,300 were killed there in the following two weeks.

Five thousand Jews were killed outside Brisk (Brest-Litovsk) on the 4th Tammuz.

Many Ukrainians had welcomed the German invasion. On the 7th Tammuz the Germans instigated pogroms in Lvov (Lemberg) and Borislav (Poland), by reminding the local population of the assassination of their previous independence leader, Petlyura (see 5678/1918), who was killed by a Jew in 1926. More than 2,000 Jews were killed in these pogroms, and 3,500 Jews were killed by Ukrainians in Zlotchov (Poland) on the 8th Tammuz.

Four hundred Jews were killed by the German Nazis in Drogobych (Ukraine) (see Elul 5702/1942) on the 8th Tammuz; 3,000 were killed in a fortress outside of Lutzk (Poland) on the 9th (see Elul 5702/1942); and 5,000 were killed in Tarnopol (Poland) (see Iyar 5702/1942) in the week following the 9th Tammuz.

German and Rumanian troops captured Chernovitz (Rumania) from the Russians on the 10th Tammuz, and they massacred over 2,000 Jews. Two hundred Jews were killed in Czortkow (Poland) on the same day (see Tishrei 5702/1941), and German and Rumanian troops shot 2,000 Jews in Hotin (Bessarabia, Russia) on the 12th Tammuz.

Twelve hundred Jews were killed by the Nazis on the outskirts of Slonim (Poland) on the 22nd

Tammuz (see Elul 5701/1941). Three thousand Jews of the port town of Libava (Latvia) (see Kislev 5702/1941) were killed at the lighthouse on the 29th Tammuz, and 700 Jews were killed outside of Oshmyany (Lithuania) on the 1st Av.

Many Rebbes (Admurim, "Tzadikim") were killed by the Nazis (see Elul 5702/1942), and some escaped (see Adar2 5700/1940, 5701/1940, Tishrei 5704/1943, Kislev 5705/1944).

Adm.R.Ben Tziyon (ben Shlomo) of Bobov (see 5636/1876) was killed on the 4th Av, and his son Adm.R.Shlomo escaped and succeeded him (after the war, in the United States).

The Nazis killed 900 Jews of Vilkovishk (Lithuania) on the 4th Av, and 400 on the 8th Av (Erev Tisha B'Av); they killed 500 Jews six days later in Kishinev (Russia) and 3,000 in Ostraha (Poland) (see Elul 5701/1941) on the 11th Av; 1,000 Jews of Kovno (Lithuania) were killed on the 14th Av (see Tammuz 5701/1941), 1,500 Jews of Zambrov (Poland) on the 26th (1,000 were killed there two weeks later), and 350 Jews in the outskirts of Koretz (Poland) (see Sivan 5702/1942) on the 27th; 1,400 Jews were killed near Tiktin (Poland) on the 2nd Elul; 7,000 Jews were killed in Marijampole (Lithuania) and 2,500 in Ostraha (Poland) (see Av 5701/1941, Cheshvan 5702/1941) on the 9th Elul, 1,700 in Radomyshl (Poland) on the 14th, and 9,000 on the outskirts of Slonim (Poland) on the 22nd (see Tammuz 5701/1941). A few who escaped from the large pits into which they had been thrown came back to the ghetto hospital, but were seized by the Nazis, returned to the pits and shot.

There had been 30,000 Jews in Zhitomir (Russia) before the war, and the Nazis killed all (except for those who had fled) on the 27th Elul.

5702 / 1941

Twenty-eight thousand Jews of the vicinity of Vinitza (Russia) were killed there on Rosh HaShana.

The methods used by the Nazis for killing Jews did not meet their desired standards of efficiency (see Sivan 5702/1942), and so at this stage they began using poison gas in the Auschwitz death camp (see Sivan 5700/1940). They also extended the camp (by including Birkenau) in order to increase the intake capacity.

34,000 Jews of Kiev were massacred and buried at Babi Yar.

On the 8th and 9th **Tishrei** (Erev Yom Kippur) the Nazis machine-gunned 34,000 Jews on the outskirts of Kiev into the ravine of Babi Yar, where they were buried, many while still alive (see Elul 5701/1941). The total number of Jews eventually killed and buried there was 100,000.

When the Nazis ordered the Jews of Tuchin (Poland) to assemble on the 12th Tishrei, the heads of the Judenrat decided that everyone should revolt. Many were killed when the Nazis broke into the ghetto, but 2,000 escaped to the forests. Three hundred returned when the Nazis promised to allow volunteer returnees to live in the ghetto, but they were taken to the cemetery and shot. Many others were delivered back to the Nazis by local Ukrainians.

All 30,000 of the Jews of the Berditchev (Russia) ghetto were killed by the 14th Tishrei (Erev Sukkot), and 500 Jews were killed outside of Peremyshlany (Ukraine) on that day.

Ten thousand Jews were killed in the Jewish cemetery in Stanislav (Poland) (see Shvat 5703/1943) on Hoshana Rabba (21st Tishrei). The head of the Judenrat in Czortkow (Poland) (see Elul 5702/1942), Shmuel Kruh, was also killed on that day, for his strong stand against cooperating with the Nazis (see 4 Cheshvan 5703/1942).

Rumanian Legionnaires (see Sivan 5701/1941) entered Odessa (Russia) on the 25th Tishrei, and killed 8,000 Jews. They killed another 40,000 within the next ten days.

Twenty five hundred Jews were killed outside Kossov (Poland) on the 25th and 26th Tishrei, and all 1,700 Jews of Kaidanov (Russia) were killed on the 30th Tishrei.

Three thousand Jews were killed in Ostraha (Poland) (see Elul 5701/1941) on the 4th **Cheshvan**, 4,000 were killed in Kletzk (Lithuania) (see Av 5702/1942) on the 5th Cheshvan, 5,000 were killed in Nesvizh (Lithuania) (see Av 5702/1942) on the 9th Cheshvan, and 2,500 were killed in Nadvorna (Poland) on the 16th, the day that 18,000 Jews of Rovno (Poland) (see Tammuz 5702/1942) were machine-gunned by the Nazis in a forest. Twelve thousand Jews from the ghetto of Minsk (Russia) were killed in a similar manner on the 17th, and another 5,000 two weeks later (see Adar 5702/1942). Their houses were used by the Germans to settle Jews who had been deported from Germany and Austria.

The Nazis killed 1,500 Jews in Mir (Russia) on the 19th Cheshvan, 800 Jews were killed in Zaleshchiki (Poland) on the 24th Cheshvan, and 700 Jews from the ghetto of Lubavitch (Russia) were killed.

On the 10th **Kislev** 10,500 Jews of Riga (Latvia) were shot to death in a nearby forest; another 16,000 (including the historian Simon Dubnow) were killed during the ensuing week, and 1,500 Jews were killed in the forest near Borislav (Poland) (see Tammuz 5701/1941, Adar1 5703/1943). Four hundred Jews of Novogrodek (Russia) (see Av 5702/1942) were killed on the 17th Kislev, 3,500 Jews were killed in Libava (Latvia) (see Tammuz 5701/1941) on the first and second days of Chanuka (25th and 26th Kislev), and 900 Jews were killed outside of Zobalotov (Ukraine) on the 2nd **Tevet** (the last day of Chanuka).

5702 / 1942

More than 15,000 Jews were killed in Drobitzky Yar outside of Kharkov (Russia) in Tevet and Shvat, 1,400 Jews of Novi Sad (Yugoslavia) were shot and dumped into the icy waters of the Danube on the 5th **Shvat**, and 3,000 Jews were killed in Brailov (Russia) by the Germans on the 25th Shvat.

The Nazis sank the *Struma*, a ship with 769 Jewish refugees on board, which the British had turned back from Eretz Yisrael (see 5699/1939), in (or near) the Black Sea on the 7th **Adar** (see Cheshvan 5701/1940).

The Nazis killed several thousand Jews (including all the children in the orphanage) in Minsk on the 13th Adar (see Cheshvan 5702/1941, Av 5702/1942). The Jews in the Minsk (Russia) ghetto underground were well organized, and they eventually helped 10,000 Jews escape to the forests, despite the harsh reprisals the Nazis imposed if they were discovered.

Many Jews – some say over 25,000 – formed partisan groups (armed guerrillas) in the forests, and they attacked the Nazis sporadically (see Nissan 5703/1943, Cheshvan 5705/1944).

Fifteen hundred Jews were killed on Purim (14th Adar) in Dolhinov (Poland) (see Sivan 5702/1942), 800 Jews were killed in Radoshkovichi (Poland) on the 22nd Adar, and 1,000 were killed in Ilya (Poland) on the 28th.

Two thousand Jews were killed outside Rogatyn (Poland) on the 2nd **Nissan**, 1,500 Jews were killed near Horodenka (Poland) on the 17th (the third day of Pesach), and 900 were killed in Kitev (Poland) when the Germans set fire to Jewish houses on the 23rd Nissan.

On the 29th Nissan the Nazis proclaimed the Crimean peninsula – where some 60,000 Jews had lived before the war – to be Judenrein ("free" of any Jews); they did not consider the Kra'im (Kara'ites) living there to be Jews (see 5613/1853).

One thousand Jews were shot in a forest near Tarnopol (Poland) (see Tammuz 5701/1941) on the 8th **Iyar**; over 2,800 Jews of Dunayevtsy (Ukraine) were killed by the Nazi Germans on the 15th Iyar; all the Jews of Dokshytz (Poland) were taken outside the town and killed on the 18th Iyar (Lag B'Omer); and 2,000 Jews from Radin (Lithuania) were killed on the 23rd Iyar. Twenty-two hundred Jews were killed in Koretz (Poland) (see Av 5701/1941) on the 5th **Sivan** (Erev Shavu'ot); over 2,500 Jews were killed in Dolhinov (Poland)

see Adar 5702/1942) on the 6th (Shavu'ot); 1,500 Jews were killed in Radziwillow (Poland) on the 13th; 4,000 were killed in Kobrin (Poland) (see Cheshvan 5703/1942) on the 17th; and 3,000 Jews were killed by the Nazis in Braslav (Poland), in the three days commencing the 18th Sivan (see Adar2 5703/1943).

The chief Nazi exterminator of Jews (Reinhard Heydrich) was killed in Sivan by Czechoslovak partisans. The Nazis accelerated the massive extermination of the Polish Jews. They had been gassing Jews in vans by way of exhaust fumes but replaced this with the more efficient system of gassing rooms (see Tishrei 5702/1941) and cremating furnaces. Trains brought 6,000 to 10,000 Polish Jews a day to the death camps, mainly Treblinka and also Maidanek, Belzec, Sobibor, Chelmno, and Auschwitz. The latter began operating at its peak of efficiency in the extermination of Jews (at a rate of 10,000 a day) on the 5th Tammuz (see Tishrei 5702/1941).

On the 2nd **Tammuz** the Nazis shot at Jews escaping from the ghetto in Druya (Lithuania), and they set fire to the ghetto killing all 1,500 Jews. Twenty-five hundred Jews were killed outside Glubokoye (Poland) (see Av 5703/1943) on the 4th Tammuz, and the Nazis killed 5,000 Jews of Rovno (Poland) on the 28th (see Cheshvan 5702/1941).

The first transport of Dutch Jews arrived at Auschwitz on the 3rd **Av**, and Nazi leader Heinrich Himmler himself supervised their gassing. One thousand Jews were killed in the ghetto of Kletzk (Lithuania) (see Cheshvan 5702/1941) when the Nazis set it afire on the 7th Av. The Jews remaining in the ghetto of Nesvizh (Lithuania) (see Cheshvan 5702/1941) tried to resist the Nazi Germans, on the 8th Av (Erev Tisha B'Av), but most were killed and only a few escaped to the forests.

The mass deportation of Jews from the Warsaw ghetto (see Kislev 5700/1939, Sivan 5702/1942) to the death camps began on Erev Tisha B'Av, at a daily rate of 5,000 or more (see Elul 5702/1942). The Nazis lured the starving people to the assembly points with food and promises for resettlement, although most Jews had grave doubts. Adam Czierniakov, head of the Judenrat (Nazi-approved Jewish self-government of the ghetto), committed suicide rather than cooperate with the deportations. Most of the Jews were deported 100 kms. away to the Treblinka death camp where they were killed.

More than 200 Jews were killed in Ivye (Poland-Lithuania) on the 9th Av (Tisha B'Av); 10,000 Jews of Minsk were massacred on the 14th Av (see Adar 5702/1942, Shvat 5703/1943); over 5,000 Jews of Novogrodek (Russia) (see Kislev 5702/1941) were killed on the 24th Av; and 40,000 Jews from Lvov (Lemberg) Poland were killed in two weeks, commencing on the 27th Av (see Tammuz 5701/1941, Sivan 5703/1943).

Seven hundred Jews were killed in Gorlice (Poland) on the 1st **Elul**; 600 Jews were killed (when thousands were deported) in Drogobych (Poland) (see Tammuz 5701/1941) on the 4th Elul; 17,000 Jews were killed on a hill outside Lutzk (Poland) (see Tammuz 5701/1941) in five days commencing on the 6th Elul; and 1,000 were killed in Minsk-Mazowiecki (Poland) on the 8th Elul. Five hundred Jews (children, the sick, and the elderly) were killed in Czortkow (Poland) (see Tammuz 5701/1941) on the 15th Elul, when thousands of others were transported to the death camps; 4,000 Jews were killed in the prison courtyard of Ludmir (Poland) beginning on the 19th Elul, and another 14,000 were killed within two weeks outside of the town. One thousand Jews were killed in Dzialoszyce (Poland), and thousands more were deported on the 21st Elul, and on the same day over 600 Jews were killed in Lachva (Poland-Lithuania) when they resisted the Nazi invasion of the ghetto, though many escaped to the forests.

The Nazis killed all of the 11,000 Jews of Stolin (Russia), including Adm.R.Moshe of Karlin/Stolin (see 5552/1792), on the 29th Elul, Erev Rosh HaShana (in a nearby forest).

90,000 Jews were deported from the Warsaw ghetto (see Av 5702/1942) on Erev Rosh Ha-Shana, completing a total of 300,000 deportations

and killings in fifty-three days (see Nissan 5703/1943). Hillel Zeitlin, a writer and thinker who had returned to Jewish religious observance wore his *Tallit* at the deportation assembly point, and his exhortations of the young to fight created an immediate skirmish. He was killed on Erev Rosh HaShana in Treblinka; Shaindel, the daughter of Adm.R.Yosef Yitzchak of Lubavitch (see Adar2 5700/1940), was killed there on the second day of Rosh HaShana 5703.

5703 / 1942

Three thousand Jews of Baranowice (Poland-Lithuania) were killed by the Germans on the day after Yom Kippur (11th Tishrei).

The Jews of Kobrin (Poland) (see Sivan 5702/1942) attacked their Nazi killers on the 3rd **Cheshvan** (see Adar2 5703/1943); the Jews of Bereza Kartuska (Poland) set their ghetto on fire on the 4th Cheshvan, when the Nazis came to remove them, and members of the Judenrat (see Av 5702/1942) took their own lives. The Nazis killed many of the Jews in the burning ghetto, and 1,800 Jews were killed outside of the town.

The Germans shot the 300 Jewish children of the orphanage in Cracow, together with the patients of the Jewish hospital and the old age home, when they were selecting 6,000 Jews to be sent to Belzec death camp, on the 17th Cheshvan.

The last 16,000 Jews in Pinsk (Russia) were killed by the Nazis on the 18th Cheshvan, and the last 3,000 Jews of Baranowice were killed on the 9th **Tevet**.

5703 / 1943

Two hundred and fifty children and old people were shot by the Nazis in the ghetto of Czestochowa (Poland) on the 27th Tevet (see Elul 5699/1939), the day after some Jewish resistance fighters fought a battle there. Hundreds of Jews were shot in Radomsk (Poland) on the 28th Tevet, when they resisted the deportation of thousands of Jews to the Treblinka death camp. Ten thousand Jews were killed in Stanislav (Poland) (see Tishrei 5702/1941).

The turning point of World War II came when the Germans lost the battle for Stalingrad and surrendered to the Russians on the 25th **Shvat**. Over 250,000 German soldiers were killed, and almost 100,000 were captured (including twenty-four generals) in the battle.

Fifteen hundred Jews of Minsk (Russia) were killed by the Germans on the 26th Shvat (see Av 5702/1942); 2,500 Jews of Buczacz (Poland) were killed outside the town on the 26th and 27th Shvat; 600 Jewish women, children, and elderly were killed in the Borislav city slaughterhouse (Poland) on the 11th Adar1 (see Kislev 5702/ 1941); 2,000 of the last Jews in the Cracow ghetto (see Kislev 5700/1939) were killed on the 6th **Adar2** and 8,000 were sent to the death camps; and 900 Jews were killed in the cemetery of Sambor (Poland) on the 7th Adar2.

On the 8th Adar2, the Nazis began transporting the 44,000 Jews of Salonika (Greece) to the death camps. Some Jews of Braslav (Poland) (see Sivan 5702/1942) resisted deportation (see Cheshvan 5703/1942) on the 12th Adar2, until they ran out of ammunition. One hundred twenty-seven Jews were killed in Czestochowa (Poland) on the 13th Adar2, and 750 Jews were killed outside of Skalat (Poland) (see Iyar 5703/1943) on the 2nd **Nissan**.

The remaining Jews in Warsaw staged a massive uprising.

Word of the fate of deported Jews was smuggled back to the Warsaw ghetto (see Av 5702/1942), and there had been some resistance to the Nazis.

R. Menachem Zemba and other rabbis had declared Erev Rosh Chodesh Nissan as a day of fast and repentance, in light of the impending doom.

On the 14th Nissan (Erev Pesach) the remaining 35,000 Jews in the Warsaw ghetto (from an original 450,000) staged an organized uprising, and drove back the Nazis with a rain of bullets when

they came to begin the final removal of all Jews. The Jewish resistance lasted for almost a month.

On the same day, a train filled with deportees was derailed in Belgium by the Jewish underground (partisans, see Adar 5702/1942) and non-Jewish rail workers. Hundreds of Jews were saved from being transported to the death camps. R.Menachem Zemba, a great Torah scholar respected by the Rogatchover Gaon (who was renowned for his condescending comments about other scholars), had reportedly declined offers of escape from the Warsaw ghetto, and was killed there in Nissan during the uprising which he is said to have supported.

Mordechai Anilevitch, the 24-year-old commander of the Warsaw Ghetto uprising, was killed during the fighting on the 3rd **Iyar**, and the uprising came to an end on the 10th. Although the ghetto was burned to the ground, some stray survivors hid in the rubble and fired at the Nazis for two months longer.

Six hundred sixty Jews were killed in Skalat (Poland) (see Nissan 5703/1943) on the 4th Iyar; 1,000 were killed in the cemetery in Stry (Poland) on the 17th; 3,000 Jews were killed in the cemetery in Tluste (Poland) on the 22nd Iyar, and another 1,000 on the 3rd **Sivan**.

Most of the remaining Jews in the ghetto of Lvov (see Av 5702/1942) were killed in a six-day massacre that began on the 18th Sivan. Four thousand Jews of Disna (Lithuania) were killed outside the town, and 2,000 escaped to the forests (where they joined partisan groups), although most of them were eventually captured by the Nazis.

On the 2nd **Tammuz**, the Vilna ghetto underground freed their leader Yitzchak Wittenberg from Nazi captivity, an act which almost triggered a (previously planned) uprising. The Nazis immediately threatened to wipe out the whole ghetto and its population; Wittenberg decided that such dramatic loss of life was inexpedient, and surrendered. Two months later the Vilna ghetto underground resisted (for a few weeks) the massive deportation of Jews to the death camps.

Five thousand Jews were killed in Kamenka-Bugskaya (Poland) on the 7th Tammuz, and 500 were killed in the Jewish cemetery in Czestochowa (see Tevet 5703/1943), on the fast of the 17th Tammuz.

The prisoners of Treblinka death camp revolted and escaped.

The prisoners of Treblinka staged a revolt on the lst **Av**, triggered off a crucial hour earlier than planned, because of a mishap. Nevertheless hundreds of prisoners escaped, although most were caught within a few weeks and only fifty survived until the end of the war. (Estimated total killed in Treblinka: 750,000.) The Jews of Bendin (Poland) attempted to resist their deportation to the death camps on the 3rd Av.

An organized uprising began in the Bialystok ghetto.

An organized uprising broke out in the Bialystok ghetto on the 15th Av but was suppressed after a few days; the Nazis deported all the remaining 40,000 Jews (see Tammuz 5701/1941) to the death camps. When the Jews of Glubokoye (Poland) (see Tammuz 5702/1942) attempted to resist deportation on the 19th Av, the whole ghetto was set afire by the Nazis, and over 1,000 Jews perished.

Over 7,000 Jews escaped across the sea from Denmark to Sweden with the help of the Danes and their fishing boats in the three weeks before Rosh HaShana 5704/1943, and when the Germans came to round them up on the night after Rosh HaShana, fewer than 500 were left. Most of them survived the war.

5704 / 1943

Jews escaped in the Sobibor death camp uprising.

Three hundred forced laborers were left in the Sobibor death camp when the transports of new victims ceased, and realizing that they were no longer needed and were about to be killed, they staged an uprising on the 15th **Tishrei**; 170 escaped alive, although all but 30 were recaptured and killed. (Estimated total killed in Sobibor: 250,000.) The Germans subsequently shut down the Janowska Road camp near Lvov on the 22nd **Cheshvan**, for fear of an uprising. They removed all traces of the particularly brutal death camp, where Jews had been tortured for the entertainment of Nazi officers.

Adm.R.Aharon (ben Yissachar Dov) of Belz (see 5615/1855) had managed to move from ghetto to ghetto during the course of the war until he escaped to Eretz Yisrael via Hungary.

5704 / 1944

Three hundred thousand Hungarian Jews were killed in three months.

The Germans invaded Hungary, their previous ally (see Sivan 5701/1941), on the 25th **Adar**, and deportations of Hungarian Jews to Auschwitz started shortly thereafter. The Nazis convinced these Jews, with the assistance of Jewish collaborators (see Kislev 5705/1944), that because Germany was losing battles in the war, they were no longer killing Jews but merely resettling them. This tactic speeded up the deportations to the death camps (mainly Auschwitz), and 300,000 Hungarian Jews were killed within three months.

Many Jews escaped from the Koldychevo concentration camp on the 27th Adar, and ten Nazi guards were shot.

The Nazis forced all the Jews of the ancient community of Canea (Crete) into a boat, which was towed out to sea and sunk on the 9th **Sivan**.

Almost one year after the Italians had removed Hitler's friend, Mussolini, from power, the Allied forces pushed back the German armies and entered Rome (the first capital city to be liberated from the Nazis) on the 13th Sivan. Those Jews of Rome who had survived the deportations emerged from their hiding places.

The retreating Nazis began evacuating some of the death camps and marching the inmates to other locations. Many of the captives died on the way. The Nazis also killed many of their Jewish slave laborers, 3,000 of them at Ponary (see Sivan 5701/1941) on the 12th Tammuz.

The Nazis discovered on the 15th **Av**, the Amsterdam hideout of Anne Frank and her family and their friends. She was a 15-year-old Jewish (German refugee) girl whose diary, discovered after the war, was published and became known internationally. She died in Bergen-Belsen during a typhus epidemic.

R.Levi Yitzchak Schneersohn, a direct descendant of the Tzemach Tzedek, whose many written comments and notes were later published by his son (and disciple) Adm.R.Menachem Mendel of Lubavitch, had been sent into Russian exile four years earlier (after having already spent a year in prison) for fulfilling his duties as a rabbi (see 5680/1920). He died on the 20th Av in Alma Ata (Asian Russia).

R.Michal Dov Weismandel, a son-in-law of the Rav of Nitra, and a Czechoslovakian Jewish resistance leader who worked to rescue Jews, had tried to warn the Hungarian Jews of their impending doom. He was found and captured by the Nazis, shortly after he had sent from his cave a letter, including maps, to the outside world, demanding that the Allied forces bomb the Auschwitz death camp in order to destroy its capabilities. He escaped by jumping off the transport train headed for Auschwitz and later settled in the United States.

5705 / 1944

Jewish uprising in the Auschwitz death camp.

On the 20th **Tishrei** those Jews who had been forced to assist in cremating the bodies at the Birkenau/Auschwitz death camp (see Tishrei 5702/1941), staged an uprising and killed some Nazis. Some escaped,but none survived.

Chanah Senesh, a 23-year-old Hungarian girl who had settled in Eretz Yisrael, was executed in Budapest on the 20th **Cheshvan**. She had been caught parachuting, with thirty-one others, into Nazi territory to help partisans (see Adar 5702/1942) and to rescue Jews.

The Nazi Germans released two transports totaling 1,686 Jews – 318 on the 29th Av 1944, and 1,368 (from the Bergen-Belsen concentration camp) on the 20th **Kislev** 5705/1944 – and those Jews were allowed to leave Europe. Their release was secured by Rudolf Kasztner, head of the Zionist rescue operations in Hungary, who was permitted to travel around Europe (including Germany) by the Nazis. After the war, in a prolonged trial, he was accused of collaborating with the Nazis, and of knowingly allowing (and assisting in) the deportation of hundreds of thousands of Hungarian Jews to the death camps (see Adar 5704/1944), in return for the release of this relatively small number of Jews.

Adm.R.Yoel of Satmar was among the Jews released from Bergen-Belsen; he traveled to Eretz Yisrael and later settled in New York in 1947.

5705 / 1945

The Auschwitz death camp was captured and liberated.

Raoul Wallenberg, a Swedish diplomat who used his position to rescue tens of thousands of Hungarian Jews from the Nazi killings, disappeared on the 3rd **Shvat**, when he was taken by the advancing Russian army.

The Russians liberated the Auschwitz death camp on the 12th Shvat. There were 2,819 Jewish survivors in the camp (see Sivan 5700/1940, Tishrei 5702/1941). (Estimated total Jews killed there: 2.5 million.)

On the 17th **Nissan**, the Nazis killed Maria of Paris, a Russian nun who had saved many French Jews from Nazi extermination.

271

Nazi Germany was conquered, and World War II ended.

After the Russians had liberated the Lublin and Auschwitz death camps (see Sivan 5704/1944, Shvat 5705/1945), the U.S. Army liberated the Buchenwald death camp (29th Nissan) with 20,000 Jewish survivors; the British liberated the Bergen-Belsen death camp (2nd Iyar) with 40,000 survivors; Dachau was liberated by the U.S. Army (16th Iyar); and Mathausen was liberated on the 24th **Iyar**, the same day that Germany surrendered unconditionally.

The Theresienstadt ghetto (which had served as a massive staging area for the deportation of some 140,000 Jews to the death camps) was liberated three days later, on the 27th Iyar.

Many surviving Jews died after the camps were liberated, from weakness, disease, and the inability to properly digest food after years of starvation.

Jews from all over Europe who had survived the wartime massacre of six million, the Holocaust, were placed by the victorious Allied forces into special camps for displaced persons. Most of them began looking for surviving relatives and friends, and for a new country to call their home. Besides the vivid memories of horror that they carried in their minds, and the loss of loved ones that left an emptiness in their hearts, most of them carried serial numbers on their arms – tattooed there by the Nazis. The Germans had reduced the significance of a Jew to a number, the ultimate aim of this being to reach the number zero.

Many of the Nazi murderers were not captured, or managed to escape (see 5707/1946).

Adm.R.Yekutiel Yehuda of Klausenberg (Cluj) (Rumania), a great-grandson of the Divrei Chaim (Tzanzer) and a son-in-law of Adm.R.Chaim Tzvi of Sighet, survived the war (although he lost his wife and eleven children) and he later remarried. He settled in New York at first, and later in Eretz Yisrael (where he established a community called Kiryat Tzanz).

R.Mordechai Gifter, who was born in Portsmouth, Virginia (United States) was probably the first American-born Talmud scholar to become a Rosh Yeshiva (in Telz Yeshiva, Cleveland) (see Sivan 5701/1941).

R.Eliezer Yehuda Waldenberg, a rabbi in Yerushalayim, published the first volume of *Tztitz Eliezer* (*Sh'elot UTeshuvot,* dealing with many isssues involving technological and scientific advances).

5706 / 1945

The Jewish underground resistance movement against the restrictive British rule in Eretz Yisrael (see 5699/1939) attacked a British internment camp for "illegal" immigrants, and freed 208 Jews on the 3rd Cheshvan 5706/1945. The resistance also continued its attempts to "smuggle" in more Jews from the European displaced persons camps. The British, however, intercepted most of the "illegal" immigrant boats, and interned the occupants in special camps on Cyprus.

5706 / 1946

The Jewish underground resistance movement (see 5706/1945) continued to attack British military installations, as the British maintained their restrictions on Jewish immigration into Eretz Yisrael; members of the resistance blew up many bridges on the borders. As a result, many Jewish political leaders were arrested on the 30th Sivan.

Forty-two Jews who had survived the Holocaust were killed in a pogrom in Kielce (Poland) on the 5th Tammuz.

On the 23rd Tammuz, a group of Jewish underground fighters blew up British headquarters in Yerushalayim, and eighty people were killed because the British had refused to believe a message of warning.

5707 / 1946

Some of the leaders of Nazi Germany had been captured after the war, and many others had escaped (see 5722/1962). The captured were brought to trial in an international court at Nuremberg (Germany), and many of them were sentenced to death. They were hanged on the 21st Tishrei 5707/1946, for crimes against Jews and humanity during World War II.

5707 / 1947

Publication of the Talmud Encyclopedia was commenced.

The first volume of the *Talmud Encyclopedia* was published in Eretz Yisrael under the editorship of R.Shlomo Yosef Zevin. He was also an editor of *Otzar Haposkim* (comprehensive encyclopedic Halacha update, on the Even HaEzer section of *Shulchan Aruch*), together with R.Yitzchak Hertzog (Ashkenazi Chief Rabbi of Eretz Yisrael) and R.Isser Zalman Meltzer. The first volume of *Otzar HaPoskim* was also published in 1947.

Two ships arrived in Eretz Yisrael with "illegal" Jewish immigrants (see 5706/1945) on the 18th Tevet, and they were taken by the British for internment on Cyprus (see 5706/1945). On the 1st Av, the British seized the ship *Exodus 1947*, causing three deaths among its 4,000 immigrants, and forced it to return to Germany.

5708 / 1947

The United Nations divided Eretz Yisrael.

The United Nations (an organization including most countries in the world) recognized the problem of the Jewish survivors in Europe who had nowhere to go (see Iyar 5705/1945). They voted on the 16th Kislev to withdraw the mandate given to the British (see 5680/1920) over Palestine (Eretz Yisrael) and agreed to a plan dividing the country. Some of the land was to be for Jews, and some for Arabs. Yerushalayim (according to the plan) was to be an international city on its own.

Arabs attacked the Jews of Eretz Yisrael to gain territory.

Arabs living in Eretz Yisrael (backed by financial support of other Arab countries) began attacking the Jews on the 17th Kislev, the day after the United Nations voted to give the Jews a partitioned area of Eretz Yisrael. The Arabs did not approve of this arrangement and sought to forcibly occupy as much territory as possible; the British governors of Palestine (Eretz Yisrael) were, at best, neutral onlookers to the attacks (see Adar 5708/1948).

On the 19th Kislev seventy-five Jews of Aden (also under British rule) were killed in Arab anti-Jewish riots. The Jews of Aleppo (Syria) were attacked, all synagogues there were destroyed, and 6,000 fled the country.

On the 16th Tevet a ship full of "illegal" Jewish immigrants arrived in Eretz Yisrael, and was driven away by the British (see Av 5707/1947).

5708 / 1948

Many Jews were killed by an exploding bomb in the center of Yerushalayim on the 12th Adar. There were many bombings and attacks by Arabs during this time, but British complicity was also suspected in this bombing.

The roads to Yerushalayim were cut off by Arab forces, and the Jews in the city came under a virtual siege, which was broken by the 6th Nissan.

The British rule over Eretz Yisrael ended on the 5th of Iyar and their troops almost all evacuated. Thirty thousand Jews of Eretz Yisrael were already enlisted in the army, but there was a severe shortage of arms and ammunition. A few hundred Jews had been killed in the fighting with the Arabs, but Jews remained in control of major cities and roads. The road to Yerushalayim was cut off placing the city under siege once again. The Palestinian Arabs had been beaten back and defeated, and many fled from their homes in fear.

The State of Israel was established in Eretz Yisrael.

The political leaders of Eretz Yisrael, headed by David (Green) Ben Gurion, a secular Zionist, established an autonomous and independent Jewish state when the British left – the State of Israel.

The provisional government of the new state immediately acted to assure free Jewish immigration to Eretz Yisrael (see 5708/1947), and the right for Jews to freely purchase land there (see 5699/1939).

Some religiously observant Jews saw the formation of Jewish self-government in Eretz Yisrael as the beginning of the Ge'ula (messianic redemption). Others accepted it graciously, as a form of

ge'ula establishing a homeland for the many homeless Jews, yet disappointed that the ultimate Ge'ula, with the long-awaited advent of the Mashiach (Messiah), seemed to have slipped out of grasp (and that Jewish government was in the hands of secular and often anti-religious Jews).

Other religiously observant Jews were against the establishment of an autonomous Jewish state (see 5674/1913, 5739/1979) and claimed that this could not be done without the prophetic advent of the Mashiach.

Eretz Yisrael was invaded by surrounding Arab countries.

The armies of all the Arab countries surrounding Eretz Yisrael (Egypt, Jordan, Syria, Lebanon, and Iraq) invaded the day after the State of Israel was declared. Saudi Arabia joined the war a few days later, and Yemen also declared war. The intention of the Arab countries was to crush the new State of Israel and destroy the Jewish population of Eretz Yisrael. The fighting began with the bombing of Tel Aviv on the 6th Iyar.

The invading armies were fully equipped with tanks, planes, and heavy artillery, which the Jews did not have. However, despite their need to often use makeshift weapons, the Jews managed to hold most areas, except for the Jewish quarter in the Old City of Yerushalayim, and the Churvat R Yehuda Chasid synagogue (see 5597/1837) was destroyed. This section fell to the Arabs on the 19th Iyar, even though the construction of a rough new road had once again lifted the siege from Yerushalayim itself.

An American colonel, David (Mickey) Marcus who was among many Jews who came to Eretz Yisrael to fight, was killed accidentally outside his headquarters on the 3rd Sivan.

The Altalena, a ship bringing arms to Eretz Yisrael (as well as 900 immigrants), was blown up on arrival, and twenty Jews were killed. A statement by David Ben Gurion (in the provisional state council on 17th Sivan) increased the suspicion that

Jewish hands were stained in the affair (see Cheshvan, 5701/1940).

Adm.R.Avraham Mordechai Alter of Gur, the Imrey Emess (see 5701/1940), died on Shavu'ot during the siege of Yerushalayim and was buried in the courtyard of the Yeshiva he had established there (see 5685/1925). He was succeeded by his son, Adm.R.Yisrael.

Twenty Jews were killed in Cairo when a bomb was thrown into the Jewish quarters on the 13th Sivan, and over 100 Jews were killed in sporadic riots.

The last of the British armed forces left Eretz Yisrael on the 23rd Sivan.

Yerushalayim was bombed from the air on the 4th Tammuz, and newly purchased Jewish planes on their way to Eretz Yisrael bombed Cairo in retaliation on the 7th Tammuz. Yerushalayim was also under continuous bombardment from heavy Arab guns, and the water supply was cut off when the Arabs blew up a pumping station.

The fighting continued throughout the country, and a few hundred thousand Arabs fled from their homes during the battles and after Jewish victories (see Iyar 5708/1948). Most did not immediately return, because the Arab governments had vowed to drive the Jews of Eretz Yisrael into the sea and to return the whole land to the Arabs.

R.Shlomo Zalman Broin of Budapest settled in New York, and published the first volume of his *She'arim HaMetzuyanim BeHalacha* (Halacha updat. on *Kitzur Shulchan Aruch*).

Jews (survivors of the Holocaust) were attacked by anti-Jewish mobs in Plungyan (Lithuania) in a blood libel on Erev Rosh HaShana.

5709 / 1949

The British released the remaining 25,000 Jewish "illegal" immigrants (from a total of over 50,000) being held on Cyprus, on the 18th Tevet (see 5706/1945).

By this time there were 1,000,000 Jews in Eretz Yisrael, almost 300,000 more than a year earlier (see 5699/1939, 5719/1958).

The War of Independence in Eretz Yisrael ended.

The State of Israel signed separate armistice agreements with all its neighboring Arab countries (see Iyar 5708/1948), and the war was ended. Jews were in control of almost 8,000 square miles of Eretz Yisrael, compared to the 6,200 that the United Nations had originally planned (see Kislev 5708/1947). However, Yerushalayim remained divided (see 19 Iyar 5708/1948), with the Western Wall (see Av 3829/69) remaining under Arab control.

Four thousand Jewish soldiers had died in the war, and 2,000 Jewish civilians perished. Arabs continued sporadic and isolated attacks on Jews for many years (see Cheshvan 5717/1956).

5710 / 1950

Adm.R.Yosef Yitzchak Schneersohn of Lubavitch died in New York (see 5700/1940) on the 10th Shvat, after having established (from the confinement of a wheelchair as a result of his tortures, see 5687/1927) a network of organizations for the furtherance of Jewish religious observance and Torah studies in the United States, Canada, Eretz Yisrael (where he founded a settlement for his followers), England, France, Morocco, and Australia. He was succeeded by his son-in-law Adm. R.Menachem Mendel Schneersohn (see Av 5704/1944), revered for his very exceptional Torah scholarship, who most signficantly increased and expanded his father-in-law's work.

The Jews left the ancient Jewish community of Iraq.

The government of Iraq, which had treated the Jews harshly in the preceding few years (see Sivan 5701/1941, Iyar 5708/1948), allowed the Jews to leave on condition that they took none of their possessions. During the fifteen months beginning in Sivan 1950, 110,000 Jews – almost all of the Jews of Iraq – left for Eretz Yisrael (leaving behind possessions worth $200 million). This was the effective end of a Jewish community dating back to before the destruction of the first Beit Hamikdash (see 3319/442, Av 3338/423) when the country was called Babylonia.

The Jews of Yemen emigrated to Eretz Yisrael.

Sixteen thousand Jews of Yemen had emigrated to Eretz Yisrael between 1919 and 1948, and the remaining 45,000 were brought to Eretz Yisrael in a massive airlift which lasted less than a year, and ended in Elul of 1950. This effectively ended the ancient Jewish community of Yemen (see Iyar 5708/1948).

Some secular Zionists actively discouraged Jewish religious practice among these and other new immigrants, who were adapting to a completely newcultural and economic life.

5711 / 1951

The Knesset (Parliament) of the State of Israel declared the 27th Nissan as Yom HaSho'a (Holocaust Remembrance Day), in memory of the six million Jews killed by the Nazis during World War II.

5712 / 1952

Twenty-six Jews including secular Yiddish writers (see 5658/1897) were killed by the Russian authorities on the 21st Av as part of their program to eradicate Jewish religion and culture (see 5680/1920).

On the 20th Elul, the government of West Germany agreed to pay money for the losses suffered by Jews at the hands of the Nazis. The State of Israel received a total of $845 million over the next fourteen years.

5714 / 1953

R.Avraham Yeshayahu Karelitz, the Chazon Ish (see 5671/1911), who settled in Eretz Yisrael in 1933, died on the 15th Cheshvan. He had gained worldwide recognition for his Torah scholarship without serving in any position as Rabbi or Rosh Yeshiva.

R.Isser Zalman Meltzer died three weeks later on the 10th Kislev.

5717 / 1956

Jewish forces invaded Egypt and conquered the Sinai.

An increasing number of Jews were being killed in Eretz Yisrael (some 1.300 since 1949) by Arab infiltrators across the borders, many of them from Egypt.

Egypt, which was receiving large quantities of quality Russian arms and ammunition, nationalized the Suez Canal and did not allow ships to pass to and from Israel. In reaction, Israeli forces invaded the Sinai peninsula on the 24th Cheshvan and conquered most of it in a lightning strike that lasted eight days.

The Egyptian army was totally routed and fled in a completely disorganized manner, leaving large quantities of almost unused arms and thousands of soldiers dead or taken prisoner. One hundred seventy-one Jewish soldiers were killed in the campaign. Jewish forces were withdrawn shortly afterward, due to political pressure from the United States and Russia, and were replaced by troops of the United Nations who were to serve as a buffer.

Many Jews left Hungary during the unsuccessful revolt against the Communist government, in Cheshvan 5717/1956.

5718 / 1958

A serious and prolonged controversy arose in Eretz Yisrael, when it was announced that people stating that they were Jews would be registered as such, by the State of Israel, without the need for certification acceptable by Halacha. The controversy is known as *Mihu Yehudi,* "Who is (considered) a Jew."

5719 / 1958

A new water reservoir was opened in the month of Kislev to ensure Yerushalayim with an adequate water supply (see 5282/1521, Tammuz 5708/1948).

At this time there were 1,800,000 Jews in Eretz Yisrael, an increase of over one million in eleven years (see 5709/1949, 5729/1969).

5719 / 1959

R.Moshe Feinstein, who had settled in the United States (in 1937), published the first volume of *Iggorot Moshe* (*Sh'elot UTeshuvot*).

5720 / 1960

Hundreds of Jews died—some say 800—including students at the Yeshiva (of Lubavitch), in an earthquake in Agadir (Morocco) on the 2nd Adar.

More than half of the 250,000 Jews of Morocco had already settled in Eretz Yisrael, and within a few years almost all of the rest followed. Of the 130,000 Jews of Algeria, only 7,700 settled in Eretz Yisrael, most of the others emigrating to France.

5722 / 1962

Adolph Eichmann, the Nazi in charge of the German plan to exterminate the Jews during World War II, was captured (see 5707/1946) in Argentina; he was tried in a court in Eretz Yisrael and hanged.

5723 / 1962

R.Aharon Kotler (see Sivan 5701/1941), a son-in-law of R.Isser Zalman Meltzer and a leader of Torah scholars in the United States and in Eretz Yisrael, died on the 2nd Kislev.

5724 / 1964

The Arab countries had permanently placed the Palestinian Arab refugees in their countries (see Sivan 5708/1948) into refugee camps, while the Jewish refugees from Arab countries (see 5710/1950, 5720/1960) were absorbed into normal life in Eretz Yisrael.

Delegations from these Arab countries met in Egypt and established the Palestinian Liberation Organization (P.L.O.), which was to have an army (of Palestinian Arabs) to carry out attacks against Jews in Eretz Yisrael (see 5717/1956). A terrorist group called Al Fatah was independently established along the same lines as the P.L.O., but its fighters were more extreme.

5725 / 1965

Martin Buber, a famous philosopher who (although himself not a practicing religious Jew) had popularized the Chasidim and their tales and ideology among intellectual Western Jews, died on the 13th Sivan.

5727 / 1967

Yerushalayim was reunited under Jewish rule, in the Six Day War.

Terrorist attacks against Jews in Eretz Yisrael had reached unbearable proportions (see 5724/1964), and Arab armies were preparing for a battle to finally destroy the Jewish state (see Sivan 5708/1948). Egypt dismissed the United Nations force in Sinai (see Cheshvan 5717/1956), began deploying its forces against the borders of Israel, and once again (see 5717/1956) closed the Suez Canal to all ships to and from Eretz Yisrael. In the morning of 26th Iyar, Israeli planes attacked Egypt and Syria in a miraculous action that lasted three hours and destroyed 452 Arab planes (391 of them still on the ground), while losing only 19.

For six days the Jewish soldiers made spectacular advances, and completely shattered the Arab armies of Egypt, Syria, and Jordan. The Old City of Yerushalayim was captured from the Arabs (see 5709/1949), and Jews could visit the Western Wall for the first time in many years (although no one suggested the removal of the Arab mosque from the holiest Jewish place). Yerushalayim was under complete Jewish control for the first time since Bar Kochba (Bar Kuziba) (see 3887/127). Many of the Jewish holy places (synagogues, etc.) were found to have been desecrated and vandalized by the Arabs.

Twenty-seven hundred square miles of Eretz Yisrael (including Kever Rachel and Ma'arat Ha Machpela), and 23,500 square miles of Sinai, came under Jewish control (see 5709/1949) although the government of Israel indicated that captured territories could be returned, except for Yerushalayim. Tremendous quantities of arms and ammunition were captured. Seven hundred seventy-seven Jewish soldiers were killed in the war.

Earlier, Jews all over the world had been aroused in an unprecedented awaking when the threat of war became reality. Many came to Eretz Yisrael to help.

In the aftermath of the miraculous victory, many Jews were reawakened to religious observance (particularly the young), and this reawakening eventually developed into the Ba'al Teshuva movement which involved many thousands of Jews returning to Jewish Halacha observance.

R.Adin Steinsaltz, in Eretz Yisrael, published the first volume of the Talmud with many embellishments designed to make it more accessible to the untrained.

A project to enter all the available *Sh'elot UTeshuvot* into a computer, for quick and comprehensive reference, was commenced in Eretz Yisrael.

5729 / 1969

Nine Jews were publicly executed in Damascus on the 8th Shvat.

R.Aryeh Levin, often called "The Tzadik of Yerushalayim" for his kind heart and good deeds (to the sick, the poor, and others in need) died on 9th Nissan.

The Arab countries around Eretz Yisrael had been re-equipped by Russia (see 5727/1967) with arms and ammunition. They still refused to recognize the existence of a Jewish state in Eretz Yisrael, and P.L.O. infiltrators (see 5724/1964) had staged many damaging attacks and bombings. On the 4th Iyar, Egypt began a war of attrition against Israel with daily shellings across the Suez Canal.

There were 2,400,000 Jews living in Eretz Yisrael at this time (see 5719/1958, 5752/1992).

5730 / 1970

Libya ordered the confiscation of Jewish property on the 17th Tammuz.

At this point, the P.L.O (see Iyar 5729/1969) launched a new technique of terrorism, hijacking international aircraft and holding the passengers as hostages until their (often unrealistic) demands were met.

5731 / 1971

Ten Jews were arrested in Russia on Tisha B'Av, and sent to jail because they were commemorating this tragic day by visiting Babi Yar (see Tishrei 5702/1941). This was part of a series of such arrests, which did not succeed in curbing the increasing courage with which the Jews of Russia (see 5712/1952) began to speak up, particularly in their petitions and requests to leave for Eretz Yisrael. One thousand Jews were permitted to leave Russia in1970, and 14,500 were permitted to leave in 1971 (see 5735/1975).

5734 / 1973

Twenty-five hundred Jewish soldiers were killed in the Yom Kippur War.

Egyptian and Syrian troops had been gathering at the frontiers of Eretz Yisrael for a number of days, but the government of the State of Israel was convinced that this did not signal an imminent war. In the early afternoon of Yom Kippur, Egypt and Syria attacked. The Arab armies were initially successful in advancing on both fronts, due to surprise and numbers (less than 500 Jewish soldiers were defending 100 miles along the Suez Canal, and they were attacked by 70,000 Egyptian soldiers). Nevertheless, within days the Israeli defense forces staged a successful counterattack, crossed the Suez Canal into North Africa, and advanced in Syria to within firing range of Damascus. Russia (which was continuously airlifting new supplies of arms to the Arabs during the fighting) used the United Nations to intervene and stop the fighting, in which the Arabs had lost very large numbers of soldiers (18,500) and massive amounts of arms (2,100 tanks). The war was over after twenty days of fighting, in which 2,522 Jewish soldiers had been killed.

After their defeat in the Yom Kippur War, the Arab countries threatened not to sell their oil to countries that supported the Jewish state, which proved an effective weapon. The State of Israel became politically isolated (particularly in the United Nations) and found it increasingly difficult to purchase armaments.

5734 / 1974

A group of mainly young religious nationalists, calling themselves Gush Emunim, established a settlement in the newly captured Syrian territory in Iyar, in an attempt to prevent the Israeli government from withdrawing from that territory. This was their first action toward their goal of establishing settlements in all parts of (biblical) Eretz Yisrael captured since 1967, which the government of Israel had consistently maintained could be returned to the Arabs.

5735 / 1975

One hundred thousand Jews from Russia had arrived in Eretz Yisrael since 1967 (see 5731/1971, 5752/1992).

The birthrate among Jewish religious families was very high, and there were great Torah centers emerging in the United States – particularly in and around New York – and in Eretz Yisrael, only thirty years after the total destruction of the European Torah centers.

5736 / 1976

One hundred Jews who had been passengers on a plane hijacked by Arab terrorists (see 5730/1970) were held hostage in the Entebbe airport near Kampala, Uganda. They were miraculously rescued from deep in the African continent in a spectacular raid by Israeli forces.

Arab infiltrators continued their constant attacks on Jews in Eretz Yisrael and all over the world (see Iyar 5727/1967).

5737 / 1977

Adm.R.Yisrael of Gur, the Beit Yisrael, who had lost his family in the Holocaust, died on the 2nd Adar and was succeeded by his brother, Adm. R.Simcha Bunim.

5739 / 1979

The president of Egypt, Anwar Sadat, visited Yerushalayim in Kislev 5737/1977 on the invitation of the newly elected prime minister of Israel, Menachem Begin. After long negotiations, a peace treaty was signed on the 27th Adar 1979, under the auspices of the United States, under which all Jewish forces and settlements were withdrawn from Sinai (see 5734/1973). Menachem Begin then visited Cairo.

Adm.R.Yoel of Satmar, who vehemently opposed the State of Israel (on religious grounds, see Iyar 5708/1948), died on the 26th Av, and was succeeded by his nephew, Adm.R.Moshe (ben Chaim Tzvi) of Sighet, Rumania (see 5664/1904).

5740 / 1980

R.Yisrael AbiChatzira, a grandson of R.Yaakov (of Morocco), had a wide reputation for miraculous deeds. He died in Eretz Yisrael (see 5640/1880) on the 4th Shvat.

Many more Jews were allowed to leave Russia (see 5735/1975) – 17,000 in 1977, 29,000 in 1978, 51,500 in 1979 – but less than half settled in Eretz Yisrael. By this time many other Jews had also left Eretz Yisrael, mostly for economic reasons, and as many as 500,000 had moved to the United States (see 5689/1929, 5729/1969, and 5641/1881).

5741 / 1981

A nuclear reactor near Baghdad was bombed and destroyed by Israeli planes. Iraq (which had always sent troops in the wars against Israel, see Iyar 5708/1948) was threatening to gain a nuclear arms capacity.

5742 / 1982

Massive enemy arsenals were discovered in Lebanon.

Arabs were bombarding Jewish settlements near the Lebanese border with destructive rockets, besides initiating other forms of terrorist attack. Jews in many other parts of the world were also being killed by terrorist bombs and attacks in an international campaign of terror against Jews. On the 17th Sivan, Israeli defense forces invaded Lebanon to remove the P.L.O. (see 5730/1970) that had firmly entrenched itself there, and the invading Jewish forces discovered enormous arsenals of threatening weapons that greatly exceeded original estimates.

Although the P.L.O. had stationed its fighters among women and children, allowing them to illustrate to the compliant international media that Jews were killing helpless civilians, the P.L.O. terrorists were overcome and forced to withdraw from Beirut to other countries. Israeli forces later withdrew southward, not fully withdrawing from Lebanon for another three years (see 5745/1985).

5744 / 1984

The Jewish population of Yerushalayim numbered 320,000 (445,000 including non-Jews), the largest of any city in Eretz Yisrael. However, Tel Aviv with its surrounding city-suburbs had a population of 800,000.

5745 / 1985

The Israeli army completed its withdrawal from Lebanon in Sivan, three years after the invasion (see 5742/1982). Six hundred and fifty-four Jewish soldiers had been killed, many in terrorist attacks.

5742 / 1982

Adm.R.Eliezer Zusia Portugal of Skulen died on the 29th Av in the United States. He had been known for his dedicated religious leadership in Romania under Communist rule (see 5680/1920) before leaving, and he enhanced this reputation in his subsequent two decades of endeavor in which he built a network of institutions for poor nonreligious Jews in Israeli towns.

5747 / 1987

On the 26th Tevet, the President of Russia (Mikhail Gorbachev) formally announced the ongoing relaxation of many tight government controls over the basic freedoms of the people in all the countries it controlled (under the USSR – Union of Soviet Socialist Republics). This allowed for more Jewish activity (banned for 70 years, see

5712/1952). Many Jews subsequently came to Russia from Israel and the United States to teach about Judaism (they even established schools and *yeshivot*), and Jews were free to apply for visas to leave. However, this relaxation of central control also allowed nationalistic passions to emerge (in such regions as the Ukraine and Moldavia, etc.), where local pride bore a strong tone of anti-Jewish feeling and hatred. These feelings raised fears among many Jews, and coupled with dwindling food production and supplies, the number of Jews leaving the country increased dramatically (see 5752/1992.)

5749 / 1988

The controversy of "Who is a Jew" (see 5718/1958) flared again during the Israeli government elections in Cheshvan 5747/1988. Although the religious parties had splintered before the election, they gained fifty percent more delegates than they previously had, thus enabling them to decide which of the major parties would form a government. Some religious parties sought to use this opportunity, to secure a commitment to have the law defining who can claim to be Jewish (and be registered as such by the State of Israel) amended to include the need for verification acceptable by Halacha (see 5718/1958.)

The Reform and Conservative movements had taken some roots in Israel by this time, and although non-Jews that they converted were not being accepted as Jews (for ritual purposes) by the official Rabbinate (Orthodox) of Israel, the proposed amendment would have meant that such people would not be accepted as Jews by the State also.

The controversy also included the issue of decisive influence from overseas Jews. Adm.R.Menachem Mendel Schneersohn of Lubavitch was criticized for wielding disproportionate influence in Israeli government affairs by promoting the Halacha issue; and the Reform and Conservative movements were criticized for campaigning among their members in the United States (their natural base) to threaten withholding donations from Israel. (Jews in the United States had traditionally been donating very large sums to Israel.)

Although there was no amendment, the controversy generated such heat that a prominent American Jewish leader compared the process of having to decide who is a Jew by Halacha to the "*selektzia*" process, where the German Nazis would decide (at the gates of the death camps) which Jew was fit to live (for labor) and which would be sent to immediate death.

5751 / 1991

When Iraq conquered the neighboring Arab state of Kuwait in a surprise attack in 11th Av 5750/1990, it already had the largest and best equipped army in the Middle East region, as well as having arsenals of chemical weapons and delivery missiles (of the type called SCUD). With the newly captured oil wells of Kuwait, it controlled a large percent of world oil production, and was well on the way to producing nucelar weapons (see 5741/1981). As Iraq ignored continuous demands (from all nations in the United Nations, to withdraw), a multinational military force was established. It was led by the United States and also included forces from other Arab countries. On the 2nd Shvat the United States air force led this multinational force in destroying much of Iraq's military structure by pounding Iraq with bombs. In response, Iraq began firing SCUD missiles at Israeli cities (see 5710/1950); and in eighteen waves of attack 4,000 buildings were damaged, but miraculously only one or two people were killed directly (although numerous people died of heart attacks in the terror). Iraq was driven out of Kuwait after a ground invasion that only lasted 100 hours. Neither the nuclear capacity of Iraq nor the chemical weaponry and the SCUD systems were fully destroyed before the multinational force withdrew.

From the 27th Nissan Adm.R.Menachem Mendel Schneersohn of Lubavitch (see 5710/1950) significantly increased his predictions of the imminent coming of the Mashiach (Messiah). Many of his followers claimed that he was already here, and (privately at first) gave him petitions proclaiming their allegiance to him as Mashiach.

In a dramatic airlift (see 5710/1950) beginning on the 11th Sivan, 15,000 Jews were flown out of Ethiopia, after 20,000 had arrived in previous years, 7,000 of them in a similar operation in 5744/1984. Although they believed themselves to be biblical descent, there was considerable Rabbinic discussion about their ultimate acceptance as full Jews.

On the 9th Elul an anti-Jewish pogrom broke out in the Crown Heights section of Brooklyn, after a non-Jewish black child was killed in a car accident. A young Jewish student visiting from Melbourne, Australia, was killed. For three days the police stood by as anti-Jewish rioters attacked Jews and their property in the mixed neighborhood of blacks and Lubavitcher chassidim. The Jews were cautious not to retaliate with violence, although much of the media persisted in describing the event as "Jews and blacks fighting each other." Some say that media people were being purposely cautious, so as not to spread black fury. Others gave this reason for the general silence from Jews in other parts of the city and country.

On the 18th Elul the formal structure of the government in Russia (which was founded by the Communists, see 5677/1917) was changed when the rule of the Communist party was ended (see 5747/1987, 5752/1992).

5752 / 1991

After considerable political pressure was applied, the United States government was successful in arranging for Israel to meet with other Arab countries on the 22nd Cheshvan to discuss peace (see 5739/1979). It was anticipated that this process would be a long one and was based on the assumption that Israel would return to Arab rule, territories west of the Jordan River surrendered to Israel (see 5727/1967). These territories had many Jewish settlements by this time, and many more were planned.

5752 / 1992

The USSR (Union of Soviet Socialist Republics) was disbanded as the formal government of Russia, and was replaced by a Commonwealth of Independent States (CIS), which included the newly independent (Communist-free) states of Russia, Byelorussia, and the Ukraine. This did not have any immediate effect on the uncertain situation of Jews in these countries (see 5747/1987).

Adm.R.Simcha Bunim of Gur (see 5737/1977) died on the 7th Tammuz. He was succeeded by Adm.R.Pinchas Menachem, another son (from a second wife) of the Imrey Emess (see Sivan 5708/1948).

Some 350,000 Jews had left "Russia" (what was formerly the USSR) and settled in Eretz Yisrael in the previous 3 years (see 5740/1980).

There were 4,250,000 Jews living in Eretz Yisrael at this time (see 5729/1969).

Appendices

In this book, Chanuka is chronologically placed in the Jewish year 3621.

Some say [Meir.Eyn.36, 53/q.Tzem.Dav.3590] that the revolt of the Chashmona'im was not in 3621 but in 3590.

This, however, is inconsistent with the dates given in the Talmud [A.Z.9a, see Tzem.David 3621].

Some attempt to resolve the inconsistency by saying that the revolt and the subsequent miracle of Chanuka were isolated victories; that the Syrian (Greek) domination and religious persecution did not cease, but continued for over twenty years until the establishment of the Kingdom of the Chashmona'im, at a later date which would coincide with the time frame of the Talmud–3622 [A.Z.9a]. Accordingly, they say, none of the brothers were kings or rulers (except for Shimon, the last brother, who ruled in a limited way), because the Syrian (Greeks) were still in power ["Chanukah" Artscroll Mesorah Series, N.Y. 1981, p.34, 81–86].

This attempt at reconciliation, however, is inconsistent with:

1) the Talmud [Shab.21b], which refers to the *Kingdom* of the Chashmona'im at the time of the miracle of Chanuka, and makes the specific point of[1] inserting the word "Kingdom" (Malchut) into the text (of Megillat Ta'anit) that it is quoting;

2) the Ramban [Br.49.10 (Quoted in "Chanukah," Artscroll, pp. 87, 88, and apparently misread)], who *clearly* refers to all of the brothers as *rulers*, who suffered the consequences of their rule (because they were Kohanim, not from the tribe of Yehuda, and therefore not supposed to rule);

3) Rashi, who refers to them all in regal terms, as *rulers* [Dan.11.20];

4) the prayer of "Al-HaNissim" composed very shortly after the miracle by Yochanan Kohen Gadol (see 3622/–139, 3623/–138, and Appendix B). This prayer (which has a *specific number of words*) indicates that only *after* they had successfully defeated their enemy *(V'achar Kach)* did they take to the dedication of the Beit Hamikdash and light the lights of the Menora [KolBo Chan.44 p.44b, Gimat.122. p.926/Roke'ach 225 p.127/Mmn.Hakd.Pir.Mi.chap.6].

Much of the weight of evidence produced by the previously mentioned work ("Chanukah," Artscroll) is based on the account of the events in the anonymous books of Chashmona'im (Maccabees). These books are part of the Apocrypha, a series of books some of which are assumed to have been written in Hebrew originally, but are now only available in Hebrew translations from the Greek (and Latin).

It seems that the books were available, in some form, in the 1500s, because they are supposedly quoted in *Tosaphot Yom Tov* [Meg.3.6] (although he refers to *Sefer Maccabi*, and may be referring to something else)[2] and in *Tzemach David* [3590]; both authors were living in a similar time span (1550–1650 C.E.). The fact that the *Tosaphot Yom Tov* and the *Tzemach David* have quoted from them is used as proof of their acceptability to traditional Talmud scholars.[3]

---

[1]Megillat Ta'anit itself distinguishes between "Beit" Chashmona'i [2.17,27, 9.3,27], "Bnei" Chashmona'i [3.17], and "Malchut" Chashmona'i [12.13]; one must therefore assume significance in the Talmud's insertion of the word "Malchut" (Kingdom).

[2]The following accounts of Chanuka are referred to, or are actually extant:

a) *Megillat Antiochus* [Siddur Otzar HaTefillot] reportedly written originally in Aramaic, and supposedly predating Chashmona'im [see footnote there].

b) *Megillat Chashmona'im,* referred to by the Halachot Gedolot (see further in this appendix). (Some say that this is the Megillat Antiochus.)

c) *Midrash Ma'asei Chanuka* [Manuscript, Munich].

d) In Chashmona'im [Macc.2.25] there is reference to five other works describing the story of Chanuka.

It is therefore quite possible that there were other works also available.

[3]"Chanukah," Artscroll [p.34] also mentions (as proof of their assumption of the Talmudic acceptability of Chashmona'im) that *Eliyahu Rabbah* [O.C.671.1 - should be 670.1] also quotes them. In fact his quote is virtually

In fact, however, it is remarkable that they (Chashmona'im) are so *rarely* referred to by Talmudists – *particularly* by the Tzemach David, who was writing history. It is equally important to note that one of those few occasions in which he does quote Chashmona'im is with regard to the chronological placement of Chanuka, yet *he overrules that opinion.*

The Halachot Gedolot (*BaHaG*) (see 4519/759) mentions a *Megillat* Chashmona'im that was written by the authors of *Megillat Ta'anit* [Hil.Sof. p.282b]. It is

_____

verbatim to that of the *Tosaphot Yom Tov,* and he also calls it *Sefer Maccabi.*

If Eliyahu Rabbah, in fact, saw the *Sefer Maccabi* that he quotes, then it is *definitely* not (see footnote 2) the *Sefer Chashmona'im* (Maccabees), because both he and the Tosaphot Yom Tov are quoting identical words to describe an event, words not found in Chashmona'im in the description of the same event [Macc.I 4.38-58, II 10.2-11].

If he is quoting from the *Tosaphot Yom Tov,* which he often did [Shem.Hag.1.Yud.92, p.52], then the *Eliyahu Rabbah* cannot be used as an *additional* endorsement of the Talmudic acceptability of Chashmona'im.

unlikely (see footnote 2) that this is the same book of Chashmona'im (Maccabees) referred to here, because Chashmona'im differs with *Megillat Ta'anit* on such a fundamental issue as how the revolt of the Chashmona'im began. *Megillat Ta'anit* [chapter 6] ascribes it to a personal persecution about to be perpetrated on the family of the Chashmona'im, whereas Chashmona'im [Maccabees I 2.17-29] ascribes it to circumstances involving a public event with an altar and an idol.

The book *Me'or Einayim* (whose author also lived in the 1500s C.E.) also bases its chronological placement of Chanuka on the book of Chashmona'im. However, the negative attitude of Talmudists (particularly R.Yosef Karo) to *Me'or Einayim* is clearly stated by the Chida [Machazik Bracha O.C.307, p.133a]; and the Maharal of Prague categorically rejects its historical calculations [Ba'er HaGola Chap.6 p.127-141, Yerush.1971].

_____

This chronology is based on Biblical, Talmudic, and post-Talmudic sources, and all evidence in such sources clearly places the date of the revolt of the Chashmona'im in the year 3621.

The Talmud mentions Yochanan Kohen Gadol many times, without clearly identifying who he was and at what time he lived.

In fact there is a difference of opinion in the Talmud [Ber.29a] as to his identity, which is described here:

1) The Rambam (Maimonides), in his introduction to his explanations of the Talmud [Pirush Ha-Mishna, Zer.], devotes a chapter [Chapter 6] to clarification of identities in the Talmud. In this chapter (where he would have been especially precise and accurate) he clearly states that Yochanan Kohen Gadol was the son of Mattityahu ("the famous, mentioned in the prayers," presumably the "Al-HaNissim" prayer). The Rambam also mentions Yochanan ben Mattityahu [in Chapters 4 and 7] as being a leading scholar of that time.

The Roke'ach, in discussing Chanuka [225,p.127], states that Chanuka transpired through Yochanan Kohen Gadol. He later points out[1] that Yochanan Kohen Gadol composed the "Al-HaNissim" prayer.

The Levush [Hil.Chan.670], says that the Chashmona'im, which means Yochanan Kohen Gadol, recaptured and entered the Beit Hamikdash.

It seems obvious that both the Roke'ach and the Levush concur with the opinion of the Rambam that Yochanan Kohen Gadol was the son of Mattityahu, and that because he became Kohen Gadol rather than a political leader like the other brothers he was perhaps therefore not commonly identified, as they were, with military or political accomplishments.

This can be reinforced by the indication in the Talmud [R.H.18b] that, after the victory of the Chashmona'im, it was customary to use a standardized introduction on legal documents. The statement read "In the year . . . . . since Yochanan Kohen Gadol . . ."

However, the Rambam [Hil.Mas.9.1] says " . . . Yochanan Kohen Gadol, who was after Shimon HaTzadik . . .," and the Bertinura [Mas.Shen.5.15] follows this statement. The Kesef Mishna (R.Yosef Karo), however, immediately explains that the Rambam wrote this in order to distinguish[2] between the first Yochanan Kohen Gadol and the second Yochanan Kohen Gadol, who became a Tzeduki. It is above all impossible to suggest that Yochanan Kohen Gadol was directly after Shimon HaTzadik, because of the events related in the Talmud [Min.109b] regarding the jealousy of succession after Shimon HaTzadik's death (see 3488/−273). (And this would probably explain why the Kesef Mishna found it necessary to comment on the historical point, when it does not affect the Halacha aspect at all.)

2) There are those who say that Yochanan Kohen Gadol was the father of Mattityahu [Yuch.1.16, 62/Sed.Had.Sed.Tan.VeAm. Yoch.K.G./possibly the Bertinura Mas.Shen.5.15].

The Yuchasin quotes the Rambam [Chapter 6], and claims that it is a mistake, and should read Yochanan the "father" of Mattityahu, not the "son." (He interprets the words "the famous, mentioned in the prayers" as referring to Yochanan, when in fact it seems obvious that it is referring to Mattityahu.)

Would the Yuchasin claim that Chapters 4 and 7 in the Rambam are also mistakes?

Toldot Am Olam [2.412] questions the Yuchasin, but also relies on saying that the words of the Rambam [Chapter 4] are inaccurate [Tol.Am.01.2.410] and really refer to the son of the son (grandson) of Mattityahu (in a circumspect way). He does not quote Chapter 6, yet it is precisely in this chapter that the Rambam would not use circumspect ref-

---

[1]The Roke'ach claims a very long line of information transferral direct to him from Shimon HaPakuli (see 3836/76) [Shem.Hag.1. Alef.219 p.21-22].

[2]It is probable that the Rambam used *this method* of identification–even though Yochanan Kohen Gadol was much later than Shimon HaTzadik–because he was paraphrasing the Talmud [Yom.9a], which lists them together because they were both famous and of long tenure.

erences to a grandson as a son while attempting to clarify and be specific about identities.

Furthermore, what would be the explanation of the (aforementioned) Talmud [R.H.18b], which indicates that Yochanan Kohen Gadol was being used as a dating "beacon" *after* the revolt of the Chashmona'im?

It is also clear that[3] Rashi [Sot.33a] maintains that Yochanan Kohen Gadol was after the revolt of the Chashmona'im.

3) Others say that Yochanan Kohen Gadol was Yochanan Hyrkanos (see 3642/–119), the son of Shimon, who was in turn the son of Mattityahu [Dor.Har.2.444/Tol.Am 01.2.227, 410].

Most agree that this Yochanan (II) was the Kohen Gadol who the Talmud says became a *Tzeduki* [Yuch.1.14,62/Tzem.David 3646/Sed.Had./Dor.Har.2.442, 444/Tol. Am 01.2.254].

There is a difference of opinion in the Talmud [Ber.29a] as to whether Yochanan Kohen Gadol was the one who became a *Tzeduki*. All seem to agree that Yannai was, or became, a *Tzeduki*. Was Yochanan the same person as Yannai, or was he not? Abbayé says he was. Rava says he was not. The Talmud appears to conclude with the opinion of Rava (as would be customary).[4]

None of the above possibilities readily accounts for a Yochanan Kohen Gadol to have served (a full) eighty years, as related in the Talmud [Ber.29a, Yom.9a]. This remains unclear.[5][6][7]

———

For the purposes of a Talmudic chronology, it is preferable to accept the clear statements of the Rambam, Roke'ach, and Levush, that Yochanan Kohen Gadol was the son of Mattityahu the Chashmona'i.

It is plausible that there would be a blurring of identities [Tal.Ber.29a] between Yochanan Kohen Gadol (the son of Mattityahu), and his nephew, Yochanan Hyrkanos Yannai, if they succeeded each other—which they probably did.

———

technically *possible* that Yochanan *could* have become a *Tzeduki*, but that in fact he did not.

[5]The *Tiferet Yisrael* [Tal.Av.2.4(33)] says that Yochanan Kohen Gadol *lived* for eighty years. The Talmud, however, clearly states that he *served* as Kohen Gadol for eighty years [Tal.Ber.29a, Yom.9a].

The Steinsaltz Talmud points to a possible solution [Yom.9a, Ber.29a], saying that Yochanan Kohen Gadol refers to a "group" of people, or to a period. This is more plausible in *Yoma* than in *Berachot*, and would be accepted if stated by a Rishon (Early Scholar). Rashi [Ber.29a], however, accepts the meaning as simply stated.

[6]The Maharsha [Pes.57a] suggests yet another possible identity for Yochanan Kohen Gadol.

[7]The Me'iri [Peticha (introduction) L'Avot] appears to contradict himself. Once he says Yochanan Kohen Gadol was the son of Mattityahu [p.28 Yerush.1964], and later he says that he was the father of Mattityahu [p.34 Sed.Hat.,Dmai].

———

[3]It appears, however, that Rashi accepts that there was only one Yannai, which raises questions resolved by Tosaphot, who indicate there were two [Rashi Sot.22b, Ber.48a, Kid.66a, Shab.16b/Tos.Yom.18a, Yev.61a].

[4]It is also apparent from the *Kesef Mishna* [Hil.Mas.9.1] that the conclusion of the Talmud is that they were two different people, and it was established that it was

Ten great Tanna'im were brutally killed by the Romans, and their memory has become legend in Jewish history, particularly through a prayer that is said on the holiest day of the Jewish calendar, Yom Kippur, during the *Mussaf* service. It is generally accepted [Sed.Had.3880] that these Ten Martyrs *(Asara Harugei Malchut)* include the following Tanna'im:

1) R.Shimon ben Gamliel I

2) R.Chanina Sgan HaKohanim

3) R.Yishmael (Kohen Gadol)

4) R.Akiva[1] (ben Yosef)

5) R.Yehuda ben Bava[2]

6) R.Chanina ben Tradyon[3]

7) R.Chutzpit HaMeturgeman

8) R.Yesheivav HaSofer

9) R.Elazar ben Shamu'a

---

[1]R.Akiva was imprisoned for an extended time (see 3894/134), and then he was tortured to death by having his skin peeled off with hot metals [Tal.Ber.61b].

[2]When all Jewish religious practice was banned, and an emphasis placed on the ban of Torah study, R. Yehuda ben Bava gathered together R.Meir, R.Yehuda (ben Ila'i), R.Shimon (bar Yochai), R.Yossi, and R. Elazar ben Shamu'a (disciples of R.Akiva, who was already in prison [see Dor.Har.4.641-4]). He met them at a point between two towns, to give them Semicha (ordination), because the Romans had threatened to annihilate any town in which Semicha was given. He told them to escape (which they did, see 3894/134, except that apparently R.Elazar ben Shamu'a was later captured). R.Yehuda ben Bava was caught and speared there (many times) to death [Tal.San.13b-14a, also San.11a].

[3]R.Yossi ben Kisma was respected by the Romans (apparently others were as well, such as R.Yochai, father of R.Shimon [Tal.Pes.112a]; and when he died many of them attended his funeral. Upon the Roman's return, they found R.Chanina ben Tradyon studying and teaching Torah. They took him, wrapped him in a *Sefer Torah* scroll, piled bundles of twigs around him, and before setting him afire they placed damp woolen cloths on him to prolong the agony of being burned to death [Tal.A.Z.18a].

There is considerable difference of opinion as to who was the tenth great Tanna killed by the Romans.

Some say that it was R.Yehuda ben Teima, others say it was R.Eliezer benDama, and some say that R.Yehuda ben Teima was also called ben Dama. There are yet others who say that R.Chanina ben Chachinay was one of the martyrs, others who say R.Yehuda HaNachtum, and others who include R. Tarfon [Yuch, Abarbanel, Yal.Reuv., q. Sed.Had. 3880].

It is known that R.Shimon ben Gamliel I (1 in the foregoing list) was no longer living at the time of the destruction of the second Beit Hamikdash [see the following], and that R.Akiva (listed as 4) was alive at the time of the Bar Kochba revolt many years later (see 3887/127). It is therefore assumed that not all ten martyrs were killed during the same period in history.

R.Yitzchak HaLevi Rabinowitz (see 5674/1914) raises some important questions (in Dorot Ha Rishonim [3.177-181, 199-202, 4.615-20]) with regard to the previously accepted list of Martyrs. His questions are as follows:

1) If they were killed at different times, over a period of approximately sixty years (from 3827/67 until after 3894/134), a time when millions of other Jews were killed by the Romans; why were *they* grouped together and memorialized as ten? Furthermore, why does the aforementioned prayer of Yom Kippur describe it as the result of the ruthlessness of a single ruler, a single judgment, and as ten consecutive murders?

2) Shmuel HaKatan (see 3836/76), one of the Tanna'im who saw the destruction of the second Beit Hamikdash, was eulogized by R.Gamliel and R.Elazar ben Azaryah [Tal.Smach. 8(47a)], (presumably) when they were both leaders of the Sanhedrin-Academy, (well) after the destruction of the Beit Hamikdash (see 3844/84). Yet on his deathbed, Shmuel Ha Katan predicted the deaths of R.Shimon and R.Yishmael [Tal.San.11a, Smach.8(47a)], who were

(undisputedly) the first two martyrs. If so, he could not have been referring to R.Shimon ben Gamliel I, and R.Yishmael ben Elisha (listed as 3), because R.Shimon died before the destruction, and R.Yishmael immediately after the destruction. They therefore had both obviously died before Shmuel HaKatan was on his death-bed, and he was presumably referring to another R.Shimon and R.Yishmael.

3) R.Shimon ben Gamliel died (in Yerushalayim) [Maharsha Sot.49a] before R. Yochanan ben Zakkai escaped from the *internal* siege of Yerushalayim (see 3827/67, 3828/68), to establish the Sanhedrin Academy at Yavneh (with the approval of the Romans), for it was R.Shimon's son, R.Gamliel II, who presided there. Furthermore, how could he have been killed by the Romans who were still (at that stage) in the northern part of Eretz Yisrael?

4) *The Halachot Gedolot* [Hilchot Tisha B'Av and Ta'anit] mentions R.Shimon ben Gamliel, R.Yishmael, and R.Chanina Sgan HaKohanim, as having been killed on the 25th Sivan. Yet in the various places where the murder of the Martyrs is mentioned [Tal.Smach.8(47a), Av.Dr.Nat.38.3/ T.D.B.E.30/ Mech. Shmot.22.22], the name of R.Chanina Sgan Ha Kohanim does not appear. Where, then, did the Halachot Gedolot (one of the Ge'onim living many years after the Talmud [see 4519/75] [Sed.Had./Shem.Hag.2.61 p.26]) find the name of R. Chanina Sgan HaKohanim, to include him?

R.Yitzchak HaLevi therefore concludes that the reference to R.Shimon was in fact R.Shimon ben HaSgan (the son of R.Chanina). His name in abbreviated form would have appeared as RShBHS"G, and some scribes, not recognizing the abbreviation, assumed it was a mistake and copied it as RShB"G, the (very common) abbreviation for R.Shimon ben Gamliel. It was known that R.Shimon ben Gamliel II did not die a violent death; hence it was assumed that the reference was to his grandfather, R.Shimon ben Gamliel I. This having been assumed, then the reference to R.Yishmael (with whom he was killed) was taken to refer to R.Yishmael Kohen Gadol who served in the Beit Hamikdash. The *Halachot Gedolot*, however, could have had a manuscript with a reference to HaSgan, and assumed it to mean R.Chanina Sgan HaKohanim.

He further concludes that it is possible that R.Shimon ben Gamliel I was in fact killed, not by the Romans, but in the civil war raging in Yerushalayim during the internal Jewish siege (see 3827/67). (The Romans did not kill even Yochanan of Gush Chalav, R.Shimon ben Gamliel's supposed ally, even though he was one of the factional *leaders* [see 3827/67] of the rebellion against them [see Chapter 9, 3829/69]. Why then would they have killed R.Shimon ben Gamliel, who was not a leader of the uprising?)

According to R.Yitzchak HaLevi's explanation, all of the Asara Harugei Malchut would have been killed at the same period in history, during (or after) the Bar Kochba revolt (R.Yishmael referring to the R.Yishmael who was a colleague of R. Akiva); the incidence of their deaths, all within a short span of time as implied by the Talmud [R.H. 23a-end] has led to the title Asara Harugei Malchut (Ten Martyrs).

Jewish history is divided into general eras that tend to coincide with developments in Torah; and the scholars of those eras are identified with them, such as the Tanna'im at the time of the Mishna, and the Amora'im at the time of the Gemara.

The beginning of the era of the Rishonim (which included Rashi, the Rif, Rambam, and Tosaphot, among others) is clearly defined by the death of R.Hai Gaon, with the subsequent decline in the centrality of the Babylonian Torah centers, and the rise of new centers in France, Germany, and Spain.

After the Rishonim (early Talmud scholars) there followed a tekufa of Acharonim (later Talmud scholars). There is, however, a blurring of the line drawn between the Rishonim and the Acharonim, with no particular event or date clearly set to mark the end of one era and the beginning of the next.

In fact, opinions regarding the time of the transition between the Rishonim and the Acharonim range from as early as the early 1300s (the latest date for the end of the era of Tosaphot), to 1563 (the printing of the Shulchan Aruch).

Such demarcation dates fulfill a role in the study of Torah in that the scholars of one era treat the opinions of scholars in a preceding era with unquestioning respect. Such demarcations exist in the distinction between the Chumash (Five Books of Moses) and the T'nach (Prophets), the Mishna and the Gemara, and the Gemara and the Ge'onim. In fact these eras are generally accepted to represent decreasing levels of Ru'ach HaKodesh (prophecy, and lower levels of quasi-prophecy) [Ramban B.B.12a].

Acharonim generally treat the words of the Rishonim with this deep respect, but the perception of who is or is not classified as a Rishon is affected by the over 250-year span of doubt.

The matter could become a dilemma, even if we are to accept a clear date for the conclusion of the era of the Acharonim (such as the near-destruction of European Jewry in 1940-1945).

If we then accept an early date for the conclusion of the Rishonim (say 1310), it would lead us to include the Torah scholars and Poskim of our century in the same era of Acharonim (and, by implication, the same level of Ru'ach HaKodesh) as the Tur, the Maggid Mishneh, the Ran, Rivash, Rashbatz, and the Nimukei Yosef (all of whom were before 1492), as well as the Shulchan Aruch, Radvaz, Eyn Yaakov, Ramak, Ari'zal, Shitta MeKubetzet, R.Moshe Alshich, Maharshal, Maharsha, Maharam, Levush, Sma, Maharal (of Prague), Shaloh HaKadosh, Tosaphot Yom Tov, Bach, Shach, Taz, Chelkat Mechokek, Reishis Chochma, Sefer Charedim, plus many others.

Even if we accept a relatively late date for the end of the era of the Rishonim (say 1492), we would still find most of those aforementioned scholars coexisting in the same era (Acharonim) as scholars from our century.

This possibility is virtually denied by the deep respect the latter scholars display toward the former.

a) Certainly, no Poskim (Halacha authorities) of our century would contradict any of the rulings of the Shulchan Aruch or its commentaries, such as the Shach and Taz.

b) As early as the Ba'al Shem Tov (1698-1760) and his disciples, we find a deep reverence for the words of the Ari'zal (1532-1570) and his contemporary, the Reishis Chochma.

c) R.Shneur Zalman of Lyady, the Ba'al HaTanya VeShulchan Aruch (1745-1813), is quoted as saying that all the authors of major works up until and including the Shach and the Taz (printed in 1646), wrote with Ru'ach HaKodesh.

The dilemma thus becomes more complex than simply setting a date for the end of the Rishonim, for even the latest date (1563) would leave the Shach and the Taz in the era of Acharonim.

This dilemma has led to the conclusion that there may in fact be an era between the Rishonim and the Acharonim.

What single event could we consider to be the end of the era of the Rishonim?

A massive tragedy – such as the expulsion of the Jews from Spain with the subsequent redistribution of Jewish communities to new locations in the expanding Ottoman Empire including Turkey, Greece, Eretz Yisrael, and North Africa, which all developed vibrant Torah centers – certainly signals the end of one era and the beginning of another.

When viewed in a broader perspective – that the expulsion from Spain was the culmination of a series of major expulsions from Europe (England 1209, France 1394, Austria 1421, and numerous local expulsions [see index for "Expulsions"] from the cities and provinces of Germany, Bohemia, Moravia, Switzerland [see 5251/1491], and Italy); and that the Jews from many of these central European areas moved eastward to Poland-Lithuania, where a new vibrant Torah center emerged in the 1500s – there is compelling reason to place the end of an era in Jewish history at the Spanish expulsion in 1492.

The printing in 1646 of the *Shach* and the *Taz* (commentaries on the *Shulchan Aruch*) clearly consolidated the place of *Shulchan Aruch* as the final word in Halacha. Two years later, the thriving Jewish communities of Poland-Lithuania received a major economic and spiritual setback in the devastating massacres of the Cossack uprising under Chmielnitzki. Jews in Poland-Lithuania (and later in Russia) never recovered the status they had had in the pre-1648 era, and were relegated to a miserable second-class socioeconomic existence.

In the 156 years between 1492 and 1648 we find the following scholars and works:

The Shulchan Aruch, Radvaz, Eyn Yaakov, Avodat HaKodesh (Kabbala), Ramaz (Remez, Kabbala), Ramak (Pardes), Ari'zal, Shitta Me Kubetzet, R.Moshe Alshich, R.Yaakov Pollak, Maharshal, Maharsha, Maharam, Levush, Sma, Maharal (of Prague), Shaloh HaKadosh, Tosaphot Yom Tov, Bach, Shach, Taz,Chelkat Mechokek, "Reishis Cochima," and Sefer Charedim.

By their names alone, they represent an outstanding era in Jewish history. If, however, we look at their accomplishments, we find an even more remarkable phenomenon.

1) The *Shulchan Aruch* was, without question, the consolidation of Halacha. The contributions of its author, R.Yosef Karo, its "editor," the Ramo, and its commentaries, the Sma, the Shach, the Taz, and the Chelkat Mechokek, all combined to seal yet another phase in the development of Torah. The *Shulchan Aruch* today is a consolidated work of Halacha, referred to with a reverence similar to that accorded the Mishna in the time of the Gemara, and to the Gemara in the time of the Ge'onim.

2) The teachings of the Ari'zal (and the Pardes of the Ramak) had a similarly profound impact on the study of Kabbala; and they rank, with the Zohar, as the major works of Kabbala.

3) The works of the Maharsha, the Maharshal, and the Maharam, along with the pilpul style introduced into Poland-Lithuania by R.Yaakov Pollak, and the works of the Shitta Mekubetzet, all contributed to the styles and trends of Talmud study that have prevailed to this day.

4) The Bertinura (R.Ovadya) and the Tosaphot Yom Tov have had a basic and lasting impact on the study of the Mishna.

5) The *Eyn Yaakov* created a concept of its own, with regard to the study of Agada; and the *Matanot Kehuna* and the *Yefei To'ar*, both the major commentaries on the Midrash Rabba, have increased the accessibility of the Midrash.

It becomes clear, then, that the era between 1492 and 1648 is more than a period between major upheavals in Jewish life. It was an era of Torah consolidation that left a major impact in the development of Torah.

The perspective of distance is often necessary before the full impact of the historical contribution of an era can be fully appreciated. Perhaps distance has only recently allowed a fresh clarity of perspective.

If we are to say that the era from 1492 to 1648 belongs neither to the Rishonim nor the Acharonim, but represents an era of Torah consolidation that stands on its own, it would need to be suitably named.

After the consideration of many possibilities, the name *Kov'im* (consolidation and setting) appears to most appropriately describe the impact of that era in Jewish history.

The following outstanding individuals lived in the 150 years from 1342–1492 (Rishonim), the 156 years from 1492–1648 (Kov'im), and the 150 years from 1648–1798 (Acharonim).

These lists can contribute to a perspective of the remarkable accomplishments in Torah that took place in the years 1492–1648, in comparison with similar time spans both before and after.

The lists include those scholars who had a major lasting impact on Jewish (Torah) history, and places them in the time frame of their major activity (for example, R.Ovadya Bertinura, who was born in or around 1445 but whose major work was finished after 1492; and R.Avraham Zacuto, who wrote his *Sefer Yuchasin* in 1504, although he was by then in his sixties). They are listed in order of birth. In case of doubt, the earliest possible date of birth and the latest possible date of death have been listed.

TORAH SCHOLARS

Rishonim
1342–1492

Secular Year Born		Secular Year Died
1275?	Tur (R.Yaakov ben Asher)	1349?
1288	Ralbag	1344
1290?	Ran (R.Nissim)	1380?
?	Nimukei Yosef	?
1365?	Maharil	1427
1380?	R.Yosef Albo (Halkkarim)	1444?

TORAH SCHOLARS

Kov'im
1492–1648

Secular Year Born		Secular Year Died
1437	Abarbanel (R.Yitzchak)	1508
1440?	Yuchasin (R.Avraham Zacuto)	1515
1440?	Mizrachi (R.Eliyahu)	1525
1445?	Bertinura (R.Ovadya)	1524?
1450?	Eyn Yaakov	1516?
1463?	Radvaz	1573?
1488	R.Yosef Karo (Beit Yosef)	1575
1510?	Maharshal	1573
1512?	Maharal of Prague	1609
1520?	Shitta Mekubetzet	1593?
1522?	Ramak (R.Moshe Cordovero)	1570
1525?	Ramo (R.Moshe Isserles)	1573?
1530	R.Mordechai Yaffe (Levush)	1612
1534	Ari'zal	1572
1540?	Sma (R.Yehoshua Falk)	1614
1543	R.Chaim Vital	1620
1545	Lechem Mishneh	1588
1550?	Kli Yakar	1619
1555	Maharsha	1631
1560?	Bach (R.Yoel Sirkes)	1640
1560?	Shaloh HaKadosh	1630
1579	Tosaphot Yom Tov	1654
1586	Taz	1667
1605?	Chelkat Mechokek	1658
1621	Shach	1663?

TORAH SCHOLARS

Acharonim
1648–1800

Secular Year Born		Secular Year Died
1630?	Beit Shmuel	1700?
1637?	Magen Avraham	1683
1641	Siftei Chachamim	1718
1660?	Seder HaDorot	1747?
1680	Pnei Yehoshua	1756
1689?	Me'am Lo'ez	1732
1690?	R.Yonatan Eybeshutz	1764
1696	Or HaChayim	1743
1697?	R.Yaakov Emden	1776
1698	Ba'al Shem Tov	1760
1698?	Maggid of Mezeritsch	1772
1707	Ramchal (R.M.Ch.Luzzatto)	1747
1707	Korban HaEida	1762
1710?	Pnei Moshe	1781
1713	Noda BiYehuda	1793
1720	Vilna Gaon	1797
1724	Chida (R.Ch.Y.D.Azulai)	1806
1727?	Pri Megadim	1792
1745	The Rav (of Lyady)	1813
1745?	Ketzot HaChoshen	1813
1759	Chavat Da'at	1832
1761	R.Akiva Eger	1837
1762	Chassam Sofer	1839

Glossaries

Terminology

Calendar: How the Jewish (Lunar) Months
Coincide with the Secular (Solar) Months

Abbreviated Reference Names

Acharon

Literally "last." Refers to Jewish scholar and authority during the period leading into the twentieth century (see Appendix D).

Acharonim

Plural of *Acharon*.

Adar

The name of a Jewish month (see Glossary calendar).

Adm.

Used in this book as an abbreviation of the title *Admur* (see below).

Admur

Abbreviation of the words *Adoneninu* (our master), *Moreinu* (our teacher), *veRabeinu* (our rabbi). Leader (or spiritual "master") of a chasidic group. Usually charismatic, and not restricted to scholarly leadership. Also called "Rebbe" or "Tzadik" (see 5520/1760, 5575/1814).

Admurim

Plural of *Admur*.

Agada

Parables, stories, and statements conveying moral lessons. Many pages of the Gemara are devoted to this, and this style forms the body of Midrash.

Akeda

Literally "binding." Refers to Yitzchak's being bound up by his father, to be brought as a sacrifice (see 2084/−1677).

aliya

Emigration to Eretz Yisrael.

Amora

Scholar of the Gemara section of the Talmud (see 3990/230, 4111/351).

Amora'im

Plural of *Amora,* (see left-hand column).

Anshei

Literally "people of." *Anshei Knesset Hagdola* refers to "the people of the Great Assembly," a Sanhedrin-type body (see 3426/−335, 3448/−313).

Anussim

Literally "forced ones." Once referred to Jews who accepted other religions under threat of death, but maintained some religious observance in secret (see Index for *Marranos* and *secret Jews*).

Av

The name of a Jewish month (see Glossary calendar). Also "head," as in head of the court, *Av Bet Din*.

Avoda Zara

Literally "idol worship." Also the name of a section (tractate) of the Talmud dealing with that subject.

Avot

Literally "fathers." A section (tractate) of the Talmud dealing with ethics.

Avot D'Reb Natan

Similar to the Talmud tractate of Avot, see above.

ba'al

Literally "owner," also "author."

Ba'al Shem

Owner of a (good) name. Title used on rare occasions for person reputed to have mystical use of spiritual words and names.

299

ba'al teshuva

Someone who "owns" teshuva. Refers to a person who has returned to a lifestyle consistent with Halacha.

ba'alei

Plural of *ba'al*. Ba'alei Tosaphot–authors of the Tosaphot.

Bet Din

Jewish religious court

Beit Hamikdash

The holy temple in Yerushalayim (Jerusalem).

bnei

Literally "children of." Bnei Yisrael–Children of Israel.

ch'ramim

Plural of *cherem* (see below).

Chabad

Initials of the Hebrew words *Chochma* (wisdom), *Bina* (understanding), *Da'at* (perception).

Chacham

Wise person. Among Sephardi Jews it is used as a title similar to Rabbi.

Chachamim

Plural of *Chacham*. Also used as a general term for sages.

chasid

A pious person. Since the mid-1700s it has been used as a noun for followers of the movement started by the Ba'al Shem Tov (see 5520/1760).

chasidic

See *chasid*. Pertaining to the movement.

chasidim

Plural of *chasid*. Used as a noun for followers of an *Admur*.

chasidut

The teachings of the movement of the Ba'al Shem Tov (see *chasid*).

cherem

Excommunication. A Jewish court of law is required to establish this, and a court is required to remove it. Mostly used as a form of punishment and/or socioreligious isolation.

Cheshvan

The name of a Jewish month (see Glossary calendar).

chidushim

Literally "new things." Refers to the scholarly achievement of attaining new interpretations and/or rulings in the study of Torah.

Chol HaMo'ed

The intermediary days of the festivals of *Pesach* (Passover) and of *Sukkot* (Tabernacles). These days, although part of the festival, manifest a lesser holiness than the first and last days.

chozeh

Literally "seer." Chozeh of Lublin–the seer of that city, who earned the name by reputation.

Chumash

The "five books of Moses." *Chamesh* = five.

daf

Page. Daf HaYomi–"The Daily Page" of Talmud study.

dayan

Judge. Member of a court.

Elul

The name of a Jewish month (see Glossary calendar).

eretz

"The land of." Eretz Yisrael – the land of Israel.

erev

Literally "evening." Usually refers to the day preceding a Holy Day or festival.

Gaon

Literally "genius." It was the formal title for the head of a major Metivta (yeshiva) in Bavel after the Talmudic era (see 4349/589).

Ge'onim

Plural of *Gaon*.

Gemara

Part of the Talmud (see 4111/351, 4152/392, 4187/427).

ha

A Hebrew prefix meaning "the."

Hagada

The text which is recited on the first two nights of Passover.

Halacha

Jewish law, which includes religious, social, and civil law.

Hallel

Literally "praise." Refers to a (small) section of Psalms that is recited during prayers on Jewish festivals.

HaNagid

A title given to Jewish statesmen.

HaNassi

The president (of the Sanhedrin).

HaNavi

The prophet.

Hashem

Literally "the name," meaning *The Name*. A term used to refer to G-d, without mentioning His name.

Haskala

Literally "pertaining to intellectual scope." A name used for the "intellectual enlightenment movement." (See definition of *maskil* in this section, and see *Haskala* and *maskilim* in Index.)

Heter Iska

A manner of structuring a loan as a joint business venture, whereby interest payments, in fact, become profit sharing, and are therefore not forbidden under Jewish law (Halacha).

Hoshana Rabba

The seventh day of the festival of *Sukkot* (Tabernacles).

Iyar

The name of a Jewish month (see Glossary calendar).

Judenrat

A form of local Jewish self-government under Nazi occupation. The Nazis used these groups to administer their plans.

Kabbala

Torah mysticism (see 5050/1290, 5490/1730).

Kara'ites (See *Kra'im* in this section.)

kashrut

As in kosher. Refers to adherence to Jewish (dietary) laws.

Kedusha

Literally "holiness." Refers to a prayer recited by reader and congregation, when all are required to stand.

Kiddush

The prayer and benediction recited over wine on Shabbat and major festivals.

Kislev

The name of a Jewish month (see Glossary calendar).

kohanim

Plural of *kohen*.

kohen

Literally "priest." Descendants of Levi (see *levi'im*), and more specifically descendants of Aharon. They performed the major priestly role in the Beit Hamikdash.

Kohen Gadol

High priest (see *kohen*).

Kov'im

See introduction to Chapter 13. A new term used in this book to refer to major scholars of the era 1492–1648 (see Appendix D).

Kra'im

A sect of Jews who claimed adherence to the Written Laws of the Torah only (see 4523/763, 5613/1853).

Lag B'Omer

Literally "the 33rd day of the Omer counting." The Omer counting begins after the first day of Pesach (Passover) and continues for 49 days, until *Shavu'ot* (Pentecost). *Lag B'Omer* is a minor Jewish festival, commemorating the end of the killing of R.Akiva's disciples (see 3880/120), and the death of R.Shimon bar Yochai.

levi'im

Descendants of Levi (see 2195/–1566, 2332/–1429) who performed a minor priestly role in the *Beit Hamikdash*.

levites

Same as *levi'im* above.

maggid

Preacher. A role that was often distinct from the role of rabbi. The rabbi decided matters of Jewish law, whereas the maggid was the preacher.

Mar

A respectful title in Aramaic.

marrano

Secret Jews of Spain and Portugal (see Index).

maskil

Person who identified and followed the *Haskala* (see definition). Many displayed an unintellectual and biased attitude against traditional Jewish values (see *maskilim* in Index).

maskilim

Plural of *maskil*.

mechutan

A person "connected by marriage."

Megilla

Literally "scroll."

meshumad

Apostate.

Midrash

Work of *Agada* (see definition).

Minyan Shtarot

Literally "counting of documents." A dating system counting the years on Jewish documents which lasted over 1500 years (see 3449/−313).

Mitnagdim

Those who opposed the movement of *chasidim* (see definition, see Index).

motza'ei

The night after.

Mussaf

Additional prayer, recited on Shabbat and festivals.

mussar

Literally "chastisement." Refers to the teaching of discipline and ethics, often in a manner of reproof.

nassi

President. Usually refers to president of the Sanhedrin.

nazir

Literally "special devotion." Refers to a person who takes an oath to refrain from drinking wine, having his hair cut, and coming in contact with items that are ritually impure.

Nissan

The name of a Jewish month (see Glossary calendar).

Nistarim

Plural of *nistar*—"hidden."

Parshat Chukat

The Torah is divided into weekly readings. The week is often referred to by the name of the upcoming reading. Chukat is the name of one such portion.

Perushim

Literally "separate ones." Refers to the Pharisees who adhered to Jewish law (Halacha) and thus kept a degree of separateness in order to refrain from contact with items of spiritual impurity (see 3570/191 and Index).

Pesach

The festival of Passover.

piyut

A prayer in poetic form. The author often began every line following the alphabet, or with a consecutive letter of his name.

piyutim

Plural of *piyut*.

R.

Abbreviation used in this book for "Reb" or "Rabbi."

Raban

A title, with increased reverence, for Rabbi.

Rbn.

Abbreviation used in this book for *Raban*, see above.

Rbnu.

Abbreviation used in this book for the title "Rabbenu," which means literally "our teacher/rabbi." Was traditionally used only in instances of special reverence.

Rebbe (See *Admur* in this section.)

Rishon

Literally "first." Refers to Jewish scholar and authority during the period of 1040–1492 (see Appendix D).

Rishonim

Plural of *Rishon*.

Rosh HaShana

The New Year festival.

Sanhedrin

The Jewish high court (see 3995/235, see also Index).

Savurai

The generation of Talmud scholars immediately following the Amora'im (see 4236/476, 4320/560).

Sh'elot UTeshuvot

Literally "questions and answers." Local rabbis addressed their Halacha questions (in writing) to scholars of greater authority. A large collection of written answers were often published (by the author, or his disciples and/or descendants).

Shavu'ot

The festival of Pentecost. Literally means "weeks" because it occurs seven weeks after the first day of Pesach (Passover) (see *Lag B'omer*).

shi'urim

Literally "measures." Refers to regular sessions of Torah study.

Shma

Shma Yisrael. The most famous passages of the Chumash (Bible)–"Hear O Israel . . . ." As the most important prayer, recited at least twice daily.

shmad

Conversion of a Jew to other religions.

Shmitta

The seventh year which has religious significance.

shochet

A person trained to ritually slaughter kosher animals.

shochtim

Plural of *shochet*.

Shofet

Literally "judge." A title given to Jewish rulers at a certain stage in history (see 2533/–1228).

Shoftim

Plural of *Shofet*.

shtadlan

A Jew who maintained extensive political connections, which were used to assist fellow Jews particularly in times of need.

Shvat

The name of a Jewish month (see Glossary calendar).

Simchat Torah

Literally "the rejoicing of the Torah." The last day (appended) to the festival of Sukkot (Tabernacles).

Sivan

The name of a Jewish month (see Glossary calendar).

Sukkot

The festival of Tabernacles.

T'nach

Abbreviation for Torah, Nevi'im, Ketuvim. Although this symbolizes the three sections of the Bible–Torah (The Five Books of Moses), Nevi'im (The Prophets), and Ketuvim (Hagiographa)–it is commonly used to refer to the two latter sections.

tallit

Prayer shawl.

Tammuz

The name of a Jewish month (see Glossary calendar).

304

Tanna

Scholar of the Mishna section of the Talmud (see 3729/−32, 3949/189).

tanna'im

Plural of *Tanna.*

Tashlich

Prayers recited on Rosh HaShana near a body of water and usually a distance from town.

Tefillin

Phylacteries. Specially prepared black leather boxes (with scriptures on parchment inside), bound on the arm and the head.

tekufa

Era.

tekufot

Plural of *tekufa.*

teshuva

Refers to a return to a lifestyle consistent with Halacha.

Tevet

The name of a Jewish month (see Glossary calendar).

Tishrei

The name of a Jewish month (see Glossary calendar).

Tish'a B'Av

The ninth day of Av. A day of many tragedies in Jewish history (see 3338/−423, 3829/69).

Torah

Generally refers to the whole body of Jewish religious knowledge.

Tosaphot

Literally "additional." Commentary on the Talmud (see 4865/1105, 5050/1290).

Tosephta

Additional material to the Mishna.

Tzadik

Righteous person. Also used to refer to an *Admur* (see definition).

Tzadikim

Plural of *Tzadik.*

Tzeduki

Sadducee. Member of a sect or group which (later) claimed adherence only to the Oral Laws of the Torah. (See 3530/−231, 3628/−133.)

Tzedukim

Plural of *Tzeduki.*

Yovel

The fiftieth year has religious significance and follows a cycle of seven times seven years (49) (see Shmitta).

Tishrei

A 30-day month that can start as early as September 5 and end as late as November 3.

Adar2 begins as early as March 2 and ends as late as April 10. This balances out the 11-day difference between the lunar and the solar calendar (see 1657/−2104).

Cheshvan

A 29- or 30-day month (it varies) that starts as early as October 5 and ends as late as December 2.

Nissan

A 30-day month that starts as early as March 12 and can end as late as May 10.

Kislev

A 29- or 30-day month (it varies) that starts as early as November 4 and ends as late as January 1.

Iyar

A 29-day month that starts as early as April 11 and can end as late as June 8.

Tevet

A 29-day month that starts as early as December 4 and ends as late as January 30.

Sivan

A 30-day month that starts as early as May 10 and can end as late as July 8.

Shvat

A 30-day month that starts as early as January 1 and ends as late as March 1.

Tammuz

A 29-day month that starts as early as June 9 and can end as late as August 6.

Adar   Adar1
              Adar2

The regular month of Adar is a 29-day month that can start as early as February 1 and end as late as March 29.

When it occurs at the earlier date, there is a 29-day leap-year month called Adar2; the first Adar is then called Adar1 and has 30 days.

Av

A 30-day month that starts as early as July 8 and can end as late as September 5.

Elul

A 29-day month that starts as early as August 7 and can end as late as October 4.

A.Z. = Avoda Zara
Ant. = Antiquities
Av. = Avot
Av.Dr.Nat. = Avot D'Reb Natan
B.B. = Bava Batra
B.Hab. = Bedek HaBayit
B.HaMa. = Ba'al HaMa'or
B.K. = Bava Kama
B.M. = Bava Metzia
B.Turim = Ba'al HaTurim
B.Y. = Beit Yosef
Bam. = Bamidbar
Bech. = Bechorot
Ber. = Berachot
Bert. = (R.Ovadya) Bertinura
Besh. = Beshalach (Sidra)
Bet. = Betza
Bik. = Bikkurim
Br. = Bereishit
Caf.Hachym. = Caf HaChayim
Chab. = Chabakuk
Cha. = Chagai
Chag. = Chagiga
Chan. = Chanuka
Chal. = Challa
Chav.Yair. = Chavat Ya'ir
Ches. = Chesronot HaShas (Hashmatot)
Chosh.Mish. = Choshen Mishpat
Chov.Umaz. = Chovel Umazik
Chul. = Chulin
Cri. = Critot
D.E. = Derech Eretz
D.H. (I or II) = Divrei HaYamim
D.YbY = Dvar Yom BeYomo
Dan. = Daniel
Dev. = Devarim
Dma. = Dmai
Dor.Har. = Dorot HaRishonim
Ed. = Edut (Hil.)
E.H. = Even HaEzer
Encyl.Jud. = Encyclopedia Judaica
Erch. = Erachin
Eruv. = Eruvin
Est. = Esther (Megillat)
Eych. = Eycha
Ez. = Ezra

Gd.Ppl. = Guide for Perplexed (Moreh Nevuchim)
Gevrt.HaSh. = Gevurot HaShem
Gimat. = Gimatriyot
Gir. = Girushin
Git. = Gittin
Hag.Bach = Hagahot HaBach
Hag.M. = Hagahot Maimoniyot
Hag.R.B.Rans. = Hagahot R'Betzalel Ranchburg
Hakd. = Hakdama (Introduction)
Hakd.L'Yad = Hakdama L'Yad (HaChazaka)
Hil. = Hilchot
Hor. = Horiyot
Hosh. = Hoshea
Ibn Ez. = Ibn Ezra
Igg.R.Sher.Gaon = Iggeret Rav Sherira Gaon
Igg.Teman = Iggeret Teman
Ish. = Ishut
Kel. = Kelim
Kes.Mish. = Kesef Mishneh
Ket. = Ketuvot
Kid. = Kiddushin
Kid.Hach. = Kiddush HaChodesh
Klly. = Klalei
Koh. = Kohelet
Korb. HaE. = Korban HaEida
Kuz. = Kuzari
Lech.Mish. = Lechem Mishneh
Lik.Sich. = Likutei Sichot
M.K. = Mo'ed Katan
Mach.Vit. = Machzor Vitry
Mag.Av. = Magen Avraham
Mag.Mish. = Maggid Mishneh
Mak. = Makot
Mal.Velov. = Malveh VeLoveh
Mam. = Mamrim
Manscpt.Ed. = recent edition from manuscript
Mas. = Ma'aser
Mas.Hak. = Ma'asei HaKorbanot
Mas.Shen. = Ma'aser Sheni
Mat.Keh. = Matanot Kehuna
Mech. = Mechilta
Meg. = Megilla
Meg.Tan. = Megillat Ta'anit
Me'i. = Me'illa

Mel. (I or II) = Melachim
Metz.Dav. = Metzudat David
Mhrl.MiPrg. = Maharal of Prague
Mhrm. = Maharam
Mhrshl. = Maharshal
Mi.Zer. = Mishnayot Zera'im
Mich. = Michah
Mid. = Midrash
Mido. = Midot
Mik. = Mikva'ot
Mil. = Milchamot
Min. = Minachot
Mish. = Mishna
Mmn. = Maimonides (Rambam)
Mord. = Mordechai
Mrsha. = Maharsha
Naz. = Nazir
Nech. = Nechemyah
Ned. = Nedarim
Nid. = Nida
Nizk.Mam. = Nizkei Mamon
O.C. = Orach Chayim
O.Hat. = Or HaTorah
Otz.Hag. = Otzar HaGedolim
Otz.Nechm. = Otzar Nechmad
Ovad. = Ovadya
Par. = Para
Pea. = Pe'a
Pek. = Pekudei (Sidra)
Pes. = Pesachim
Pir. Dr.El. = Pirkei D'Reb Elazar
Pir.Mi. = Pirush HaMishna
Pn.Mosh. = Pnei Moshe
q. = quoted in
R.H. = Rosh HaShana
RaN. = Rabbenu Nissim
Rab. = Rabba
Re = R'eh (Sidra)
Rut. = Ruth
S.K. = Se'if Katan
SMaG = Sefer Mitzvot (HaGadol)
Saad.G. = Saadya Gaon
Sam. = Samchuni
San. = Sanhedrin
Sed.Had. = Seder HaDorot
Sed.Hat. = Seder HaTanna'im
Sed.Ol. = Seder Olam (Rabba)

Sed.Ol.Zut = Seder Olam Zuta
Sed.Tan.VeAm. = Seder Tanna'im
　　VeAmora'im
Sef.Hak. = Sefer HaKabbala
Sef.Mitz. = Sefer HaMitzvot (Maimonides)
Sh. = Shmot
Sh.Hsh. = Shir HaShirim
Sh.Mkbtzt. = Shitta Mekubetzet
Sh.Up. = Sh'ela Upikadon
Shab. = Shabbat
Shek. = Shekalim
Shem.Hag. = Shem HaGedolim
Shev. = Shevu'ot
Shilt.Gib. = Shiltei Giborim
Shl. = Shlach (Sidra)
Shm. (I or II) = Shmuel
Shmitt. = Shmitta
Shof. = Shoftim
Shvi. = Shvi'it
Sif. = Sifri
Sif.Chach. = Siftei Chachamim
Smach. = Smachot
Sof. = Sofrim
Sot. = Sota
Suk. = Sukka
T.D.B.E. = Tanna DeBei Eliyahu
TBY. = Tur Beit Yosef
Tal. = Talmud
Tal.Tor. = Talmud Torah
Tan. = Ta'anit
Tan. = Tanchuma
Targ.Yon. = Targum Yonatan
Teh. = Tehilim
Tem. = Temura
Tetz. = Tetzaveh (Sidra)
Tfi. = Tefilla
Tif.Yis.Bo. = Tiferet Yisrael–Bo'az
Tol.Am.Ol. = Toldot Am Olam
Tor.HaOl. = Torat HaOla
Tor.Tem. = Torah Temima
Tos. = Tosaphot
Toseph. = Tosephta
Tos.Y.T. = Tosaphot Yom Tov
Tsh. = Teshuvot
Tsh.Hag.Zich.LeRi. = Teshuvot HaGe'onim,
　　Zichron LeRishonim
Tze. = Tzephanya

Tzed.Lad. = Tzeida LaDerech
Tzem.Dav. = Tzemach David
Vay. = Vayikra
Vayish. = Vayishlach (Sidra)
VeAm. = VeAmora'im
Vik. = Viku'ach
Yad. = Yadayim
Yad. = Yad HaChazaka (Mishneh Torah)
Yad.Mlchi. = Yad Malachi
Yal. = Yalkut
Yal.Reuv. = Yalkut Re'uveni
Yam.Sh.Sh. = Yam Shel Shlomo
Yech. = Yechezk'el

Yef.To. = Yefei To'ar
Yer. = Yerushalmi
Yes.Hat. = Yesodei HaTorah
Yesh. = Yeshayahu (Isaiah)
Yev. = Yevamot
Yir. = Yirmiyahu
Yit. = Yitro (Sidra)
Yom. = Yoma
Ysh. = Yehoshua (Joshua)
Yuch. = Yuchasin
Zech. = Zecharyah
Zev. = Zevachim
Zoh. = Zohar

Text Plates

The following plates are reproductions from classical Jewish texts. Since Jewish texts are often composites of commentaries from a number of sources, these plates indicate the origins of each source.

Figure A. *Chumash* (Bible) with commentaries.
Figure B. *Mishna* with commentaries.
Figure C. *Mishna* with commentaries.
Figure D. *Talmud Bavli* (Babylonian Talmud).
Figure E. *Talmud Yerushalmi* (Jerusalem Talmud).
Figure F. *Halachot* of the Rif.
Figure G. *Halachot* of the Rif.
Figure H. *Yad HaChazaka* (Mishneh Torah) of the Rambam (Maimonides).
Figure I. *Yad HaChazaka* (Mishneh Torah) of the Rambam (Maimonides).
Figure J. *Shulchan Aruch,* Orach Chayim section.
Figure K. *Shulchan Aruch,* Yoreh Deya section.
Figure L. *Shulchan Aruch,* Even HaEzer section.
Figure M. *Shulchan Aruch,* Choshen Mishpat section.
Figure N. Commentaries of the Maharsha, Maharam, and Maharashal.

וַאֲרִין מַהַהוּא זַמְנָא לְסָכְבֵי עֵנוֹי וּמְרָא יַת עֵשָׂו בְּרֵיהּ רַבָּא בְּאַרְבְּיסַר בְּנִיסָן וַאֲמַר לֵיהּ הָא בְּרִי דֵין עֵילָוֵי מְשַׁבְּחִין לְמָארֵי עַלְמָא וְאוֹצְרֵי טַלִין מִתְפַּתְּחִין בֵּיהּ וַאֲמַר לֵיהּ הָא נָא : ב וַאֲמַר הָא כְּדוֹן סִיבַת לֵיהּ אֲנָא יָדַע יוֹם מוֹתִי : ג וּכְדוֹן סַב כְּדוֹן זַיְנָךְ מָאנֵי בֵיתְיָנָךְ וְקַשְׁתָּךְ וּפוּק לְחַקְלָא וְצוּד לִי צֵידָא : ד וְעֵיבַד לִי הַבְשִׁילִין הֵיכְמָא דִרְחֵימִת וְתַעֵיל וְאֵיכוֹל בְּגִין דִּתְבָרְכִנָּךְ נַפְשִׁי עַד לָא אֵימוּת : ה וְרִבְקָה שָׁמְעַת בְּרוּחַ קוּדְשָׁא כַּד מַלֵּיל יִצְחָק עִם עֵשָׂו בְּרֵיהּ וְאָזַל עֵשָׂו לְחַקְלָא לְמֵיצַד צֵידָא לְאַיְתָאָה : ו וְרִבְקָה אֲמַרַת לְיַעֲקֹב בְּרָהּ לְמֵימַר הָא לֵילְיָא הָדֵין עֵילָאֵי מְשַׁבְּחִין לְמָארֵי עַלְמָא וְאוֹצְרֵי טַלִין מִתְפַּתְּחִין

פי' יונתן

רש"י

רשב"ם

שפתי חכמים

דעת זקנים מבעלי התוספות

רמב"ן

אבן עזרא

אור החיים

כלי יקר

אבי עזר

ספורנו

Figure A. **Chumash** (Bible) with commentaries (Mikra'ot Gedolot edition, see 5276/1516).

אונקלוס

עֵינָיו מֵרְאֹת וַיִּקְרָא אֶת־עֵשָׂו | בְּנוֹ
הַגָּדֹל וַיֹּאמֶר אֵלָיו בְּנִי וַיֹּאמֶר אֵלָיו
הִנֵּנִי: ב וַיֹּאמֶר הִנֵּה־נָא זָקַנְתִּי לֹא
יָדַעְתִּי יוֹם מוֹתִי: ג וְעַתָּה שָׂא־נָא
כֵלֶיךָ תֶּלְיְךָ וְקַשְׁתֶּךָ וְצֵא הַשָּׂדֶה
וְצוּדָה לִּי צָיִד: ד וַעֲשֵׂה־לִי
מַטְעַמִּים כַּאֲשֶׁר אָהַבְתִּי וְהָבִיאָה
לִּי וְאֹכֵלָה בַּעֲבוּר תְּבָרֶכְךָ נַפְשִׁי
בְּטֶרֶם אָמוּת: ה וְרִבְקָה שֹׁמַעַת
בְּדַבֵּר יִצְחָק אֶל־עֵשָׂו בְּנוֹ וַיֵּלֶךְ עֵשָׂו
הַשָּׂדֶה לָצוּד צַיִד לְהָבִיא: ו וְרִבְקָה
אָמְרָה אֶל־יַעֲקֹב בְּנָהּ לֵאמֹר הִנֵּה
שָׁמַעְתִּי אֶת־אָבִיךָ מְדַבֵּר אֶל־עֵשָׂו

בְּרֵי וַאֲמַר לֵיהּ הָא אֲנָא :
ב וַאֲמַר הָא כְּעַן סִיבִית
לֵית אֲנָא יָדַע יוֹמָא
דְאֵמוּת : ג וּכְעַן סַב כְּעַן
זֵינָךְ סַיְפָּךְ וְקַשְׁתָּךְ וּפוֹק
לְחַקְלָא וְצוּד לִי צֵידָא :
ד וַעֲבֵיד לִי תַבְשִׁילִין
כְּמָא דִי רְחִימִית וְתָעֵיל
לִי וְאֵיכוּל בְּדִיל דִי
תְבָרְכִנָּךְ נַפְשִׁי עַד לָא
אֵימוּת : ה וְרִבְקָה שְׁמַעַת
כַּד מַלֵּיל יִצְחָק עִם עֵשָׂו
בְּרֵיהּ וַאֲזַל עֵשָׂו לְחַקְלָא
לְמֵיצַד צֵידָא לְאֵיתָאָה :
ו וְרִבְקָה אֲמַרַת לְיַעֲקֹב
בְּרַהּ לְמֵימַר הָא שְׁמָעִית
יָת אֲבוּךְ מְמַלֵּיל עִם עֵשָׂו

בעל הטורים

כי כהות עיניו יזיד והוא לבת שוה מפשוטו ...

רש"י

אלו (שהיו מעשנות ומקטירות לע"א) ד"א כשנתקד ע"ג
המזבח והיה אביו רוצה לשחטו באותה שעה נפתחו השמים
וראו מלאכי השרת והיו בוכים וירדו דמעותיהם ונפלו על
עיניו לפיכך כהו עיניו . ד"א כדי שיטול יעקב את הברכות :
(ב) לא ידעתי יום מותי . א"ר יהושע בן קרחה אם
מגיע אדם לפרק אבותיו ...

שפתי חכמים

כיתה נתיבה כז כדפרש"י (מהרש"ל) ול"נ דלדידי רש"י ל"ג ...

אור החיים

ליטול יעקב הברכות ע"ד סיבה זו ולא בידיעת ילחק כי מזה
סובבו כמה סיבות ...
בנו הגדול . נתינת טעם למה לא קרא ליעקב כי זה הבכור ...

כלי יקר

ולבכרם בנו כא כיעים על כן אמר באן ילחק שלפי' לפם זקנתו ...

2
3
ר' עובדיה מברטנורה
כלאים קרחת פרק ד
תוספות יום טוב
קיט
אם העומד מרובה על הפרוץ מותר. ואם הפרוץ מרובה על העומד כנגד הפרצה אסור: ה הנוטע שורה של חמש גפנים. בשא כרם. ובהא אינו כרם עד שיהו שם שתי שורות. לפיכך הזורע ארבע אמות שבכרם בית שמאי אומרים קידש שורה אחת. ובית הלל אומרים קדש שתי שורות:
מלאכת שלמה
יכין
תפארת ישראל
בועז
משנה ראשונה
תוספות רע"ק
תוס' אנשי שם

Figure B. Mishna with commentaries (a standard edition).

1. Text of the Mishna
2. Bertinura (see 5248/1488)
3. Tosaphot Yom Tov (see 5377/1616)
4. Tiferet Yisrael (see 5597/1837)

Figure C. Mishna with commentaries. (This edition appears at the end of Volume One of the standard Babylonian Talmud. It comprises the Mishna section of Zera'im [agriculture law], which has no Gemara following the Mishna.)

1. Text of the Mishna
2. Rash (see 4948/1187)
3. Rambam (see 4965/1204)

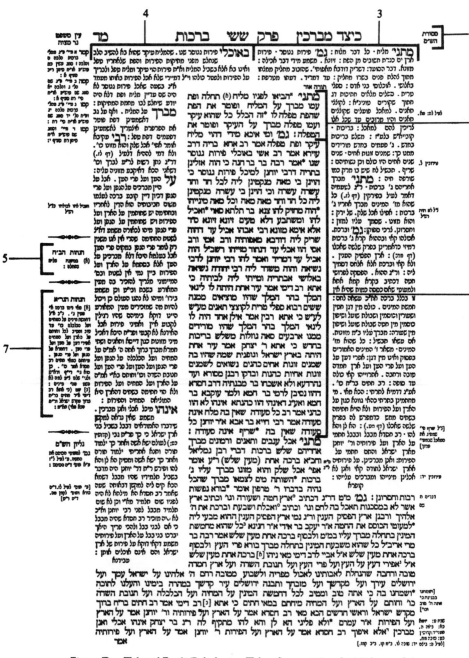

Figure D. **Talmud Bavli** (Babylonian Talmud) comprising the Mishna and the Gemara, with commentaries (standard edition).

1. Text of the Mishna
2. Text of the Gemara
3. Rashi (see 4865/1105)
4. Tosaphot (see 5050/1290)
5. (Hagahot Ha)Bach (see 5400/1640)
6. Mesorat HaShas (see 5449/1689)
7. (Hagahot Ha)Gra (see 5558/1797)

318

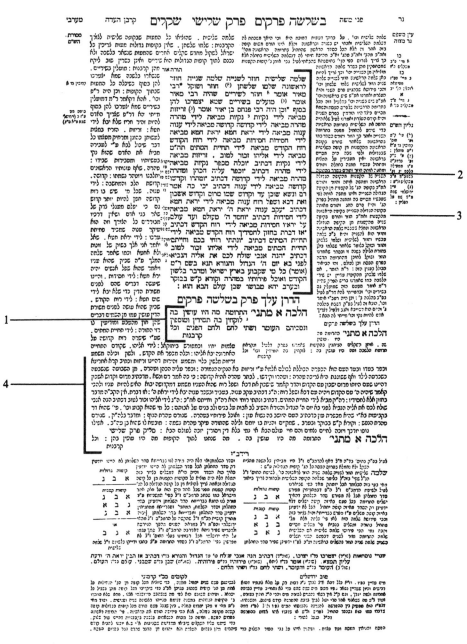

Figure E. **Talmud Yerushalmi** (Jerusalem Talmud) comprising the Mishna and the Gemara, with commentaries (standard edition).

1. Text of the Mishna
2. Text of the Gemara
3. Pnei Moshe (see 5541/1781)
4. Korban HeEida (see 5503/1743)

Figure F. Halachot of the Rif (standard edition, on the sections with the commentary of the Nimukei Yosef).

1. Rif (see 4863/1103)
2. HaMa'or (see 4910/1150)
3. Nimukei Yosef (see 5153/1393)
4. (Hagahot Ha)Bach (see 5400/1640)

2

1

רש"י

שהשבועות דלות על דבר שאין בו ממש
כדבר שיש בו ממש מה שאין בו בנדרים
כיצד אמר שבועה * שאיני למלזין ישלא
אוכל מא אוכל ושלא אוכל אוכל אכילנה צדקה
לעני משבע מדר סיני הוא ולא חייל
עלה שבועה אלא מצוה לעשר : שאיני
ישלא אישן אוני הוא אמר ר' יודען האומר
שבועתן שאיני אישן שלשה ימים מלקין אותו
וישן לאלתר הום אמר שלשה ימים והכאלאאמר
בשלמא
* איתמר שבועה שיש פלוני צרד לים
שבועה שלא זרק רב אמר חייב שמואל
אמר פטר רב אמר איתיה בלאו והן (ברשון)
ישמאל אמר פטר לותיה בלבזה :

...

(דף ג:)

אביי אמר
אלא

Figure G.** **Halachot of the Rif** (standard edition, on the sections with the commentary of the Ran).

1. Rif (see 4863/1103)
2. Ran (see 5104/1344)

Figure H. **Yad HaChazaka** (Mishneh Torah) of the Rambam (Maimonides) with commentaries (standard edition).

1. Rambam (see 4965/1204)
2. Ra'avad (see 4959/1198)
3. Hagahot Maimoniyot (see 5059/1298)
4. Migdal Oz (see 5096/1336)
5. Maggid Mishneh (see 5104/1344)
6. Kesef Mishneh (see 5335/1575)
7. Lechem Mishneh (see 5335/1575)
8. Mishneh LeMelech (see 5487/1727)

322

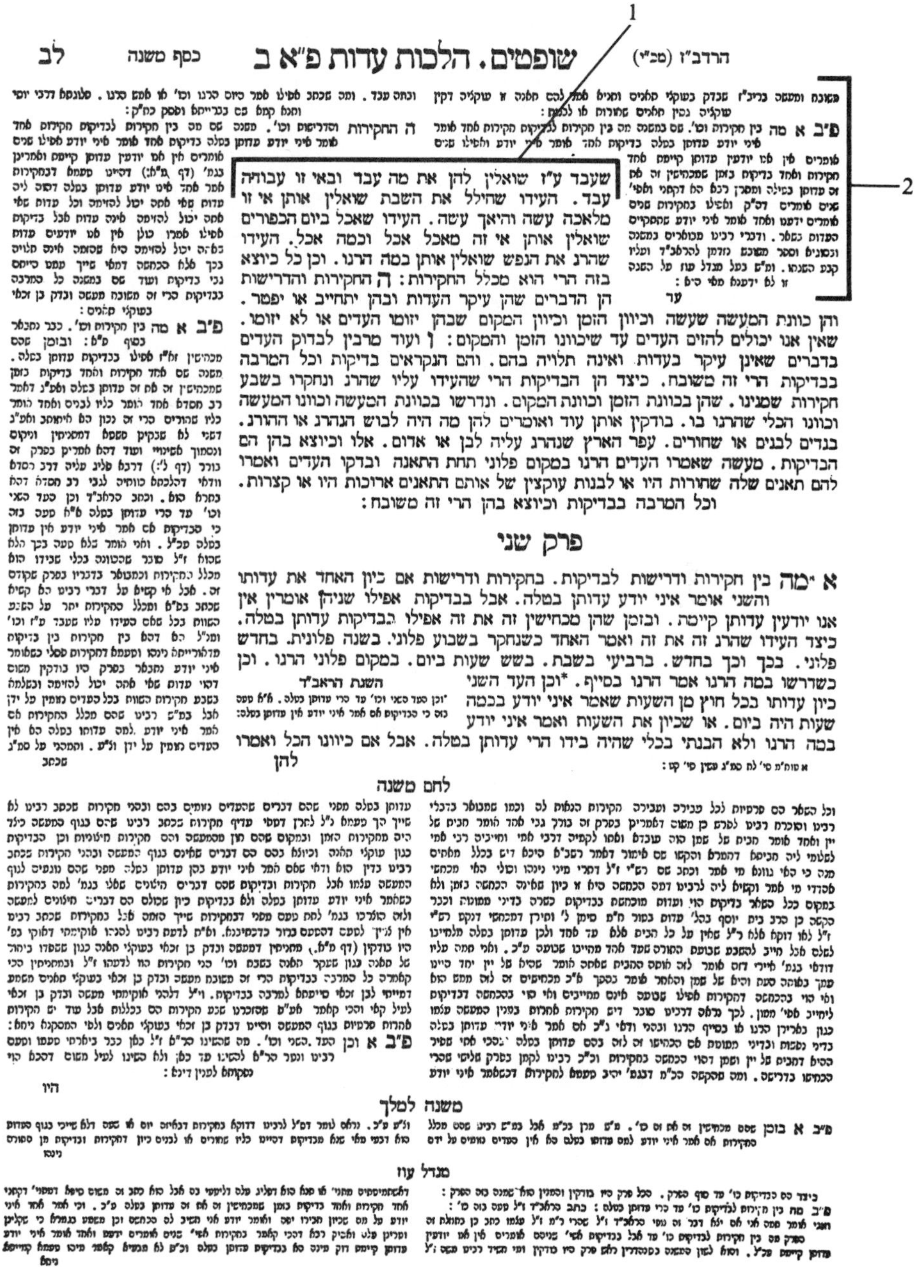

לב כסף משנה שופטים. הלכות עדות פ"א ב הרדב"ז (מכ"י)

שעבד ע"ז שואלין להן את מה עבד ובאי זו עבודה עבד. העידו שחילל את השבת שואלין אותן אי זו מלאכה עשה והיאך עשה. העידו שאכל ביום הכפורים שואלין אותן אי זה מאכל אכל וכמה אכל. העידו שהרג את הנפש שואלין אותן במה הרגו. וכן כל כיוצא בזה הרי הוא מכלל החקירות: ה החקירות והדרישות הן הדברים שהן עיקר העדות ובהן יתחייב או יפטר. והן כוונת המעשה שעשה וכיוון הזמן וכיוון המקום שבהן יוזמו העדים או לא יוזמו. שאין אנו יכולים להזים העדים עד שיכוונו הזמן והמקום: ו ועוד מרבין לבדוק העדים בדברים שאינן עיקר בעדות ואינה תלויה בהם. והם הנקראים בדיקות וכל המרבה בבדיקות הרי זה משובח. כיצד הן הבדיקות הרי שהעידו עליו שהרג ונחקרו בשבע חקירות שמינו. שהן בכוונת הזמן וכוונת המקום. ונדרשו בכוונת המעשה וכוונו המעשה וכוונו הכלי שהרגו בו. בודקין אותן עוד ואומרים להן מה היה לבוש הנהרג או ההורג. בגדים לבנים או שחורים. עפר הארץ שנהרג עליה לבן או אדום. אלו וכיוצא בהן הם הבדיקות. מעשה שאמרו העדים הרגו במקום פלוני תחת התאנה ובדקו העדים ואמרו להם תאנים שלה שחורות היו או לבנות עוקציו של אותם התאנים ארוכות היו או קצרות. וכל המרבה בבדיקות וכיוצא בהן הרי זה משובח:

פרק שני

א מה בין חקירות ודרישות לבדיקות. בחקירות ודרישות אם כיון האחד את עדותו והשני אומר איני יודע עדותן בטלה. אבל בבדיקות אפילו שניהן אומרין אין אנו יודעין עדותן קיימת. ובזמן שהן מכחישין זה את זה אפילו בבדיקות עדותן בטלה. כיצד העידו שהרג זה את זה ואמר האחד כשנחקר בשבוע פלוני. בשנה פלונית. בחדש פלוני. בכך וכך בחדש. ברביעי בשבת. בשש שעות ביום. במקום פלוני הרגו. וכן כשדרשו במה הרגו אמר הרגו בסייף. *וכן העד השני כיון עדותו בכל חוץ מן השעות שאמר איני יודע בכמה שעות היה ביום. או שכיון את השעות ואמר איני יודע במה הרגו ולא הבנתי בכלי שהיה בידו הרי עדותן בטלה. אבל אם כיוונו הכל ואמרו להן

השגת הראב"ד

*וכן העד השני וכו' עד הרי עדותן בטלה. א"א פעם כאן כי בבדיקות לא אמר איני יודע אין עדותן בטלה:

א טוח"מ סי' לג סמ"ג עשין סי' קט:

לחם משנה

משנה למלך

מגדל עוז

Figure I. Yad HaChazaka (Mishneh Torah) of the Rambam (Maimonides) with commentaries (standard edition), on sections where there is no commentary of the Maggid Mishneh, and the commentary of the Radvaz appears in its place.

1. Rambam (see 4965/1204)
2. Radvaz (see 5313/1553)

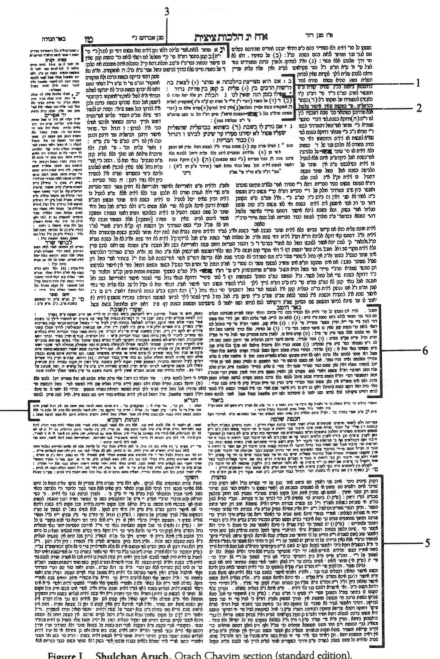

Figure J. **Shulchan Aruch,** Orach Chayim section (standard edition).

1. R.Yosef Karo (Beit Yosef) (see 5330/1570)
2. Hagahot of the Ramo (see 5330/1570)
3. Magen Avraham (see 5433/1673)
4. Gra (see 5558/1797)
5. Machatzit HaShekel (see 5567/1807)
6. Ba'er Heitev (see 5483/1723)

Figure K. **Shulchan Aruch,** Yoreh Deya section (standard edition).

1. R. Yosef Karo (Beit Yosef) (see 5330/1570)
2. Hagahot of the Ramo (see 5330/1570)
3. Taz (see 5406/1646)
4. Shach (see 5406/1646)
5. Ba'er Heitev (see 5483/1723)
6. Pitchei Teshuva (see 5616/1856)

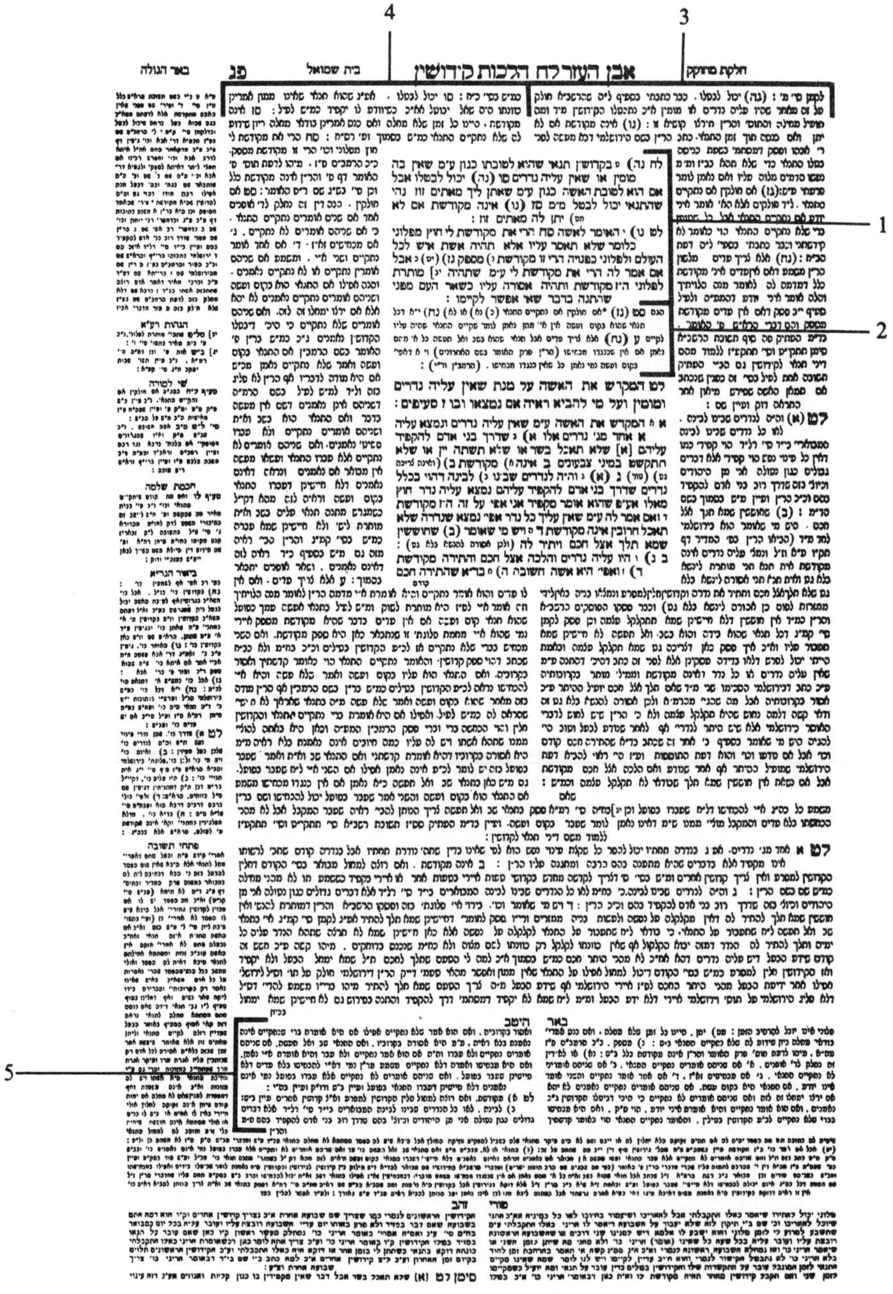

Figure L. Shulchan Aruch, Even HaEzer section (standard edition).

1. R. Yosef Karo (Beit Yosef) (see 5330/1570)
2. Hagahot of the Ramo (see 5330/1570)
3. Chelkat Mechokek (see 5400/1640)
4. Beit Shmuel (see 5449/1689)
5. Ba'er Heitev (see 5483/1723)

Figure M. **Shulchan Aruch,** Choshen Mishpat section (standard edition).

1. R. Yosef Karo (Beit Yosef) (see 5330/1570)
2. Hagahot of the Ramo (see 5330/1570)
3. Sma (see 5374/1614)
4. Ketzot HaChoshen (see 5548/1788)
5. Netivot HaMishpat (see 5569/1809)
6. Ba'er Heitev (see 5483/1723)

Figure N. Commentaries of the Maharsha, Maharam, and Maharshal, printed at the end of each volume of the Talmud (standard edition).

1. Maharshal (see 5334/1573)
2. Maharsha (see 5374/1614)
3. Maharam (see 5376/1616)

Charts

SHOFTIM – JUDGES AND EARLY PROPHETS

Jewish Year		Secular Year
2488	Yehoshua (Joshua)	– 1273
2516	Zekeinim (Elders)	– 1245
2533	Shoftim (Judges)	– 1228
2533	Othniel ben Knaz	– 1228
2573	Ehud ben Gerah	– 1188
2654	Shamgar died[1]	– 1107
2654	Devorah	– 1107
2694	Gideon	– 1067
2734	Avimelech	– 1027
2737	Tolah ben Pu'ah	– 1024
2758	Ya'ir HaGil'adi	– 1003
2779	Yiphtach	– 982
2792	Eylon	– 969
2802	Avdon ben Hillel	– 959
2810	Shimshon (Samson)	– 951
2830	Eli (HaKohen)	– 931
2871	Shmuel	– 890

[1] All others listed at beginning of reign.

KINGS OF YEHUDA

	Jewish Year
Rechav'am	2964
Aviyah	2981
Assa	2983
Yehoshaphat	3024
Yehoram II	3047
Achazyahu II	3055
Athalya Ruled	3056
Yeho'ash I	3061
Amatzya	3100
Uziyahu	3115
Yotam	3167
Achaz	3183
Chizkiyahu	3199
Menasheh	3228
Amon	3283
Yoshiyahu	3285
Yeho'achaz II	3316
Yehoyakim	3316
Yehoyachin	3327
Tzidkiyahu	3327

KINGS OF YISRAEL

	Jewish Year
Yerav'am I	2964
Nadav	2985
Ba'asha	2986
Elah	3009
Zimri	3010
Omri	3010
Ach'av	3021
Achazyahu I	3041
Yehoram I	3043
Yehu	3055
Yeho'achaz I	3083
Yeho'ash II	3098
Yerav'am II	3115
Zecharyahu	3153
Shalom	3154
Menachem	3154
Pekachya	3164
Pekach	3166
Hoshea	3187

KINGS 2882–2924

	Jewish Year
Shaul	2882
David (limited rule)	2884
Ish Boshet	2889
David	2892
Shlomo	2924

KINGS 2964–3327

King	Jewish Year	Kingdom
Rechav'am	2964	Yehuda
Yerav'am I	2964	Yisrael
Aviyah	2981	Yehuda
Assa	2983	Yehuda
Nadav	2985	Yisrael
Ba'asha	2986	Yisrael
Elah	3009	Yisrael
Zimri	3010	Yisrael
Omri	3010	Yisrael
Ach'av	3021	Yisrael
Yehoshaphat	3024	Yehuda
Achazyahu I	3041	Yisrael
Yehoram I	3043	Yisrael
Yehoram II	3047	Yehuda
Achazyahu II	3055	Yehuda
Yehu	3055	Yisrael
Athalya Ruled	3056	Yehuda
Yeho'ash I	3061	Yehuda
Yeho'achaz I	3083	Yisrael
Yeho'ash II	3098	Yisrael
Amatzya	3100	Yehuda
Uziyahu	3115	Yehuda
Yerav'am II	3115	Yisrael
Zecharyahu	3153	Yisrael
Shalom	3154	Yisrael
Menachem	3154	Yisrael
Pekachya	3164	Yisrael
Pekach	3166	Yisrael
Yotam	3167	Yehuda
Achaz	3183	Yehuda
Hoshea	3187	Yisrael
Chizkiyahu	3199	Yehuda
Menasheh	3228	Yehuda
Amon	3283	Yehuda
Yoshiyahu	3285	Yehuda
Yeho'achaz II	3316	Yehuda
Yehoyakim	3316	Yehuda
Yehoyachin	3327	Yehuda
Tzidkiyahu	3327	Yehuda

KINGS AND RULERS OF THE CHASHMONA'IM DYNASTY

	Jewish Year
Yehuda HaMaccabi	3622
Yonatan	3628
Shimon	3634
Yochanan Hyrkanos	3642
Yehuda Aristoblus	3668
Alexander Yannai	3670
Shalomit	3688
Aristoblus II	3696
Hyrkanos II	3700
Antigonus	3721

ROMAN CLIENT KINGS AND RULERS OF THE HERODIAN DYNASTY

	Jewish Year
Herod	3725
Archelaus	3761
Roman Procurators only[1]	3770–3781
Agrippa I	3781
Agrippa II	3804

[1] There were no official Jewish leaders during this period – only Roman Procurators.

NESSI'IM – PRESIDENTS OF THE SANHEDRIN

	Jewish Year
Yosef (Yosee) ben Yo'ezer	3550
Yehoshua ben Perachya	3610
Shimon ben Shatach	3688
Hillel	3729
Shimon (ben Hillel)	3769
Rbn. Gamliel I (ben Shimon)	3769
R.Shimon ben Gamliel I	3810
R.Gamliel II (ben R. Shimon)	3828
R. Elazar ben Azaryah[2]	3844
R.Shimon ben Gamliel II	3878
R.Yehuda HaNassi	3925
R.Gamliel III (ben R.Yehuda)	3949
R.Yehuda Nessia I (ben Gamliel)	3949
R.Gamliel IV (ben Yehuda)	3990
R.Yehuda Nessia II (ben Gamliel)	3990
R.Gamliel V (ben Yehuda)	4060
R.Yehuda Nessia III (ben Gamliel)	4069
Hillel II (ben Yehuda)	4119
R.Gamliel VI (ben Yehuda)	4189

[2] Approximately twenty years of his leadership were shared (see 3864), and he was the only Nassi from the time of Hillel, who was not his direct descendant.

MAJOR RISHONIM

	Secular Year Born		Died
Rbnu.Gershom Me'or Hagolah	960?	–	1070?
Rbnu.Chananel	985?	–	1057?
R.Shmuel HaNagid	993	–	1056?
Rif (Alfasi)	1013	–	1103
Rashi	1040	–	1105
Rashbam	1080?	–	1174?
R.Avrahim ibn Ezra	1089?	–	1164
Rabbenu Tam	1100?	–	1171
Ri (R.Yitzchak)	1120?	–	1200?
Ra'avad	1120?	–	1198
Ba'al Halttur	1120?	–	1193?
Ba'al Hama'or	1125?	–	1186
Rambam (Maimonides)	1135	–	1204
R.Yehuda HaChasid	1150?	–	1217
Roke'ach (R.Elazar)	1160?	–	1237?
Radak (Kimchi)	1160?	–	1235?
Rbnu.Yona (Gerondi)	1180?	–	1263
Ramban (Nachmanides)	1194?	–	1270?
Maharam MeRothenburg	1215?	–	1293
Rashba	1235?	–	1310?
Mordechai (Pirush)	1240?	–	1298
Hagahot Maimoniyot	1240?	–	1298
Me'iri (R.Menachem)	1249?	–	1315?
Rosh (R.Asher)	1250?	–	1327
Rbnu.Bachya II	1265?	–	1340?
Tur (R.Yaakov ben Asher)	1275?	–	1349?
Ralbag (Gersonides)	1288	–	1344
Ran (R.Nissim)	1290?	–	1380?
Rivash	1326	–	1408?
Maharil	1360?	–	1427
Rashbatz	1361?	–	1444

KOV'IM

	Secular Year		
	Born		Died
R.Yitzchak Abarbanel	1437	–	1508
Yuchasin	1440?	–	1515
R.Ovadya Bertinura	1445?	–	1524?
Eyn Yaakov (R.Yaakov ibn Chaviv)	1445?	–	1516?
R.Yaakov Pollak	1460?	–	1530?
Radvaz	1463?	–	1573?
Beit Yosef (R.Yosef Karo)	1488	–	1575
Maharshal	1510?	–	1573
Maharal of Prague	1512?	–	1609
Shittah Mekubetzet (R.Betz.Ashkenazi)	1520?	–	1594?
Ramak (Cordovero)	1522?	–	1570
Ramo (R.Moshe Isserles)	1525?	–	1573?
R.Mordechai Yaffe (Levush)	1530	–	1612
Ari'zal (R.Yitzchak Luria)	1534	–	1572
Sma (R.Yehoshua Falk)	1540?	–	1614
R.Chaim Vital	1542?	–	1620
Lecnem Mishneh (A.Avraham di Boton)	1545?	–	1588
Kli Yakar (R.Shlomo Ephrayim)	1550?	–	1619
Maharsha (R.Shmuel Edels)	1555	–	1631
Bach (R.Yoel Sirkes)	1560?	–	1640
Shaloh (R.Yeshayahu Horowitz)	1560?	–	1630
Tosaphot Yom Tov (Lipman Heller)	1579	–	1654
Taz (R.David ben Shmuel)	1586	–	1667
Chelkat Mechokek (R.Moshe Lima)	1605?	–	1658
Shach (R.Shabbetai Kohen)	1621	–	1663?

MAJOR ACHARONIM

	Secular Year	
	Born	Died
Beit Shmuel (R.Shmuel)	1630? –	1700?
Magen Avraham (R.Avr.Abele Gombiner)	1637? –	1683
Siftei Chachamim (R.Shabbetai Bass)	1641 –	1718
Mishneh LeMelech (R.Yehuda Rosannes)	1657? –	1727
Pnei Yehoshua (R.Yaakov Yehoshua Falk)	1680 –	1756
R.Yaakov Culi (Me'am Lo'ez)	1689? –	1732
R.Yonatan Eybeshutz	1690? –	1764
Sha'agat Aryeh (R.Aryeh Leib Gunzberg)	1695? –	1785
Or HaChayim (R.Chaim (ib)n Attar)	1696 –	1743
R.Yaakov Emden	1697? –	1776
Korban HaEida (R.David Frankel)	1707 –	1762
Pnei Moshe (R.Moshe Margolis)	1710? –	1781
Noda BiYehuda (R.Yechezk'el Landau)	1713 –	1793
Vilna Gaon	1720 –	1797
Chida (Azulai)	1724 –	1806
Pri Megadim (R.Yosef Te'omim)	1727? –	1792
R.Shneur Zalman (Rav of Lyady)	1745 –	1813
Ketzot HaChoshen (R.Aryeh Leib Heller)	1745? –	1813
Chayei Adam (R.Avraham Danziger)	1748 –	1820
Yismach Moshe (R.Moshe Teitelbaum)	1759 –	1841
Chavat Da'at (R.Yakv.of Lissa/Netivot)	1759? –	1832
R.Ephrayim Zalman Margolis	1760 –	1828
R.Akiva Eger	1761 –	1837
Chassam Sofer	1762 –	1839
Tiferet Yisrael (R.Yisrael Lipshutz)	1782 –	1860
Tzemach Tzedek (of Lubavitch)	1789 –	1866
Divrei Chaim (of Tzanz)	1793 –	1876
Chidushei HaRim (of Gur)	1799 –	1866
Minchat Cinuch (R.Yosef Babad)	1800? –	1874
Kitzur Shulchan Aruch (R.Shl.Ganzfried)	1804 –	1886
Malbim (R.Meir Leib(ush))	1808? –	1879
Pitchei Teshuva (R.Avraham Tzvi Hirsch)	1813 –	1868
Aruch HaShulchan (R.Yechi'el Epstein)	1829 –	1908
Sdei Chemed (R.Chaim Chizkiyah Medini)	1832? –	1904
Ben Ish Chai (R.Yosef Chaim Al-Chakkam)	1833? –	1909
Chafetz Chaim (R.Yisrael Meir Kagan)	1838 –	1933
Darkei Teshuva (R.Tzvi Hirsch Shapira)	1845? –	1913
Sfass Emess (of Gur)	1847 –	1905
R.Chaim Brisker	1853 –	1918
Rogatchover Gaon (R.Yosef Rozin)	1858 –	1936
Torah Temima (R.Baruch Epstein)	1860 –	1942

MAJOR ADMURIM AND CHASIDIC LEADERS

	Secular Year Born		Died
Ba'al Shem Tov	1698	–	1760
Maggid of Mezeritsch (R.Dov Ber)	1698?	–	1772
R.Avraham Gershon of Kitev	1701?	–	1761
R.Nachman of Horodenka	1705?	–	1765
R.Elimelech of Lizensk	1717?	–	1786
R.Zushya of Annopol	1718?	–	1800
R.Yechi'el Michel of Zlotchov	1721?	–	1786?
R.Yaakov Yosef of Polannoe	1724?	–	1784?
The Shpoler Zeideh	1725	–	1812
R.Shmelke of Nikolsburg	1726?	–	1778?
R.Pinchas of Koretz	1728	–	1790
R.Menachem Mendel of Vitebsk	1730?	–	1788
R.Nachum of Chernobyl	1730	–	1797
R.Pinchas Horowitz	1730	–	1805
R.Yisrael (Maggid) of Kozhnitz	1733?	–	1814
R.Aharon of Karlin	1736	–	1772
R.Shlomo of Karlin	1738	–	1792
R.Levi Yitzchak of Berditchev	1740	–	1810
R.Avraham of Kalisk	1741	–	1809
Adm.R.Yitzchak Aisik of Kalliv	1744?	–	1821
R.Shneur Zalman (Rav of Lyady)	1745	–	1813
Chozeh of Lublin	1745?	–	1815
R.Baruch of Medzibuzh	1753?	–	1811
Adm.R.Avraham Yehoshua Heschel of Apta	1755	–	1825
Adm.R.Menachem Mendel of Rymanov	1755?	–	1815
Yismach Moshe (R.Moshe Teitelbaum)	1759	–	1841
Adm.R.Meir of Apta	1760	–	1827
Adm.R.Naftali Tzvi of Ropshytz	1760	–	1827
Adm.R.Klonymos Kalman of Cracow	1763?	–	1823
Adm.R.Asher of Stolin	1765	–	1826
The Yehudi of Pershisskha	1766	–	1814
Adm.R.Simcha Bunim of Pershisskha	1767	–	1827
Adm.R.Mordechai of Chernobyl	1770	–	1837
R.Nachman of Bratslav	1772	–	1811

MAJOR ADMURIM AND CHASIDIC LEADERS (cont'd.)

	Secular Year	
	Born	Died
Adm.R.Dov Ber of Lubavitch	1774	– 1827
Adm.R.Shalom of Belz	1779	– 1855
Adm.R.Meir(el) Premishlaner	1780?	– 1850
Bnei Yissachar (of Dynov)	1783?	– 1841
Adm.R.Elazar Nissan Teitelbaum	1786?	– 1856
R.Mendel of Kotzk	1787	– 1859
Tzemach Tzedek (of Lubavitch)	1789	– 1866
Divrei Chaim (of Tzanz)	1793	– 1876
R.Yisrael of Ruzhin	1797	– 1850
Chidushei HaRim (of Gur)	1799	– 1866
Adm.R.Shlomo of Radomsk	1803	– 1866
Adm.R.Aisik of Komarno	1806	– 1874
Adm.R.Yekutiel Yehuda of Sighet	1808	– 1883
Divrei Yechezk'el (of Shinev)	1811?	– 1899
Adm.R.Yitzchak of Skvira	1812	– 1885
Adm.R.Menachem Mendel of Vizhnitz	1830	– 1884
Adm.R.Shmuel of Lubavitch	1834	– 1882
Adm.R.Chananyah Yom Tov Lipa of Sighet	1836	– 1904
Adm.R.Avraham of Sochatchev	1839	– 1910
Darkei Teshuva (of Munkatch)	1845?	– 1913
Sfass Emess (of Gur)	1847	– 1905
Adm.R.Shlomo of Bobov	1848	– 1906
Adm.R.Sholom DovBer of Lubavitch	1860	– 1920
Adm.R.Avraham Mordechai of Gur	1866	– 1948
Adm.R.Chaim Elazar of Munkatch	1871?	– 1937
Adm.R.Aharon of Belz	1880	– 1957
Adm.R.Chaim Tzvi Teitelbaum of Sighet	1880?	– 1926
Adm.R.Yosef Yitzchak of Lubavitch	1880	– 1950
Adm.R.Yoel(ish) of Satmar	1888	– 1979
Adm.R.Yisrael of Gur	1894	– 1977
Adm.R.Simcha Bunim of Gur	1896	– 1992
Adm.R.Menachem Mendel Schneersohn	1902	–
Adm.R.Moshe of Sighet	1915	–
Adm.R.Pinchas Menachem of Gur	1925	–

Index

This index gives the year in which an item is mentioned (not the page).

The index does not provide any specific indication for the many instances that an item appears twice in the same year. It is advisable to read the whole year given in the index.

(A)	= Amora		(Q)	= Queen
(E)	= Exilarch		(R)	= Rishon
(G)	= Gaon		(S)	= Shofet (Judges)
(K)	= King		s.	= son of
(L)	= Acharon		(T)	= Tanna
(P)	= Prophet		(V)	= Savurai

Years listed in *italics* refer to the Jewish calendar year.

Years not in italics are secular calendar dates.

INDEX

345

משנות דור ודור

יצחק מתתי׳ קאנטאר

𝒜

ג׳עסון אהרונסון, מו״ל
נערטבעל, ניו ג׳ערסי
לונדון